71 0

LEEDS

GREAT CITIES OF THE WORLD

BY WILLIAM A. ROBSON

The Government and Misgovernment of London
The Governors and the Governed
Local Government in Crisis
Nationalized Industry and Public Ownership
Politics and Government at Home and Abroad
The Relationship of Wealth to Welfare
The Law of Local Government Audit
Justice and Administrative Law
The Development of Local Government
The British System of Government
The University Teaching of Political Science
Civilization and the Growth of Law

WITH C. R. ATTLEE

The Town Councillor

CONTRIBUTOR TO

British Government Since 1918

EDITED BY WILLIAM A. ROBSON

Problems of Nationalized Industry
The Civil Service in Britain and France
The British Civil Servant
Public Enterprise
Social Security

JOINT EDITOR WITH H. J. LASKI AND W. I. JENNINGS

A Century of Municipal Progress

GREAT CITIES
OF THE WORLD
THEIR GOVERNMENT, POLITICS
AND PLANNING

EDITED BY

WILLIAM A. ROBSON

AND

D. E. REGAN

VOLUME ONE

London
GEORGE ALLEN & UNWIN LTD
RUSKIN HOUSE   MUSEUM STREET

First published in 1954
Second Edition (Revised and Enlarged) 1957
Third Edition (Revised and Enlarged) 1972

© George Allen & Unwin Ltd 1972

ISBN 0 04 350024 2

Printed in Great Britain
in 12 point Bembo type
by Alden & Mowbray Ltd
at the Alden Press, Oxford

'It now only resteth, having brought our city to that dignity & greatness, which the condition of the Scite and other circumstances afford unto it: that we labor to conserve, to maintaine and uphold the dignitie and greatnes of the same.'

Giovanni Botero: *A Treatise Concerning the causes of the Magnificencie and greatness of Cities*, done into English by Robert Peterson (London, 1606).

CONTRIBUTORS

Ali Ashraf   Arne F. Leemans
Ruth Atkins   Hjalmar Mehr
J. J. N. Cloete   Carlos Mouchet
Winston W. Crouch   Milton Rakove
Abhijit Datta   D. E. Regan
Paul Delouvrier   José Arthur Rios
Robert C. Fried   William A. Robson
Leslie P. Green   Masamichi Royama
Eric Hardy   Wallace S. Sayre
Axel Holm   H. C. Swaisland
J. N. Khosla   Fouad Diab Abdel Tawab
Živorad Kovačević   Emidio Tedesco
Aprodicio A. Laquian   Sylwester Zawadzki

A*

Measurement of Length and Area

I Kilometre is approximately $\frac{5}{8}$ of a mile, so 8 kilometres may be regarded as 5 miles

I square kilometre = ·386 square mile = 100 hectares

I hectare = 2·471 acres

Currency Values as at March 1971

	National Currency	Equivalent of one Pound Sterling	Equivalent of one U.S. Dollar
ARGENTINA	Peso (of 100 Centavos)	9·6	4·0
AUSTRALIA	Dollar (of 100 Cents)	2·1	·91
BRAZIL	Cruzeiro (of 100 Centavos)	12·0	5·0
BRITAIN	Pound (of 100 New Pence)	—	·42
CANADA	Dollar (of 100 Cents)	2·4	1·0
DENMARK	Krone (of 100 Öre)	18·1	7·5
FRANCE	Franc (of 100 Centimes)	13·3	5·6
INDIA	Rupee (of 100 Paise)	18·0	7·5
ITALY	Lira (of 100 Centesimi)	1500	600
JAPAN	Yen	864	359
MEXICO	Peso (of 100 Centavos)	30	12·5
NETHERLANDS	Guilder (of 100 Cents)	8·7	3·6
NIGERIA	Pound (of 20 Shillings, 240 Pence)	·86	·36
PHILIPPINES	Peso (of 100 Centavos)	15·5	6·5
POLAND	Zloty (of 100 Groszy)	9·6	4
SOUTH AFRICA	Rand (of 100 Cents)	1·7	·71
SWEDEN	Krona (of 100 Öre)	12·5	5·2
UNITED ARAB REPUBLIC	Pound (of 100 Piastres)	1·04	·425
U.S.A.	Dollar (of 100 Cents)	2·4	—
YUGOSLAVIA	Dinar (of 100 Paras)	36·0	15·0

PREFACE TO THE THIRD EDITION

IT IS gratifying that the demand for this book continues to the extent that a new edition has been requested by the publishers.

The purpose of this third edition of *Great Cities of the World: their Government, Politics and Planning* is essentially the same as that of the previous editions: namely to describe in depth the local governments of a selected group of the world's great cities and to consider whether, and if so how far, these vast communities are confronting common problems arising from similar causes; and what steps, if any, they are taking to overcome them. As in the earlier editions, the contributors of the studies of individual cities have in all cases lived and worked in them, often for most of their lives.

In recent years there has been a substantial increase in the generalized study of metropolitan government. We have therefore included a select bibliography on metropolitan government in general in addition to the bibliographies on the individual cities. Much of the recent work in this field is by American scholars whose approach bears the unmistakable influence of the American idiom and is usually orientated to the American scene. *Great Cities of the World* remains the only book at present available which brings together the knowledge and experience of many authors of different nationalities concerning more than a score of metropolitan areas scattered throughout the world.

Despite the continuation of the basic purpose, the present edition contains much new work. The synthesis in Part One has been extensively revised and enlarged, although the framework remains unaltered. Part Two deals with twenty-seven cities compared with twenty-three in the second edition. Nine cities appear for the first time (Belgrade, Birmingham, Cairo, Delhi, Ibadan, Manila, Mexico City, Pretoria and Warsaw). Of the eighteen cities included in the second edition, only five are covered again in the present volume by the same authors; they are Copenhagen, Los Angeles, Osaka, Rio de Janeiro and Tokyo. The other thirteen are dealt with by entirely new contributions by different authors (Amsterdam, Buenos Aires, Calcutta, Chicago, Johannesburg, London, Montreal, New York, Paris, Rome, Stockholm, Sydney and Toronto). In many instances the original authors were not available to undertake the extensive revision needed, but in some cases we felt it desirable for other reasons to obtain entirely new chapters. We were compelled regretfully to omit studies of Moscow and Manchester which we had commissioned owing to the failure of the authors to submit the manuscripts or to inform us of their inability to do so.

11

Our scope has been deliberately world wide in the present as in the earlier editions of the work. We could easily have obtained studies of more European and North American cities than are included, but we were determined that the work should not be overbalanced in favour of these areas. Competent authors for studies of many African, Asian and Latin-American cities are, however, difficult to secure. We are particularly disappointed not to be able to include Karachi; an author was found who later withdrew.

All our contributors were given a detailed editorial statement as a guide to the content of their chapters. On the whole this has been followed reasonably well but some authors had difficulty in obtaining information on certain aspects of the city on which they were writing. A degree of variation in a book of this kind must be recognized as inevitable, and is usually due to differences of education, outlook and experience. There are also certain differences in the dates of the statistics and some of the factual information given in the various chapters. This is explained by the fact that the preparation of the third edition took from 1966 to 1971 to complete.

We decided to omit all photographs from the present volume mainly because a great number of each city would have been needed in order to illustrate the text in a significant manner, and this is not commercially feasible. We have instead included maps of each city.

We owe sincere thanks to all the contributors to the present volume for their willing co-operation.

We are indebted to Miss M. Maureen Evans, Miss Elizabeth Walton and Mrs. Dorothy Regan for drafting maps, and to Mrs. Constance and Mr. Brian Dear for making the finished maps for publication.

We are also grateful to our colleague Dr. G. F. D. Dawson for translating the chapters on Copenhagen and Stockholm from the Danish and Swedish respectively; to Mr. Ronald Robson for assistance with the general bibliography, to our secretaries Mrs. Elaine Steinhart and Mrs. Linda Snowden for their indispensable role of typing, filing and reminding; and to Mrs. D. H. Easterling and Mrs. W. Grollman for additional typing assistance, and to Mr. A. J. A. Morris for editorial assistance.

WILLIAM A. ROBSON

D. E. REGAN

London School of Economics and
  Political Science
July 1971

CONTENTS

Contents

Contents

MAPS

(Drawn by Constance and Brian Dear)

PART ONE

The Great City of Today

WILLIAM A. ROBSON

WILLIAM A. ROBSON

Educated University of London (London School of Economics and Political Science). B.Sc.(Econ), 1922; Ph.D., 1924; LL.M., 1928. Barrister-at-Law. Formerly Professor and now Professor Emeritus of Public Administration in the University of London. Honorary Fellow London School of Economics.

Has been Visiting Professor in the Universities of Chicago, North Carolina, California (Berkeley), Patna, the Indian Institute of Public Administration, the Hebrew University of Jerusalem, the International Christian University of Tokyo, and the Federal University of Lagos. Has received honorary degrees from the Universities of Lille, Grenoble, Paris, Algiers, Durham, Manchester and Birmingham.

President, International Political Science Association (1952–55); Vice-President, Political Studies Association; Vice-President, Royal Institute of Public Administration; Member of Council, Town and Country Planning Association.

During the Second World War he served in the Civil Service in several departments including the Ministry of Fuel and Power and the Air Ministry. He has acted as adviser to the governments of Lebanon, Turkey, Nigeria, India and Tokyo.

A list of his published books is given on page 4.

He has been a member of many official committees.

The Great City of Today

THIS book is concerned with the government, politics and planning of a selected group of great cities in Europe, America, Asia, Africa and Australia. Its purpose is not only to gain knowledge of a neglected field but to see how far the great city produces problems of more or less universal significance. I believe that the studies will provide some valuable comparative material on matters of general interest.

A MODERN PHENOMENON

Men have lived in towns for thousands of years, but the great city of today is a very modern phenomenon. The vast aggregations of population, numbering millions, to be found in the largest towns could not have been supplied with enough food to keep them alive for a single day before the advent of modern means of transport. The railway, the motor car, the cargo ship driven by steam or oil, are the veritable founders and supporters of the great modern city. We are equally dependent on modern technology for the conveyance, filtration and distribution of the enormous quantities of water required by the citizens of every large city for domestic, industrial and commercial uses. The Pont du Gard in Provence is a superb relic of a Roman aqueduct which successfully carried water a considerable distance; but the Romans would have been totally unable to provide London or Paris with the quantities of water they consume today.

Much the same is true of the garbage collection and sewage disposal services of the great modern city. They too are the result of modern technology. And without power-driven factories and mills, mechanized offices, telecommunications, and swift local transport, it would be impossible for such vast populations to earn their living in concentrated urban centres.

The cities described in this book cover a very wide range of size, both as regards population and area. Table I shows the population and the territory contained within the legally defined boundaries of the cities. These boundaries bear little relation to the real size of the city regarded as a social and economic aggregation.

There is, of course, no definition of a great city, in terms of its minimum size. The conception will usually have some relation to the total population of the country in which the city is situated. Zürich, for example, with an estimated population of 432,000 in 1968, ranks as a great city in a small country like Switzerland, whereas it would be regarded as of only medium size in the United States. Size is, however, only one of the characteristics of the great city. Its economic significance, either in regard to manufacturing industry, commerce or financial power, is generally a dominant factor. A third

TABLE I
Population and Area of the Cities
Metropolitan Areas are shown only where they are local government units.

	Population	Date	Area (sq. miles)	Area (sq. kilometres)
Amsterdam	830,853	1970	79·8	206·6
Belgrade	745,000	1967	81·1	210
Greater Belgrade	1,046,000	1967	934·1	2,420
Birmingham	1,075,000	1969	80	207
Buenos Aires	3,100,000	1970	77·2	200
Cairo	4,219,835	1967	81·8	212
Greater Cairo	4,965,514	1966	121·9	316
Calcutta	3,439,887	1962	37	142·8
Chicago	3,550,404	1960	224·2	580·3
Copenhagen	824,200	1969	45·6	118·1
Delhi Union Territory	2,658,612	1967	573	1,484·4
Ibadan	635,011	1963	40	103·6
Johannesburg	1,390,000	1970	195	505
London	7,763,820	1968	616·4	1,596·9
Los Angeles	2,781,829	1970	463	1,199·5
Manila	1,582,300	1970	99·2	38·3
Mexico City DDF	7,425,000	1969	572	1,481·9
Montreal	1,222,255	1966	60	155·4
Montreal Urban Community	1,923,178	1970	190	492
New York	7,991,500	1965	320	826·2
Osaka	3,067,700	1969	78·4	203
Paris	2,607,625	1968	38·6	99·7
Paris Region	9,250,674	1968	4,632	12,000
Pretoria	608,000	1970	224	580·3
Rio de Janeiro	4,000,000	1968	452	1,171
Rome	2,477,367	1966	582·1	1,507·6
Stockholm	756,697	1969	72·0	185·9
Greater Stockholm	1,418,267	1968	1,067	2,787
Sydney	157,200	1967	Not available	Not available
Tokyo	11,353,724	1969	780·9	2,029
Toronto	697,422	1967	40	103·6
Toronto Metropolis	1,881,691	1966	240	621·8
Warsaw	1,278,000	1968	172·3	446·2

feature is its cultural eminence. A city which is merely large and wealthy lacks the quality of greatness unless it can show signs of distinction in the arts and sciences. This explains the urge on the part of public authorities or public-spirited citizens to establish or develop a university; to have a symphony orchestra, some fine museums, art galleries and other displays; to have an opera house, a leading theatre and other manifestations of culture, even though a public subsidy is needed to support them.

Lastly, there is the political importance of the great city. Professor Mackenzie regards the potential dominance of the great city in the sphere of national politics as one of the chief problems calling for consideration.[1] He points out that the domination of great cities has been accepted as one of the marks of the Western way of life; and yet the political problem which they present has been largely ignored, despite its urgency.

The political importance of the great city does not necessarily derive from its position as a national capital. Indeed, only fourteen of the twenty-seven cities dealt with in this book are national capitals. It arises rather from the massive concentration of highly organized power which the great city is able to exert. When that concentration of power and resources is associated with the prestige and authority of a capital, the result is formidable in the extreme.

The great city may not be a capital, but it is almost certain to be a metropolitan area, in the modern sense of the term. This connotes a great commercial, industrial, cultural or governmental centre surrounded by suburbs, housing estates, dormitory towns or villages. Large numbers of people who work in the city reside in these outlying areas beyond its boundaries. They and their families use the shops, hospitals, universities, colleges or schools, theatres, concert halls and other institutions provided by the 'mother-city'.[2] Conversely, the outlying areas supply the city with market garden and dairy produce; and they offer those who dwell in the city open spaces, playing fields, golf courses, camping grounds and many different kinds of rural amenity. There is also sometimes a centrifugal movement of people who live in the city and work in the outlying areas, but this is usually of less substantial proportions. There will often be some relatively self-contained urban centres providing both homes and workplaces for many of their inhabitants. The satellite new towns come into this category.

[1] W. J. M. Mackenzie: *The Government of Great Cities*, p. 2 (Percival Lecture, 1952); 93 Memoirs and Proceedings of the Manchester Lit. and Phil. Society, No. 5.

[2] Dr. Victor Jones defines a metropolis as 'a mother-city from and toward which people move to establish suburban aggregations on the periphery. Many of the people who live in the suburbs work in the central city; and they and their families use the cultural, recreational, trade, professional and commercial facilities of the mother-city almost as freely as do those who live within its boundaries'. *Metropolitan Government* (University of Chicago Press, 1942), p. 2.

THE METROPOLITAN COMMUNITY

The economic and social reality we have to bear in mind is that of a metro-politan community living in a metropolitan area of the kind mentioned above. This again is the result of modern improvements in transportation and communication. Never before has the townsman been able to live a considerable distance from his work. The age-long distinction between the way of life of the town-dweller and the countryman has almost ceased to exist in the typical metropolitan area. People who live in the country receive frequent deliveries of goods by motor van from the great city; they enjoy electric light, gas supply, main drainage, motor cars, the telephone, radio, television, daily postal deliveries, laundry and cleaning services, metropolitan newspapers, travelling libraries, refrigerators, local cinemas—all this and heaven too.

Despite the growth of suburbs and increasingly distant housing estates, despite a relative and sometimes absolute decline of population in the inner core compared with the outer belt—a decline sometimes applying to the population of the entire 'mother-city'—the original city has not merely held its own but even increased its dominance as a commercial and financial centre, a magnet which attracts those in search of employment, amusement and culture. 'The whole increasing population', wrote T. H. Reed, '—the overtaken farmer as well as the invading suburbanite—more and more seek the stores, churches and professional services of the centre to the detriment of the crossroads store, the wayside church and the county doctor. A nation has been put on wheels, and its mobility has created metropolitan regions with common political problems and no adequate machinery to solve them.'[1]

The growth of metropolitan areas has occurred in every part of the world. One finds metropolitan cities in the West and in the Orient; in all the con-tinents; in developed and underdeveloped countries; under capitalism and under communism; in new countries and in old. It is a movement peculiar to our age and has now assumed vast quantitative importance. Thus in 1968, 64·6 per cent of the total population of the United States were living in Standard Metropolitan Statistical Areas; of this proportion 29·4 per cent were residents of central cities and 35·3 per cent in the suburban rings.[1] I am critical of the basis on which these figures are compiled, but they nevertheless give a broad indication of the position.[2] In England and Wales, 16 million people, or one-third of the total, live in London and five other metropolitan

[1] 'Metropolitan Areas'. *Encyclopaedia of the Social Sciences* (1st edition) Vol. X, p. 396.

[2] *Trends in Social and Economic Conditions in Metropolitan Areas*, U.S. Department of Com-merce, Series P. 23, No. 27, February 7, 1969.

areas recognized as conurbations by the Registrar-General.[1] Paris embraces nearly a fifth of the population of France.

In Australia, the metropolitan communities have been increasing in population at a more rapid rate than either the separate states or the Commonwealth. Between 1961 and 1966, the population of Australia increased by 9·9 per cent, while that of Australian metropolitan communities increased by 15·5 per cent. During this period in every Australian state the population of metropolitan urban areas increased at a faster rate than that of the state. In consequence the proportion of the total population living in metropolitan areas has been rising, and in 1966 exceeded 58 per cent.[2]

The proportion of the metropolitan community living within the city boundaries is indicated in some of the studies presented in this book. Thus, the population of Greater Amsterdam was 1,043,051 in 1970, of which 866,421 lived within the confines of the city. The metropolitan area extends to 58,587 hectares which is nearly three times as large as the city's area. The city of Belgrade contains 745,000 residents and another 300,000 live in the suburban areas. Greater Cairo has a population of approximately 5 millions, of whom 4,219,835 live in the city. In Calcutta the disproportion is much greater: 3 million people live in the city and 7,500,000 in the metropolitan district. Metropolitan Manila has a population of 2,989,300, of which less than half (1,138,611) lives in the city of Manila. The city of Paris has a relatively stable population of 2,790,091, but the population of the Paris region has grown to 9·2 millions. The city of Montreal had a population of 1,222,255 in 1966, while the population of the Montreal metropolitan area was 2,436,817 in 1966. The three municipalities of Copenhagen, Frederiksberg and Gentofte which form the capital of Denmark have a total population of 847,800, while the metropolitan area, which includes nineteen suburban municipalities, has 1,382,100 inhabitants. The city of Los Angeles has a resident population of 2,781,729 out of a total of 7,087,677 for the metropolitan area.

The tendency in most metropolitan areas is for the suburban ring to grow more rapidly than the central city, which may even decline in terms of its resident population. In the United States, the population of metropolitan areas grew from 112·4 millions in 1960 to 128·0 millions in 1968. The population of central cities increased only from 57·8 millions to 58·2 millions while the suburban rings grew from 54·6 millions to 69·9 millions.[3] These figures

[1] The Registrar-General's Statistical Review of England and Wales for 1967, Part II, Table E, p. 16, H.M.S.O. The conurbations range in size from Tyneside with 848,780 to Greater London with a population of 7,880,760.

[2] Census of the Commonwealth of Australia. June 1966. Census Bulletin nos. 6 to 11, and 9.1.

[3] Trends in Social and Economic Conditions in Metropolitan Areas. U.S. Department of Commerce. Series P. 23. No. 27. Feb. 1969.

are symptomatic of the increasing tendency for large numbers of persons to live outside the central core of the old city, whose boundaries remain fixed for long periods of time.

It is, however, impossible to present the position of metropolitan cities in its proper quantitative significance because there are seldom areas which adequately represent them for census purposes. For example, the area known as Greater London is used by the Registrar-General for population statistics, but the metropolitan region extends far beyond this. The same is doubtless true of Greater Stockholm, Greater Buenos Aires, and all the other metropolitan areas. The Royal Commission on Local Government in England recently identified three metropolitan areas in England outside London. They are (1) West Midlands metropolitan area, containing 3,014,000 people in 1968 in an area of 984 square miles. This is based on Birmingham, whose present population is 1,100,000; (2) South-East Lancashire and North-East Cheshire metropolitan area based on Manchester. This comprises a population of 3,232,000 in 1968 within an area of 1,048 square miles, compared with Manchester's estimated population in 1966 of 625,250 and an area of 43 square miles; (3) Merseyside metropolitan area centred on Liverpool, whose estimated population in 1966 was 712,040 in an area of 43 square miles. The metropolitan area would contain 2,063,000 people in an area of 614 square miles.[1] The people of the Perth–Fremantle area in Western Australia are becoming 'metropolitan-conscious and aware of metropolitan needs.' But an Australian scholar reports that few of them could give a precise answer to the question: What is our metropolitan area?[2] The same would doubtless be equally true in Rome, Boston, Brussels, Cairo, Madrid or Johannesburg.

If the typical metropolitan area consisted of a continuous built-up area, it would be far easier to define and to describe in terms of population and territory; but actually no metropolis is composed of a single compact urban concentration. And just because the metropolitan community is so attenuated, spreading farther and farther afield in ever-widening circles like the ripples on a pond, it becomes increasingly hard to define, to measure, to comprehend, and to govern.

An urban region has been described not simply as an overspill of the city or as a territorial unit, but rather as 'a population living as an organic group of people whose jobs, economic activities, social institutions, leisure time and mobility are working in a highly integrated fashion'.[3] This may be helpful

[1] Report, Vol. I of the Royal Commission on Local Government in England, H.M.S.O. Cmnd. 4040/1969, Annex I, Table 1.
[2] J. R. H. Johns: *Metropolitan Government in Western Australia* p. 1.
[3] *The Regional City*: edited by Derek Senior, London, 1966, p. 9, quoting Frederick Gutheim.

as a concept which emphasizes the interdependence of people and their activities rather than the unified physical structure of the region but it is of limited use for the practical purposes of planning and governing the urban region. It may be contended that while all metropolitan areas are urban regions, not all urban regions are necessarily metropolitan areas. A metropolitan area must have at its heart a great city, definable not only in terms of function but also in a territorial sense, which serves as a centre for the entire region in respect of those facilities, services and activities which require a very large clientele or a high degree of specialization or very large resources.[1] It will also provide a high proportion of jobs in many vital branches of industry, trade, government, finance, publishing, communication and the professions.

In the United States a good deal of research has been devoted to metropolitan areas; and the usual means of defining such areas is by laying down a minimum figure of aggregate population combined with a density minimum for the surrounding districts.[2] So crude a method is clearly unsatisfactory.

The method of defining 'Standard Metropolitan Statistical Areas' used by the United States census in 1960 was to take a county or group of counties which contained at least one city of 50,000 inhabitants or more, or 'twin cities' with a combined population of at least 50,000. (In New England, towns and cities were used instead of counties.)

There are two manifest weaknesses in this definition. First, a county or group of counties may not be continuous with the true limits of a metropolitan area but may extend far beyond it, thereby inflating the population figure for that metropolitan area. Secondly, the figure of 50,000 is so small that it robs the word 'metropolitan' of any sociological and political significance; and the definition takes no account whatever of the functions which should be performed by a metropolitan area worthy of the name. It should be either a great political and governmental centre, or a commercial and industrial centre, or a cultural centre, or all of these, or at least two of them.

The effect of the United States census definition is shown by the fact that by applying it in the 1960 census no fewer than 212 Standard Metropolitan Statistical Areas were enumerated, of which only 60 contained populations exceeding 400,000, 53 exceeding 500,000, while no less than 89 contained fewer than 200,000 persons. They included such insignificant places as Fort Smith, Alabama, with a population of 66,685 and Great Falls, Montana, with 73,418.[3]

[1] *Ibid.*, p. 17.
[2] Paul Studenski: *The Government of Metropolitan Areas in the United States*, p. 9.
[3] Statistical Abstract of the United States, 1968, Section 33, Tables 1 and 2, Washington.

In our view, in a country as large and highly developed as the U.S.A., only metropolitan areas with a central city of not less than 300,000 and a total population of at least 400,000 should be regarded as possessing metropolitan status. To place a vast mass of small fry in the same category as the great metropolitan communities of New York, Chicago, Los Angeles, Philadelphia, Detroit, Boston and so forth does not assist the serious study or understanding of the problem of the metropolitan city.

Only in five or six of the world's great cities has any serious attempt been made to provide the metropolitan community with a system of government designed to satisfy its present and future needs in regard to organization, services, finance, co-ordination, planning or democratic control and even in these exceptional areas the measures taken are barely adequate. Elsewhere the great city is usually struggling along with an out-of-date structure vainly trying to grapple with mounting difficulties and to solve problems which cannot be overcome without drastic reforms. Meanwhile, the population washes outward over the irrelevant administrative boundaries like the ocean tide washing over submerged breakwaters. The inhabitants of the outlying suburbs, dormitory towns, communes, housing estates and villages flood into the central city each day, scarcely aware when they cross the boundary. The outward growth of the metropolis is not checked by the frontiers of counties, states or even countries. Metropolitan New York sprawls over much of New Jersey, Connecticut and other states. Detroit is partly in the United States and partly in Canada. The development of civil aviation, and particularly the helicopter, will accentuate this problem. It is already possible to imagine businessmen living on the French coast and flying daily to and from their work in London. And if the housing situation is difficult in Copenhagen, why should one not live in Norway or Sweden and fly every day to the Danish capital?

The picture we have tried to paint of the great city outgrowing its boundaries should be regarded as prolegomena to an understanding of the government and administration, the politics and planning, of the modern metropolis. We should think of the metropolitan community which lives, works and plays in a widespread metropolitan area as being the basic social and economic reality. This is the great city of today, not the narrowly confined part of it which happens to live within the obsolete legal and administrative boundaries laid down in a former age.

We shall return to the political, governmental and administrative implications of this problem after we have considered the present methods of local government.

The task of governing a very large city is fundamentally different from that of governing one of small or medium size. After a certain stage is reached, quantitative differences produce qualitative differences. The great city of today is so large that it is difficult to evoke from its citizens or inculcate in them the spirit of community. People often do not know their neighbours, and so the sense of neighbourhood, of belonging to the same place and sharing common interests, is lost. There is a danger that the city council and its executive organs may seem remote and aloof from the daily life of the citizens, with whom they are not in close contact. In consequence, apathy is often shown towards municipal policies and municipal elections. It is difficult for local government to flourish in an atmosphere of indifference, suspicion or distrust. In some cities, such as Belgrade and Warsaw, special neighbourhood units have been established to overcome this difficulty. Also in cities like New York, where the political process is exposed to the mass media, remoteness may be less pronounced.

SPECIAL CONSTITUTIONAL FEATURES

The great city is sometimes, but not always, distinguished from other towns either by reason of its constitution or because of its relations with the national government, or both. Thus, the Ville de Paris differs from all other French communes by virtue of the fact that it has no mayor, all executive power being in the hands of either the Prefect of Paris or the Prefect of Police. Moreover, the former has acquired many powers which are usually possessed by the municipal council in a French commune. His powers in regard to the elected council of the city are greater than those accorded elsewhere to prefects.

Tokyo has a different form of government from other large cities in Japan. The Tokyo Metropolitan Government combines the powers of a city with those of a prefecture, which outside the capital are exercised by separate organs. The Tokyo Metropolitan Government has jurisdiction over the entire area, but its powers are greater in the special wards than elsewhere. In the special ward area functions are divided between the Tokyo Metropolitan Government and 23 elected ward councils which are subordinate to the metropolitan authority. Outside the ward area are 17 cities, 13 towns, 2 villages and 3 islands in Tokyo Bay, over all of which the Metropolitan Government exercises prefectural powers.

London has a two-tier structure specially designed for the capital city in 1963. Proposals have been made in a 1970 White Paper that a somewhat similar type of structure should be applied to five other metropolitan areas in England.[1]

---

[1] Reform of Local Government in England. Cmnd 4276/1970. H.M.S.O.

In Yugoslavia, there is a two-tier system of local government for Belgrade but elsewhere the district assemblies have been abolished and only the municipalities remain. A new city charter was adopted in 1968 for nearly the whole metropolitan area. This enables the city of Belgrade to undertake responsibilities elsewhere entrusted to municipalities, which in the capital consist of the lower-tier authorities; and furthermore, to perform tasks which were previously within the competence of the republican government.

Buenos Aires, like Washington, D.C., has been placed in a special district under the federal legislature. After the 1966 revolution, the city council was dissolved and all its powers concentrated in the President as 'the immediate and local head of the Federal Capital'. A somewhat similar situation existed in Rio de Janeiro when it was the national capital, but after Brasilia was built and became the capital, Rio was embodied in the State of Guanabara, which took over the territory of the former federal district. Rio de Janeiro thus became a city-state with a constitutional system similar to that of other states in Brazil.

Delhi is another capital which has special constitutional characteristics. It is a Union territory under the Indian constitution, and is administered by the President acting through an administrator. It has three multi-purpose local authorities. One of them is the Municipal Corporation of Delhi, the principal organ of metropolitan government, whose jurisdiction includes 94 per cent of the area and 89 per cent of the population. This follows the normal pattern laid down by the Municipal Corporations Act, 1957. A second local authority is the New Delhi Municipal Committee, created in 1933 to administer the new governmental and residential city adjoining old Delhi which the British raj constructed after its decision to move the capital of India to Delhi. Its members are nominated by the central government, and 5 of the 11 members are officials. When it is realized that the great complex of central ministries known as the Secretariat, the Presidential residence, the Houses of Parliament, the foreign embassies and missions, the official residences of the Prime Minister and other ministers, Members of Parliament, and senior civil servants, are all located in New Delhi, the reasons for this tight central control over the area become clear. The third local authority is the Cantonment Board, which carries out local government services in the part of Delhi known as the Cantonment, where the military troops are accommodated. The Cantonment is administered under statutory arrangements laid down as long ago as 1924. They provide for a board, half of whose members are elected and half nominated, with the commanding officer of the station acting as its head under the supervision of the Ministry of Defence.

Mexico City follows the example set by several other federal constitutions of having a special federal district for the national capital known as the Departamento del Distrito, or D.D.F. This includes the city of Mexico and a number of *delegaciones* or separate areas each governed by a *delegado* appointed by and responsible to the Governor of the District. The Governor, who is himself appointed by the President of the Republic and is subordinate to him, is directly responsible for the administration and development of the main city. There is no elected element in the governance of Mexico City but the citizens possess voting rights for the federal legislature.

Cairo has the same form of organization as other governorates in U.A.R., but the governor enjoys a higher status and has closer relations with the President and ministers of the central government than officials holding similar posts elsewhere.

The city government of Rome differs surprisingly little from the local government of other Italian towns, except for the requirement (often found in the countries of continental Europe) that the financial estimates must be approved by the central government instead of by the provincial authority. Moreover, the Minister of the Interior exercises control over all matters of wide economic importance affecting Rome. In Copenhagen, which also belongs to the county borough species, the executive organs are rigidly separated from the city council, whereas in other Danish towns the mayors and aldermen are chosen from among the councillors. The separation of powers is also reflected in the provision that committees of the council do not participate in administration. Warsaw and Pretoria do not display any special constitutional features.

Among the cities which are not national capitals, one finds that Montreal has been the subject of special legislation passed by the province of Quebec, while the province of Ontario has created a new form of metropolitan government for Greater Toronto. Sydney also depended on special legislation until the Local Government (Areas) Act, 1948, brought the city into line with the ordinary local government system of the state. New York City has a constitution peculiar to itself which was adopted in 1961; but in the United States the principle of 'home rule' is so widely applied to local government, that this is a very commonplace occurrence.[1] Johannesburg, Amsterdam, Osaka, Sydney, Manila, Ibadan, Birmingham and Los Angeles follow the system of local government generally applicable in their respective countries or states.

From this brief survey it appears that the tendency is for capital cities[2] to

[1] See Harold Zink: *Government of Cities in the United States*, pp. 121-30.
[2] I refer here to national capitals, and not to state capitals in countries with a federal form of government.

B

have a special form of local government different from that of other cities in the country. Great cities which are not capitals usually have the system of local government applied in their country to substantial towns. Both these propositions are subject to exceptions.

It is usually true that a capital city tends to enjoy a lower degree of self-government than other cities in the same country. The explanation is not far to seek. A capital city is the seat of the national government; it contains the diplomatic representatives of foreign countries whose security is a national responsibility; and possession of the capital is often the key to political control over the entire country. For these reasons the national government often exercises a much greater degree of control over the capital than over other large towns. Paris is the classic example of this; but one might equally well cite Buenos Aires or Washington, D.C. In London the police force, elsewhere administered by the police or watch committee of the local authority, is administered by the Commissioner of the Metropolitan Police who is under the control of the Home Secretary.[1]

THE ELECTED COUNCIL

In local government, as in government at higher levels, we normally look for both the representative element and the executive element. The representative element is found in the city council. The degree to which a municipality can be regarded as endowed with democratic local government depends on the existence, composition and functions of the council, and the extent to which the executive organs are subject to popular control either by the council or by the electorate.

All but four of the great cities comprised in this volume have an elected council. The exceptions are Buenos Aires, Mexico City, Ibadan and New Delhi. All except the last-named have in the past had elected councils but for various reasons these have been abolished. None of these four cities has any local self-government. Cairo has a partly elected and partly nominated council.

The city councils vary greatly in size, the qualifications required of candidates, tenure of office, remuneration, and also the franchise. The size of the council ranges from 15 persons in Los Angeles to 710 in Warsaw. The councils fall into the following three groups in regard to size:

---

[1] The only exception is the small area of the ancient City of London, where the Corporation of the City is permitted to maintain its own police force.

TABLE II

Number of Councillors

Below 50	Between 50 and 100	More than 100
Manila 20	Copenhagen 55	Tokyo 120
New York 37	Belgrade 100	Birmingham 156
Johannesburg 42	Osaka 94	Delhi Municipal
Pretoria 30	Rome 80	Corporation 106
Amsterdam 45	Calcutta 100	London 116
Los Angeles 15	Stockholm 100	Warsaw 710
Metropolitan	Paris 90	
Toronto 33	Chicago 50	
Sydney 21	Cairo 85	
Montreal 48		

The size of the council is a matter of great importance. It affects not only the effectiveness of the deliberative body but also the relations between the city council and the citizens. In New York City, where a councilman represents on an average over 300,000 citizens, it must be much harder for the elected representative to keep in close touch with his constituents than in Amsterdam, for example, where the ratio is rather less than 1 to 20,000 voters.

One of the most serious disadvantages usually associated with the great city is, indeed, the steep reduction in the number of citizens who participate directly in the process of government. Birmingham has a representative on the council for every 7,000 citizens; while in South-East Lancashire there is an elected councillor for every 1,500 citizens. The Ville de Paris has one councillor for every 30,000 citizens, but in the communes of neighbouring departments the ratio is one to fewer than 1,000 persons. Hence one can infer that the amalgamation of outlying areas with the city will usually cause a decrease in the ratio of councillors to citizens, thereby reducing the number of men and women taking an active part in local government.

This problem has been solved by two methods. One is the establishment of a two-tier structure which provides, in addition to the major council, a lower tier of elected councils exercising functions in their own districts. There are thirty-two local councils in Greater London,[1] and as a result there is an average of one representative for every 3,500 persons. Before the reform of London government in 1963 the metropolitan boroughs had one representative for an average of 2,250 persons.

Warsaw also has a lower tier of 7 district people's councils, each of which has 80 elected councillors. A district councillor represents between 2,000 and

[1] There is also the ancient City of London.

2,600 inhabitants according to the size of the district. The people's council for the city has 710 members, which works out at one for about 1,800 inhabitants. This compares with one member of the Greater London Council for about 68,000 inhabitants. The low ratio of councillors in relation to population in Warsaw has been achieved by creating a council many times larger than that of any other great city included in the present edition of this book. A similar system is found in the Soviet Union, where an even larger number of councillors are elected to the Moscow Soviet.

There are obvious disadvantages in having so large an assembly as the principal governing body of the municipality. Its sheer size makes detailed discussion impracticable, debate is difficult, and oratory offers the most effective way to influence. Members can reveal streams of opinion in such an assembly, voice the discontent of their constituents and express popular needs. By such means policy can be influenced and administrative action determined. But the business of very large assemblies is almost always decided 'off-stage'; and the agenda and resolutions are usually managed by the executive committee. We may conclude, therefore, that while Warsaw, Moscow and some other great cities of Eastern Europe have apparently solved the problem of popular representation to a greater extent than elsewhere, in doing so they have transformed the city council from a council of city fathers into a mass meeting. Much more thought and study must be given to this aspect of metropolitan government if genuine democracy is to be attained in the great city.

Belgrade is one of the most interesting cities from the standpoint of its constitution and structure. In addition to the city council which is in charge of metropolitan functions, there are 13 municipalities acting as lower tier authorities. The lower tier municipalities execute such tasks as local health services, welfare services, social assistance, child care, the provision of primary schools, public libraries, cultural services of various kinds, recreational amenities, minor communal facilities such as side streets, squares, playgrounds, public gardens, telephone booths and so forth. The city council is in charge of all the functions which relate to the metropolis as a whole, both in the sphere of planning and in that of administration. In addition to the 13 municipalities there are 108 neighbourhood communities in Belgrade. These communities are not local government units but self-governing organizations of citizens established to deal with their everyday problems. Their activities cover a surprisingly wide field, including child-minding, organizing of excursions and vacations, voluntary work connected with playgrounds, care of old and disabled persons, provision of classes for illiterates, health education, cultural and artistic performances, helping to bridge the gap between the home and the school, construction and maintenance of the smaller local amenities. All or many of these activities form part of the responsibilities of the municipalities, which in consequence encourage the neighbourhood communities and give them funds for the purpose of carrying them out.

Another novel and indeed unique feature of Belgrade was the creation in 1967 of five separate chambers within the city council. These comprise the city or general chamber with 100 councillors, the economic chamber with 80 representatives, the culture and education chamber with 50 councillors, the social and health chamber with a similar number of councillors and the public services chamber with 40 councillors. The councillors of the economic chamber are elected by citizens working in industry, agriculture, transport, catering and several other vocations; those of the culture and education chamber are elected by the personnel working in primary and secondary schools, universities, scientific institutions, museums, libraries, theatres, broadcasting stations, films, etc. Councillors of the social and health chamber are elected by citizens working in hospitals, health centres, medical centres, pharmacies, health protection centres, social insurance institutions, social centres, etc. The public services chamber is elected by officials in state administration, the law courts, the defence forces and the like. I will describe on a later page how the system works;[1] here I am concerned only with the notable way in which Belgrade combines a two-tier structure of general local councils with a functional delegation within the metropolitan government.

The two-tier structure possesses definite advantages for a great city quite apart from the increase of popular representation which it makes possible. In a city with a population of more than, say, half a million, the city council finds great difficulty in maintaining a close contact with the citizens. The town hall, the councillors and officials, seem to become remote and aloof: and the citizens see the city government as 'they' rather than 'we'. However good the intentions of the councillors may be, the bureaucratic element tends to prevail as the size of the city becomes really large. This tendency is assisted by the increasing scope, magnitude, and complexity of municipal functions. The Royal Commission on Local Government in England stated that in their view a local authority with a population much above 1,000,000 would encounter serious difficulties of management and also of maintaining democratic local government. They therefore recommended that this should be the upper limit of size for unitary authorities, and the larger metropolitan areas be provided with a two-tier structure.[2]

[1] *Post*, pp. 48, 64.   [2] Report, H.M.S.O. Cmnd. 4040/1969, paragraphs 266–76.

The introduction of a lower tier of secondary councils is a method of decentralizing power in respect of purely local matters to district organs. These organs are in a position to know much more than the city council about their own districts; and they should be able to keep in close and intimate touch with their local affairs. If well organized, and free from corruption and nepotism, they should be able to conduct purely local functions in a more efficient and democratic manner than the major council. I therefore believe a two-tier structure to be right in principle as a form of government for the largest cities.

Cairo has a two-tier system. The upper tier consists of a governor and governorate council described later in this book,[1] and the lower tier of five district councils. Each district has its own council, some members of which are *ex officio* representatives of central government ministries, some are selected for their leading capacities in the district, and some are elected. There are 20 elected members and they must constitute a majority. They must be committee members of the Arab Socialist Union. The lower tier is firmly controlled by the superior governorate council and the central government, but the district councils can and do carry out many activities within their areas. Dr. Fouad Abdel-Tawab is on sound ground when he states that 'it would be difficult for one council to maintain a close contact with citizens. . . . These district organs are in a position to know more than the city council about their own districts'. This is true whatever the nature of the politico-economic regime may be.

Even the highly centralized government of Paris has always had its *arrondissements*, although they are not separate local authorities but mere administrative units under the control of mayors appointed by the Prime Minister. The mayors, indeed, are executives of the central government, and the town halls are branch offices of the prefecture. Their activities relate to such matters as the census, notifying conscripts, keeping the electoral register up to date, issuing certificates, etc.

Paris has a two-tier system in a much more significant sense when one considers the District of the Region of Paris which was established in 1964. This development will be referred to in a later section.[2]

A two-tier form of organization is especially necessary in a metropolitan area. For this consists of an extensive region based on a great city, which forms the commercial, industrial, political and cultural centre, surrounded by suburbs, dormitory towns, satellite towns, housing estates, villages, market-garden areas and so forth. By whatever means the need for a unified government over the whole metropolitan area may be met—and we shall

[1] *Post*, pp. 59–60.   [2] *Post*, pp. 57, 58 and 69.

discuss this later—the need for the purely local government of all these diverse places will remain. It can best be satisfied by means of a two-tier organization conferring the greatest possible amount of local autonomy consistent with the well-being, good government, co-ordination and planned development of the whole metropolitan area.

A move in this direction was taken some years ago in Toronto. The Municipality of Metropolitan Toronto, which began to operate on January 1, 1954, consisted at first of a metropolitan council responsible for certain services in an area comprising the city of Toronto and twelve suburban municipalities. The council's services included the supply and wholesale distribution of water to the component municipalities, trunk sewers and sewage disposal plants, and major highways. Public transportation and town planning were also dealt with on a metropolitan scale by *ad hoc* bodies. The twelve outlying municipalities were separated from the county of York in which they were formerly situated, and the services previously carried out by the county transferred to the metropolitan council. These included the provision and upkeep of court houses and jails, the hospitalization of indigent patients, and post-sanatorium care of tubercular patients.

The changes initiated in 1954 left the local authorities then existing untouched except to deprive them of some of their functions. The metropolitan council based on the federal principle was superimposed on the existing structure, but no attempt was made to rationalize the lower tier of local authorities. The metropolitan council consisted of a chairman and twenty-four members drawn from the municipal units concerned. The city of Toronto had twelve representatives consisting of the elected mayor, two of the controllers elected at large, and the alderman gaining the largest number of votes at the last election in each of the nine wards in the city. The twelve suburban towns were represented by their mayors or reeves. This allocation of seats on the metropolitan council resulted in substantial inequity, for the outlying municipalities had populations ranging from 8,000 to nearly 100,000, and their differences of size and importance were not reflected in their representation on the major authority. By 1963 the largest suburb had thirty-two times the population of the smallest. The city of Toronto accounted in 1954 for 60 per cent of the population in the metropolitan area but was allocated only twelve representatives out of 24.

In 1967 the metropolitan council was enlarged to 32 members plus the chairman. The city of Toronto's representation continued to number twelve, a proportionate loss only partly reflecting the decline in population of the city relative to that of the suburbs. The 12 suburban municipalities were amalgamated into 5 more substantial units, and these were given representation on the metropolitan council in proportion to their sizes, ranging from 2 from East York to 6 from North York. The chairman is elected by the council.

The original allocation of functions was not based on rational principles. Some services requiring large-scale organization, such as the police and fire brigades, were left to the constituent local authorities in order to avoid increasing the tax rates in the suburban municipalities. On the other hand the metropolitan council was given certain functions, such as the provision and maintenance of homes for the aged, the maintenance of neglected children and of women committed to industrial refuges, which could quite well be carried out by secondary authorities of reasonable size and resources. The position has been greatly improved by the subsequent changes which have given Metro[1] additional functions. These include control of air pollution, traffic lights, isolation hospitals, the police force, sites for garbage disposal, emergency and ambulance services, welfare assistance, regional libraries and the financing of public schools. Many functions are shared between the two tiers: for example, metropolitan expressways are the responsibility of the metropolitan council while local streets are entrusted to the second tier of authorities. A sharing of functions also applies to (regional) open spaces and neighbourhood parks, trunk water mains and distribution systems, main sewers and local drains.

Several of the metropolitan functions are carried out not by the metropolitan council and its departments but by *ad hoc* bodies of various kinds or by voluntary organizations.

Metropolitan government cannot rest entirely on indirect election if it is to be satisfactory from a democratic standpoint, although a combination of direct and indirect election may have certain advantages. The absence of any members directly elected to the metropolitan council is a defect of the Toronto reforms. In London, Warsaw, Belgrade, Stockholm and Tokyo the metropolitan and the borough, ward, district or county councils are separately elected.

To return to the council. We will not trouble the reader with all the minor variations in regard to such matters as the qualifications of candidates, the franchise, tenure of office, remuneration of councillors and so forth. These are not without interest; but little would be gained from a summary of the different practices.

In order to understand the role of the city council we must consider its relation to the executive power. There are fundamental differences to be found in different city constitutions, and they are of crucial importance. We

---

[1] The Metropolitan Council is usually known as Metro.

may preface our remarks by pointing out that in many countries the separation of powers is applied in city government inasmuch as the executive power is entrusted to an organ which is separate from the council. Where this occurs, the council is frequently regarded as a deliberative body which discusses policy, legislates by enacting ordinances or by-laws, passes the budget, approves proposals submitted to it and is responsible for approving or making certain appointments. This is a typical situation which is subject to many variations.

The constitutions of the great cities dealt with in this book can be divided into five main classes as regards the executive power and its control.

THE CITY COUNCIL AS EXECUTIVE

This is the universal principle to be found among all local authorities in Great Britain. It applies to the Greater London Council, to the London borough councils, and also to Birmingham. The essence of the system is that the council possesses full executive power within the limits laid down by law, and has complete control over administration. This control is exercised in practice by committees of the council dealing with specified functions such as education or public health. The committees report to the full council, which can either accept their proposals, reject them or refer them back for reconsideration. The council will, however, often delegate to a committee the power to decide matters without referring them to the council for prior approval. Under this system the council elects the mayor (or chairman of the Greater London Council) who presides over the council and occupies a position of great dignity and civic prestige. But he possesses no executive authority and does not control the administration.

In Birmingham the city council elects the mayor annually. It appoints and dismisses the town clerk, the chief professional, salaried, non-political officer of the city. It appoints the committees, of which there are 26. The council has delegated decision-making powers to these committees except the making of by-laws or city ordinances, the levying of rates or raising loans. The committees all report at regular intervals to the council.

The standing committees have immense power both to control administration and to determine administrative policy subject to the overriding authority of the council.

All members of the council serve on the committees, and outside persons may be co-opted to any committee except the finance committee. The chairmen of the committees usually belong to the party with a majority on the council, and this is the practice in Birmingham.

B*

The committee system in British local government has tended over the years to proliferate too many committees and sub-committees, thereby imposing an excessively heavy burden on councillors. Criticism has been levelled at this tendency and many councils, including Birmingham, have recently substantially reduced the number of their committees.[1]

The problem of co-ordination has become increasingly important with the growth in the scope and complexity of municipal functions. The Greater London Council has introduced several devices to achieve a high degree of co-ordination. It has set up a policy steering committee concerned with the larger policy questions. Even more important is the leader's co-ordinating committee, which, unlike any other G.L.C. committee, is manned only by members of the majority party on the council. Its twelve members are all chairmen of committees. The planning and transport committees have been merged because of the close relation between physical development, highways and transport. There is also a strategic planning committee to work out long-term strategies.

The London borough councils all work through the committee system, although each of them has its own peculiar features.

Finance is the prime responsibility of the finance committee, to which all other committees must submit their proposals both for revenue expenditure and capital projects. The ultimate authority over finance, as over all other matters, is the city council.

The British system has been adopted in some of the Commonwealth countries. We find it applied in Sydney, except that there is no co-option on the municipal committees. The mayor is directly elected but he has no executive powers except in case of an emergency. His position is essentially similar to that of an English mayor, and executive control is exercised largely through a number of functional committees.

AN EXECUTIVE APPOINTED BY THE COUNCIL

The nearest thing to the British committee system is the method of entrusting executive power to a committee appointed by the city council. The simplest case exists in Warsaw, where there is no mayor. In that city an executive committee (the praesidium) elected by the people's council is the executive and administrative organ. It consists of eleven members, including a chairman, five deputy chairmen and a secretary, all of whom work full time. The remaining four members are part time. It is primarily responsible for

[1] This has been mainly due to the recommendations of the Maud Committee on the Management of Local Government which reported in 1967.

planning and directing the work of the municipality, and full executive powers have been delegated to it by the people's council. It prepares and convenes meetings of the council, carries out the directives of higher authorities, co-ordinates the work of the administrative departments, and supervises and directs the praesidia of the district councils. It reports to the council of the city on the fulfilment of their policies and programme.

Although the executive powers are delegated to the praesidium, the Warsaw City Council appoints a large number of standing committees, nearly all of which are engaged in supervising the work of the departments. These committees can submit criticisms and proposals concerning any of the city's departments to the council, the praesidium, or the department. They thus act as watchdogs of and advisers to the council, which meets rather infrequently and is of great size.

In Pretoria and Johannesburg executive control is entrusted to a management committee of 5 members appointed by the council from among the councillors. The management committee serves for 5 years unless replaced sooner by a resolution of the council. The management committee was introduced in South Africa in 1960 in place of the many committees which previously existed in the large cities. A city council may, with the approval of higher authority, appoint other committees, and Johannesburg has appointed 4 such committees; but these must report to the council through the town clerk to the management committee. A proposal to set up a management committee on somewhat similar lines in English local authorities was made by the report of the Maud Committee on the Management of Local Government in May 1967 but this recommendation has not been accepted by any local authority in Britain. The reason for its rejection is that it would fatally weaken the power and reduce the status of the functional committees which at present comprise the executive under the aegis of the council.[1]

In Montreal, the city council appoints an executive committee, consisting of six of its members, and a chairman. This body is in charge of the city's administration, although certain powers of supervision are accorded to the mayor. It reports to the council on all matters within its jurisdiction; submits by-laws to the latter for approval; and prepares the annual budget and capital development programme. It appoints all heads of departments and approves the appointments of most other officials. It is responsible for enforcing the law and many administrative duties. The mayor is entitled to nominate six council members but the appointment rests with the council. The mayor is a member of the executive committee but he may not act as chairman.

[1] *Recent Reforms in the Management Arrangements of County Boroughs in England and Wales,* Institute of Local Government Studies, Birmingham University, March 1969, p. 5.

The Mayor of Montreal is directly elected on a popular vote for a four-year term of office. He is the first magistrate of the city, and represents the city on ceremonial occasions. He presides over the council and can submit recommendations to the executive committee and to the council. He is required to superintend, investigate, and control all departments of the municipality to ensure the laws are properly and impartially enforced; and he can suspend municipal employees. But his executive authority is circumscribed, not only by the executive committee but also by the executive secretary, who is appointed by the council and who is a non-voting member of the committee. The executive secretary, the highest salaried officer, is responsible for city administration and keeps the departments in touch with the executive committee. This committee ultimately controls the administration.

On January 1, 1970 the Montreal Urban Community was established by provincial legislation. Under its provisions the Montreal Urban Community Council has come into existence. It consists of 82 members, comprising the directly-elected Mayor and Councillors of Montreal City (53 in all), the heads of 28 suburban municipalities on Montreal Island; and the Chairman of the Executive Committee who is appointed by the provincial government. The Executive Committee of the Community is composed of this Chairman, all seven members of the City's executive committee, and five other elected members. This executive is a hybrid and difficult to classify. It is in part directly elected (the Mayor and heads of suburban municipalities); in part nominated (the Chairman); and in part elected either by the Montreal Urban Community Council or by the City Council of Montreal.

Copenhagen also comes into this category. In the Danish city the executive council (*magistraten*) is composed of a chief mayor (*overborgmester*), five other mayors (*borgmestre*), and five aldermen (*radmaend*). All of them are elected by proportional representation for eight years by the city council. Anyone is eligible who is qualified to vote for the lower house of Parliament. The present practice is to choose mayors from among members of the city council. A councillor who is elected to be a mayor or alderman must vacate his seat on the council.

The mayors and aldermen are the repositories of executive power in municipal affairs. They act partly through the executive council, over which the chief mayor presides, and partly through their individual departments or jurisdictions. The chief mayor and each of the other mayors is at the head of a department. There are six departments, and the municipal statutes lay down the distribution of functions among them. Thus, to the chief mayor's department belong municipal accounts, audits, wages, pensions and local rates;

he also acts as city treasurer. The third department, to take another example, embraces public assistance, social insurance and the child guidance service. An alderman is allotted to each department.

Each mayor has charge of all matters referred to his department. He can act independently and on his own responsibility and no appeal lies from his decision to the executive council.

Questions affecting the municipality as a whole, such as by-laws or statutes and the annual budget; or matters which concern several branches of the city's administration; or which are of vital importance to the city or its economy, go to the executive council for decision. The executive council also deals with the appointment and discharge of officials, except the chief officers, who are appointed by the town council on the nomination of the executive council.

The mayors possess great executive power, both individually and collectively. It will be noticed that they are not tied to committees appointed by the elected council, which happens in some cities. The aldermen act as the link between them and the council, and seek to reconcile the bureaucratic and the democratic points of view. In the executive council the aldermen are in a position of equality with the mayors and their votes are of equal weight. The aldermen are largely occupied with committees on which they serve as representatives of the executive council.

Despite this concentration of power in the hands of the mayors and the executive council, Dr. Holm assures us that 'the centre of gravity in the administration of Copenhagen lies not only nominally but actually in the town council'.[1] The city council elects the mayors and aldermen. It appoints ten standing committees and any others which may be required. It appoints the highest municipal officials on the nomination of the executive council. It alone can grant money or approve the raising of loans.

Stockholm is another Scandinavian example of the same species, though it differs in several important respects from Copenhagen. In the Swedish capital, the city council elects an executive board of aldermen (*stadskollegiet*) consisting of twelve members of the council. Their duty is to prepare all business going to the city council and also to exercise general control over the municipal administration. This executive board is the central authority of the city and wields greater power than might appear from the city charter, by reason of the fact that all the party leaders on the council are members of it. In consequence, its proposals are generally accepted by the council. The aldermen receive an attendance allowance of 50 kroner and the chairman and vice-chairman receive salaries of 14,000 and 7,000 kroner.

[1] *Post*, p. 382.

Stockholm has no mayor, but has instead eight city commissioners elected by the council for four years. They must not be aldermen but they may be councillors. They are usually chosen by the political parties in proportion to their strength on the council. They must have special insight and experience in public affairs. They receive the highest salaries paid in the Swedish public service—about 125,000 kroner, which is considerably more than those paid to ministers of the Crown.

Each commissioner is in charge of a municipal department. The commissioners are not, however, simply officials but occupy a politico-administrative position more akin to that of municipal ministers. They participate in the meetings of the city council and of the executive aldermanic board, to which they report on departmental matters. They also form a board of their own, presided over by the commissioner in charge of finance.

The city commissioners possess great power, but they do not exercise undivided authority over their departments. The most important decisions are taken by separate administrative committees or boards elected by the city council to take responsibility for the various spheres of municipal activity. Each of these administrative boards or committees is made up of members nominated by the political parties in proportion to their relative strengths on the council. Members of a board may be councillors, but a great proportion of them are drawn from outside occupations. They bear some resemblance to the committees of a British municipality, except that a commissioner generally acts as chairman of the board or boards[1] which deal with his department. The point to notice is that a commissioner cannot dictate the decision of an administrative board, if the members are opposed to his opinion. On the other hand, an administrative board has nothing like the political influence of the executive board of aldermen, and therefore cannot rely on the city council accepting its recommendations. Nevertheless, an administrative board or committee exercises a considerable amount of independent administrative power, as we should expect in Sweden, which is accustomed to give a large measure of autonomy to boards at all levels of government. Hence, the administrative boards can take decisions which neither the city council nor the board of aldermen can change, except in the long run by the replacement of members whose term of office has expired, or by control over finance.

This structure of numerous committees and boards is typical of Swedish local government, and appears to outside observers as excessively complex.

---

[1] There are usually several boards for each department. Thus, in the social welfare department there are committees for rehabilitation, for unemployment, for temperance, for child welfare, for public social welfare, for care of the elderly and a legal assistance board.

Underlying the system lies a deep distrust of municipal bureaucracy and the desire to secure the participation of a considerable number of citizens in the administration of local affairs.

The intention is that powers should be divided between the city council on the one hand, and the executive aldermanic board, the city commissioners and the administrative boards on the other. In practice, the board of aldermen acts largely as a committee of the council. In theory, policy should be decided by the city council and administrative matters determined by the other authorities. In fact, many of the council's decisions, including the budget, are based on the advice of the administrative boards.

The system of city commissioners, which is peculiar to Stockholm, has been under discussion from time to time. There is some controversy about whether the combination of political and full-time administrative posts is desirable in a city government. A similar combination existed in Germany under the former *bürgermeister* system, which in my opinion had many disadvantages.[1] It is also found in another form in the American 'strong mayor' towns which we shall presently describe. In Britain, local government is based on the assumption that a sharp dividing line should be drawn between the political or democratic element, consisting of the elected representatives, and the bureaucratic or administrative element, consisting of the salaried professional officials; but this is difficult to establish in places where a different tradition prevails. Another question which has been raised in Stockholm is whether it would not be better to replace the present method of electing city commissioners according to political party representation on the council by a responsible cabinet system, whereby the political party with a majority on the council would nominate all the commissioners.

The Municipality of Rome falls under the same heading. The city council is the fundamental organ of the municipality; and its approval is required for all important questions involving policy. It passes the budget, and must approve the estimates of all administrative agencies to which the commune contributes money. It supervises all institutions created for the benefit of the citizens.

Executive power is confided to an executive committee (*giunta*), composed of the mayor (*sindaco*) and 14 councillors (*assessori*), together with 4 substitute members, who are elected by the council. The mayor is also elected by the council from among its members. The alderman who receives the most votes in the election of the executive committee becomes deputy mayor. The mayor is head of the municipality and presides over both the council and the executive committee. He signs all municipal contracts, when they have been

[1] See William A. Robson: 'Local Government in Germany', in *Political Quarterly*, Vol. XVI, No. 4 (October–December 1945), p. 277.

authorized by the council, and is responsible for enforcing all municipal regulations and by-laws. He inspects municipal offices and institutions. But he does not exercise power independently of the executive committee and the council. Except in case of an emergency, the mayor is always subordinate to these bodies. In a few matters he acts as an officer of the central government, e.g. as registrar for births, deaths and marriages in the municipality. The mayor and the executive committee are appointed for 5 years, but they can be recalled at any time by an adverse vote in the council, and this is by no means an infrequent event.

Amsterdam has a municipal executive which combines an aldermanic element elected by the city council with a mayor appointed by the central government. The system contains some features displayed by the municipalities dealt with in this section—i.e. those in which the executive is appointed by the city council; but on balance we consider that Amsterdam falls into the category of cities whose executive organ is appointed by the central government.

The unusual constitutional structure of Belgrade city government has already been described. An understanding of this is necessary in order to explain how the executive is formed. Formerly, local authorities in Yugoslavia had executive committees which may have resembled the praesidium in the Soviet Union or Poland; they were small bodies with a chairman exercising great authority. It was found that this resulted in the city council being little more than a voting machine. A system of some twenty committees of the council was introduced in 1952 in place of a single executive organ. They had a mixed membership and democratized the decision-making process. At that time the council had only two chambers, but in 1967 the present organization of a multi-chamber assembly was introduced and it was thought unnecessary to have committees covering the fields dealt with by the five chambers. In consequence the number of committees was reduced to five. They deal with internal affairs, national defence, town planning, social planning and finance, and general administration. These committees act as executive bodies in these spheres of activity, while outside these spheres the several functional chambers control the administration in their respective spheres. Dr. Kovačević remarks that many students of local government regard a functional committee as a better instrument for carrying out the political-executive function than one of the much larger chambers attached to the council.

THE ELECTED MAYOR AS EXECUTIVE

A third type of constitution to be found among great cities is that in which a directly elected mayor possesses the executive power. This system embodies the twin doctrines of the separation of powers, and popular choice of the executive. It is much favoured in the United States, particularly in the larger cities which have not adopted the city manager plan.

New York is an example of the 'strong mayor' form of government. The mayor is elected on a popular vote and is regarded as the chief executive officer; but until the adoption of the 1961 charter, his powers were often more apparent than real. On the one hand he has to work with the board of estimate, and on the other hand many of the administrative functions of the city are in the hands of appointed officials such as the police commissioner, the traffic commissioner, the superintendent of schools or the planning commissioner who possess a high degree of independence of the mayor, even though he was responsible for their appointment. Some of the city's officials are elected by the voters, the most prominent among them being the comptroller, who exercises autonomous fiscal powers.

The board of estimate consists of the mayor, the president of the city council, the comptroller and the presidents of the 5 boroughs of which the present city of New York is composed. The boroughs at one time exercised many functions which have now been transferred to the city but they continue to be constituencies for the election of the presidents who sit on the board of estimate. The charter of 1936 which determined the city's constitution strengthened the position of the board of estimate *vis-à-vis* the mayor and he was often unable to override or overcome opposition to his policies or programmes by this 'guardian of borough interests'. The charter of 1961 has substantially reduced the powers of the board of estimate and increased those of the mayor and council. The mayor has now much greater control over the budget and over the organization of the administrative agencies running the municipal services.

While New York must be placed in the category of cities in which the elected mayor is the chief executive, his position has always been affected by two characteristic features of American city government. One is the application of the doctrine of checks and balances to the exercise of political power, displayed in New York by the countervailing power of the board of estimate and of the comptroller; the other is the fragmentation of government shown by the existence of numerous separate bodies such as the board of education, the housing authority, the board of water supply and the civil service commission. Despite these limitations on and dispersal of his powers, the people of New York look on the mayor as the man responsible for running the city.

Chicago is supposed to have a 'weak mayor' constitution, signifying that the council has much greater powers than in the 'strong mayor' system. The mayor is nonetheless the city's chief executive officer. He directs the municipal departments and with council approval appoints their heads and also the members of separate agencies. He presides at council meetings and has a casting vote. He prepares the budget and administers it after it has been passed by the council. There is a separately elected treasurer who is responsible for safeguarding the finances of the city, but the city comptroller is an appointed official and so too is the city collector. As in New York there are a number of separate commissions appointed by the mayor. In Chicago, therefore, the mayor is not only the chief executive and head of the municipal administration: he is also the presiding officer of the council.

Any deficiencies in the constitutional and legal powers of the mayor are counteracted by the domination of the Democratic Party in Chicago over the entire apparatus of city government. With the mayor also holding the office of Chairman of Cook County Democratic Central Committee he is unquestionably in control of the executive arm of government as well as of many other sources of power. His constitutional powers are reinforced by his political power as party boss.

In Los Angeles the mayor possesses very large ostensible authority, but in practice he exercises little direct power over the departments, which are headed (as in Chicago) by boards or commissions of citizens. The mayor appoints the members of these boards and commissions with the approval of the council, but the city charter gives them a considerable degree of independence which they guard jealously, and the mayor is unable to exercise much control over their activities. The usefulness of boards and commissions is hotly disputed in Los Angeles, and many attempts have been made to give the mayor direct authority over the departments. So far they have not succeeded owing to the opposition of business groups who believe their interests are better looked after in the hands of the separate boards and commissions.

In Chicago and Los Angeles a few services which might be regarded as municipal are provided by the respective county. Thus, Cook County provides welfare services in Chicago, builds and maintains county roads. There are also *ad hoc* bodies appointed by the county for such purposes as air pollution and flood control. As county government in the United States is regarded as part of state government, these intrusions into the territory of metropolitan areas do not affect the position of the executive in the great city.

Both in Tokyo and Osaka the chief executive of the city is directly elected by all the voters. This system was introduced in 1947 under the influence of the U.S. occupation forces in Japan. The chief executive and the assembly stand on an equal footing and in some respects reflect the American belief in the system of checks and balances. But apart from this common feature there are profound differences in the municipal government of Tokyo and Osaka

First, the Metropolitan Government of Tokyo is both a prefectural government and the administration of a large city. For this reason the chief executive of Tokyo has the title of governor instead of mayor. The city of Osaka on the other hand is a municipality within the territory and jurisdiction of the prefecture of Osaka—fu, which has a separately elected governor and prefectural council. The prefecture exercises certain functions in the city of Osaka. Second, the metropolis of Tokyo has a two-tier structure, which differs between the ward area and the remaining parts of its territory. In the ward area the administration is divided between the Tokyo Metropolitan Government and the 24 special ward elected councils; while elsewhere in the metropolis the lower tier consists of numerous cities, counties, villages and islands.

In Osaka, by contrast, there are no local authorities below the city government, only some 22 administrative wards which are not self-governing authorities but administrative divisions of the city, comparable to the *arrondissements* in Paris. Third, owing to the fact that Tokyo is the national capital, the relations between Tokyo Metropolitan Government and the central government differ from those appertaining to other great cities. Thus, the central government has set up the National Capital Regional Development Commission which is intended to prepare development plans for the whole vast region and to co-ordinate policies and programmes of the central government with these plans. Again, the metropolitan police department is in a special position. The superintendent-general is appointed by the national public safety commission with the approval of the metropolitan public safety commission and the consent of the Prime Minister. He and the top officials of the metropolitan police department are treated as national public service personnel, although they are supervised by the metropolitan public safety commission as the watchdog of citizen interests in Tokyo.

The governor of Tokyo is the chief executive of the capital city, although he depends in certain respects on the approval and co-operation of the metropolitan council. The council must pass the budget, enact, repeal or amend by-laws, approve the accounts, and consent to local taxes, rents, fees and so forth. It must approve the appointment of vice-governors proposed by the governor, and it has refused its approval in two instances in the recent past. The assembly appoints numerous committees to advise on bills and other measures relating to a wide range of functions, and these committees are authorized to investigate the work of the relevant administrative departments.

There are two other cities included in this book which have an elected mayor as chief executive. They are Manila and Rio de Janeiro.

Manila follows the American pattern of the mayor–council system of city government. The mayor is elected by direct vote of the citizens and he is the chief executive. He controls the executive functions of the administrative departments subject to the general supervision of the President of the Philippines. There is also an elected vice-mayor who deputizes for the mayor when necessary and presides over the municipal board, which is the legislative council of the city. The mayor's executive powers are restricted in practice by the fact that many of the city's administrative departments are headed by officials of the national ministries instead of by the city government's own employees, and this obviously reduces his powers of control over them. The mayor is nevertheless an official possessing great legal and political power. He can often overcome deficiencies of formal authority by means of political influence.

The system of government in Rio is the result of the transfer of the federal district and the capital to Brasilia. As already explained, Rio de Janeiro became the city-state of Guanabara after this event with its own constitution, and with the same territory as the former federal district. It was given a governmental system similar to that of other states in the Brazilian Federation. It thus has its own legislature, executive and judiciary. The executive power is in the hands of an elected governor, who acts as mayor. The constitution permits the governor to appoint a mayor with the approval of the assembly, but this post has never been filled, and is clearly unnecessary. The governor indeed has much greater power than any mayor: his approval is required for all the laws passed by the state legislature; he has the final voice on the budget and the financial programme; and he sanctions all decisions about the state's indebtedness, credit operations, the acquisition of public property, and charges for public services.

AN ELECTED COMMITTEE AS EXECUTIVE

A fourth type of city constitution is one in which, instead of an elected mayor wielding executive power, we find a small group of individuals being elected to the highest executive positions by the direct vote of the citizens.

In the city of Toronto (not to be confused with the Municipality of Metropolitan Toronto), a board of control has general responsibility for the administration. This board consists of the mayor, who is elected each year by the city at large, together with four other members elected in a similar manner. The board of control prepares the annual estimates, supervises revenue, expenditure and investment. It awards municipal contracts and considers by-laws. It recommends to the council appointments to the heads of departments and sub-departments; it can also recommend the dismissal of chief officers. The city council in Toronto possesses power to override the board of control in several respects by a two-thirds vote: for example, by such means it can make appropriations or authorize expenditure not recommended by the board; and it can refuse to sanction the dismissal of a senior official. A two-thirds vote in the council is necessary to confirm the removal of a municipal auditor, or to award a municipal contract. In Toronto we see a mixture of the American predilection for a separation of powers and a directly elected executive, with the British preference for entrusting authority to a committee rather than to an individual.

A similar system *mutatis mutandis* has been applied in the Municipality of Metropolitan Toronto. There an executive committee occupies a position comparable to that of the board of control in the city, but its composition is different. The city has the right to five places on the executive committee. Prior to 1969 the city was represented by the mayor, two of its four elected controllers, and two city aldermen chosen by the metropolitan council. Since the election in December 1969 the city has been represented by the mayor and the four controllers. Each of the suburban municipalities is represented by its mayor, and the full-time chairman of the metropolitan council also serves *ex officio* as a member with full voting rights of the executive committee. The present arrangement weights the executive committee in favour of the city, whose population is now only about 40 per cent of the population of the entire metropolis. As in the city of Toronto, the metropolitan council has a number of standing committees dealing with such matters as parks and recreation, welfare and housing. The reports of the committees are considered by the executive committee before submission to the council.

AN EXECUTIVE APPOINTED BY THE CENTRAL GOVERNMENT

The several forms of government which we have so far considered are those in which executive power is given either to the elected city council, or to an organ elected by the council, or to a person or body elected by the citizens. These are all different types of local self-government.

We now turn to the great cities in which executive power is given, wholly or partly, to an officer or organ appointed by a higher authority. This higher authority is either the central government, or, where a federal constitution is in force, the state or national government. It is obvious that cities which are governed wholly by such means do not enjoy local self-government; while those which are governed partly by such methods do not enjoy full self-government. For this reason they must be distinguished from those which we have examined above. It will be found, however, that in some instances an elected council is associated with a centrally appointed municipal executive. Where this occurs, the character of the regime depends on the balance of forces between these two elements.

We have already explained that the executive system in Amsterdam is of a mixed type.[1] The constitutional feature which has caused us to classify Amsterdam with the great cities whose executive is appointed by the central government is the arrangement whereby the mayor or burgomaster is appointed by the Crown for a period of six years, on the recommendation of the cabinet council. He can be reappointed for a further period of office. The mayor presides over the city council, and he can in law be a member of it, but in practice this rarely happens. His right to vote depends on whether he is a member of the council, but he can always participate in the deliberations of the council.

The mayor is chairman of a body known as the Board of Burgomaster and Aldermen, which controls the executive machinery of the city. This board consists of the burgomaster, who presides, and seven aldermen, who are elected by the councillors from among their own ranks. The aldermen are usually chosen from the political parties in accordance with their relative strengths on the council. Thus, all the members of the board except the mayor are appointed by the municipal council, and must be members of the council.

The aldermen receive full-time salaries, and it is customary to entrust each of them with the direction of an important branch of the administration, such as education, finance or public works. Strictly speaking, the aldermen have no legal authority either individually or collectively, except when they are sitting with the mayor as the board of mayor and aldermen.

It would be wrong to regard the division of powers between the council and the board as based simply on the distinction between 'legislative' or deliberative functions on the one hand and administrative functions on the other. 'Both in the field of legislation and in that of administration, the council's powers are primary', wrote Mr. Oud, a former Mayor of Rotterdam.[2] The law confides all authority in these two fields to the council, except

[1] *Ante*, p. 48.
[2] In a paper on 'The Netherlands Burgomaster' prepared for the Congress of the International Political Science Association held at The Hague, September 8–12, 1952. Printed in *Public Administration*, Vol. XXXI, Summer 1953.

where the Municipal Act expressly confers powers either on the board of burgomaster and aldermen, or on the mayor personally. The council may, of course, delegate some of its powers to the board or to the mayor. The board is chiefly concerned with day-to-day administration, and in particular with executing the decisions of the council. Moreover, the law has conferred on the board of burgomaster and aldermen numerous powers in the exercise of which it is legally independent of the council. The entire machinery of administration is under the control of the board of burgomaster and aldermen.

Broadly speaking, the task of the board is to formulate and prepare policies which are in harmony with the views the council has expressed or is likely to hold. It is also the board of management for the city government.

The mayor is at once the representative of the city and an agent of the central government. Apparently no one, not even a minister, can give him orders, though he can be dismissed by the Crown. He is in no sense an official either of the central government or of the municipality, but occupies rather the position of a public officer who takes his instructions only from the law itself. What is important is that he possesses a large and increasing range of powers which have been conferred upon him in his individual capacity, and for these he is not accountable to the council. He is head of the municipal police force; he has many administrative functions vested exclusively in him, especially those relating to public order. Even in regard to some matters in which the council retains certain regulatory powers, such as theatres, public houses, etc., it is the mayor alone who is charged with the task of enforcing them. The office of the Mayor of Amsterdam thus partakes of that 'dual capacity' which is found so frequently in the countries of continental Europe.

The role of the mayor in Amsterdam is to provide general leadership to the city government, to initiate and support municipal initiatives, to co-ordinate and integrate policies, and to reconcile divergent views on the executive board. He also exercises certain representational functions at home and abroad. To perform these tasks effectively calls for great tact and discretion, an absence of party political bias in his official capacity, and an ability to identify himself with the interests and aspirations of the city.

Yet the mayor is not politically neutral, and it has frequently happened in the past that the council have been displeased with the choice of the individual or dissatisfied with his political views. However, in recent decades a socialist has been appointed as mayor in view of the strong socialist representation on the council. Obviously, if care were not taken, his political views might upset the political balance on the board of burgomaster and aldermen. The violent disturbances which took place in Amsterdam between young demonstrators and the police in 1966 resulted in the dismissal of the mayor, and his position and status also became a burning issue. Public opinion in the city felt strongly that the people of Amsterdam should participate in the appointment of the mayor, and the government gave way to this demand to the extent of consulting the council before appointing his successor, the present mayor—a change which Dr. Leemans describes as 'a remarkable deviation from former governmental attitudes'.

In Buenos Aires there is no local self-government at all. An organic law of 1882 provided for the constitution of an elected municipal council with considerable powers of deliberation, policy-making, legislation and finance. The council has undergone many vicissitudes, and it was dissolved—not for the first time—by the revolutionary junta in 1966. Since then there have been no representative bodies in the capital city or in the other municipalities of Argentina. The powers of the city council of Buenos Aires have been transferred to the President of the Republic; those of the other municipalities in the Province of Buenos Aires to the provincial governors who are appointed by the President.

The Mayor of Buenos Aires has never been elected either directly by the people or indirectly by the municipal council, when it existed. He was always appointed by the President, but before 1966 the consent of the national senate was required. That body was also abolished in 1966. The reason that the office of mayor has never depended on direct or indirect election was the President's apprehension of the difficulties he would encounter if he were faced with an intransigent mayor whom he could not dismiss. A similar system applies in the capitals of the other provinces. Conflict and friction between the mayor and the council existed immediately prior to the 1966 revolution.

Some of the powers previously belonging to the council are now exercised by the President. These include approving the annual budget, approval or modification of city ordinances, borrowing money, approving the terms and conditions of employment of the municipal staff, regulations affecting contracts for public works and the granting of concessions for municipal services.

Ibadan is another instance of a democratic system of local government being abolished and replaced by an administrator appointed by the military governor of the Western Region. This also occurred in 1966. As the civil war in Nigeria has ended so recently it is impossible to foresee when a civil administration will replace military rule in the cities, or what area will be placed under its jurisdiction. But Dr. Green is confident that local government in Ibadan will not revert to the system which existed before 1952 when a district council composed of tribal chiefs and the *Olubadan* administered a vast territory.

The position in Delhi is complicated. I have already described the three separate local authorities administering New Delhi, the Cantonment, and the much larger population coming under the Municipal Corporation. All of them are located in the Union territory of Delhi which is governed by the President of India acting through a lieutenant governor. The latter is assisted by a deputy commissioner and various secretaries and heads of departments who form the Delhi Administration. The budget, taxes and any necessary legislation for Delhi must be authorized by the Union Cabinet and the national legislature.

In the Delhi Municipal Corporation a strict separation of powers is in force. The administration is in the hands of a municipal commissioner appointed by the central government for a period of five years and thereafter renewable annually. The commissioner can be removed by a special resolution of the council backed by a three-fifths majority. The commissioner is the chief executive, and it is a strange fact that the average length of service in the position is only $2\frac{1}{2}$ years. So short a period of service in so important an office cannot produce satisfactory results. Several of the other top positions are held by officers seconded from the Indian Administrative Service. This must severely limit the ability of the corporation to control its officials which is indispensable for genuine local self-government. In the Cantonment, executive control is in the hands of the cantonment board headed by the officer commanding the station, while in New Delhi the nominated committee and its official President ensure that government control over the executive is firmly maintained.

Calcutta has a similar system to that obtaining in Delhi Municipal Corporation. The entire executive power is in the hands of a municipal commissioner, who is appointed by the state government on the recommendation of the State Public Service Commission. He holds office for a period of five years, but the corporation can by a majority pass a resolution asking for his removal. Apart from that they have no control over him.

In Paris, executive power is vested in the Prefect of Paris and the Prefect of Police, who are administrative agents of the central government. Like all other prefects in France, they are appointed and dismissed by the Minister of the Interior, and are answerable to him. Their power is enormous and the Council of Paris has neither an elected mayor nor any other municipal executive.

As a consequence of all these centralizing tendencies, the elected Paris Council is in a relatively weak position. It cannot debate many questions which are of concern to the citizens of Paris but is limited to those enumerated by law. These comprise broadly the city's budget, accounts, taxes, loans, contributions to public works carried out by the state, subsidies and other financial matters; the method of administering public services of an industrial, commercial or social character; agreements concerning the operations of large-scale services of an industrial or commercial nature, such as public utilities, the management of municipal property, the programming of public works and plans for new highways. Nowhere else is an elected council so restricted in the scope of its deliberations as in the French capital.

In regard to the above-mentioned matters the council has powers of decision. In other matters the council may be invited to express an opinion by the Prefect of Paris or the Prefect of Police. Here it acts in a purely consultative role.

The reforms carried out by the law of July 10, 1964, have *inter alia* abolished the General Council of the Seine, of which the Paris municipal councillors were also members—the former Department of the Seine included Paris and 80 communes surrounding the city—and Paris now has the status of both a department and a commune. But the strong hand of the central government has not relaxed its grip on the city, and the Paris council is still very clearly subordinate to the dominant executive power of the central government, exercised through the two prefects. In the 20 districts or *arrondissements* the mayors are not officers of the commune but executives of the central government appointed by the Prime Minister on the recommendation of the Minister of the Interior. Their town halls are branch offices of the Paris prefecture.

The Prefect of Paris has wider powers than those of other prefects. He prepares the draft budget for the city and authorizes expenditure. All the officials and agents of the municipality are under his orders. He is responsible for the construction, maintenance and safety of highways, for public hygiene, sanitation and health, education, housing and town planning, and many other social services. He is the official representative of the city of Paris.

The jurisdiction of the Prefect of Police extends beyond the city of Paris to the adjoining departments of the Hauts-de-Seine, Seine-Saint-Denis and Val-de-Marne. His functions in the city include general police administration, public order and state security, the regulation of places of worship, entertainments, sporting events, the supervision of prisons, traffic regulation, wholesale food markets, etc. He is also responsible for certain aspects of public health, since he has to supervise sanitary conditions in furnished apartments, etc.

The most decisive and symbolic power of the Prefect of Paris is his power in certain circumstances to suspend the meetings of the council for a period up to three months, or to suspend its activities altogether, or to dismiss councillors from office. The prefect would not, of course, exercise such arbitrary powers except in the most serious circumstances, and no doubt only with the support of the Ministers concerned; but such considerations touch only the question of expediency, not of the distribution of power between the central government and the municipality. The distribution is, indeed, vastly unequal, and Paris cannot be regarded as in any real sense a self-governing city.

In Cairo executive power is in the hands of the governor (or *muhafez*). He is appointed and dismissible by presidential decree, which means in effect that he is an officer of the central government. This is emphasized by the fact that he has the status of a deputy minister. He represents the executive power of the state within the city of Cairo and reports to the Minister for Local Administration in respect to local government matters and to the Minister of the Interior on matters of security. Other ministers may delegate some of their powers to him. The governor's office is clearly modelled on that of the French prefect.

The governor nonetheless has to share powers with the governorate council, over which he or his deputy presides. This body has an unusual composition: of its 85 members, 44 are elected by the 22 districts of the city, in each of which is a committee of the Arab Socialist Union. The elected members must be members of such a committee. Of the remaining members, 24 represent the ministries whose personnel are doing work for the city, and 16 are men of exceptional ability drawn from the regional services; they may be either civil servants or private citizens, but they must be active members of the Arab Socialist Union. Half the membership is supposed to consist of farmers and workers according to the National Charter of the U.A.R.

This mixed council has numerous functions involving administrative activities. They include the administration of education, health and social affairs within limits prescribed by regulations; the exploitation of local resources and the increase of productivity in the city; the provision of work for the unemployed, the protection of motherhood and childhood, and assisting the aged and disabled; the management of state services and enterprises in accordance with government directions; the support of libraries, museums and other centres of culture and education; and the provision of financial or other forms of assistance to voluntary societies performing charitable or benevolent activities.

The governorate council is obviously intended to be a check on the governor's power, but it is difficult to discern the amount of influence it exerts and how much of that influence represents a point of view which is independent of and different from that of the central government, which is itself heavily represented on the council. The merging of technocratic, official, non-official and party henchmen in the governorate council could produce widely ranging consequences affecting the actual power of the governor, who is in theory unquestionably the chief executive.

Mexico City comes under the authority of the Department of the Federal District known as the D.D.F., which is virtually part of the Mexican federal government. The President of the Republic is the supreme head of the D.D.F. but the governor of the district is in immediate charge of its administration. The governor is appointed by the President and is often an important person in political circles as well as the working head of the federal capital.

The governor possesses many legal powers and much discretion in the exercise of them. He has at his disposal a large budget and a large staff; he does not have to face opposition or criticism from an assembly representing the city, for none exists. His discretion and leadership are unlikely to be questioned, and he has the support of a party which will endeavour to legitimize and justify his actions. He is, therefore, in a highly favourable position of almost unchallenged power subject to the one condition that he receives the continuous support of the President. Without it he may run into trouble with the Treasury, the press, the dominant political party, labour unions and other interest groups, with other federal departments and even the police. So while the governor is a political figure of some stature, he is dependent on presidential support. He can be dismissed by the President, and this happened in 1966. Hence, while the governor may be regarded as the chief executive, the city is under the thumb of the central government.

It is a disturbing fact that in eight out of twenty-seven great cities included in this book the executive organ is appointed wholly or partly by the central government. This group of metropolitan areas, comprising Paris, Buenos Aires, Calcutta, Amsterdam, Cairo, Mexico City, Ibadan and Delhi, is a major category in the classification we have attempted above. Here we have a group of famous cities, situated in Western Europe, in South America, in Africa and in Asia, where the executive authority is not entrusted to councillors elected by the local body of citizens, or to a person or persons chosen by them and responsible to them, or to a mayor or other high officer voted into office. How comes it that in these vast metropolitan cities with their millions of inhabitants, their high cultural attainments, their relative economic prosperity, their proud history and traditions, their busy industrial and commercial life, the democratic spirit burns at so low an ebb that the aspiration to govern itself which has inspired every great city since the days of ancient Greece has not been achieved? This indeed affords food for reflection, especially if one believes, as the writer does, that without successful self-government in the local sphere, a country is unlikely to attain a satisfactory standard of self-government at the national level.

We should be fully aware of the fact that the cities referred to above present vast differences not only in the formal machinery of government but also in the spirit which informs its working. In Amsterdam, for example, the city council exercises a most important influence on the entire organization of the municipal administration, and everyone is familiar with the political maturity and democratic outlook of the Dutch people. Moreover, the mayor is associated with a group of aldermen appointed by the city council to the board of burgomaster and aldermen. There is a vast contrast between Amsterdam, whose constitution contains many of the elements of self-government, and which operates within a democratic national regime, and Buenos Aires, where power is asserted in arbitrary and degraded forms and the true spirit of democracy is at present lacking at all levels of government—federal, state and local.

But when full allowance has been made for these differentiations, it is impossible to regard a city in which the executive power is possessed by an organ appointed by higher authority as enjoying democratic local government.

The explanation of the position lies partly in the immense increase in the importance of the great city both in the national economy and in the national polity. The sheer size of the modern megalopolis, especially if it is a capital, and its preponderance of resources of all kinds, has made the state regard it as a potential threat to the central government. Indeed, the possession of Paris has in the past often determined the fate of the French regime; while Mussolini's so-called 'march on Rome' was a decisive act in his seizure of power, despite the fact that he made the journey in a railway sleeping compartment. Historical facts and contemporary fears combine to make national governments anxious to keep control of the government of the capital city; and this desire expresses itself most frequently in the direct or indirect retention of executive authority. The city council, if there is one, may be permitted to do the talking; but a mayor or governor appointed by a minister or the head of the state, better still a prefect, will in time of emergency do what he is told by the government of the day.

MUNICIPAL SERVICES

For what functions is the municipal government of the great city responsible? This is obviously a question of large importance to our inquiry, and one would like to be able to give a reply which would be at once comprehensive and simple. Unfortunately, it is almost impossible to give such an answer. One reason is that in many of the cities some functions are carried out by independent or semi-independent boards which are often linked in one way or another with the city government, and it is exceedingly difficult to decide whether such functions should or should not be regarded as performed by the city government. To rule out all such functions would often be to give a totally misleading picture of the city government. On the other hand, they can be distinguished from the services under the direct control of the city council or its executive. A second reason is that while about eighteen or twenty services are commonly carried out by the municipalities of great cities, and about another eight or nine are found in several of them, there is a wide range of functions which are peculiar to a particular city, and are not to be found elsewhere.

The most widespread services administered by the municipalities of great cities are public health, hospitals, city planning, water supply, sewerage and sewage disposal, public cleansing, education, highway construction, street maintenance and lighting, public assistance, welfare, police forces, fire fighting, the provision of public housing and housing regulation, parks and playgrounds, recreational and cultural amenities, public transport, markets, abattoirs, cemeteries and crematoria. These services form the central core of local government, although all of them are not everywhere entrusted to the municipal government of the great city.

The list of services most commonly provided by the governments of great cities gives no indication of the scope or standard of performance. In one city 'education' may mean little more than overcrowded primary schools, in another it may include primary, secondary, technical, higher and further education, special schools for handicapped children, teacher training colleges, and many other institutions. 'Public health' may signify very little or a great deal. A sewage system may be provided for the entire metropolis or for a few favoured districts. Recreational and cultural amenities may or may not include municipal art galleries, museums, theatres, opera houses, concert halls, libraries, a planetarium, radio stations and many other activities; while sporting and athletic facilities can cover playing fields, athletic stadia, tennis courts, swimming pools, gymnasia and much else. It would be impossible to describe the scope, depth and standard of performance of all these functions for each of the cities included in this volume.

The governments of all great cities exercise a large number of regulatory functions concerning an immense variety of activities. Theatres, music halls, dance halls, night clubs, massage establishments, restaurants and hotels, employment agencies, saloon bars and public houses, taxi-cabs, noxious trades, air pollution, the removal of snow, the keeping of animals, the closing hours of shops, safety precautions in buildings, street signs and advertisements—these and a multitude of other matters are regulated by municipal ordinances, though not all of them in any one great city.

I have already pointed out that in several of the cities comprised in this book some functions are entrusted to independent or semi-independent boards which are linked with the city government. In Chicago, for example, in addition to the city government, there is Cook County, the Forest Preserve District, the Chicago Park District, the Board of Education, the Junior College District and the Metropolitan Sanitary District of Greater Chicago. Some of these bodies are directed by boards appointed by the mayor, others are elected by the citizens. All of them have the right to levy taxes and possess a substantial amount of independent power. A similar situation exists in Los Angeles.

This fragmentation of functions derives from the notion of checks and balances, and the fear of too great a concentration of power in any single organ of government, which characterizes American political thought and tradition. It has spread to Canada where local government services are subject to a similar kind of fragmentation. Thus in all parts of Canada responsibility for certain services, notably education, is given to bodies which are not under the full control of a municipal council. In Toronto the hydro-electric system is run by the Toronto Electric Commissioners, consisting of the mayor and two outside persons appointed by the council. The parking authority consists of three appointed commissioners chosen by the council from outside their own members. The harbour commission is appointed partly by the city of Toronto and partly by the Canadian government. Housing, public libraries and city planning also have separate boards with a minority of their members drawn from the city council which is the appointing authority. These local boards attached to the city administration demonstrate what Mr. Eric Hardy describes as 'the substantial erosion of the direct exercise of local government responsibilities by the city's elected representatives'.[1] Such fragmentation appears to be confined to North America. In Mexico City, by contrast, there is an absence of the fragmentation of functions and authority which characterizes local government in the United States and Canada. There, the threat to local government arises rather from the ever-spreading tendency towards centralization. Nearly all the services provided by Mexico City are duplicated, supplemented or overshadowed by the related or competing activities of federal departments and agencies.[2]

[1] *Post*, pp. 1007, 1012.   [2] *Post*, pp. 658, 659.

A similar trend has occurred in Buenos Aires, where the municipality provides or controls relatively few services. Many functions which are usually regarded as part of local government, such as fire fighting, abattoirs and slaughterhouses, sewage disposal and water supply, are in the hands of national agencies.

In Sydney, it is the State Government of New South Wales which does the overshadowing. Basic services such as education, police and public housing are provided by the state government. In the metropolis of Sydney municipal functions are even more restricted than in the principal country towns where local councils are empowered to provide the water supply, fire protection, aerodromes and other services which in Sydney are entrusted to state boards, commissions or departments.

Some of the services provided in great cities are of a public utility character; they are often called municipal trading services or municipal utilities. They include the supply of water, gas and electricity; the operation of public transport services within the city and its environs; wholesale food markets, municipal slaughterhouses or abattoirs; a port or harbour undertaking where one exists; with sometimes an airport as a modern addition. These services are nowadays less frequently the responsibility of the city government than formerly. They are, or can usually be made to be, financially self-supporting or even profitable. In consequence, municipal enterprise in the trading services is often rejected in favour of a commercial company operating for profit and regulated by public utility legislation or bound by the terms of a concession. Another alternative to municipal enterprise is an *ad hoc* authority, particularly the public corporation, which has become extremely popular in one form or another for public utility undertakings requiring management of a commercial or industrial kind.[1]

In Belgrade all the basic functions are performed within the city to the exclusion of federal or republican administration. But a majority of services are provided and financed by independent organs and not by the City assembly or the municipalities. The role of the City and municipal authorities is to prepare plans and lay down development programmes, to ensure that appropriate institutions are available to carry out tasks allocated to them, to subsidize those unable to pay their way, to see that all agencies observe the law, and to inspect and supervise the activities of the independent bodies.

Direct municipal ownership and administration is in my opinion the most satisfactory method of operating public utility services in the great city, if certain conditions are satisfied. First, the local government must cover a

[1] See W. A. Robson: *Nationalised Industry and Public Ownership* (2nd edition, 1962), London. George Allen & Unwin.

sufficiently large part of the population and territory of the metropolitan area to enable the services to be provided on a basis of economy and efficiency. In this connection it is clear that for certain functions, such as electricity generation, much larger areas even than a great metropolitan city are required for optimum efficiency. But although the generation of electricity has usually outgrown the boundaries of even a great metropolis, distribution can and should remain under the ultimate control or supervision of the municipal authority. Secondly, the city government must be democratic, honest and able to provide capable management. Thirdly, public utility services should not be run primarily for profit to relieve taxation, but in order to provide good service at the lowest possible cost to the citizen.[1] Well-run municipal enterprise is far better than the concessionaire company, which all too often is unwilling or unable to replace obsolete plant and equipment because of the uncertainty of its future position in relation to the undertaking. Whenever one sees in a city antiquated, obsolete tramways or motor buses, one can usually assume that they are owned by a company which is nearing the end of its franchise. Municipal enterprise, at its best, can be superior to the public corporation running a nationalized industry. For the opportunity for effective democratic control over the undertaking is direct and immediate when it is run by the municipality. The voters, who are also the consumers, know that responsibility for the service rests with a body (the city council, the mayor, etc.) which they can influence not only by their votes but also by their protests and representations. A public corporation, independent board or commission, is a much more remote body to the ordinary citizen. The man in the street, and still more the woman in the home, is scarcely aware of its existence; and its non-elective directors are remote from any living contact with the common man.

These three main groups of services do not exhaust the functions of the city government. There is, in addition, a great variety of functions which are peculiar to individual cities and which scarcely reveal a common pattern. One finds municipal universities in some cities; municipal pawnshops, savings banks, laundries, restaurants and hotels in others. Rome has a municipal funeral undertaking, chemists' shops and a municipal zoo. Sydney has a municipal golf course. Stockholm organizes vacations for housewives. Birmingham inspects premises used by child-minders. Tokyo provides financial assistance to small businesses. Belgrade assists shops selling food-stuffs and other commodities. The promotion of tourism is a municipal function here and there.

[1] See *The Management of Public Utilities by Local Authorities*, Vols. I and II. Proceedings of I.U.L.A. Congress, Bangkok, February 6–11, 1967, The Hague.

C

THE NEED FOR INTEGRATION

The task of providing a great city with the major services required by a civilized community has produced immense problems of a technical, administrative and financial character. The teeming millions of Tokyo, Paris, New York or London expect to be provided with an adequate water supply, an efficient main drainage and sewage system, highways adapted to modern traffic needs, housing accommodation on a continually rising standard, and good transport facilities. It is becoming increasingly difficult to provide these and other basic services like education on a scale which will satisfy their ever-growing demands. And in all great cities there is a rising demand for an improved environment and a decrease of pollution in all its many forms.

A special difficulty which confronts the great city is the need to provide services for the army of workers of all classes and occupations which pours into the city on every weekday. These hordes of workers in offices, shops and factories require water, drainage, police protection, highways, fire brigades, traffic and transport facilities, food regulation and inspection, and many other costly services; but they reside outside the boundaries of the city, and in consequence escape wholly or in large part the taxes levied by the city government, in particular those which fall on the houses or flats in which they live. This phenomenon has intensified the financial problem of the great municipality. It has also aroused the desire of the city government to extend its boundaries in order to incorporate the outlying suburbs, towns, villages, housing estates and other places within the metropolitan area.

There are many technical or administrative reasons connected with municipal functions which support and reinforce the desire of the great city on financial grounds to absorb the neighbouring areas outside its boundaries. Town and country planners, for example, are agreed that today a great city should not be planned in isolation from the surrounding suburban, rural or semi-rural hinterland. Accordingly, a development plan should cover the whole metropolitan area and indeed the region of which it is the centre.

Technical education is a service which requires for a high standard of achievement a wide range of differentiated institutions containing expensive equipment and highly trained specialist staffs. These can only be provided by a large local authority disposing of great resources. Where the great city provides technical education, people living in the outlying districts will seek to benefit from the superior facilities afforded by the large municipality, particularly if they work in the city. Where they are permitted to do so, the result is usually to the financial disadvantage of the large city, since such services are often subsidized out of local taxation. Moreover, technical education should be carefully related to the needs of local industry or commerce; and the requirements of outlying areas may differ from those of the central municipality. They may not be taken into consideration unless the entire metropolitan community is treated as a whole for this purpose.

To supply a great city with water often means bringing supplies from long distances at great cost; while to provide it with main drainage may mean transporting vast quantities of sewage to large disposal plants or outfalls. Sewage works and main drainage systems require high capital expenditure, great engineering works, and skilled personnel far beyond the reach of small local authorities. Modern methods of disposing of domestic and trade garbage also demand costly incinerating plants or reclamation schemes. The technical reasons for treating the entire metropolitan community as a single entity in respect of such services are very strong. Similar considerations apply to main highways and bridges. The system of public transport services within the region should clearly be organized as a whole. It is not simply the travelling needs of their own citizens which must be considered by the government of the great city, but also those of the entire metropolitan community of which it forms the traffic focus and radiating centre. There are several other services which should also be planned and administered over the entire metropolitan area, such as major housing schemes, fire brigades, the police, public libraries, large parks and open spaces, the distribution of gas and electricity, hospital services, and certain health services requiring highly specialized organization.

Of greater significance than these functional needs is the fundamental change in urban life which has taken place in the twentieth century. Modern methods of transportation have for the first time enabled people to live far away from their place of work; they have enabled men and women living in remote suburbs or distant villages to make frequent journeys to the great city for purposes of business or pleasure, education or social intercourse, medical treatment or aesthetic experience. Conversely, the inhabitant of the great city can travel twenty, thirty or more miles in pursuit of recreation: to play golf, to spend a day or a weekend at the coast, to visit friends, to enjoy a picnic or a walk in the woods, to go sailing or fishing in stream or lake, to climb mountains or go skiing. The big shops in the big city deliver goods to customers living within a large region; the metropolitan newspapers circulate within that region. This is the regional city, the most characteristic urban phenomenon of our time. It reveals the breakdown of the traditional form of self-contained, compact city and the birth of a much more mobile, scattered and diverse type of human settlement.

The great task confronting legislators and statesmen is to provide the metropolitan community with a regional government designed to satisfy modern needs in regard to organization, planning, co-ordination, finance and the other prerequisites for a satisfactory performance of the municipal functions on which the civilized life of urban man largely depends.

Important changes have taken place in a few of the cities included in this book. In Toronto, London, Paris, Belgrade and Stockholm steps have been taken to solve the metropolitan problem in various ways. I have already described the creation of the Municipality of Metropolitan Toronto and the improvements which were subsequently made in its structure. A strange anomaly in Toronto, however, is that although the metropolitan munici-pality was intended to coordinate the planning and development of local government services throughout the metropolitan area, the traditional notion of fragmented local government through the use of local boards was nevertheless made an essential feature of the new system. Schools, public transport, the police, licensing and child welfare were all hived off to boards or voluntary bodies not forming part of the metropolitan munici-pality.[1] Integration followed by disintegration is indeed a contradiction in terms.

In London a more drastic reform took place in 1963 when the Greater London Council and 32 London borough councils[2] were created by the London Government Act, which abolished a multitude of local authorities of various kinds which previously littered the ground. The London reforms are the most far reaching which have occurred hitherto in that the structure of both tiers of local authorities is entirely new. The system is not perfect and it could be improved in several respects, but it represents an immense improve-ment on the chaotic situation which previously existed in London and which still exists in most of the world's great cities.

The essential features of the London reforms are that there is a directly elected council covering the entire built-up area of the metropolis, and 32 directly elected London borough councils forming a second tier. The Greater London Council is responsible for such metropolitan functions as strategic planning, metropolitan roads, fire fighting, ambulances, major parks and open spaces, sewerage and sewage disposal, refuse disposal, traffic regulation, public transport, overspill housing, etc. The London boroughs are responsible for planning their own areas in conformity with the strategic plan, health and welfare services, refuse collection, education,[3] housing, local roads, swimming

1 *Post*, p. 1012.

2 The Corporation of the ancient City of London still exists, making a lower tier of 33 local authorities in Greater London.

3 In the former area of the London County Council, education is entrusted to an Inner London Education Authority, a unified organ which represents both the G.L.C. and the 12 London boroughs concerned.

pools, public libraries, etc. Certain services such as town planning, housing and highways are shared between the Greater London Council and the boroughs.

The administration of Paris has always been controlled by the central government, and this tradition persists in the recent reform of the District of the Paris Region, a large area containing a population of over 9 millions. In 1964 seven new departments were created to replace the former departments of the Seine and the Seine-et-Oise. One of these is the Ville de Paris. Each of the new departments has a prefect and an elected council. A new regional district embraces all the new departments and the official in charge of it is the Prefect of the Paris Region. He also bears the title of Delegate General and is directly responsible to the Prime Minister.

Within the Paris region are 1,305 communes. They are directly elected local authorities each with its mayor and councillors. Many of them are quite small and have few resources. The District has an administrative board consisting of 54 members drawn from the elected councillors in the communes and departments. The net effect of these reforms is to impose a powerful centrally controlled regional superstructure over the departments and communes, to rationalize the prefectural organization, and to leave untouched the obsolete system of communes.

In Tokyo the regional problem has been entrusted to the Capital Region Development Commission set up in 1956 and later revised in 1967. This commission consists of the Minister of Construction and four other members nominated by him. It is an agency of the central government and contains no element of local government or any link with the Tokyo Metropolitan Government. The region covers Tokyo and the 7 prefectures which surround it within a radius of about 100 kilometres of Tokyo Station. It contained a population of almost 30 millions in 1965. The Capital Region Development Commission is a weak and ineffective body. It is responsible for regional planning, but it has no powers of planning control, enforcement or development. It has a very small staff, a very small revenue and little political influence or power. Meanwhile, the metropolis of Tokyo is left to struggle with immense problems with an obsolete structure, insufficient finances and inadequate powers.

A scheme has been adopted to establish a large county council (*landsting*) in the Stockholm region, taking effect at the beginning of 1971. The new county council contains 49 local authorities, including the city of Stockholm, and it has 149 councillors (including alternate representatives) elected for a three-year term of office. The council is in effect a new type of organ with more numerous and extensive duties than those of other county councils in Sweden. It is responsible for regional planning, overall traffic organization, hospital services, the planning of schools other than primary, water and sewage planning, the public dental service, assistance for disabled and handicapped persons, legal aid, welfare services of specified kinds, and the co-ordination and support of local housing associations.

Many of these functions have hitherto been in the hands of the local authorities. The latter will continue to provide many basic services within their respective areas, such as city planning, roads and parks, recreational services, housing, gas and electricity supply, school and cultural activities, development of the environment, and many welfare services.

Not the least remarkable feature of the new regional system is that it was the outcome of an agreement in principle reached between the Stockholm City Council and the county council, and it was at their request that the Riksdag was asked to pass legislation creating the 'Greater County Council'.

The metropolitan areas of the United States are in a position of extreme difficulty, for any comprehensive integration is ruled out by sentiments and forces which are virtually insuperable. As Professor Wallace Sayre points out, New York City today experiences 'along with almost every other large American city, the urgent problems of policy and administration which accompany the status of a "central city" in a metropolitan region much larger in area and population'.[1] The New York Metropolitan Region has a land area of nearly 13,000 square miles and a population of approximately 19 millions. It contains more than 1,500 separate governments, the great majority being local authorities of one kind or another. This region is an urbanized area which confronts many urgent and pervasive problems but it has no effective governmental institution for dealing with these regional problems. The New York metropolitan region is at present characterized more by governmental fragmentation, specialization and parochialism than by integration; and this state of affairs is likely to continue. A similar situation exists in Chicago.

The position is made especially difficult by the fact that the metropolitan area of New York sprawls over the three States of New York, New Jersey and Connecticut, while Chicago Metropolitan Area extends over Illinois and Indiana. No integrated authority which derogated from the territory or powers of these states could be considered. A second and more general obstacle arises from the fact that political sentiment in the United States believes that local communities on the outskirts of a city should not be merged unless they agree to do so by means of a referendum. There is no law or constitutional provision to this effect. It derives from the American conception of

[1] *Post*, p. 691.

democratic rights. The opposition to any such proposal is likely to be very strong.

In Los Angeles the official metropolitan area is coterminous with the boundaries of the county, but the true region extends far beyond the county of Los Angeles to the counties of Orange, San Bernardino, Riverside and Ventura. Even within the county of Los Angeles the government of the metropolitan area is distributed among numerous local units, notably the county and the city, 77 suburban cities, the Los Angeles City School District and the suburban school districts. There has been no attempt to integrate all these local government units.

In Denmark, the adjoining municipalities of Copenhagen, Frederiksberg and Gentofte have long been recognized as 'the capital'. The division of the capital among three independent municipalities created some serious problems, but the metropolitan area now extends to 19 suburban municipalities which has so exacerbated these problems that a more rational organization of the metropolis for administrative, transport, planning and financial purposes is now under consideration. In the Netherlands the metropolitan area of Amsterdam consists of a large number of independent municipalities, and here again integration is completely lacking at present although it is under consideration.

The local government of the Calcutta Metropolitan District is fragmented amongst hundreds of urban and rural bodies. This makes it impossible to undertake the planning and administration of the functions affecting the entire metropolis. In Osaka there is a jumble of authorities and the urban complex is divided among many government authorities. As Professor Royama remarks, 'There is no integration and co-ordination among the government services performed by those authorities and confusion and ambiguity in the division of responsibility are apparent'.[1]

The situation described in these cities is typical of the position which exists in most metropolitan areas. An integrated, rational organization is the exception rather than the rule. Meanwhile, the difficulties accumulate to such an extent that the problems can no longer be ignored, and a solution cannot be postponed indefinitely. The fundamental question is therefore what kind of solution will sooner or later be adopted.

The obstacles to the integration of the local authorities in and around a great city in some form of metropolitan government are of various kinds. Sometimes (as in Manila and Copenhagen) they arise from the opposition of some or all of the municipalities concerned to what is proposed, or their inability to agree on a viable scheme. More often they are due to apathy or

[1] *Post*, p. 973.

hostility on the part of the central government (or the State government in a federal constitution), or to a fear that a metropolitan authority would be too powerful to be easily controlled. An interesting feature of the recent reforms in the Stockholm region is that the initiative came from the City Council and the County Council after they had reached agreement on the principles involved.

THE ATTEMPT TO EXPAND

The expansion of the principal municipality to cover the metropolitan area is a development which might appear at first sight to be the most obvious solution to the problem of metropolitan government. As a general proposition, the principle that political and governmental institutions should expand in order to keep pace with the enlarged scale of human activity, is incontestable. Among smaller units of local government, the principle often prevails. When, however, attempts are made by great cities to extend their territories, their efforts meet with such fierce resistance that this method has proved of small use as a means of providing metropolitan areas with appropriate organs of local government except where expansion has been imposed by a higher level of government, often in the face of severe opposition in the localities concerned. New York city has annexed no territory for more than seventy years; Philadelphia is only one-tenth of a square mile larger than it was in 1854; San Francisco is the same size as it was in 1856; Chicago occupies the same territory as it did in 1889.

There are only a few exceptional instances of success in this direction. In Bombay, for example, the policy of boundary extension, first advocated in 1918, was adopted in 1950 by the amalgamation with the city of a number of neighbouring communities. This assured Bombay of sufficient land to meet all its housing requirements that could be foreseen. Manchester, after repeated efforts, at last induced Parliament in 1930 to extend the city's boundaries so as to include land now occupied by the garden suburb of Wythenshawe. Sydney, by invoking statutory powers enacted in 1948, secured the amalgamation of eight municipalities in the industrial suburbs adjoining the city but the city of Sydney has recently been *reduced* in size by the State government. Los Angeles was an outstanding case of large-scale territorial expansion, especially in the years between 1913 and 1925, but this was due to the difficulty of obtaining water in a semi-arid region. Los Angeles was drawing its water supply from areas more than 150 miles away, and this involved expenditure on a scale beyond the resources of any save a very large and wealthy city. In order to share in the benefits of this water supply, outlying areas were ready and even anxious to come within the territory of the city; and many of them actually applied for annexation. Nevertheless, more than 3 million people now live outside the city limits.

There are only a few rare instances where a great city has succeeded in expanding its boundaries to include the metropolitan community and in a few exceptional cases the city has under its jurisdiction a substantial tract of unbuilt territory.[1] 'The large American cities', writes Dr. Victor Jones, 'have never been able to keep pace, by means of annexation or consolidation, with the accumulation of population on the margin of the city'.[2] The prospects today are less favourable even than in the past that the process of amalgamation will bring any substantial part of the metropolitan population under the jurisdiction of a true metropolitan government. There is, indeed, a continued proliferation of small local authorities in the outlying parts of the principal metropolitan areas of the United States.

A similar situation is reported from Australia. 'It is unlikely', observed Dr. J. R. H. Johns, 'that the problems of metropolitan local government in Western Australia will be solved, at least in the near future, by either a Greater City Movement or the adoption of Regionalism.'[3] The only example of a large expansion of a major city was in 1925 when the Greater Brisbane Council was given exclusive powers in an area of 375 square miles. Local parochialism, the refusal of the wealthier areas to share their rating resources with the poorer local authorities, and the indifference of elected councillors towards projects which may result in their loss of office, are among the reasons which make amalgamation of local government areas with the central city almost impossible to achieve.[4] Professor Atkins has more recently noted a mild interest in the creation of regional authorities in some states, but the only practical result appears to have been the deconcentration to regional offices of State government activities.[5]

In view of this it is not surprising to learn that the distribution of the metropolitan population in Western Australia has occurred without any corresponding changes in local government boundaries of fiscal resources. Since 1900 only one municipality and four road board districts have been incorporated. 'Changes in the status of local authorities have been rare and boundary adjustments few. Structural changes in local government have lagged behind changes in function and fiscal need.'[6]

[1] e.g. Rome, Belgrade, Pretoria. Rio de Janerio, and Delhi.
[2] Victor Jones: *Metropolitan Government* (1942), p. 129.
[3] J. R. H. Johns: *Metropolitan Government in Western Australia*, p. 73.
[4] *Ibid.*, p. 59.
[5] 'Local Government' in *Public Administration in Australia* Ed. R. N. Spann, pp. 175-176.
[6] J. R. H. Johns: *Metropolitan Government in Western Australia*, p. 6.

C*

It is obvious that a large municipality, surrounded by a multiplicity of small local authorities of various kinds, cannot hope to meet the social, political or administrative needs of a great metropolitan area. A medley of scattered and disintegrated local authorities cannot provide the unity required for a coherent scheme of development. Many small areas will be unable to obtain the range or standard of services which demand large-scale administration or substantial resources of money, population, specialized institutions and highly trained personnel.[1] It has been truly remarked that 'disintegrated local government in metropolitan areas results in unequalized services, in a disparity between need and fiscal ability to meet the need, and in a dispersion and dissipation of political control of the development of social, economic, and political institutions'.[2]

Opposition to the expansion of the great city is essentially political. It is often founded on a sense of separateness on the part of the inhabitants of the outlying suburban areas, who do not identify themselves completely with the metropolitan community, although they may work in the great city, use it for shopping, recreation, and many other purposes. The local politicians, councillors and officials usually try to fan the flames of such resistance and their attitude may be quite sincere in that they themselves fail to identify their district with the larger metropolis of which it forms a part. On the other hand, their attitude is sometimes due to self-regarding motives springing from a desire to retain an official appointment or to remain a councillor at all costs, regardless of the wider public interest involved. When a full account has been taken of such considerations, the stark fact remains that amalgamation usually results in the absorbed unit ceasing to be a separate entity, and thereby losing its local government institutions. Instead of having its own elected council, mayor, chairman or city manager, it becomes an insignificant fraction of a vast city governed from a remote centre with which it has little contact. Is it surprising that, faced with such a prospect, the small towns, urban and rural districts, villages, etc., should resist what appears to them to be the lethal encroachments of an advancing tide? From their point of view, it is a fight for life.

Technical, financial and administrative considerations concerning efficiency or economy, the equalization of services and resources, the broadening of the incidence of taxation: all these count for little compared with the primitive emotions which are aroused by the urge to survive.

All kinds of arguments both true and false, and all manner of accusations,

---

[1] This was emphasized by the Ontario Municipal Board in its decisions and recommendations on the Toronto metropolitan question. See report dated January 20, 1953, p. 14.

[2] Victor Jones: *op. cit.*, p. 52.

are employed by the spokesmen of suburban or outlying areas to oppose absorption by the great municipality. These arguments and allegations vary from place to place and from time to time.[1] They are for the most part, however, mere surface phenomena, and as such scarcely warrant detailed study. They usually represent an attempted rationalization of underlying currents of feeling which are often subconscious.

By far the best way of meeting these objections is by means of a two-tier system of local government. There are substantial advantages in establishing a major authority for the planning, co-ordination and administration of large-scale functions, while leaving all the purely local services to a lower tier of minor authorities. The arguments for a two-tier system in a great metropolitan area are overwhelming, for only by such a method is it possible for the suburban and outlying districts to retain their institutional identity and communal life whilst becoming part of the metropolitan area for the larger governmental purposes.

Only by this means, moreover, can we hope to find a solution to the problem of providing the metropolitan area with a democratic system of local government while also giving the citizen a smaller and more easily comprehensible unit of community life in whose government he can participate. It is perfectly feasible and logical to aim simultaneously at both larger and smaller units of local government in metropolitan areas; and to evoke in the citizens a sense of civic interest in both the larger community and the smaller. It may even be worth while establishing a federal type of metropolitan council, in which a proportion of the members would be elected by the local authorities in the area, although we would insist that not less than half of them would be directly elected by the electors for the metropolitan area, in order to ensure an adequate representation of the regional outlook.

THE 'AD HOC' AUTHORITY FOR SPECIAL PURPOSES

The English-speaking countries have made considerable use of the *ad hoc* authority set up to perform a single function, or sometimes more than one,

---

[1] For an analysis of the reasons formulated by politicians and various organizations in outlying areas in U.S.A. in opposing amalgamation, see Victor Jones: 'Politics of Integration in Metropolitan Areas', in *The Annals of the American Academy of Political and Social Science*, Vol. 207, January 1940, pp. 161–4. For an example drawn from Canada see the Report of the Ontario Municipal Board dated January 20, 1953, summarizing the objections by outlying municipalities to amalgamation with the city of Toronto. The opposition to the reform of London government is set out in the report of the Royal Commission on Local Government in Greater London (H.M.S.O. Cmnd. 1164/1960). See also Frank Smallwood: *Greater London. The Politics of Metropolitan Reform* (1965), Gerald Rhodes: *The Government of London. The Struggle for Reform* (1970).

over a larger area than that in which the city government exercises power. In London, for example, there is the Port of London Authority, the Metropolitan Water Board, the London Electricity Board, the North Thames Gas Board, London Transport[1] and several others. In Los Angeles there is the Metropolitan Water District, the Water Pollution Board, the County Air Pollution Control District, the Flood Control District, and one or two other 'special districts' as these bodies are called in the United States. Metropolitan Toronto has a Metropolitan School Board, the Metropolitan Toronto and Region Conservation Authority, the Toronto and York Roads Commission, the Ontario Housing Corporation, a similar body for student housing, and the Toronto Transit Commission. In Montreal we find a Transportation Commission controlling all surface transport facilities throughout the metropolitan area, and the Metropolitan Commission, set up to control the finances of all the municipalities on the Island of Montreal. Sydney has had a Metropolitan Water and Sewerage Board since 1880; a Main Roads Commission; and many other *ad hoc* bodies to provide transport, fire protection, abattoirs, hospitals and public health services, maritime services and housing. There are trusts set up to administer parks, sanctuaries, cemeteries and crematoria in the metropolitan area. In Calcutta there is the Metropolitan Water and Sanitation Authority. In metropolitan Chicago there are several *ad hoc* bodies, of which the Sanitary District of Chicago is the best known.

The Port of New York Authority is a leading example of a vigorous *ad hoc* authority exercising functions in a district covering about 1,500 square miles and containing about twelve million persons. It was established in 1921 by a compact between the States of New York and New Jersey to deal with the complex transport problems which have arisen in the metropolitan area. Six unpaid commissioners are appointed by the governor of each state with the approval of the state senate. The Port of New York Authority provides cross-river bridges, marine terminals for shipping, the great international airports serving New York, the air terminals, terminals for motorbus services, motor truck transport and rail freight. It constructed and operates the Hudson tunnels, and has recently taken over a local commuter railway. The Metropolitan Transportation Authority is a major body concerned with mass public transportation facilities in New York City and 7 neighbouring counties.

In the United States *ad hoc* authorities have proliferated to an alarming extent. Professor Robert G. Smith stated in 1964 that there were more than

[1] London Transport was transferred to the Greater London Council in 1969, but its services extend far beyond the area of the G.L.C.

18,000 special districts and single-function public authorities operating in every state of the Union. The distinction he drew between the two kinds of bodies was financial: the special districts rely primarily upon special taxes levied in their districts, whereas public authorities rely primarily on revenue-bond issues which are amortized by the charges paid by those who use the service or facility provided by the authority.[1] Both special districts and public authorities are *ad hoc* bodies operating outside the regular structure of government. They are not politically responsible; and they are performing functions which properly belong to the organs of local or state government.

There are several reasons why they have come into existence in such very large numbers, and why they are today the most rapidly increasing type of governmental agency in the United States. One very important reason is the inadequacy of the existing organization of local government, especially in the metropolitan areas, and the almost insuperable difficulty of reforming the structure. An additional reason has been a desire to escape from the legal limits imposed on the borrowing powers of city governments. Furthermore, they appeal to people who think that this is the most efficient way to get a particular job done by specialists without the delay and the conflicts which the regular processes of democratic government frequently encounter.

In Tokyo several important functions are being carried out by public corporations. Among them are the Teito Rapid Transit Authority, the Japan Housing Corporation, the Tokyo Expressway Corporation, the Tokyo Metropolitan Housing Corporation and the Tokyo New Town Development Corporation. Sometimes a public corporation has been created to undertake a particular project, such as the construction of the Shinjuku business centre in Tokyo. In Japan the creation of public corporations is often seen as the easiest way of solving a problem which could and should be solved by other methods. For example, the borrowing powers of Tokyo Metropolitan Government are unduly restricted by the central government. So a public corporation is sometimes established because it has greater freedom to raise loans.

In Australia a similar trend can be observed. In Sydney *ad hoc* bodies are responsible for several major functions in the metropolis, such as ferry services, water supplies, sewerage and drainage, cemeteries and crematoria. Cairo also relies on such bodies for transport, water supplies and sewage disposal. In Belgrade all the public utilities and many of the social services

---

[1] Robert G. Smith: *Public Authorities, Special Districts and Local Government*. National Association of Counties Research Foundation (Washington, D.C.) pp. xii, xviii. See also the same author's *Public Authorities in Urban Areas* (produced by the same publisher in 1969).

and cultural activities are entrusted to independent self-managing organizations separate from the City and municipal authorities but guided, supervised, inspected and subsidized by them.

In Britain the movement towards the *ad hoc* authority has swung forward in the course of nationalizing several major industries and services. There are now numerous regional gas boards, regional electricity boards, regional hospital boards and licensing authorities for road transport vehicles, operating over very large areas and exercising functions which were in many instances formerly carried on by city councils.[1]

There are several different types of *ad hoc* body among those which have been or might be mentioned. Dr. Thomas H. Reed distinguished the following four main categories:[2]

(1) Those appointed by and responsible to the central government, or, in the case of a federal constitution, to the state government. Examples of this type are the Metropolitan Police Commissioners in London, who are appointed and controlled by the Home Secretary; and the Japan Housing Corporation.

(2) Those composed of representatives of the constituent bodies, such as the London Metropolitan Water Board, the Montreal Metropolitan Commission and the New Town Development Corporation in Tokyo.

(3) Those directly elected by the voters. In this category come the Sanitary District of Chicago, and the East Bay Municipal Utility District of California.

(4) Those where the governing body represents chiefly the interests concerned in its activities. Examples of this type are the Port of London Authority and some of the boards set up in Australia which contain members representing producers, consumers, employees, and other interests.

The *ad hoc* authority has been widely adopted as an easy solution to the problem of metropolitan government. In this connection I will venture to quote the following passage on the subject from my book, *The Government and Misgovernment of London*.[3]

The attractiveness of the *ad hoc* idea is not difficult to understand in a situation such as that which exists in London. The ground is littered with multifarious elected authorities possessing jurisdiction over utterly inadequate areas. Each one of those authorities is a centre of potential opposition to any rational scheme of reform. On the other hand, the technical needs of a service—water, transport or whatever it may be—are easily ascertained and strongly urged by responsible administrators or independent experts who at least desire to promote the efficiency of that service. Hence the wary politician, the timid civil servant and the technical

---

[1] See W. A. Robson: *Nationalized Industry and Public Ownership*.
[2] 'Metropolitan Areas', *Encyclopaedia of the Social Sciences* (1st edition), Vol. X, p. 398.
[3] Second edition, pp. 333–4.

specialist readily turn to the *ad hoc* authority as the easiest way out of their difficulties. 'Ministers have almost ceased to apologize', writes Mr. Herbert Morrison, 'for creating Greater London authorities for purposes which, if local government were rationally organized in the area, could have been discharged under normal local government auspices. Indeed, some enthusiasts with specialist minds occasionally bob up demanding yet another Greater London authority in respect, for example, of housing or town planning. There are people who believe that the establishment of a special authority will solve most problems for co-ordination, whereas it may have done little more than create a salary list.' Sometimes the more pressing technical difficulties may be assuaged for a time. But ultimately the *ad hoc* body gives rise to as many problems as it solves.

The most serious drawback of the *ad hoc* body is that there is no method of co-ordinating its work with related activities carried out by other bodies. It has one, and only one, object in view; and it is in a sense failing to discharge its duty if it attempts to take a comprehensive view of things. Yet the services of a great modern city are becoming more interrelated every day, and even their efficiency is determined to no small extent by the degree of co-ordination that is attained. Housing, planning, transport, highways—how can one separate such a group as this? And housing in turn involves education, drainage, public health, gas and electricity and many other services. There are hundreds of other points of contact between the various public and social services where 'the single eye' is needed to obtain the best result.

Professor Reed[1] agreed that the metropolitan problem as a whole cannot be solved by the creation of special districts, though he rightly pointed out that the services rendered by many *ad hoc* authorities are of immense value. He considered that where several important functions have been entrusted to a single *ad hoc* authority, the result is a close approach to what he called 'the federated city'. He cited as an example the Massachusetts Metropolitan District Commission, which has been made responsible for sewers, water supply, parks and planning in Greater Boston. But this commission is in no sense an organ of local self-government, for its members are appointed by, and responsible to, the governor of the state. In consequence, it has the overwhelming disadvantage of failing to satisfy the basic criterion of local democracy. On this ground alone we must reject such a solution of the problem of metropolitan government.[2]

The same objection would not apply to a directly elected, or even an indirectly elected, *ad hoc* authority gradually acquiring the power to perform a wide range of functions, and thereby becoming in effect the principal

---

[1] *Encyclopaedia of the Social Sciences: op. cit.*

[2] See J. R. H. Johns: *Metropolitan Government in Western Australia* (1950), p. 67. 'A widening range of metropolitan services is rendered by statutory boards which are subject to diverse directions in the composition of the controlling agency and have varying degrees of fiscal and administrative autonomy. The future good government of the Metropolitan Area and indeed of the State demands an examination of the functions which have been removed from local control and the selection of those which local government is competent and willing to administer.'

organ of metropolitan government. But is there any reason to believe that such a movement would not meet with fierce opposition on the part of all the minor local authorities, and in addition the chief municipality, whose interests would be jeopardized by such a development? They would, I believe, resist this movement for the same reasons as the former resist the expansion of the great city. Indeed, from their point of view the ultimate result would be almost identical.

The *ad hoc* authority operating within a special district which is larger than the municipality attempts to solve the technical, administrative and financial problems arising in connection with a particular service by isolating it from the complex of municipal services of which it forms a part. It may solve that problem, but only at the cost of weakening the general structure of local government in the great city and its environs, whereas the real need is to strengthen it.

The *ad hoc* authority appears to have emerged chiefly, but by no means exclusively, as a method of dealing with metropolitan areas. In some instances the *ad hoc* organ is regarded as likely to provide more efficient management. In some countries the motive has been to restrict the scope of the powers conferred on local government authorities.

It is possible that a prefect or other local representative of the central government may sometimes act as a unifying influence in an urban centre divided among numerous local authorities. This was clearly the object in creating the District of the Paris Region and appointing a regional prefect to take charge of it. In the Scandinavian countries the governor or intendant provides a central point of reference which fosters local unity.[1] In our view the disadvantages and dangers to local self-government which the prefect or intendant brings in his train outweigh any possible advantages which the system may have. Similarly the principle of 'democratic centralism' which governs the relations between the People's Council of Warsaw and the higher authorities in Poland may provide an explanation of why it is not necessary to establish *ad hoc* organs in the Polish capital. This principle originated in the Soviet Union and is now found in most of the communist countries in Eastern Europe.

OTHER ATTEMPTS TO SOLVE THE PROBLEM

There are many other devices which either exist or can be introduced to

[1] In Sweden the county administration is an organ of state authority operating at the county level. It is directly under the Ministry of Home Affairs and exercises important co-ordinating and supervising functions. *Post*, p. 884; W. J. M. Mackenzie: *op. cit.* p. 11.

overcome the difficulties arising from the lack of an integrated metropolitan government. One such device is for the great city to provide the
outlying districts or towns with some of its services, although there is a
physical limit to what can be done in this direction. It is quite common for
large cities which own and operate motor bus, trolley bus and tramway
undertakings to provide services to points far beyond the city boundaries.

Manchester City Council brings water to the city from a distance of 100
miles, and supplies in bulk many other districts and also the neighbouring
town of Salford. In Buenos Aires, municipal services are usually extended to
suburbs outside the city limits as the metropolis expands. Legal permission
has usually to be obtained from higher authorities before activities of this
kind can be carried out.

A similar result is attained when the great city permits residents from outside areas to use its municipal services, on payment of an appropriate sum
by the outlying local authority or by the person concerned. This arrangement
is easily applied to services which are rendered to specific individuals, like
technical or higher education, hospital treatment, libraries and so forth.
Arrangements of this kind must usually be negotiated and agreed between
the local authorities concerned.

Large cities also sometimes acquire property outside their boundaries,
such as water reservoirs, hospitals, greenhouses, parks and playing fields.
Sometimes they are even authorized to exercise regulatory or police powers
in outlying areas.[1]

A further development of more recent date is the provision of housing to
take the overspill of the great city's population in outlying areas within the
metropolitan region. Where insufficient land is available in the great city to
enable slum clearance, the abolition of overcrowding and good housing
standards to be achieved, arrangements are sometimes made whereby the
municipality provides or finances housing accommodation for its citizens in
outlying areas. The former London County Council built a great many
housing estates outside its own boundaries and this policy has been continued
on a big scale by the Greater London Council.

Where this occurs the great municipality becomes a colonizing power,
planting its citizens in alien lands beyond its own borders. In the past, these
colonizing activities have often been unwelcome to the 'receiving' local
authorities, who were obliged to provide schools, hospitals, police forces,
fire brigades and many other services for the overspill. This not only cast a
financial burden on the receiving local authority, but also created a problem

[1] Albert Lewpawsky: *Urban Government* (National Resources Committee, Washington,
1939), Vol. I, p. 34.

of assimilation, where large numbers of families were uprooted from a slum district in which they had long resided and were suddenly transplanted to an area which was quite new to them and in which they had neither friends nor relatives. The Town Development Act, 1952, which seeks to encourage town development in county districts in order to relieve congestion or over-population elsewhere, should remove some of these causes of friction in England. The Town Development Act enables big cities to enter into agreements with smaller towns which are willing to expand whereby a big city can provide substantial financial contributions, and also technical aid if required, to promote the construction of additional public housing, in exchange for the right to nominate tenants of the new housing units. The central government gives housing subsidies to the expanding towns and can also contribute towards the cost of providing or extending certain services like water supply, main sewerage and sewage disposal plants. These town development schemes provide for industrial expansion of the towns, and tenants with appropriate industrial skills are given priority by the exporting authority.

Not only Greater London, but also Birmingham, Bristol, Liverpool, Manchester, Newcastle, Wolverhampton and Salford have entered into agreements of this kind. In London by the end of 1967, 27,500 London families had moved to new homes in 31 expanded towns, where jobs were also available. Birmingham has entered into such agreements with 38 local authorities, involving the transfer of factories as well as workers. The schemes under this legislation are always of substantial size. An example is the agreement between Birmingham and Droitwich for the subsidization of 2,000 new houses. Another and more ambitious scheme concerns Daventry, which is planned to grow from a population of 7,000 to 36,000 by 1981. In this case Birmingham City Council is building the houses which will be sold at cost price to the Daventry Borough Council.

These diverse arrangements, whether legal, financial, or administrative, are essentially devices for overcoming the lack of unity and coherence in the government of the metropolitan region, and the congestion which so often afflicts the great city. They are not solutions of the problem; but rather substitutes for a solution. Regarded merely as expedients, they have much to commend them; but if they are regarded as attempts to cope with some of the greatest problems of modern urban life, they are puny and insignificant. Moreover, they bring great disadvantages in their train. It is not obvious wherein lies the good sense or justice in permitting or encouraging the Greater London Council or Birmingham City Council to impose taxes on their citizens in order to subsidize the accommodation of their fellow-citizens in housing estates in other towns and to transfer factories, etc., to those towns. Such activities do not strengthen local government in the metropolitan area; and it is doubtful if they even enhance the sense of community among the people in the metropolitan region. On the other hand, they help to relieve the congestion in some parts of the great city and thereby facilitate rehousing and slum clearance schemes at lower densities and in an improved environment.

One other method of attempting to solve the problem which we may note is by amalgamating the city with the county in which it is situated. This approach is familiar in the United States, where proposals to consolidate the county with the city have been put forward in recent years in a number of great cities, including Pittsburgh, Detroit, Cleveland, Milwaukee and St. Louis. This usually means reorganizing the county, which in the United States is a unit of state government, and making it the basis of a metropolitan municipality. Some important cases of city–county unification have occurred in New York City, Washington, D.C., New Orleans, Denver, Philadelphia and San Francisco. It is clear, however, that the reorganization of the great cities of America cannot be satisfactorily effected by this method because too many counties are involved. New York metropolitan region extends over 31 counties, Los Angeles over 5 or 6. Where a metropolitan area covers several counties the development of county government would not solve any of the problems demanding a metropolitan approach. In San Francisco, city–county consolidation has done nothing to lessen the acute need for an effective form of overall planning and administration embracing the entire area of the bay. The Chicago metropolitan area extends even beyond the State of Illinois to Indiana, and this trend will continue. The greater part of Cook County consists of the city of Chicago, but in addition it contained in 1966 486 governmental units of various kinds.[1] Professor Rakove points out that despite this medley of public authorities and a population explosion in the suburbs, there is little prospect of a serious move towards a metropolitan government possessing real political or administrative power.[2] There are still some enthusiastic exponents of city–county consolidation as the way forward, but it is impossible to see any rational ground for their belief that this will solve the metropolitan problem in America.[3]

POLITICS IN THE GREAT CITY

The growth of party politics in the great city can be observed all over the

[1] *Post*, p. 360.   [2] *Post*, p. 363.
[3] See my foreword to *Metropolitan Problems* (published by Drew University, Madison, New Jersey).

world. This phenomenon is an aspect of the general movement towards the increase of political parties and party organization which has occurred during the twentieth century. Municipal politics have become the subject of intense organization and propaganda in many countries during the last thirty or thirty-five years to a much greater degree than formerly. Moreover, the political party machines have become much more closely integrated than hitherto at the municipal, provincial and national levels.

These tendencies are particularly strong in the great cities, for reasons which are easy to understand. Political control of a great municipality—especially a capital city—is in itself a considerable prize, a substantial asset in the struggle for power. Moreover, such control possesses great propaganda value and prestige in the wider sphere of national politics. Indeed, so important are these influences in the municipal election campaigns which take place in great cities, that sometimes the main object of the conflict is to demonstrate that public opinion is strongly in favour of, or opposed to, the party which controls the national (or state) government rather than to gain control of the city council. These secondary effects can become the primary objects of the political contest within the municipality. Thus Mexico City has been the passive prize of victory in national politics rather than an active contender for national power, whereas Rio de Janeiro and Manila have been strongholds for the opposition.

This tendency is fortified by the close relationship which exists in most countries between the great municipality and the central (or the state) government. This relationship takes various forms and many different threads are woven into the pattern; but the general trend is towards increased control of the city by higher authority, and greater reliance by the municipality on grants of money contributed by the national or state government. One result of this has been to assimilate municipal and national or state politics, especially in regard to such matters as the social services, public expenditure, economic planning and fiscal policy. Sydney has been the victim of party politics in the State of New South Wales. Professor Atkins observes that general party guides in politics are not adequate for local affairs.

The emerging picture is one in which the national political parties participate in the municipal elections, and usually nominate the candidates. The 'independent' holder of municipal office without specific party ties has become a rarity; and it is extremely difficult, if not impossible, for anyone to get elected to the council without the support of a powerful party.[1] All or

---

[1] There are, however, some exceptions to this general tendency. In Canada federal and provincial parties are not acceptable at the local level, and both Montreal and Toronto have evolved their own municipal parties. Los Angeles has a non-partisan system of city government.

most of the main political parties are nowadays represented on the city council; and executive organs, committees, commissions or boards appointed by the council usually reflect the relative strengths of the various parties on the council. Where the mayor is directly elected by the citizens, he will usually be a party candidate, and his executive powers will be immensely reinforced by his political influence as a party chief.

There is nothing inherently wrong with these tendencies. They are merely the result of the drive for better party organization to cope with the enormous size of the modern electorate, and for more coherence to deal with the greater scope and complexity of municipal activity. Political parties can be as useful to the local government of a great city as they are to democracy at the national or state level. The value of political parties can be tested by what happens in their absence. In Los Angeles, and in the adjoining county, municipal government is conducted on a non-partisan basis. The result, we are told, is that all kinds of pressure groups representing commercial, vocational, ethnic, labour and other interests exert an influence on the conduct of city affairs, and the newspapers have a dominant voice in determining policy. This may well be a less desirable state of affairs than a straightforward party system, provided the parties are not corrupt.

There are, however, some very undesirable consequences which sometimes flow from the intrusion of party politics in city affairs. First, there is the tendency to sacrifice questions of genuine municipal importance to irrelevant national controversies. Municipal elections should be fought on municipal issues; and where the intervention of national parties has the effect of substituting national questions the quality of political life within the city is lowered. It is absurd to conduct a municipal election campaign about such matters as foreign policy, rearmament or the national budget, for the city council exercises no power in such matters, which are outside its jurisdiction. Yet this is quite a common occurrence. In London, Dr. Regan observes 'Most people use their municipal vote to register protest at, or approval of, central government activities.'

In Sweden national politics have permeated local politics and local government initiatives not only in Stockholm but in other parts of the country. But conversely, Stockholm has been leading the way in demanding national reforms. So the interactions and the political pressures between the capital and the nation are reciprocal. Dr. Hjalmar Mehr makes the interesting suggestion that the larger the local authority the greater the differences of outlook and policies between the parties.[1] One feature of special importance in Sweden which may help to assimilate national and local politics is that the

[1] *Post*, p. 886.

councillors of the county councils and six county borough councils elect members to the Upper House of the Parliament.

A quite different situation exists in Copenhagen, which is administered largely on bi-partisan lines. In Amsterdam again the local parties are largely independent of the national parties, and the tendency is towards a consensus among the parties on the council. It is not surprising, however, that in South Africa, where racial questions dominate party politics, the more liberal racial attitude of the United Party, which has a majority on the City Council of Johannesburg, should permeate municipal elections and the municipal policy of that city.

A second and more serious defect of party politics in city government is the tendency in some places to treat every municipal question, great or small, as a party question, even when no political principle is involved. Dr Swaisland goes so far as to say that in Birmingham nine-tenths of local government business does not lend itself to party politics. There are many cities to which this statement would not apply, even in regard to such humdrum matters as refuse collection or water supply. But everywhere there are some questions which can best be decided on technical rather than political grounds.

In several cities the main distinction between the parties concerns the scope of municipal activity and the level of taxation. The labour, socialist or social democratic parties normally favour a more generous or extensive provision of social services, such as public housing, education and medical facilities, irrespective of the increase in local taxation which may result, whereas the more conservative parties tend to urge restraint under both head-ings. But other differences in party attitudes sometimes make their appear-ance. Thus, a party representing the better-off electors may urge large expenditure on motorways while a party of the lower middle class and working class may favour improved public transport facilities, slum clear-ance and nursery schools. In Rome the left-wing parties are concerned not only to ensure that municipal powers are used to tackle social problems, but they also strive to restrict central government controls over local authorities and to achieve a greater decentralization of functions. Conservative or right-wing parties normally favour private enterprise in contrast to municipal enterprise whenever this is possible. There are no fewer than nine political parties which put forward candidates for municipal elections in Rome and other large Italian cities, in addition to locally sponsored candidates. This proliferation of parties must result in a complex and confused situation.

In several of the cities included in this book party politics in the ordinary sense of the term does not exist either because political parties have been abolished, or because the democratic system of election has been suspended.

Thus Ibadan is under the military regime which holds sway throughout Nigeria at the present time. In the U.A.R. political parties are not allowed, and therefore a non-partisan system of municipal government obtains in Cairo. The Arab Socialist Union, which is not regarded as a political party but is clearly a political movement, prevails in the capital and no one can be elected to the governorate council unless he is a member. In Argentine all political parties were dissolved by the revolutionary junta in 1966 and since then democratic methods of election have been abolished throughout the country. In the previous edition of this work we stated that: 'In Buenos Aires the party system appears to have degraded municipal government to a point at which it became almost unworkable.'[1] The changes levelled against the municipal politicians in Buenos Aires included not only an excessively partisan attitude to the needs of the city, but also allegations of widespread incompetence and corruption.

There are other cities in which patronage or corruption are rampant. In Mexico City all the chief officials are political appointees and no attempt is made to ensure a politically neutral administration. All the officials and workers employed by the city are expected to be active supporters of the ruling party.

Chicago has never enjoyed a reputation for clean government and Professor Walker described the politics of Chicago as 'bawdy, corrupt, and unashamed'.[2] The political life of the city was dominated by strong political bosses, sometimes resembling a mercenary army, resulting in great waste and inefficiency in municipal administration. Party supporters were appointed to public offices regardless of their incompetence or dishonesty. Professor Rakove in his study in the present edition paints a much more favourable picture of the high standard achieved under Mayor Daley's regime in the performance of such vital functions as police, highways, fire protection, street lighting, public transportation and traffic control. At the same time the mayor is not averse to jobbery and patronage. He is concerned that friends, neighbours, supporters and politicians should get jobs on the public payroll. The apparent paradox is explained by the fact that while the constitutional structure of city government is weak, decentralized and lacking in real power, the political organization of the Democratic Party, which is dominated by Mayor Daley, is highly organized, powerful and authoritarian—not a satisfactory model for the government of a great city.

In the communist countries of Eastern Europe party politics do not exist in the Western sense of the term. There may be discussion and dispute about policies or particular measures, but there is no attempt to dislodge the ruling

[1] p. 73.   [2] p. 74 of the previous edition of this book.

party at an election, and no official opposition. This situation prevails in Warsaw and in Belgrade. This does not mean that there are no separate parties or contested elections. In Warsaw, for example, there are three political parties known as the Polish United Workers' Party, the United Peasant Party and the Democratic Party. These parties, and trade unions and co-operative societies, are legally entitled to propose candidates for election, but all candidates are actually nominated by the National Unity Front on which all these bodies are represented, together with associations of progressive Catholics. The National Unity Front is committed to the consolidation and development of socialism in Poland. In consequence, although there is a genuine choice among the candidates put forward by the Front—220 candidates were nominated for 150 vacancies in the 1965 elections—it is difficult to see how there can be any basic differences of outlook or purpose among the parties.

The situation described above is entirely different from the bi-partisan system which exists in Osaka, for example, where the directly elected mayor, who controls the municipal executive, is supported by both the Radical and the Conservative Parties. In those conditions opposition is only held in check and can be resumed at will.

It is easy to blame political parties for various evils and maladies in the government of great cities and to assume that if party politics were abolished municipal government would become miraculously transformed and everywhere exhibit qualities of truth, goodness and beauty. In fact, however, political parties reflect the civic qualities—or the lack of them—to be found in the electorate. Where the citizens are indifferent to the public weal, politically immature, not averse to corruption or patronage, and ready to take advantage of every weakness in the city government, the party politicians will possess the characteristics familiar in Buenos Aires or Tammany Hall in its heyday.

Dr. Rios points out that administration and politics in the city of Rio de Janeiro cannot be understood apart from the national pattern, and this is true of cities in most other countries. Brazil has not had a democratic regime for more than 30 years. Under the presidential system which has existed, nepotism and other political maladies have flourished, and municipal as well as federal government has suffered severely from these practices.

DIVIDED CIVIC AND POLITICAL INTEREST

The impact of the social, psychological, ethnic, religious and educational background on the political regime is a matter of which we are all aware both in a general way and through our individual experiences. This is the realm of political sociology, which has thrown much light on the subject. What has not been sufficiently studied are the reasons which cause apathy towards city government and an undeveloped sense of community among the denizens of the great city, as compared with those who live in smaller towns.

The most important factor in our view is the inadequacy of the local government institutions in metropolitan areas. Nowhere do the local authorities correspond to the social, economic and political realities of the area. In consequence, large numbers of men and women live in one municipal area and work in another. Their interest, their loyalty and their allegiance are divided. They suffer from a kind of political schizophrenia which weakens their desire to participate actively either as citizens or as councillors. The sense of community among those who live in the great city is diluted by the presence of the invading hordes of workers who swarm in each day. Those who live in the suburbs beyond the city are, in a sense, escapists: they no longer feel any sense of responsibility for the well-being of the great city nor do they participate in its government. On the other hand, their interest in the local government of the area in which they dwell cannot be very strong and vital, because they spend so much of their time and energies elsewhere.

In a biographical sketch of her parents Lady Chorley has given an interesting description of the effect which 'moving out' of Manchester to the exclusive suburb of Alderley Edge had both on the well-to-do businessmen who could afford to go there and on the corporate life of Manchester. The exodus spoilt the appearance of Manchester by vacating the fine Regency houses in the older residential parts of the city. These quarters soon degenerated in the usual way when they were abandoned by the better-off families. But the 'moving out' process had deeper effects by depriving the city of many vigorous and capable leaders. When they lived in Manchester, the city was the centre of their lives; they had a civic pride which was more than mere philanthropic zeal. They founded colleges and a university, picture galleries and libraries; they established the Hallé symphony orchestra and supported its famous concerts. They sought to make the city proud and beautiful. 'But when the sons of these nineteenth-century citizens moved out they could no longer carry on the tradition. The city became the place they worked in by day and abandoned in the evening as quickly as might be. Their leisure interests and recreations were elsewhere and the time they gave to civic duties dwindled. The city was no longer the centre of their cultural lives and though . . . they still contrived to run a host of charities, they tended to withdraw their services from the city council. They grumbled enough about its quality . . . but it never occurred to them that they as individuals were perhaps to blame.'[1] The history of Lady Chorley's own family typified the process. Her grandfather had been an alderman and mayor, but none of his sons served on the council.

There was clearly an element of personal irresponsibility in thus evading the problems of the city which provided the labour, the wealth and the property which made it possible to build the large and luxurious houses at Alderley Edge. But part of the blame must also rest on the governments and parliaments which have refused for so long to recognize the problem which is epitomized in the story of Manchester and Alderley Edge. A similar process has taken place, and is now taking place at an enhanced tempo, in nearly all the great cities of the world. And with a few exceptions almost nothing is being done to counteract the social and political disintegration which results. If a proper system of metropolitan government were introduced, the Alderley Edges would become part of the Greater Manchesters to which they belong, and the 'moving out' process would not necessarily produce such unfortunate results.

The expedients which have been introduced in metropolitan areas to overcome the difficulties of local government without drastic reform have produced an extraordinary tangle of areas and authorities. The medley of uncoordinated units which exists outside the narrow boundaries of the city proper, the welter of *ad hoc* authorities set up to administer a whole series of services, add to the sense of confusion, incoherence and disharmony in the mind of the average citizen when he thinks about the government of the great city in which he lives. How can we expect to find in the minds of men and women that sense of identity on which community is founded if we do nothing to develop and express it through appropriate political institutions?

The very size of the great city today makes the task of creating or enhancing a sense of community among its inhabitants much more difficult than in a small town. The sheer scale of the metropolitan area, in terms both of population and territory, is in some respects a handicap to good government. For although the resources of the great city make it possible to employ the best and most highly qualified officers, to undertake developments requiring immense sums of capital expenditure, and to provide services (in the spheres of education and health, for example) which are quite beyond the power of smaller authorities, there are countervailing disadvantages. It is extremely difficult, if not impossible, for the city government to keep in close touch with the mass of citizens, to be aware of their attitude towards the services which are provided, or of their unsatisfied needs.

In Warsaw the people's councils for the city and the districts have a much

<hr>

[1] Katharine Chorley: *Manchester Made Them*, p. 139.

lower ratio in the proportion of councillors to citizens than in any of the other cities included in this volume, and this should facilitate contacts between the citizens and their representatives. An additional feature of some interest is the introduction of self-government in the housing estates of the city, which form the basic units of the social structure. These estates contain 6,000 to 12,000 inhabitants, who elect a tenants' council, sometimes supplemented by committees for single houses or blocks of apartments within the estate. House and block committees are directly elected at general meetings of the inhabitants, whereas the housing estate committees (or tenants' councils) are indirectly elected.

The object of these minor units is to strengthen the ties between the citizens and the district people's councils. They s^e that dwellings and other buildings are properly used and maintained; th ey bring about improved living conditions by obtaining more or better equipment; they foster good neighbourly relations by encouraging mutual assistance among tenants and settling disputes in a peaceful manner; they provide good conditions for children and young people to work and play. The tenants' self-government movement has paid special attention to developing educational work with children at their place of residence, including children's self-government by organizing courtyard teams. In this sphere the estate committee co-operate with voluntary associations concerned with children's welfare. Professor Zawadzki emphasizes that the social education of the tenants is the most important feature of these small units of community self-government.

Belgrade has a somewhat similar system of neighbourhood communities. As in Warsaw, they have an average of 6,000 to 12,000 inhabitants. They are recognized in the city's charter; they are legal entities and can own property, make contracts, etc., but they are not local authorities with statutory powers. They elect their own council and committees, and sometimes have a paid secretary. The scope of their activities varies greatly and depends on the interests, energies and imagination of the members. Arrangements for child care and baby minding, the provision of playgrounds, excursions, summer vacations, the care of old and disabled persons, is one category of activity. Another consists of organizing courses for illiterates or slow learners, courses in domestic economy for girls and women, and courses in health education. Artistic performances can be arranged by and for the neighbourhood community. A third type of activity consists in providing service centres, such as workshops in which citizens can carry out repairs to household articles or share in the use of household appliances. Some communities improve the amenities of the neighbourhood by providing a local park or sports ground, planting trees and so forth. These tasks are all within the powers of the municipality, but for one reason or another are overlooked or neglected. The work of the neighbourhood communities therefore supplements that of the local authorities, which give financial aid, usually in the form of a grant to cover a proportion of the cost of specified projects.

There is no doubt whatever that the communist regimes of Eastern Europe have advanced much further than other countries in bridging the gap between the governors and the governed in the great metropolis. The neighbourhood unit as a basis of community is in accord with the findings of research carried out for the Royal Commission on Local Government in England. This was a national survey of community attitudes in England. The major finding was that more than three-quarters of the persons interviewed were conscious of living in a local community which was defined as the 'home area'.[1] This community area is much smaller than the local government areas in which they reside. In urban areas three-quarters of the electors identified their 'home area' as being no larger than a ward, and a majority of them defined its extent as a group of streets in their immediate neighbourhood, or even less.

The Moscow Soviet attempts to bridge the gap between the governors and the governed by enlisting the help of a large number of voluntary workers to assist the deputies on the various committees. These so-called 'activists' are co-opted to a particular committee, such as that dealing with health, housing or education; and their duty consists largely of visiting municipal institutions such as schools, colleges, blocks of flats, hospitals or clinics, and ascertaining the standard of efficiency and also the public attitude towards them. These activists, together with the deputies whom they assist, number some 4,000 persons—a substantial political force for maintaining public relations and communications between the principal city soviet and the people of Moscow. This figure does not include the district soviets, whose 3,000 deputies are assisted by a further 10,000 activists.

A similar system exists in other cities of the Soviet Union. In Leningrad there are 5,836 deputies in the city and district (or *rayon*) soviets, of whom 4,630 serve on committees. They are assisted by 27,000 'activists'.[2] This has been described as mass participation in local government.

RELATIONS WITH HIGHER AUTHORITIES

The relations between the government of a great city and higher authorities reflect to a considerable degree the general relations between central and

[1] Report of the Royal Commission, H.M.S.O., Cmnd. 4040/1969 paragraph 233. Research Studies Vol. 9, H.M.S.O., 1969, p. 24.

[2] David T. Cattell: *Leningrad: A Case Study of Soviet Urban Government* (1968), pp. 61–2.

local government prevailing in the country concerned. There may also be, however, certain special factors which can influence the position. The most important of these exists where the great city is a national capital, for this may lead to a much greater degree of central control, as in Paris, or to the supersession of the democratic organs of local government, as in Buenos Aires. It may result, in a federal constitution, in a special district being established for the capital under the direct control of the national legislature, as in Mexico City or New Delhi. It may result, as in Tokyo and London, in a special organization of local government not found elsewhere.

Even where the great city is not a capital, or at any rate not a national capital, it may occupy a special position. This occurs particularly in federal types of constitution, where the higher authority for local government is the state or province. Frequently there is a conflict between the city and the state government which arises from the under-representation of the former in the state legislature. Montreal and Chicago are examples of cities located in provinces or states in which a rural minority has been able to dominate an urban majority on account of the over-representation of the former in the legislature. A typical result of this situation is that rural areas are favoured in matters of taxation, in the administration of federal aid through state or provincial governments, or in the calculation of subventions by the latter.

Pure autonomy for any municipality, however large, is of course impossible; for unlimited freedom would be tantamount to national sovereignty and we should then have the city-state of ancient Greece. Hence, the autonomy of a city is always limited, and the most usual method of determining or controlling it is by legislation emanating from the higher authority (national or provincial). State law and state constitutions thus impose limitations on even the 'home rule' cities of the U.S.A., which enjoy an exceptionally high degree of freedom. Under the Soviet system there are no specific limitations on the powers of the local authorities in Moscow; but the latter are subordinate to the higher authorities and must conform to their plans and directives in every respect, and this is the all-important fact. The same system exists in Poland. The principle of democratic centralism makes the executive organ of a city responsible not only to the people's council at its own level but also to the executive organ of the next higher level of government.

The general trend of central-local relations is one of increasing control by higher authority, but great differences in the degree, the methods and the comprehensiveness of central control nevertheless exist, and are likely to continue. At one end of the spectrum there are great cities whose administration is in the hands of the central government, or of a high official appointed by and answerable to the head of state or the national government. Mexico

City, New Delhi and Buenos Aires are examples. At the other end of the spectrum is Belgrade, which is unique in that the higher levels of government in Yugoslavia, whether federal or republican, have no administrative or operational powers over the city council, except to question the legality of municipal regulations by bringing them to the attention of the constitutional court. Belgrade does not even receive grants-in-aid from the higher authorities.

Between these extremes come a great many gradations due to differing historic and political circumstances. In Japan there was a high degree of centralization before the Second World War and the Mayor of Tokyo, elected by the council, was placed under the double supervision of a prefectural governor appointed by the central government and indirectly of the Minister for Home Affairs. It was not until after the war that a directly elected governor was given control of the metropolitan executive and the powers of a prefectural governor in the metropolis. Thenceforth, the central government was supposed to exercise only legislative and judicial control but this is far from the reality of the situation. The central government tries to control the Tokyo Metropolitan Government in a thousand different ways, and the capital city's financial dependence on grants, subsidies and permission to borrow money is so great that this gives the central government a dominating position in several spheres.

The tradition of strong central control of Paris exercised in the past by the Prefect of Police and the Prefect of the Seine has not changed perceptibly with the reorganization of the region. The Regional Prefect, the Prefect of Paris and the prefects of the other departments in the district continue to be the dominant forces in the administration of the metropolitan area, with the councils of the communes, the departments and the district playing a subordinate part.

The authors of the studies of Cairo, Rome, Manila, Calcutta, Johannesburg, Delhi, Osaka, London and Birmingham all report strong central government control of one kind or another. In Rome the actions of the municipal council are subject to the legal control of the prefect, who can annul any act he considers unlawful. If the city's budget is not balanced it can be controlled by the provincial executive and by the central commission on local finance. The Mayor is required to carry out certain functions on behalf of the central government and can be replaced by a commissioner if he fails to do so. The council can be dissolved if it fails to maintain public order or is in default of its duties. In Delhi the municipal corporation lives in a state of 'uneasy intimacy' with the central government, which has considerable powers of control, many of which have been delegated to the lieutenant governor. These include the making of ordinances, the appointment or approving the appointment of chief officers, the sanctioning of municipal loans, the giving of directions and the supersession of the municipal corporation. Similar powers are possessed by the government of West Bengal in respect of Calcutta, quite apart from the power which the state government exercises of appointing a commissioner to control the City's administration.

In Australia, the state can regulate the organization of local government in Sydney. It lays down rules governing the procedure at council meetings, determines the qualifications and status of local government officers, and settles many other details. The municipality cannot make its own ordinances, regulations or by-laws. It must obtain the approval of the State Department of Local Government for loans and bank credits; the state examines the annual statement of accounts, the qualifications and integrity of local government officers. A somewhat similar situation exists in Canada in regard to the relations between Toronto and the provincial government. The Department of Municipal Affairs and the Ontario Municipal Board are the provincial organs responsible for supervising the city government. The department is concerned with the general operation of the law. It has power to regulate methods of accounting, estimates and auditing. The municipal board must approve loans and zoning ordinances; it hears appeals against assessments for city taxes, and arbitrations regarding the acquisition of land by the city. It supervises the operation of the city's public utility undertakings. The appointment and dismissal of some of the chief municipal officers are subject to the approval of the provincial government.

Turning to the countries of Northern Europe, we find that although in principle Amsterdam can legislate on all matters of local interest which have not been regulated by the provincial or central government, there is nevertheless a considerable amount of central control. The approval of the provincial government ('deputed states', as they are called) is required for the budget, for decisions of the city council concerning municipal property and various other matters. The Crown—that is, the central government—can suspend or annul decisions of the city which it considers to be illegal or not in accordance with the public interest. The city's housing quota is allotted by the provincial government. In future, Amsterdam is likely to be bound even more closely than at present by the policy of the central government, largely owing to its increasing financial dependence on the centre. The loss of financial independence is certain to be followed by diminished municipal autonomy.

From Denmark comes a similar report that the influence of the central government on municipal administration is steadily increasing. The formal relations between Copenhagen and the state are determined by constitutional law, which declares that the law shall establish the right of municipalities to govern their own affairs under the supervision of the state. This means that the rules according to which Copenhagen is governed are contained in acts of the Danish Parliament, and municipal regulations must be approved by the Home Office. These regulations include the creation or abolition of all the higher posts in the city. Home Office approval must be obtained for any loans required for capital expenditure, and also for the purchase or disposal of municipal property.

The general duty of the state to supervise the municipality is carried out in Copenhagen by the lord lieutenant (*overpraesident*) who acts as superintendent on behalf of the central government. He can attend the meetings of both the city council and the executive committee, and reports to the Home Office any matter which he regards as illegal or undesirable. 'The local administration', observes Dr. Holm, 'is in practice largely dependent on the central administration.' The principal reason for this is to be found in the realm of finance. The municipality of Copenhagen, it appears, has no real authority as regards taxation. The provisions which determine municipal rates and taxes are enacted by national legislation and the administrative rules for their application are laid down by the central government. This relates particularly to the income tax, which has gradually become the principal source of municipal revenue. The rules governing taxes on property are also outside the control of the municipality. Finally, such services as education, public assistance and social insurance are all deeply rooted in national legislation.

In Sweden there is a strong tradition of local self-government which is jealously guarded. Some of the functions carried out by the city government of Stockholm are based on national legislation, which lays down precise provisions regarding each service. In these circumstances the municipality has little discretion in respect either of policy or of the scale of expenditure. On the other hand, in certain spheres of activity, such as public utility undertakings and the management of real property, the city is much freer and enjoys a high degree of independence.

Stockholm is a county as well as a city; (it corresponds to a county borough in England). For that reason it has, like other counties, its own lord lieutenant or governor (*överstathallare*) who is appointed by the central government. The approval of this high official must be obtained for certain decisions of the administrative organs. He can also disallow a decision of the council concerning the budget or the rate of tax on grounds of illegality, although he cannot substitute his own decision in its place. Loans for periods over five years require government consent. The general position is, however, that the central government exercises no direct power of a positive kind over the city administration and little general control.

The main reason for the independence which Stockholm enjoys lies in the financial strength of the city government. The city receives grants-in-aid, in respect of housing for example, and subsidies for other services such as schools, roads and welfare; and these involve various forms of state control. But the financial strength of the municipality is so great that the city, if forced to do so, could dispense with state grants and rely on its own resources. In consequence, the city is able to maintain a considerable measure of independence in its dealings with the national government. Manila is also relatively independent of the Central Government as regards finance, and this must undoubtedly colour all its relationships.

In Britain, as in Sweden, there is a strong tradition of local self-government, and historically local government preceded central government in point of time. Nevertheless, local authorities are subject to a considerable amount of control by the central government and this has been increasing in recent years. There is, however, a strong demand voiced in local government circles and also among politicians for a reduction in the amount of central control. It is generally believed that the reform of the structure of local government which is expected to take place in the 1970s will be followed or accompanied by a relaxing of certain types of central government control.

The constitution, franchise, areas and powers of local authorities in Britain are laid down by Acts of Parliament. Greater London is unique in that it has a special constitutional system prescribed by the London Government Act, 1963. Birmingham has a charter and is subject to the constitutional provisions of the Municipal Corporations Acts. All the principal services, such as housing, education and public health, are the subject of Parliamentary statutes which lay down the national policy in these spheres, prescribe the powers and duties of local authorities, and also confer powers on ministers. Lastly, municipalities have the right—which the larger ones like the Greater London Council and Birmingham City Council exercise frequently—of petitioning Parliament for a Private Bill: that is, a law applying only to their area, and giving them powers which are not generally accorded elsewhere.

The central ministries exercise a considerable degree of control over local authorities; and this applies to London and Birmingham in much the same way as elsewhere, with one important exception. The Greater London Council does not have to obtain permission from the Department of the Environment before borrowing money. Instead it presents its loan-raising requirements in an annual Bill which goes before Parliament. This places the

D

Greater London Council in a more favourable position than other cities, for the loan sanction is one of the most potent instruments of central control.

Grants-in-aid have reached very high proportions in relation to local taxation, but the largest of the grants—now called the rate support grant—is calculated according to an elaborate formula of need and can only be varied in any particular case by blatantly abnormal behaviour by a local authority, which can be ignored for all practical purposes in regard to London or any other large city. Some specific grants still remain, such as those for housing, the police and central area redevelopment, and these can be and are used as instruments of control (though not as regards the police in London since this is under the direct control of the Home Secretary). An example of central control was the refusal of the Government in 1969 to allow the Greater London Council to raise the rents of their houses and flats beyond a specified figure which was far less than the council wished; and to limit the number of houses the council might sell to tenants.

In Birmingham or London one finds no official corresponding to the prefect or governor of a continental city, nor does the central government have any voice in the appointment of the lord mayor or chairman of the council. The municipal budget does not have to be approved by a higher authority; and the central government cannot suspend or dissolve the council. There are no officials who act in a dual capacity as officers of the municipality and representatives of the central government. All these well-known forms of central control are absent.

Central government departments have statutory powers of many different kinds affecting the activities of local authorities. Thus, Birmingham City Council, the Greater London Council and the 32 London borough councils must submit their development plans for approval to the Department of the Environment and their school development plans to the Department of Education and Science. The Department of Education makes regulations laying down the standards to be observed by local authorities in building new schools. Birmingham and London must pay school teachers such salaries and require such qualifications as the Minister approves. The appointment and dismissal of the medical officer of health and certain other chief officers employed by the local authority must be approved by the appropriate Ministry. The accounts of all the local authorities in London (except the ancient City Corporation) and some of the accounts of Birmingham City Council are audited by a central government auditor, who can disallow unlawful or excessive expenditure and recover the sums in question from the responsible persons. In some spheres of activity, Ministers have 'default' powers: that is, if the local authority fails to carry out its duties they can intervene and arrange for the function to be carried out by another agency. Many individual acts of the local authority require the assent of a minister.

The municipal authorities in London and Birmingham are subject to the general requirements of this complex relationship between local and central government. It bears on them less heavily than on many smaller towns for several reasons. First, they are highly efficient and progressive municipalities, leading the way for the country as a whole in many activities; they therefore do not have to be goaded or prodded into activity by the central government in order to achieve the national minimum standards of health, housing, education, etc.: it must be recognized that the enforcement of a national minimum is the object of many of the central controls mentioned above. Second, they are very wealthy cities, and the magnitude of their financial resources gives them a degree of independence not usually possessed by the poorer municipalities.

In the past the cities of the United States were more free of intervention by higher authorities than those of any other country. Here too the relationship has changed, although the emerging pattern is very characteristic of American attitudes. As Professor Wallace Sayre points out, 'the urbanization and metropolitanization of the United States has been mainly responsible for a transformation of the federal system during the past four decades into a system of intricately shared powers among the three tiers. . . . In this new and still evolving system, governmental powers are so extensively shared by the three tiers that no one level of government can plan or govern without consulting and bargaining with the other two levels. Nor is it possible to assert that one level is more powerful than another; the center of gravity in influence varies from function to function, from issue to issue, from time to time.'[1] The U.S. federal government has become involved in numerous municipal functions since the end of the Second World War. These include highways, education, welfare, housing, urban renewal and the prevention or cure of poverty. The mode of intervention varies; in some instances the federal department deals directly with the city government, in others indirectly through the state government. The state governments are themselves involved both separately and in combination with the federal agencies or departments; yet many state governments are indifferent or even hostile to the needs of the cities. This is partly due to the over-representation of rural areas in the state legislatures and traditional American beliefs about the wickedness of urban life compared with the moral purity of the countryside. Reapportionment of constituencies is taking place or has taken place following a decision of the U.S. Supreme Court, and this should in time modify

[1] *Post*, p. 719.

the position. The persistent participation in one form or another of the federal government is partly due to the neglect by the states of the problems of the cities, especially in the metropolitan areas.

But the dominant influence in the U.S., as in other countries whose political history and constitutional development have been quite different, is the recognition that central and local authorities, or central, state and local authorities, form a partnership which is necessary and unavoidable. The terms of the partnership vary from country to country and often from function to function; but in the major municipal services neither local nor central government can satisfy the public need in isolation.

The central or provincial government should not be conceived as a single entity acting in a uniform and consistent manner in all its dealings with the municipality. It is usually a number of ministries which pursue their own particular policies in an unco-ordinated way. This is certainly the case in Tokyo just as it is in Toronto, Montreal and elsewhere. Sometimes the role of a higher authority towards a municipality is restrictive, sometimes it is directive in laying down policies or objectives, sometimes it is stimulating or fostering by inducing action in a particular direction, sometimes it is regulatory in prescribing or approving procedures, schemes, plans or priorities, sometimes it is enabling by providing grants or other subventions from national or state taxation, or securing changes in legislation.[1] Everywhere financial aid from national funds has become indispensable to local government, and nowhere is this more evident than in the great cities. The most obvious failure on the part of higher authorities has been their refusal, in all but a few instances, to carry out the reform of the structure and functions of local government in the metropolitan areas which is essential for the planning and administration of municipal services at a satisfactory standard. It does not follow that because the higher authorities exercise strong control over the administration and finances of the great city that they also recognize the problems which confront it and are willing to assist in solving them. Indeed, quite the contrary may be the case.

MUNICIPAL FINANCE

This brings us to the subject of municipal finance. In no sphere is there greater diversity among the cities comprised in this volume. The methods by which great cities obtain their revenue, and the amount and objects of their expenditures, differ so greatly that it would be futile to attempt any kind of

[1] The best detailed study of one country is J. A. G. Griffith: *Central Departments and Local Authorities*, Allen & Unwin, London, 1966.

comparison or generalization. A mere description of the phenomena would be tedious and unilluminating. We shall only attempt, therefore, to draw attention to a few outstanding points.

Real property is by far the commonest subject of local taxation, and taxes on land and buildings are often the chief source of municipal revenue. Nevertheless there are some striking exceptions. Thus, Copenhagen relies for most of its revenue on a municipal income tax. Hence about 60 per cent of its revenue from taxation came from this source in 1966–67. In Ibadan it would be impractical to impose a tax on real property owing to the traditional system of land ownership and occupation. In Belgrade the bulk of the City's revenue is derived from personal income tax and a retail sales tax. Calcutta imposes a small tax on professions and vocations which is 'a sort of miniature income tax'.

A graduated tax on income has many financial and social advantages over taxes levied on real property, whether assessed on annual or capital value; and this has led a number of people to advocate a municipal income tax. Whatever the theoretical merits of the proposal may be, it is considered by many people to be politically impractical in countries such as Britain, where income tax levied by the central government for national purposes has already attained levels which are oppressive. It may not be an accident that Denmark is a country whose national expenditure on defence is relatively low. It is worth noting that since 1929 Dutch municipalities have been prohibited by law from raising local income tax and surtax on government income tax. In place of this, a municipal fund was established fed by a special tax and distributed to local authorities according to their population. Sydney relies on the rating of land values—that is, the unimproved capital value of land—as its main source of revenue. In Cairo the largest item of local taxation consists of licence fees on transport vehicles. The major source of local revenue in Johannesburg and Pretoria is the sale of goods and services. In Buenos Aires the most important source is the tax on profitable activities in business, industrial and professional undertakings.

Despite the predominance of taxes on real property, no country except Britain relies on them exclusively for municipal revenue derived from local taxation. Elsewhere one finds a wide variety of local taxes. Amsterdam has municipal taxes on entertainments, dogs and fire insurance; Chicago has taxes on entertainments for which admission charges are made, and also a tax on motor vehicles. Taxes on sales are a common method of raising municipal revenue. Thus, Los Angeles derives nearly 16 per cent of its total revenue from a municipal sales tax, Montreal has a shared sales tax which contributes nearly 13 per cent of the city's revenue, while New York City

has a sales tax which in 1966–67 produced about 9 per cent of the total resources compared with 30 per cent from taxes on real estate, and a tax on
businesses which also yielded about 9 per cent. The Ville de Paris levies a
wide range of taxes. Some Paris municipal taxes are added to those collected
by the state on, for example, furnished rooms, rents and business premises.
The municipality can at its discretion tax balconies, domestic servants, the
consumption of gas and many other articles or services. The city is obliged
to impose taxes on entertainments, cafés, bars, stamp duties and, most important of all, on business transactions. Rome employs equally diverse methods
of financial municipal services by means of taxes on rent receipts, building
sites, family wealth, industry, trade, the professions, domestic servants, dogs,
pianofortes, billiard tables, coffee-making machines, advertising posters and
billboards, stamps on official documents and even a hearth tax. Tokyo has a
purchase tax on motor cars, and taxes on diesel oil, hunting, hot baths and
business undertakings as well as on real property. There is also a resident tax.
Cairo taxes a great variety of objects, including hotel occupancy, ferry boats
and houseboats, entertainments, and properties benefiting from public
improvements, but most of these yield only small sums. Buenos Aires raises
part of its municipal revenue from taxes on motor cars, offices, sporting
events, construction of buildings and the consumption of gas and electricity.

A tax on real property has the advantages of certainty, stability, convenience and economy of collection. On the other hand, it possesses several disadvantages. It is usually regressive so far as residential property is concerned, and is inelastic compared with rising costs, increasing municipal
expenditure and other crucial factors in local government finance. From
Osaka comes the complaint that faced with an enormous demand for services
the municipality is facing a very difficult financial situation because it lacks a
sufficiently elastic system of taxation and does not receive special treatment.
Yet Osaka has in addition to property taxes a gasoline tax and other sales
taxes.

Of all the cities included in this book, Belgrade has the greatest degree of
freedom and independence in regard to taxation. Permitted sources of revenue
are laid down by law and municipalities are free to decide for themselves
which of the authorized taxes and contributions shall be used and also their
amount. The federal government has the right to restrict the rates of municipal taxes but in 1968 the only intervention concerned the maximum permissible rate of turnover taxes. Belgrade has an entirely self-contained financial
system, for it receives no grants from either the federal or the Serbian government. The Republic and the city jointly maintain a few museums and art
galleries of special interest.

Without attempting to evaluate the merits of all these diverse taxes, it is clearly an advantage for local authorities to be able to draw their revenue from several different sources. London and Birmingham are at a disadvantage here, compared with Tokyo or Paris. Indeed, the rigid and exclusive emphasis which the British system lays on real property as a source of local taxes contrasts unfavourably with the wider basis of municipal taxation permitted to practically every other great city comprised in this book.

The inadequate and unsatisfactory basis of the rating system in Britain partly explains the much greater role which grants-in-aid from the central government play in municipal finance there compared with other countries. In 1966–67 government grants amounted to 52 per cent of expenditure by local authorities, taking the country as a whole. The proportion is expected to rise to 57 per cent by 1970–71. The wealthier municipalities receive a smaller amount from grants-in-aid in proportion to their total revenue than the poorer areas. Greater London is by far the wealthiest part of Britain, and in 1966–67 the Greater London Council received only 12 per cent of its revenue from central government grants. The London boroughs and the City of London received grants amounting to 33 per cent of their income. Birmingham City Council received 28 per cent of its revenue from this source. Chicago also received almost 28 per cent from state and federal aid, New York City received about 26 per cent of its total revenues in 1968–69 from New York State and about 14 per cent from the federal government. Osaka received grants from the central Treasury and the Prefecture of Osaka amounting to 18 per cent of its total income. Metropolitan Toronto receives less than 10 per cent of its revenue from Dominion and Provincial grants and subsidies. At the other extreme we find Manila, which is relatively independent of the central government in matters of finance; while Rome, Johannesburg and Pretoria receive negligible amounts from this source.

The position of Amsterdam calls for special comment because local government revenue is mainly drawn from the Municipal Fund and from Exchequer grants. The Municipal Fund is a nationally operated fund fed by a specified percentage of the central government's total receipts from taxation. Allocations are made to each municipality from the fund on the basis of its population, area, density and the costs of its welfare and social services. In the case of Amsterdam certain additions are made because the city's finances have been showing a deficit in recent years. These additions are only payable if the taxes and charges levied by the city council exceed a prescribed minimum. The Municipal Fund is an arrangement for integrating local and central taxation. It is distinct from Exchequer grants which are also paid in the Netherlands to local authorities.

The financing of municipal services in the great city presents a problem of very great difficulty. This is as true in the wealthiest and most industrialized centres like New York or Tokyo as it is in much poorer cities such as Ibadan or Calcutta. 'The financing of government in large American cities is a difficult task', Professor Wallace Sayre remarks, 'and that of New York City, as befits its size and complexity, is one of the most difficult.'[1] The city of Chicago, we are told, is in excellent financial condition, but this statement refers only to such criteria as municipal indebtedness, the levels of taxation and the budgetary position. It tells us nothing about the scope, scale or standards of the services provided for the citizens. It is theoretically possible for the finances of a city to be in a satisfactory condition and for the services it provides to be deplorably inadequate. This indeed seems to be the situation in Ibadan, where Dr. Green considers the city council's revenue position to compare favourably with local authorities in most other parts of the world. Yet the information he gives about the municipal services is far from favourable. The Department of the Federal District, which is responsible for administering Mexico City, has as a result of conservative fiscal policies shown a surplus on its current account each year since 1952 and has redeemed the whole of its funded debt. Yet financial constraints have prevented the department from meeting some of the most essential needs of the capital. Hundreds of thousands of men, women and children are living in squatter settlements under the most primitive conditions without schools, markets, piped water, drainage, sewerage, paved and lighted roads. Similar conditions can be found in many other cities in Central and South America, Asia and Africa. It is less surprising that such conditions should exist in the large cities of the poorer countries than that the richest cities of the wealthy nations should be unable or unwilling to provide the elementary conditions of a civilized life. Why does homelessness and squalor exist in London on a substantial scale? Why do the slums of Harlem and the badly lighted, poorly paved streets of Chicago persist in the world's richest country? Why does the sewage system of Tokyo serve less than a third of the special ward area? Why are the transport and traffic facilities of nearly all metropolitan areas unable to meet the travelling needs of the inhabitants with reasonable comfort and expedition? One could go on to ask many similar questions about other functions and other great cities.

The reasons for these shortcomings are complex. First, it is probable that the cost of providing many services increases disproportionately in the great metropolitan centre:[2] we have in mind the enormously expensive works

[1] *Post*, p. 715.
[2] For statistics showing that the cost of urban government in the U.S.A. varies directly with

required to provide the huge modern city with main drainage and sewage disposal, highways capable of carrying the continually growing mass of motor vehicles, water supplies which may have to be brought a distance of a hundred miles or so, housing and slum clearance, and so forth. Secondly, as the transport and traffic facilities improve, the number of workers coming into the city from outside each day increases, and these daily migrants must be provided with expensive services to the cost of which they contribute little or nothing. Thirdly, the huge rise in the value of land increases enormously the cost of providing municipal works or services for which land is required,[1] such as housing, highways, parks and open spaces, schools and playgrounds. Indeed, the cost of these services has risen so much in some of the largest metropolitan centres that no serious attempt is being made to provide them on an adequate scale. On Manhattan Island the motor traffic has almost seized up; the motor car has become the slowest and most tiring method of transport, because the streets are too narrow. If anyone should suppose this to be due to the fact that Manhattan is a narrow island, he will find a similar situation in central London. Paris and Moscow enjoy a much more favourable position in regard to main highways; but the housing shortage in those cities is deplorable.

It is for such reasons as these that central or provincial governments have been led in many countries to make grants-in-aid towards the cost of municipal services even in the largest and wealthiest cities. If, however, grants-in-aid become too large in relation to sources of taxation within the control of the local authorities they lead to central domination which endangers the independence, freedom and responsibility of the municipality.[2]

The method of sharing taxes on an agreed basis between the local authority and the national or state government has certain advantages, since it does not necessarily lead to any great increase of central control. Among cities sharing taxes with higher authorities are Chicago and Los Angeles, which receive

the size of cities, not only in the aggregate but also function by function, see Albert Lewpasky: *Urban Government* (National Resources Committee, Washington, 1939), Vol. I, p. 33.

The Ontario Municipal Board, after an exhaustive inquiry into the local government of the metropolitan area of Toronto, concluded that in the larger municipalities with complex administrative problems costs tend to increase with the size of the municipality, chiefly because of the larger number of employees per unit of population. *Report of Decisions and Recommendations* dated January 20, 1953, p. 29.

[1] The cost of land in Tokyo is so high that it presents almost insuperable difficulties to planning and development policies. In the Tokyo region in 1969 the price of residential land within a 6 to 12 mile radius of the city centre ranged from £46 to £75 for 10 square feet of floor space. Land prices rose in the Tokyo area by more than 25 per cent in 1968 and in some of the more popular districts by more than 85 per cent.

[2] For the position in England in this respect see W. A. Robson: *Local Government in Crisis*, Allen & Unwin, 2nd edition, 1968, pp. 59–75.

D*

part of the state petrol tax from Illinois and California respectively; Montreal, which gets a share of the sales tax levied by the provincial government; Manila, which shares in no fewer than eight national taxes; Delhi, which shares in the property taxes and terminal taxes on commodities; and Paris, which has the right of additional centimes added to national taxes. Many taxes are shared in Buenos Aires between the national government and the municipality, such as income tax, excess profits tax, sales tax, racecourse tax and capital gains tax.

Lastly, mention should be made of the equalization systems in operation. In Denmark, an inter-municipal adjustment fund was established in 1937. Into this fund are paid moneys derived from special inter-municipal taxes levied on all ratepayers in all municipalities. Contributions are made from this fund to the cost of public assistance, hospitals and education provided by the municipalities. In addition there is an equalization arrangement whereby municipalities with a low level of wealth and a high expenditure on public assistance receive contributions from those which are richer and with a lower expenditure on public assistance.

In England, the principal Exchequer grant (at present known as the Rate Support Grant) is based on a complicated formula. One element in the calculation is related to local taxable resources so that areas with a low level of rateable value per head receive a higher proportion of the grant than those above the national average. Another element is based on the needs of the local population weighted in accordance with a formula and supplemented by various factors.

In addition to these national schemes, there are special schemes applicable to the capital cities of the two countries. In the Danish capital the object is to equalize the proceeds from a number of rates and taxes in the three adjoining municipalities of Copenhagen, Frederiksberg and Gentofte, which are separate local authorities but together comprise the capital. In Greater London, the object of the equalization scheme is to reduce the disparities of taxable capacity among the 32 London boroughs and the City of London. In Metropolitan Toronto, 70 per cent or more of the tax burden has been pooled.

PLANNING THE GREAT CITY

Most of the world's great cities grew up without any serious attempt at planning in the modern sense of the term, although this does not mean that there was a complete absence of public regulation. It was obviously necessary to control in the social interest the width and building line of streets, the height and construction of buildings, the provision of open spaces, nuisances and noxious trades, the disposal of refuse, the drainage of water and many other vital aspects of urban life; and such matters have been subject to municipal regulation for centuries. But it is a far cry from these elementary necessities to the positive control over growth and development which is inherent in modern town and country planning. Very few great cities bear the marks of deliberate planning of a creative kind: Paris, Washington, Moscow, Stockholm, London and a few others are exceptional in this respect. The rectangular pattern of streets found in most American cities is a form of deliberate control over the layout and development of the city, though it is a long way behind modern ideas of city planning.

Often one finds in cities which are not planned in any general sense of the term particular aspects which bear the planner's imprint. The park system and the lakefront of Chicago, and the parks and squares of London, are admirable examples of the planning of important features.

The need for comprehensive planning is felt more strongly and more quickly in the great metropolitan city under modern conditions than elsewhere, for the dire consequences of unplanned development soon become painfully obvious in a vast industrial and commercial centre. It is not surprising to find, therefore, that most great cities have either adopted a master plan or are in process of doing so.

Amsterdam has had a master plan since 1935 to guide the physical development of the city. This plan provided for eight garden cities within the city's territory and these have all been constructed. It embodied a scheme for providing the city with a magnificent forest park and this is now one of the glories of Amsterdam. As population grew, and standards of housing and amenity rose, the land available for development or renewal declined and the city council had to look outside its existing boundaries for further territory in which to expand. The city's needs have been met partly by the purchase of a large area of land in an adjacent municipality for industrial and inland waterborne trading establishments; partly by amalgamation of adjoining areas; and partly by means of a regional land use plan which covers Amsterdam and four neighbouring municipalities.

In recent years much closer co-operation has taken place in regard to planning not only between neighbouring municipalities but also between the planning authorities of the three levels of government. The provincial government occupies the principal position in regard to physical planning. It draws up regional physical plans and approves plans for local extensions. The regional plans provide that the heavily urbanized centres in the area known as Holland shall be separated by green belts. Another trend in the post-war years has been the increasing concern of the Amsterdam City Council with economic and social planning.

In Chicago the modern planning movement dates from the publication of the Plan of Chicago in 1909 by a group of businessmen and civic leaders. The plan aimed at improving the aesthetic appearance of the city, its housing, transport and traffic facilities, highways, parks and amenities. There was much idealism embodied in this early plan, but its authors were reluctant to impose restrictions on the use of private property.[1] Shortly after it was promulgated, the municipality appointed an official city plan commission to carry it into effect. Since then large sums of money have been raised to finance the capital expenditure required to carry out particular features of the plan. These include the acquisition of outlying forest preserves, street improvements (including two-level highways on Michigan Avenue and Wacker Drive), parks, airports, straightening the course of the river and reclaiming the lake front. Much has been done, but much more remains to be accomplished before Chicago, which still has vast areas of derelict dwellings and slum quarters, can be regarded as a well-planned city. The idea of city planning in at least its visual aspects has, however, to some extent entered the minds of the citizens.

For many years a major defect was the weakness of the Chicago Plan Commission as a purely advisory body. The commission became an official agency in 1939. In 1957, when the department of city planning was set up, the commission was reconstituted as a policy-making organ. In 1965 the department became the department of development and planning, and given enlarged functions. The following year the department of development and planning issued a new comprehensive plan for Chicago. This is an extremely ambitious scheme which aims 'to enlarge human opportunities, to improve the environment, and to strengthen and diversify the economy'. It involves the construction of 16 development areas within the city each containing 150,000–250,000 persons. Each will have its own schools, shopping centres, parks, recreational facilities and municipal services. Highways and public transport will be improved, and a further 1,200 acres of Lake Michigan will be reclaimed for recreational purposes. Refuse disposal, sewage and pollution of air and water will be dealt with more effectively than at present.

The real problem has for long been the planning of Greater Chicago. It does not appear that this will necessarily be solved by the new proposals, since little more is promised than that efforts will be made to co-ordinate the city's

---

[1] For a severe criticism of the City Beautiful movement inaugurated at Chicago, see Lewis Mumford: *City Development* (London, 1946), p. 19; and *The City in History* by the same author (New York, 1961), p. 401.

plan with the metropolitan area planning of the North-Eastern Illinois Planning Commission. The outlook is, however, considerably brighter than in the days when the only unifying agency was an unofficial and ineffectual body known as the Chicago Regional Planning Association.

In New York City a planning commission was created in 1936. The commission was given a high degree of autonomy in order to insulate it against political influences. This was intended to strengthen the position of the commission but in practice it has had a weakening effect. The commission's record is a poor one for although it was directed to prepare a master plan for the city, no such plan has emerged after more than 30 years. Originally the commission had the duty of preparing the city's annual capital budget together with a capital investment plan for the ensuing five years which it presented direct to the board of estimate. Under the 1961 Charter this potent instrument for guiding development has been transferred from the commission to the mayor. The main achievement of the commission has been in the sphere of zoning and even here it has had only a limited success. Its status is mainly that of an advisory and exhortatory body.

The position is even more unsatisfactory in the vast metropolitan region of which New York is the central city. For here there is no official regional planning authority of any kind. In its absence reliance has to be placed on the Regional Plan Association, a voluntary organization supported by public-spirited citizens and financed by the Russell Sage Foundation. The first Regional Plan of New York and Environs was published in 1929–31 and in its day attracted great interest. A second regional plan has recently appeared. Whatever its merits, most planners and political scientists would agree that the time has passed for planning by well-intentioned voluntary agencies. Yet in the conditions prevailing in the United States a comprehensive plan cannot be carried out in a metropolitan region except through the voluntary co-operation of the many authorities concerned—a result which is almost impossible to attain.

Impediments of a similar kind exist in nearly all countries where the metropolitan area presents a major planning problem. In Denmark, for example, a town-planning law passed in 1938 requires every town or built-up area containing more than 1,000 inhabitants to prepare a town plan; but the act makes no provision for the comprehensive planning of several municipalities forming a single region, nor did it create a regional planning authority. To fill this gap in the official machinery, an unofficial committee (which some years earlier had considered the question of open spaces in Copenhagen) took on the task in 1945 of drawing up a plan for Greater Copenhagen. In 1947 it issued an outline plan for the metropolitan region. This plan envisages that future development should be connected with the railway lines which radiate from the centre of the city. This proposal would result in a formation resembling the human hand,[1] the palm consisting of Copenhagen and the five fingers representing the building developments along the five radial railways. The spaces in between these spread out fingers would be mainly devoted to green areas.

The regional planning committee which was responsible for this work possessed no executive power. It nevertheless contained members representing the municipalities of the Copenhagen region and of many other authorities and institutions interested in planning. A town development committee was appointed in 1949 to draw up another regional plan and this appeared in 1951. Many other detailed plans for the region were issued in subsequent years but they had almost no practical effect. The latest effort was an outline of the principles for a regional plan produced in 1962 by the Metropolitan Municipalities Joint Committee. A Joint Regional Council was appointed in 1967 to co-ordinate the work of the municipal, county and state planning authorities.

Paris has had a regional plan since 1934–35. Greater Paris for this purpose comprised the departments of the Seine (which included the Ville de Paris), Seine-et-Oise, Seine-et-Marne and five cantons of the Oise. The individual communes included within this extensive region were required to prepare plans to conform with the regional master plan. The communal plans, and also the regional plan, had to be submitted for approval to an advisory body known as the *Comité d'aménagement de la région parisienne*, which contained senior civil servants, representative of local authorities, members nominated by associations and experts.

Important advances have been made in the planning and development of the Paris Region since 1960, and this has been and is the principal concern of the new administrative organization known as the District of the Paris Region. The regional plan is described in considerable detail in the section on 'Paris and its Region' in the chapter on Paris which Monsieur Delouvrier has contributed to this volume, and the planning of the Paris Region appears to be more sophisticated, more comprehensive, more civilized and more farsighted than comparable plans for other metropolitan regions.

In the previous editions of this book Professor Chapman remarked that 'With so rich a heritage of beauty, spaciousness, dignity and splendour, one can readily understand the tendency of town planners in Paris to concentrate on aesthetic and conservation aims'.[2] This is certainly no longer true. The new *Plan d'aménagement et d'organisation générale de la région*

[1] See pp. 373, 402.   [2] p. 92 (2nd edition).

parisienne (known as P.A.D.O.G.) is far from being an exercise in visual planning. It is concerned with land use and activities, economic location and employment , schools and the pattern of education, demographic trends, housing needs, transport and highways, social life and recreational amenities, personal mobility, and new towns. The perspective of the plan goes forward to the year 2000, but a shorter term plan for the period to 1975 has also been drawn up.

P.A.D.O.G. looks forward with boldness and imagination to the future growth and development of the region. It contemplates that the population of the Ville de Paris will remain at about its present level, and that the most significant growth and development will take place in the surrounding departments. The plan expresses a remarkable confidence and sureness of touch; its main features are rational and civilized; it emphasizes the need to organize and preserve the unity of the region as one of its three basic principles: the others are new urban centres and preferential development areas. Above all one feels that although modern techniques have been used in evolving the plan, it is not the product of computers and mechanized concepts.

The planning problem in Rome is rendered exceptionally difficult by the need to provide for the increased traffic needs of the city and to remedy the housing shortage while preserving and even improving the display of historical monuments and artistic buildings which adorn the Italian capital. Moreover, the overspill of the poorer classes from the overcrowded tenements into a ring of suburbs outside the main city has created a considerable danger, for in many of these outlying areas the general living conditions are primitive and the public services inadequate. Squalor, disease, and poverty are rampant in these suburbs, which are a potential menace to the whole metropolitan community. Several attempts have been made to produce a master plan, notably in 1931 and again in 1940–41; but so far the planning of Greater Rome—that is, the whole metropolitan area—has not been achieved, nor are there any organs available for the purpose. An ambitious redevelopment plan was drawn up in 1962 but so far little or nothing has been done to carry it out.

In Sydney an attempt to deal with the planning of the metropolis was made by the Local Government (Town and Country Planning) Amendment Act, 1945. This constituted the Cumberland and County District and provided for a county council to be elected by the councils of the cities, municipalities and shires of the area from among their own members. The county council was given responsibility for preparing a master plan for an area exceeding 1,500 square miles. The constituent municipal councils were also authorized to engage in local planning. The master plan was completed and became effective in 1951. Unfortunately, most of its recommendations were ignored, partly because of the indifference of the local authorities and partly because of the lack of support by the state government. The scheme for a green belt, for example, was eroded by allowing much of it to be used for housing purposes. In 1964 a State Planning Authority was set up in place of the county council, drawn partly from State Departments and partly from local government. Its functions include supervising and encouraging planning by local authorities, and preparing a strategic plan to guide the development of an enlarged Sydney metropolitan area. In 1967 the Authority published a somewhat vague 'Sydney Region Prelude to a Plan', which in due course is to be followed by an outline plan. The new Authority is in a stronger political position than the Cumberland County Council to plan the metropolitan area, but there are so many strong forces in New South Wales opposed to planning constraints that it is difficult to feel confident that the new regime will be more successful than its predecessor.

In Toronto a city planning board was appointed in 1942. Its plan was approved by the city council in 1949, and by the Ontario Minister of Planning and Development in 1950. The Municipality of Metropolitan Toronto Act, which established a metropolitan government for Greater Toronto, made Metro the principal planning authority; but the Act required the Ontario Minister of Planning and Development to define an even larger area for this purpose. This led to the Metropolitan Planning Board with jurisdiction over the Municipality of Metropolitan Toronto and 13 adjacent municipalities, whereby 479 square miles of territory were added to the 241 square miles of the metropolitan municipality for planning purposes.

The original Metropolitan Planning Board issued a lengthy draft plan in 1959, but this was not adopted by the metropolitan council. A revised and shorter version was in 1966 approved as a policy of council but not as an official plan. The metropolitan plan is no more than an amalgam of the separate plans made by the individual local governments. This cannot be regarded as true regional planning.

In Montreal the position is less favourable because there has been no authority or organization for metropolitan planning. In consequence, the city planning department was compelled to engage in regional planning studies which served as a background for the city's own planning schemes. The creation of the Montreal Urban Community in 1970 should in time improve the situation as the new metropolitan municipality is expected to prepare a development plan for the whole area, although the existing local planning organs will continue to function.

The planning of Warsaw was a necessity after the Second World War owing to the appalling destruction it had suffered at the hands of the Nazi invaders. Vast numbers of buildings, including the whole of the ancient historic centre, had been systematically destroyed. What remained was little more than a shell. The sheer scale of the destruction and the impoverishment of the nation made the planning and reconstruction a formidable task unequalled in any European city. It was facilitated by public acquisition of the land of the capital, a decision necessitated by the destruction of the title deeds of the private owners.

The first general town plan was submitted in 1946 to the Supreme Council for the Reconstruction of Warsaw and its basic principles were approved. It was decided from the outset that the city should be planned against the background of its region, and that the Warsaw Urban Area—which is larger than the city—should also receive consideration. The rapid development of industry in and around the capital exceeded the rate of progress in rebuilding the city centre and developing municipal services. A more balanced plan and development programme was therefore adopted by the people's council in 1956. An interesting feature of the plan was the rebuilding in its original form of the old historic quarter of the city which is today one of its most attractive centres.

In the plans for the Warsaw Urban Area and the regions, efforts have been made to diminish the inequalities in the living standards of the various districts. Warsaw is to retain its dominant position as a political, scientific and cultural centre, but in order that it shall not monopolize its possession of these advantages steps are to be taken to restrain its growth in relation to the rest of Poland. This involves not only restriction of entry into Warsaw for industry but the relocation of some factories to new sites in the Warsaw region. A question has arisen whether the administrative organization is adequate for the effective development of the urban area and the region. At present the only organ which exists is a Co-ordinating Council for the Development of the Warsaw Urban Area.

Both Johannesburg and Pretoria have engaged in town planning as a municipal function, but neither city has produced a comprehensive master plan. Hitherto the emphasis appears to have been laid on attempts to accommodate the ever-rising flood of motor cars. In 1967 the government appointed an independent Capital City Advisory Planning Committee for Pretoria and an independent Advisory Urban Renewal Committee for Johannesburg. The greatest obstacle so far in the way of greater achievement in the planning field has been lack of funds.

Tokyo has engaged in planning the physical development of the metropolis

with considerable energy. Unfortunately the efforts of the Tokyo Metropolitan Government have been frustrated by two factors: one is the lack of
any effective methods or machinery for controlling development; the other
is the immense pressure on land which has occurred during the post-war
period as a result of the enormous annual rate of population growth and
economic development. In consequence, the green-belt policy which was
adopted was abandoned, and the dwindling relics of the green belt, now renamed the green girdle, will soon disappear. The only restrictions on development imposed in practice have been a refusal to allow new factories, colleges
or universities to be established in the special ward area of the city. A new
town-planning law of 1969 is intended to strengthen planning control but it
is too early to say if it will succeed in doing so.

Meanwhile, many developments are occurring in the city which good
planning would avoid, such as the building of large numbers of office blocks
of the skyscraper type in the central area, and the construction of expressways
bringing a torrent of motor cars into the central city irrespective of the
capacity of the secondary roads to handle the resulting traffic.

Regional planning is entrusted to the Capital Region Development Commission which is composed of the Minister of Construction as chairman and
four other members. This body is authorized to prepare development plans
for the entire region covering the metropolis and seven adjacent prefectures.
The commission is, however, a weak body with little money and a small
professional staff, which is unable even to co-ordinate the policies of central
ministries in relation to regional development. Its effect on the planning and
development of the capital region has not been of great significance.

Osaka, the second largest city in Japan, published its basic proposals for
comprehensive planning in 1967; before that only sectoral plans had been
formulated by the various bureaux or departments of the city government.
The proposals cover the period until 1990; and a plan based on them is now
being prepared. The city of Osaka also forms part of three separate regions.
One is the Kinki Region, extending over an area of 37,174 square kilometres
and containing a population in excess of 18 million. There is a development
plan for the Kinki Region drawn up by a special organization appointed in
accordance with national legislation.[1] Another is the Hanshin Region, which
forms part of the Kinki Region, made up of 54 local authorities with a total
population of 9·2 million. There is no separate plan for this. The third region
is the Osaka Prefecture for which the Osaka regional plan has been made.
This covers an area of 1,839 square kilometres.

---

[1] Regional Development Liaison Council, consisting of the mayors of the three big cities,
the governors of the prefectures, and the chairmen of the assemblies.

In both Tokyo and Osaka the greatest obstacle in the way of satisfactory planning and development is the fantastic price of land. The land question underlies almost every problem concerning physical development and city government in Japan's great cities.

Town planning is in an advanced state in Stockholm, and the local authorities are in a favourable position to prepare ambitious plans and to carry them out. The fact that Sweden did not take part in the Second World War saved Stockholm and Sweden's other cities from destruction from aerial bombing, and also enabled exceptionally large resources to be devoted to the development and improvement of the capital.

Greater Stockholm has a population of over 1,400,000 and a territory of about 2,500 square kilometres. The Stockholm Region is a much larger area of about 7,700 square kilometres but it is sparsely populated. Greater Stockholm contains 28 local authorities of which the city of Stockholm is by far the greatest with about 780,000 inhabitants and providing 600,000 of the available jobs. Hitherto matters affecting the whole of Greater Stockholm have been settled by voluntary co-operation but a new type of metropolitan council has been approved by the Swedish Parliament and will come into force at the beginning of 1971. The metropolitan council will be responsible *inter alia* for regional planning, educational planning above the elementary level and the planning of sewage and water systems. The transport problem has been dealt with separately by the creation of a regional traffic authority to which all the undertakings have been transferred—the underground railways, the local services of the national railways, the bus services and the boat services serving the Stockholm archipelago.

A regional plan has already been drawn up by the local authorities through the medium of an advisory board acting on their behalf. This plan, which was approved by the government, has no statutory force but is intended to guide the local authorities in making their own plans. This method has apparently been more successful than one might expect from an advisory plan, but not sufficiently so as to preclude the creation of a directly elected regional council.

The plans now in existence involve the renewal of the inner city (excluding the old historic centre which occupies a somewhat similar position to the ancient City of London) comprising a mass of residential buildings constructed in the early years of the present century, most of which are now obsolete by modern standards. A new commercial, administrative and cultural centre is envisaged for this part of Stockholm. A body known as the General Planning Commission made up of the municipal leaders of all parties was created to carry out the surveys on which the plan was based and to co-ordinate the activities of the several administrative departments and public authorities which will participate in its realization.

A factor of extreme importance both in the past and in the future is the policy which Stockholm City Council has followed for many years of buying up large quantities of land not only within the city but also in adjacent municipalities. How many other large cities have had the money, the powers, or the foresight to acquire undeveloped land cheaply long before it is required for city development?[1] During the 1960s Stockholm had acquired about 30,000 hectares outside its own boundaries. Dr. Hjalmar Mehr remarks that in many parts of the world the expansion process begun by urbanization has been retarded by outdated local boundaries, but this has been avoided in Stockholm by the successful and active policy of purchasing land in adjoining territories as well as inside the city.

Some of the most affluent countries have failed to plan their great cities in a satisfactory manner, and metropolitan areas are often lacking in any kind of regional planning. It is also true, however, that the poorer or less prosperous cities included in this book have not achieved effective planning of their areas. For various reasons Manila, Calcutta, Rio de Janeiro, Cairo, Delhi,[2] Ibadan and Mexico City all present a picture of inability to plan, or to plan comprehensively, or to plan for the whole metropolis.

Birmingham has been a pioneer in town planning. The first law giving local authorities planning powers was passed in 1909 and a scheme prepared by Birmingham City Council was approved in 1913. Since then there has been a succession of new and more ambitious plans. No one can visit Birmingham today without being struck by the spectacular rebuilding of the city centre, and behind this reconstruction lies a vast redevelopment of other parts of the city. Beyond the immediate centre are located five comprehensive redevelopment areas which are to be cleared and rebuilt to provide improved standards of housing, open spaces and community facilities. The relocation of more than 1,500 business firms is involved. An interesting feature of the redevelopment is the provision of flatted factories for small industries. Many of these are in the jewellery and allied trades which at present occupy decayed houses.

A major problem facing Birmingham City Council is the lack of available land in the city for rehousing and other kinds of redevelopment. Birmingham is the centre of the large West Midlands region, for which there is at present

[1] Birmingham took a step in this direction in the nineteenth century when Joseph Chamberlain was lord mayor of the city. The Municipality purchased what is now Corporation Street in the heart of the city.

[2] New Delhi is excluded from this statement as it was very carefully planned in accordance with the ideas of the period when it was constructed (1910–40).

no regional authority with overriding powers. Co-operation in planning has depended on the goodwill of neighbouring counties. Since 1956 a Joint Committee on Birmingham Overspill has attempted to reconcile conflicting interests. In 1957 it was estimated that in order to reduce urban congestion to a reasonable level the city would have to move out of Birmingham 180,000 persons and 32,000 jobs. A not inconsiderable contribution to this objective has been made in the ensuing years but the rate of progress has declined since 1962, partly owing to national policy favouring other less prosperous regions for industrial development or redevelopment.

The building of two new towns is assisting Birmingham's need to deconcentrate. One of these is Telford, 30 miles to the west of the city; the other is Redditch to the south. Birmingham has also entered into agreements with numerous small local authorities to support and assist their growth by allocating houses and jobs to suitable citizens living in overcrowded conditions in Birmingham.

Considerable numbers of houses have been or will be built by Birmingham City Council in the neighbouring counties of Worcestershire and Warwickshire, but there is great opposition to this form of urban encroachment in rural or semi-rural areas. Some erosion of the green belt around Birmingham is threatened as a means of solving the housing problem. A much larger metropolitan authority (on the lines of the Greater London Council) is likely to be established in the Birmingham region in the next few years, and this may lead to a more comprehensive view being taken of the needs of the West Midlands complex.

London is in some respects a very well planned city and in other respects ill planned or unplanned. Some of the principal features of the central area, such as the squares of Bloomsbury, Mayfair and Belgravia, the Mall, Trafalgar Square and the Thames Embankment, are of the highest value. The splendid string of parks stretching from Westminster to Kensington are unique and unrivalled in any other great city. These are the creations of the eighteenth and nineteenth centuries. The worst examples of unplanned development, urban sprawl and reckless destruction of the natural environment are the outcome of the expansion which occurred between about 1870 and 1939.

During the Second World War, when London suffered very severely from aerial bombardment, new plans were produced for the County of London (which was the area of the London County Council, then the principal local authority in the metropolis) and for Greater London, a much larger area covering 2,535 square miles outside the county. The Greater London plan was the work of the late Sir Patrick Abercrombie, the most eminent planner of his time. In 1947 the ancient City of London, the small central core from which the modern metropolis has sprung, published a plan for its own area.

These three related plans have had a substantial effect on the post-war development of the capital city. The L.C.C. plan provided for the removal from the county of 500,000–600,000 persons. Abercrombie's plan added a further 415,000 to this figure, making a total of about a million inhabitants to be transferred. About three-quarters of them were to be decentralized to new towns, to smaller existing towns capable of development, and to housing estates outside the county. The remainder were to be dispersed outside the region. This vast removal was to be brought about by voluntary methods in order to provide better living conditions both to those who were to leave London and those who would continue to inhabit the capital. Underlying the proposal was a recognition of the fact that it is no longer necessarily true —if ever it was—that the bigger a city becomes the better life will be for its denizens.

The most striking feature of Abercrombie's great plan was the creation of eight new self-contained satellite towns outside the green belt. These new towns have been planned and built as complete entities at distances of between 17 and 40 miles from the centre, although the sites differ from those suggested by Abercrombie. Their total population in 1969 was about 450,000 and they have succeeded in attracting a large amount of industry. A significant beginning has also been made in attracting firms offering office employment. In consequence the great majority of the residents are employed either in the new towns or near by. Only a very small percentage commutes to London. The new towns have been built by new town development corporations on behalf of the central government, which provides the money, designates the sites and decides major questions of policy.

The Greater London Council was constituted in 1964, and it has continued to support and develop the new towns and expanded towns programmes which the London County Council had initiated. Under the expanded town programme agreements have been made between the Greater London Council and 27 small towns to build houses and admit factories, etc., in their areas for Londoners willing to move. The total number of houses included in these agreements was 80,087 (as at June 30, 1967) which would accommodate probably 250,000 Londoners.

Another major feature of the Abercrombie plan (although it was initiated much earlier) was the green belt which encircles London. This has been maintained without violation, and some local authorities are pressing for it to be extended.

Control over the location of industry was authorized by the Town and Country Planning Act, 1947, and considerable restriction has been imposed thereafter by the Board of Trade on the construction or expansion of factories in Greater London. What was not foreseen until much later was that the unrestricted construction of office buildings in the central area of London could create immense problems. For many years the number of jobs in the uncontrolled construction of office buildings in the central area of London could create immense problems. For many years the number of jobs in the central area increased by about 15,000 a year. The effect was to increase the army of workers commuting from ever longer distances, creating severe difficulties of transportation, and transforming the city centre into a mass of faceless office blocks, which tended to overwhelm and supplant houses, shops, theatres, clubs, dance halls and buildings devoted to many other activities. To remedy this situation the Control of Office and Industrial Development Act was passed in 1965, whereby office buildings are subject to controls similar to those applicable to factories. Since then office building in central London has been severely restricted.

The central government has greatly assisted the movement to reduce the population of Greater London, not only by the measures described above, but also by offering large subsidies to firms providing additional employment in other parts of Great Britain, particularly those known as the development areas in which declining industries have caused unemployment above the national average. These inducements have had some effect in reducing the pressure to expand in the South-East Region. The government has also taken the lead in decentralizing large numbers of civil servants formerly employed at the headquarter offices of Government Departments in the centre of London. The combined effect of all these measures has been to reduce the population of Greater London from 8,201,186 in 1951 to 7,763,820 in 1968.

The London Government Act, 1963, introduced an entirely new system of planning in the metropolis. The Greater London Council was required to produce a strategic plan for the metropolis; and the 32 London boroughs and the City Corporation were authorized to prepare detailed plans for their respective areas in conformity with the general guide lines laid down by the strategic plan. Such a division of functions has not been previously attempted in Britain, and it is too early to form a judgment on its success.[1] But a good deal of criticism has been levelled at the Greater London Development Plan which was published in 1969. The plan is subject to public inquiry at which all objections will be heard, and it can then be amended by the minister or

[1] See *Tomorrow's London* for a background to the Greater London Development Plan.

referred back to the G.L.C. What some critics contend is that the Greater London Council has too restricted an area for regional planning, and that the London boroughs have been given too independent a position *vis-à-vis* the Greater London Council.

It is certainly true that the machinery of planning could be improved in the metropolis and its region. It is also true that the Greater London Development Plan contains several excellent features, such as the twenty-nine new strategic shopping centres, the three new regional park projects, the development of Thamesmead as a settlement for 60,000 Londoners in an abandoned, low-lying bend in the Thames, and the proposal to create office centres in the less congested parts of Greater London. Its most controversial proposal is the construction of three rings of motorways, especially the innermost one known as the motorway box. This has already aroused a good deal of opposition and its future is uncertain.

During the present decade important decisions will have to be made on the planning and development of South-East England. The South-East Economic Planning Council has presented to the government a strategic study for planning the region and the feasibility of this has been examined by a team of civil servants and professional planners. The planning of the region will clearly have far-reaching effects on the development of Greater London, which dominates the south-east, and the converse is equally true. The South-East Region is the most rapidly growing region in Britain and part of the growth is due to the export of population from London. The planning and development of this region on sound lines is a matter of national importance. The most favourable feature of the present position is that the central government has formulated both an urban policy and a regional policy.

THE PROBLEMS SUMMARIZED

In this introductory analysis we have surveyed broadly the many different kinds of problems which confront great cities of the world today. In the chapters dealing with individual cities contained in Part Two the contributors discuss in greater detail the incidence of these problems as they exist in the circumstances peculiar to each metropolis. The details vary from country to country and from city to city; and no metropolitan community has to cope with all the problems in an intense form at any one moment. But in general there is sufficient similarity between the difficulties which have arisen in many different countries to enable us to say that great cities all over the world are facing common problems which are mainly due to similar causes.

These problems may be classified under the following five headings:

1. *Organization of areas and authorities*

Under this heading comes the question of evolving a constitutional framework for the great municipality which corresponds with the facts of population, territorial size, mobility, social and economic life in the last quarter of the twentieth century. It involves the administrative integration of the whole metropolitan area for the large-scale services which require unified planning, co-ordination or administration. It also involves smaller, more compact units of local government to perform the functions which can best be administered by smaller municipal organs. The reform of metropolitan government thus demands both more centralization and more decentralization; in other words, both larger and smaller areas and authorities. It also requires the absorption of many *ad hoc* authorities which have been created on a widespread scale to provide one or more services in a special district. The fragmentation of metropolitan government has already proceeded too far in many cities. Even where an *ad hoc* authority can be justified on rational grounds, and not merely explained by the specious excuse that this method makes it possible to avoid much-needed reforms which are too difficult politically to carry through, the proper relationship of *ad hoc* bodies with the city government still requires careful thought. 'Divide and Misrule' seems to be the maxim which legislators have hitherto followed in devising the constitutional organization of many great cities. Reforms of various kinds have taken place in London, Paris, Toronto, Montreal and Stockholm, but most great cities are left to struggle on as best they can with out-of-date structures and powers. The expansion of boundaries appears to be carried out most easily in the Communist countries of Eastern Europe where political opposition is largely absent.

2. *Popular interest and democratic participation*

The problem of evoking and holding the interest of the citizens in the affairs of the great city, and of securing their active participation in its government, is one of great importance. It has nowhere been solved, but successful efforts in the right direction have been made in Belgrade and Warsaw. Mass participation in city government and the creation of small neighbourhood units or block committees are characteristic of the communist regimes in Eastern Europe. Electoral apathy is usually more marked in the great city than in towns of smaller size; and popular interest in the government of the metropolis also compares unfavourably with that shown in government at the national level. Many of the defects of metropolitan government are directly traceable to public indifference or popular ignorance.

The low level of popular interest in, and public understanding of, the affairs of the great city even among the more educated classes largely explain the difficulty of finding men and women of high mental and moral calibre who are willing to serve on the city council or its executive organs. They explain, too, the nepotism and corruption which occur in some great cities. They account for the ease with which self-interested politicians or officials obstruct or defeat attempts at improving the constitutional organization of the metropolis. Above all, it is only the low level of civic interest in city affairs which makes it possible for great cities like Paris, Buenos Aires, Delhi, Mexico City and Calcutta to be virtually governed by prefects, mayors or commissioners appointed by the central or provincial government, with only nominal or limited power, if any, given to the representative organs.

The public apathy towards the government of the great city is the result of many different factors. One of them is the divided interest and allegiance resulting from the separation of workplace and home in different municipal areas; another is the huge size of the very large metropolis. But whatever the causes, only a deliberate and sustained effort to educate metropolitan man in the politics and government of the vast metropolitan community of which he is a member will solve the problems arising under this head.

3. *Efficiency of the municipal services*

The product or output of city government in the great municipality is by no means satisfactory. Recurring themes in the studies which follow are the inadequacy of highways to carry modern traffic, the public transport problem, congested living quarters, the growth of slums, excessive density of population in the poorer parts of the city, shortage of open spaces, housing inadequacies, the problem of overspill, difficulties of carrying out major engineering works such as those connected with water supply or sewage. The great city of today lives by a miracle. It is not operating on a satisfactory standard in regard to schools, housing, open spaces and playing fields, traffic circulation, public transport, police protection, air pollution, noise and many other services. The causes are complex and diverse. Sometimes they spring from maldistribution of functions between the great municipality, *ad hoc* bodies, and national or provincial authorities. Sometimes they derive from defective organization within the metropolitan region, particularly in the allocation of functions among many small, poor and unco-ordinated authorities. Sometimes the chief causes are corruption or sheer incompetence on the part of the city government, which are in turn due to the public apathy or ignorance already referred to. An excessive bureaucratization of the city government may result in public needs being overlooked or side-tracked by stiff-necked officials who lack high professional standards, while sheer insensitivity on the part of elected representatives often acounts for the persistence of disamenities and public nuisances. This can easily happen when the affected classes or groups are not articulate or do not possess effective methods of making their needs known to the authorities.

4. *Finance*

From many cities comes the complaint of inadequate financial resources to provide the municipal services of the great city. Wealthy New York City joins with impoverished Calcutta, Osaka with Rome, in declaring their inability to find the money required to finance current municipal services and much-needed new developments. A chronic state of financial stringency appears to be a permanent condition of many metropolitan cities. This condition is one which afflicts both the wealthiest and the poorest cities. It is this which explains the fact that in many great cities highway development lags so far behind the proved needs of motor-car traffic that it is scarcely an exaggeration to say that the central areas have almost seized up. Housing, education, water supply, the police, even street paving, are often less adequate in quantity and quality in the great metropolis than in the smaller towns, though in every branch of municipal activity some great cities have the highest achievements to their credit. The point I am making is that we cannot assume that mere size will by itself guarantee high standards of government and administration. Finance is all too often the Achilles heel of the metropolis. The cost of services and especially of land is disproportionately high in the great city, and is seldom matched by the higher yield of taxes.

5. *Planning the metropolitan region*

Many of the most difficult problems which confront the great city can be solved only by imaginative planning and drastic development or renewal. The elimination of overcrowding in the densest quarters; the provision of a reasonable amount of land devoted to parks, playing fields and other outdoor amenities; the opening up of the suffocating alleyways in the older parts of ancient cities, like Stockholm or Copenhagen, or the narrow canons which shut out light, sun and air in downtown New York or Chicago; the reclamation of slums and derelict residential, commercial or industrial areas;

the avoidance and elimination of high population densities in the central areas in order to exploit the enormous land values which accrue in the great metropolis; the reduction and prevention of long, exhausting and expensive journeys to work which waste the money, health, energy and time of those who live in the outlying suburbs of the great city; these and cognate aims to cure the maladies which are commonly found in the great metropolis can only be achieved by well considered, drastic and creative planning.

Such planning must secure control of the whole metropolitan region which is centred on the great city. It must comprise both town and country within its scope. It must be positive as well as negative: it must prescribe what shall be done and not merely what is forbidden. Authorities to carry out the plans must exist both at the regional and local levels, and they must have effective powers, adequate territorial jurisdiction and sufficient resources. Much positive development must be entrusted to them where private enterprise is unwilling or unable to carry it out. A well-designed administrative organization, the necessary legal framework and financial support must be provided by the central government.

At this stage of the argument we reach a point where the question we are discussing is really the future of the great city. For although primarily this book is concerned with the government and the politics of great cities, it is also concerned with their planning. And in considering town planning one is bound to examine the social life of the vast communities which live in these huge urban aggregations.

THE METROPOLITAN REGION OF TOMORROW

The easy-going assumption that the bigger the city the better existence would be for everybody concerned prevailed throughout the nineteenth century. It is no longer accepted in the leading centres of social and political thought. Sociologists, town planners and political scientists have in recent decades made some penetrating studies of great cities, beginning with Charles Booth's great pioneering study on *The Life and Labour of the People in London.* This was published in no less than eighteen volumes in 1903, and is a landmark of social investigation which had profound consequences both in the world of thought and the world of action. The most profound studies of a general kind are Lewis Mumford's fine book *The Culture of Cities* published in 1938 and the same author's *The City in History*, which appeared in 1961. A more journalistic and less balanced account was Robert Sinclair's *Metropolitan Man.*

Mumford delivers a coruscating criticism of the modern metropolis. He considers it to be economically unsound, politically unstable, biologically degenerate and socially unsatisfying.[1] Beneath the proud surface glitter of the great city and its artificially induced prestige and glamour he detects much that is meretricious and unreal. He sees the great city as too dependent on paper, on finance, insurance and advertising;[2] he sees the bulk of its inhabitants leading a drab and unhealthy existence too remote from the sights, sounds and smells of the countryside; he sees them wasting enormous quantities of time, energy, money and vitality on subway journeys and other debilitating forms of travel devoid of value in themselves.[3] 'The metropolitan world', he contends, 'is a world where flesh and blood is less real than paper and ink and celluloid. It is a world where the great masses of people, unable to have direct contact with more satisfying means of living, take life vicariously, as readers, spectators, passive observers. . . .'[4] The physical form of the great metropolis he declares to be shapeless: to consist of mere size without significance. Even when one finds order, design and meaning in the central area, as in Paris, Madrid or Buenos Aires, the surrounding districts present a picture of a 'vast enveloping aimlessness'.[5]

There is much truth in Lewis Mumford's indictment, though it is not the whole truth about the matter. His work is profound, imaginative, and deeply felt. That a revaluation is needed of our ideas about the great city as a habitat for man can scarcely be doubted.

In the nineteenth century, mere size was regarded as a desirable attribute of cities, and 'the bigger the better' was a maxim which embodied public opinion on the subject. There was little or no attempt to limit or control urban growth. Today, the overblown, dropsical city of elephantine proportions can no longer be regarded as desirable or even tolerable in its present condition.

The period of unqualified acceptance and unfettered growth of the metropolitan city is passing. We have already moved into an era in which the amorphous, shapeless, sprawling metropolis is being challenged by new ideas which will eventually transform it into something very different.

It is now clear that effective planning of a metropolis is assisted by placing a limit on the maximum size and population. The essential instrument for enforcing this limit is control over the location of employment. If new industry and other kinds of employment are permitted to enter the metropolitan area freely, and existing factories and office buildings are allowed to expand indefinitely, no real control over either the ultimate size of the metropolis or its design is possible.

---

[1] *The Culture of Cities*, Chapter IV, and *The City in History*, Chapter 17.
[2] *The Culture of Cities*, p. 256.   [3] *Ibid*, p. 243.   [4] *Ibid*, p. 258.   [5] *Ibid*, p. 234.

In the second place, the abolition of slums, the clearance of overcrowded tenements, the widening of narrow, airless streets, and the rehousing of the people at a reasonable standard, inevitably produces a big problem of urban dispersal and overspill. This can only be solved on rational lines by redistributing population between the overcrowded quarters of the central city and the suburbs, towns, villages and housing estates in the outlying parts of the metropolitan region or beyond.

Decongestion means decentralization; but it is senseless to move people out to the suburbs or semi-rural housing estates if they are obliged to work in the great city and to make costly, exhausting and time-consuming journeys to and from their work. It is far better also to move out the factories, warehouses, offices and workplaces, or to encourage new industrial and commercial development in satellite towns or new independent cities where the workpeople can enjoy not only good housing conditions, but an agreeable environment and easy access to the countryside. By doing so, we can once more bring together the home, the workplace, and the playground or recreational centre: that essential triad of human life which has become scattered and disunited in the welter of the modern metropolis. We shall thereby restore family life to the primacy it once enjoyed but has since long lost in the turmoil of the great city. Finally, in offering easy access to the countryside to the citizens who move out from the congested central area to the outlying towns and settlements, we must insist on drawing a clear line of demarcation between town and country, in order to ensure that rural amenities are not destroyed by those who would enjoy them. The worst feature of many metropolitan areas today is that much of their environs consists of neither town nor country, but merely of land suffering from urban blight.

When we have done all this and much else which is in the minds of our most creative planners, our most imaginative social thinkers, and our leading practical reformers, we shall find that we have transformed the great metropolis. In place of an inchoate metropolitan community continually shuttling back and forth between suburb and central city, wasting its energy, time and money in nerve-shattering journeys to and from work, or living in overcrowded apartment houses in back streets, we shall gradually create an ordered, coherent, decentralized metropolitan region.

The city centre will contain the institutions which need vast resources and the support of large numbers of people: the university, the opera house, the chief theatres; the great museums and art galleries; the principal reference libraries; the concert halls for symphony orchestras and famous musicians; the exhibitions of a specialized or highly cultivated character; the leading centres of scientific teaching and research; the superior courts of law; government and municipal offices of many kinds; the principal broadcasting and television studios; the headquarters of banks, insurance companies and other financial institutions; the most important shopping centres for such goods as furniture, jewellery, motor cars, works of art, fashionable clothes, etc.; the headquarter offices of great commercial undertakings; the principal publishers of books, periodicals and newspapers; the more elaborate and highly developed hospitals for teaching and research; and much else which can best flourish in the great city and cannot easily be decentralized. The outlying towns or settlements of the garden city type will contain houses and flats, factories and offices, shops and laboratories, schools, cinemas, local theatres, smaller concert halls, civic centres, lending libraries, and many other institutions to enable the local communities to lead a largely self-contained life for much of their time, but with recourse to the central city when occasion demands.

The metropolitan city has played a great part in the history of mankind. It can continue to play a great part in future, if we guide its destiny wisely and well. I have referred in these concluding pages to some of the severe criticisms which have recently been levelled at the metropolis. But there is much to love and to admire in the great city. It is the home of the highest achievements of man in art, literature and science; the source from which the forces of freedom and emancipation have sprung. It is the place where the spirit of humanism and of democracy have grown and flourished, where man's quest for knowledge and justice has been pursued most constantly, and truth revealed most faithfully and fearlessly.

Let us bear all this in mind, and remain the friends and lovers of the great city in all that we do to improve its government, its politics and planning, and thereby raise the quality of life of its citizens.

PART TWO

Amsterdam

ARNE F. LEEMANS

ARNE F. LEEMANS

Born 1920. Degrees: Master of Law, Leyden University, 1946; Doctor of Law, Leyden, 1967. Formerly Assistant Secretary-General of the International Union of Local Authorities, and Reader in Public Administration at the Institute of Social Studies, The Hague. Presently: Professor of Public Administration and Director of the Institute of Public Administration, University of Amsterdam.

Author of: *Integration of Policy Making in a Large City* (Eenheid in het bestuur der Grote Stad). Doctoral dissertation (in Dutch), Leyden, 1967; *Changing Patterns for Local Government*, International Union of Local Authorities, The Hague, 1967; editor of 'Administrative Reform', a special issue of *Development and Change*, Vol. II, 1, The Hague, 1971. Various papers for international conferences and numerous articles on local government.

Amsterdam

AMSTERDAM, capital of the Netherlands but not its seat of government, has for centuries occupied the special position of being the largest commercial and industrial centre of the country. The earliest historical sources of Amsterdam, dating back to the thirteenth century, refer to it as a fisherman's village, but a few centuries later it had developed into a thriving commercial city from where an enterprising fleet sailed the Seven Seas, bringing prosperity to its home town. During the sixteenth and seventeenth centuries, Amsterdam developed into one of the world's most important trading and banking centres. It played a dominant role in the Low Countries, so dominant in fact, that at times it even challenged the authority of the Sovereign.

Prosperity and a population explosion during the seventeenth century necessitated several extensions outside the original defensive canal system. In spite of this enlargement, however, the city was very densely inhabited, with a population of over 200,000.

International competition during the eighteenth century checked the development of the city, whilst the Napoleonic occupation cut off the people from the sea and thus dealt a fatal blow to the city's prosperity. Not until the second half of the nineteenth century did the city begin to awaken from its dark ages. Better communications with the open sea started a new commercial and industrial development. The population, which amounted to over 200,000 during the second half of the seventeenth century and remained almost at a standstill for nearly two centuries, began to increase rapidly: from 221,000 in 1850 to 510,000 in 1900. Finally, the city again began to extend its territory in order to accommodate the expanding population and its need for recreation and to provide harbour and industry space, and did so by annexing several neighbouring municipalities which were of a predominantly rural nature. The city's surface area thus increased considerably during the nineteenth century and the first decades of the twentieth century. After 1921, however, annexations came to a halt as they were considered to conflict with the idea of municipal autonomy and freedom. Only very recently in 1966, have new areas again been added to the territory of the city.

These territorial restrictions did not stop urban sprawl into adjacent municipalities which became increasingly urbanized, some over a period of several decades, others only in recent years. This, in addition to the industrial and harbour expansion, has caused the development of a large urban agglomeration or metropolitan area, the boundaries of which are not

133

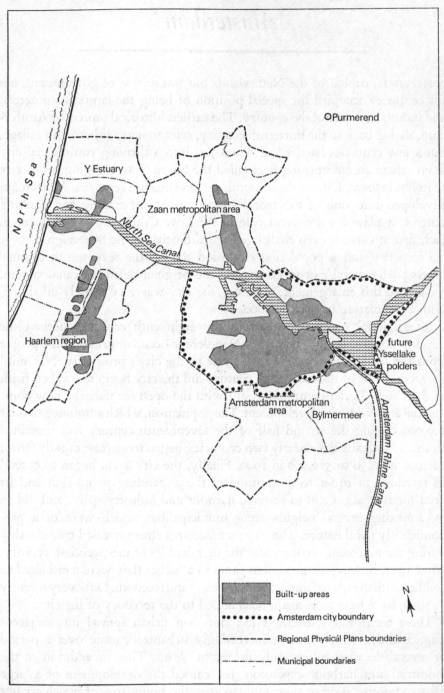

MAP I AMSTERDAM

well defined, and on the delimitation of which considerable disagreement exists.

Table I shows the growth of population and the expansion of the city territory.

It has already been stated that the city is of a mixed commercial and industrial character. The harbour for seagoing vessels and inland waterway transport plays a vital role in the city's economy. The North Sea Canal and its locks have recently been enlarged so as to take ships with a draught of 43 feet. The canal between Amsterdam and the river Rhine provides a good connection with the major industrial area of Germany, the 'Ruhrgebiet'.

TABLE I

	Surface area in hectares[1]	Population	
± 1830		± 180,000	
1850		221,111	
1890	3,252	408,061	
1900	4,395	510,853	
1920	4,630	647,427	
1930	17,455	757,386	
1940	17,455	803,073	
1950	17,455	845,266	
1960	17,455	866,342	
1967	20,664	866,421	1970
Metropolitan area of Greater Amsterdam[2]			
1967	58,587	1,043,051	1970

Although this canal was improved considerably during the 'fifties, further extension is again necessary. In spite of these improvements, however, the number of ships entering the harbour and the tonnage of goods passing through the harbour has increased but little since 1961. Shipbuilding and engineering works have always played an important role in the industrial sector. Other industries include textiles, car manufacturing and the very old and highly specialized diamond industry.

Amsterdam, formerly an international banking centre, is still important in the banking world. The city is also the cultural hub of the country; tourists, especially to the relatively well-preserved age-old city centre, represent an important element in the city's economy.

[1] 1 hectare = 2·471 acres.
[2] The Metropolitan area referred to here is only a geographical expression, not a unit of administration.

POLITICAL HISTORY AND CULTURE

Similarly to other cities in the Low Countries, Amsterdam had a strongly representative government of its own from the moment it became a chartered town in the Middle Ages. The country's sovereign authorities, whether foreign or Dutch, rarely interfered in city government affairs, although burgomasters and councillors were at times dismissed by Sovereign or Parliament after major political changes had taken place in the country. City councillors were selected mainly by co-option, and the city was consequently ruled by its commercial and later by the aristocratic élite.

After the establishment of the Kingdom of the Netherlands in 1813, representative government was developed very gradually, first on the basis of appointment by the King, later by a limited electoral system and, since 1917, by general suffrage.

A milestone in Dutch local government history was the Local Government Act of 1852, which was based on three main principles: the old and strong tradition of local autonomy, the concept of democratic representation in municipal government, and a centralizing trend which stemmed partly from French influence. Under this Act, considerable discretion was given to local authorities, who were entitled to undertake, within certain limits, anything they considered to be in the interests of the local community.

During the first few decades after the introduction of this Act, local authorities, including the city of Amsterdam, made little use of the vast opportunities which it offered for municipal action. According to the philosophy of the liberals, the politically dominant group at that time, city government should restrict its activities mainly to the maintenance of law and order. It was not until the second half of the nineteenth century that the government of Amsterdam, in which progressive liberals and representatives of religious parties played an increasingly important role, assumed a growing number of tasks. In fact, Amsterdam became one of the most progressive cities in the Netherlands and has therefore been called the 'laboratory' for new municipal action.

This trend has continued during the present century, under the influence of the socialists. The first socialist was not elected to the city council until 1902, but the party grew so rapidly that in the 1913 elections it gained approximately 43 per cent of the votes. This shift to the left continued, with the result that in the first elections after the First World War, which were conducted under the new system of proportional representation instead of the district system, the Communist Party gained 6 of the 45 council seats, the socialists having 13.

After the Second World War, the Communist Party again flourished and gained 15 of the 45 seats in 1946, as did also the socialists. It is an interesting fact that the communists are far stronger in Amsterdam than in the other large cities of the country.

Indeed, the political climate and culture of Amsterdam differs conspicuously from that of the other large cities. In fact, Amsterdam has been called the country's political boiling pot. The new progressive political currents of the second half of the nineteenth century, welfare state liberalism, and socialism, first found institutionalized expression in political associations and groups in Amsterdam. Socialism developed earlier and on a much more massive scale than in the other cities, and later communism obtained a stronger foothold in Amsterdam than elsewhere.

This exceptional political climate had quite a few causes. First, the city had traditionally a large urban proletariat which, as in other European cities, was inclined to radicalism. Moreover, a great many immigrants to Amsterdam during the nineteenth and twentieth centuries came from secularized, religiously progressive, neighbouring areas and from a politically radical province in the north of the country.

This inclination towards radicalism undoubtedly had significant effects on the functioning of the city government, and was a prime cause of the progressive public policies for which Amsterdam has been noted. Moreover, it led to the strong political differentiation of the city council and consequently to considerable opposition within the council.

THE STRUCTURE OF LOCAL GOVERNMENT

The metropolitan area of Amsterdam is formed by an agglomeration of independent municipalities. A form of metropolitan government for the whole area or for part of it does not exist, but its establishment is under consideration.

The municipalities in the area are in charge of, and fully responsible for, the conduct of most public affairs. Municipal functions can be distinguished into autonomous and 'co-government', the latter being state functions, the execution of which has been delegated to local governments. Further attention will be given to this distinction below.

Municipalities perform their functions within the limits set by law, by central government directives, or by the general interest, and are controlled by central and provincial governments in several respects. The smaller municipalities in the area are generally more strictly controlled than Amsterdam.

E*

The city government of Amsterdam is made up of three major organs: the council, the executive board, and the burgomaster.

The council

The council is the supreme organ of the municipality. Its 45 members are elected for the city as a whole, under a system of proportional representation. Interest in council membership is unfortunately limited, partly owing to the amount of time involved, and political parties consequently often have difficulty in finding sufficient qualified candidates, who must be not less than 21 years of age.

The freedom of the council to establish legally constituted committees with varied functions, powers and composition, has been increased considerably as a result of recent legislation. Non-council members may now be appointed members of committees; and committees may now even be vested with executive and rule-making powers, whereas formerly they were only of an advisory character. Thus far, however, Amsterdam's council committees still conform with the old law: they are still composed of council members and have merely an advisory function. The council is apparently reluctant to delegate powers to such committees, or to appoint non-council members.

Under the law, the council is vested with all local government powers which have not been expressly assigned to the executive board or the burgomaster. It takes the final decision in all matters except those which it has delegated or which have been entrusted to other local organs. The executive board is not legally responsible to the council for 'co-government' functions, but nevertheless submits to it most proposals of this nature.

Although much council business is conducted in council committees, and relatively few proposals made by the executive board to the council are rejected or amended, the council's plenary sessions still have considerable value. First, the annual budget debates offer political factions and their members an opportunity to review the overall policy of the city. Secondly, plenary sessions enable council factions and council members publicly to justify their votes for or against a proposal. Finally, council members may submit motions and propose amendments to proposals presented by the executive board; they may also make proposals to the council. Recent research[1] has shown that the city councillors of Amsterdam are considerably more active in this respect than their colleagues in The Hague or Rotterdam: they propose more motions and amendments and take more initiative in new

[1] See the author's doctoral dissertation: *Integration of Policy-making in a Large City*.

proposals than their aforesaid colleagues. One reason for this greater activity may be the relatively strong extreme left-wing factions in the council and the ensuing degree of dissent.

Council work is mainly concentrated in the committees, each of which deals with a certain aspect of municipal activity. At present there are twenty-one such committees in Amsterdam, most of which have a dual role. On the one hand, they enable council members to be frequently consulted on municipal matters and to influence the executive board during the policy-formulation process. On the other hand, they give the executive board an opportunity to hear the opinions of the council and thus to allow for the wishes of council members when preparing new proposals, thereby increasing the chances that these proposals will be adopted by the council in its plenary sessions.

The executive board

The executive board, which in some respects can be considered the municipal 'cabinet', is composed of the burgomaster and aldermen,[1] the latter being elected by the council from amongst its members, in principle for a four-year period of their tenure as councillors. The appointment of the aldermen takes place during the first council session after the municipal elections. At present, Amsterdam has eight aldermen.

Since the introduction of proportional representation into Dutch local government, local councils have shown a strong inclination to form a broadly based 'coalition cabinet' and to elect aldermen in such a way that political factions are represented on the executive board according to their strength in the council. In the past, exceptions to this informal rule were frequently made when the sharply contrasting political views of the various council factions caused one or more to decline membership of the council, preferring not to bear responsibility for its policy. This also occurred when members of certain parties, particularly of the extreme right or left, were found unacceptable by other factions as members of the board. The fact that, for many years, two of the larger factions had no representatives on the executive board, i.e., the communists and the liberals (the latter being somewhat conservative in the Dutch political context), is indicative of the rather strong political differences in Amsterdam's city council. Not until the 1966 elections did these two parties each gain a seat on the board. The liberals again withdrew from the board in 1970.

---

[1] 'Aldermen' is not really an adequate translation of the Dutch word *wethouder*, which means literally 'holder of the law'.

The politically representative composition of the executive board has significant implications for its operation. On the one hand, the arrangement may help the council to accept policies proposed by the executive board since the aldermen, being also members of the council and therefore of the respective political factions, can pave the way to such acceptance in their own council faction. On the other hand, when political factions hold strongly conflicting views, as in Amsterdam, a broadly based coalition cabinet is likely to affect decision-making by the board, and to hamper its policy-making.

The executive board is of a dual character. First, its task is to prepare and formulate policies in accordance with the wishes of the council, or in antici-pation of such wishes. Secondly, it is the board of management of the city government organization. Each member of the executive board is in charge of one or more portfolios which are distributed amongst them by the execu-tive board as a whole immediately after their appointment. The members manage and supervise the sections of the municipal apparatus belonging to their portfolios, which they do with a considerable degree of discretion. As a result, there is a notable amount of departmentalization in the city machinery.

The board cannot legally delegate functions to its individual members as, in principle, all decisions have to be taken by the board as a whole in order to guarantee that all viewpoints—political party as well as sectorial—are taken into consideration. Such collegial decision-making in a large city machine such as that of Amsterdam is, of necessity, often of a purely formal nature, confirming the proposals made by board members without further discus-sion. It is noteworthy, however, that in Amsterdam, more than in The Hague or Rotterdam, the executive board has tended to adhere to the attitude that all policy decisions should be taken by the board as a whole, not only formally but also in reality.

The burgomaster

The burgomaster is appointed by the Crown for a period of six years. He can be, and usually is, reappointed. He is chairman of the council as well as of the executive board. He receives a salary of 143,000 guilders paid by the municipality from funds made available by the state. One motive for the appointment system is to make the burgomaster independent of the political factions in the council, but although designated in this way, he is by no means a central government official. His relationship with central government is perhaps best described by saying that, at least in most respects, he is not responsible to central government but to the law. In fact, the burgomaster identifies himself rather with the city community, whose interests in major issues he advocates, frequently with great ardour, before central government.

In the Crown's appointment of a burgomaster, allowance is always made for the political composition of the city's population. Consequently, in view of the strong leftish groups in the city council, a socialist has always been appointed to Amsterdam during the last few decades.

The history of Amsterdam shows several serious conflicts between the burgomaster, usually a prominent citizen, and the council or population, thus proving the capital's reputation of being a difficult city. Those conflicts, often related to the maintenance of law and order under the responsibility of the burgomaster, led to the resignation of a burgomaster at the turn of the century, and resulted in the dismissal of the burgomaster by central government in 1967, an extremely rare event. Under the pressure of the opinion prevailing in Amsterdam that the people of the city should have a voice in the appointment of their burgomaster, the government decided to consult the city's council when considering the appointment of the present burgomaster—a remarkable deviation from former governmental attitudes. The present burgomaster was formerly a Member of Parliament and had held office as Minister of Justice. At the time of his appointment he was Professor of Law at Leyden University.

Legally speaking, the burgomaster plays a dual role: as a municipal officer and as agent of the state entrusted with the execution of certain central government tasks. In the latter capacity, he is in charge of police affairs and is head of the local police force.

The burgomaster is chairman, but not a member of the council, in which he has only an advisory voice but cannot vote. He is also chairman, and member, of the executive board, in which he has a full right to vote. As a member of the board, he holds one or more portfolios; in Amsterdam these usually include harbour affairs, a matter of essential importance to the city. Moreover, the burgomaster acts as spokesman of the board in the council on major occasions, such as debates on general policies and sometimes on very crucial issues. He does not usually interfere with policy preparation by the aldermen within their own fields. Thanks to these functions, the burgomaster can be very influential, depending very much on the personality of the man holding the position.

The role of the Burgomaster of Amsterdam includes the following major features: providing general leadership, developing and supporting major municipal initiatives, co-ordinating and integrating policies, and reconciling differences of opinion, particularly among members of the executive board. To enable him to carry out this work efficiently, it is considered essential that the burgomaster should preserve political impartiality as well as impartiality

between the city's sectorial fields of activity. Moreover, the burgomaster
has an important task in representing the city on major occasions in the local
community as well as abroad, and in promoting its interests with central
and provincial authorities.

The system of proportional representation encourages small political
parties and groups to register for elections. As a result, an abundance of
parties participate in municipal elections—in 1970 as many as 17 in Amsterdam. The present composition of Amsterdam's council, based on these
elections, is as follows: Labour 12 seats (the lowest since 1919), Communists
8, Liberals 6, *Kabouters* ('Gnomes', a new party mainly supported by anti-
authority oriented youth) 5, Catholics 5, Protestant parties (2) 3, Old People's
Party 2, Pacifist-Socialist 1.

Political parties in Amsterdam are generally organized in parallel to the
national parties. Most of the latter have a local branch, and several of them
have developed a municipal programme which serves as a general guideline
for local politicians. With the exception of a few extremist parties, however,
local parties are entirely free to determine their own policies, and do not
receive directives from the national party leaders.

Similarly, the link between the local party organization and the councillors
is generally not very strong. Council factions operate independently of the
local party organization and do not receive directives, except again in the
case of some extremist parties. However, several local parties convene period-
ically in order to discuss local policies, and these meetings are frequently
attended by municipal councillors.

Although policies advocated by the various parties in Amsterdam often
sharply conflicted in the past, the opinions of most parties on major political
issues now closely approximate to each other in most cases.[1] Subjects on
which major parties still differ include the type and level of local taxes and
duties, the level of charges for public utilities, housing policy and the extent
to which the municipality should assume tasks or leave them to the private
sector. Issues which, according to an inquiry held among Amsterdam's
electorate, received the greatest degree of attention during the 1966 elections,
included: the growing traffic and transport problem, housing, the youth
problem, care of the aged, the financial relationship between central and
local government and the matter of the creation of some form of metro-

---

[1] The electoral campaign for the 1970 municipal elections was marked by a sharpening of
political positions and controversies to which the new *Kabouters* party greatly contributed.

politan government. The violent clashes which took place in Amsterdam in 1966 between the youth and the police (resulting in the dismissal of the burgomaster), caused the methods of maintenance of law and order and the position of the appointed burgomaster to become burning issues.

Although the tumultuous conflicts which took place in Amsterdam's city council during the first decades of this century have since abated and the contrasts between the parties have diminished, the differences between the political parties are still more pronounced than in the other large Dutch cities. The strong groups on the extreme left have tended to pull the Labour Party in that direction, thus increasing the gap between the socialists and the parties on the right, and causing decision-making to become more difficult.

The abatement of political party strife in Dutch local government has been due to a considerable degree to centralized financing, which leaves relatively little opportunity for strongly differing points of view regarding local taxation, and also to the far-reaching central government regulation of hot political issues of the past, such as public housing and the employment conditions of municipal personnel.

MUNICIPAL POWERS AND FUNCTIONS

Under the Constitution and the Local Government Act, municipal councils can pass by-laws on all matters of local interest. These are the so-called autonomous functions, in the execution of which the city council is in principle bound only by the law and the general interest. Over the years, the government of Amsterdam has made considerable use of the almost limitless opportunities thus provided.

Apart from these autonomous functions, the city government is entrusted with powers delegated to it by central government. From the beginning of the present century, central government has gradually assumed many tasks which were originally municipal, and has then delegated the performance of such tasks to the municipalities, as co-governmental functions.

The following functions can be considered examples of autonomous functions: public utilities, provision of hospitals, homes for the aged and the like, recreational activities, cultural activities, making of general police by-laws. Some aspects of these activities may be affected by central government legislation.

Co-government functions include education, physical planning, low-cost housing, civil defence, food inspection, military conscription, keeping of civil registers. National legislation gives a considerable amount of free discretion to municipalities in some of these activities, such as in the case of physical planning; in other cases, national legislation has laid down detailed and precise rules so that the local authorities in fact merely administer higher legislation.

The distinction between autonomous and co-governmental or delegated functions developed into a doctrine in the latter part of the nineteenth and the earlier part of the twentieth century. During the last few decades, an awareness has grown that this distinction has become rather artificial in many respects. Functions of both categories have been increasingly regulated by national legislation and by central government. In general, however, central government regulations tend to be more detailed with regard to delegated functions; moreover, it is only fair to state that in the case of autonomous functions, activities are primarily undertaken on the initiative of local governments.

In addition to the activities which the government of Amsterdam itself undertakes, it has set up, or has fostered the establishment and activities of, many semi-public and private organizations and institutions, which it supports by means of subsidies. A basic principle of Dutch local government is that the municipality abstains from performing certain functions and providing certain services, if these are satisfactorily undertaken by the private sector. There may, of course, be differences of opinion between the parties about whether a service provided by private enterprise is or is not satisfactory. Through this support of private action, which implies a certain direction and control, the scope of policy-making by the city government considerably exceeds the field of direct municipal action.

Any enumeration of the wide field of city government activities is bound to be incomplete, but the following are the most important. The city government draws up its own development and redevelopment plans; it undertakes infrastructural works such as the preparation of sites for building purposes, the construction of roads, canals, bridges and sewerage. It has its own local public housing scheme (although low cost houses are mainly built by co-operative housing associations). The city government is also increasingly engaged in economic development policy; it lays out industrial sites and constructs and operates the harbours.

In the social field, the city government makes provision for public health and education, including hospitals and various types of schools; it also subsidizes private health and educational organizations and institutions. It supplies or subsidizes social services of various kinds for the aged and the young, the disabled and the deprived; and is active in the fields of culture, recreation and sports. It operates museums, etc., and subsidizes numerous cultural organizations: theatres, orchestras, arts, etc.; it constructs sports halls and lays out sports fields, which are then usually rented to sports organizations.

Finally, the government operates a number of public utilities such as electricity, gas and water, transport, street cleaning, markets, baths and wash houses, slaughterhouses, etc.

ADMINISTRATIVE ORGANIZATION AND STAFFING

By and large, the administrative machinery of Amsterdam is made up of two major elements: the central municipal secretariat and the municipal services and enterprises. As at December 31, 1969, the personnel engaged therein numbered 30,222.

The municipal secretariat is headed by the town clerk and made up of 22 sections, covering various functional activities such as public works, housing, education, health and social affairs, and some staff activities such as finance, personnel, organization and methods, and statistics. The work of these sections is primarily advisory and administrative with regard to the executive board and its various members, although some have a considerable executive task (e.g. education, for which there is no specialized service of the kind described below). The secretariat sections also act partly as liaison officers between the services and enterprises and the members of the executive board under whom the latter fall. Although the heads of these sections are formally subordinate to the town clerk, they have, in fact, become the principal staff officers of the respective board members as a result of the growing departmentalization of the city organization. This development has seriously affected the unity of the municipal secretariat, and thus also affected its co-ordinating role.

This development has had considerable effect on the position of the town clerk of Amsterdam. At present, and contrary to the situation in smaller municipalities, he is no longer effectively head of the municipal secretariat; his activities are limited rather to seeing that it functions properly. He convenes periodic meetings of the heads of the secretariat sections, at which matters of common interest are discussed. In this way, the town clerk has a co-ordinating role with regard to procedures and matters of an administrative nature, but this does not extend to policy co-ordination. As secretary to the council and of the executive board, the town clerk prepares the agenda for their meetings and has their decisions communicated to the various parts of the municipal machinery. Normally, the town clerk of a Dutch municipality is also considered to be the legal expert of his municipality, who checks the final text of council resolutions. The present town clerk of Amsterdam, however, refrains from doing so except on rare occasions.

Needless to say, the position of the town clerk in the municipal organization depends to a certain degree on his own personality. Consequently, the actual position of successive town clerks of a particular city may differ considerably.

The municipal services and enterprises, about 50 in number, are the specialized technical and administrative arms of the executive board and the council, for whom they prepare plans and execute decisions. The services differ greatly in size, the largest being the public works department with approximately 4,000 employees, which includes the town planning and city engineering sections. Other major services include the harbour service, in charge of all harbour affairs including the industries located in the harbour area, and the social affairs service. Major municipal enterprises include public transport, gas and electricity supply, and water supply.

Services and enterprises formally fall under the executive board as a whole, but actually their directors usually report to the member of the board to whose portfolio the service or enterprise belongs. The directors may be asked to attend meetings of the executive board and informal council meetings in an advisory capacity, and are always present at meetings of the council committees. Directors frequently play a very influential role in the city's policy making.

The executive board recruits and controls the personnel of the city government, although its personnel policies depend greatly on national legislation and central government regulations. Personnel may appeal to independent tribunals in certain cases if they feel their rights have been violated.

There are no *ad hoc* bodies in Amsterdam. For instance, there is no harbour authority. So-called 'functional decentralization', however, is an important issue in Dutch city government today, to which much attention is given. The only result thus far in Amsterdam has been the establishment of councils for certain fields of municipal activities, such as a sports council, a youth care council, a city planning council and a traffic council. Members of these councils are either representatives of voluntary organizations or experts in the field concerned, or both. In addition, members of the executive board and municipal officers are members of these 'functional councils'. A member of the executive board is chairman. Members are appointed by the city council. These councils have a primarily consultative character.

FINANCE

The financial management of the city of Amsterdam is characterized by a relatively large degree of discretion in determining the purposes and levels of its various expenditures within the limits set by its revenues. These revenues are restricted as a result of the Dutch system of municipal finance, whereby municipal revenues are principally derived from central government grants, divided into two categories: (*a*) allocations by the Municipal Fund, and (*b*) grants by the Exchequer.

The Municipal Fund is supplied by a certain percentage of the central government's total taxation income (in 1971: 13·72 per cent), and has the character of an equalization fund. Each municipality obtains a grant on the basis of its number of inhabitants, its surface area, the density of its built-up area, the costs of its welfare and social provisions. Amsterdam received an additional grant during the transitional period of change in the system of reallocation recently introduced. This additional grant gradually decreased and ceased altogether in 1970. Finally, Amsterdam receives yet another allowance which is given to municipalities with a deficit budget, on condition that certain taxes and duties levied by the city government exceed a minimum level set by central government.

In common with the other large cities, the city government of Amsterdam is of the outspoken opinion that grants from the Municipal Fund are quite insufficient to enable the city to provide the minimum of public services; their expenses, they claim, are increased by their position as a central town having to provide services to a large surrounding area. This insufficiency has become more pronounced as a result of the constant wage increases of municipal employees, for which proper allowance has not been made. Since 1966 the large cities have, however, received a special grant from the government in recognition of their special difficulties. The Municipal Fund also allocates an amount towards the costs of primary education in Amsterdam.

Grants by the Exchequer are earmarked for such purposes as education, police, civil defence and certain social welfare provisions. Moreover, grants are given by various ministries for cultural monuments, etc. Several of these grants have also not kept pace with the increase in costs of the services concerned. The 1970 budget shows a net loss of over 28 million guilders on services for which special grants are given by the Exchequer.

City revenues from local taxes are comparatively small as local authorities have only limited taxation powers. Amsterdam levies the following taxes and duties: (*a*) land tax on landowners, based on the assessed annual yield; (*b*) house tax on house occupiers, based on the assessed rental value and on the value of the contents of the house (these taxes are both collected by the state); (*c*) amusement tax; (*d*) fire insurance tax; (*e*) road tax, on owners of property situated along roadways; (*f*) street cleaning fee; (*g*) tax on dogs.

The taxes (*d*) to (*g*) will be replaced by a rate on real estate, introduced by an Act of 1970.

Other major revenues include fees paid by the public to municipal enterprises. Although several public enterprises formerly made considerable net profits and thus constituted a significant source of income, most of them nowadays suffer increasing losses caused by growing costs resulting from impressive new capital investments, increased rates of interest and wage increases. Socio-political considerations and the price control exercised by central government have made it impossible to increase fees for public utilities sufficiently. Amsterdam's 1970 budget consequently shows an estimated total loss of more than 42 million guilders for public utilities.

As a result of these unfavourable developments, the city government is faced with a rapidly growing deficit on its annual budget, as shown below.

	Revenues (million guilders)	Expenditure (million guilders)	Balance (million guilders)
1950 (Accounts)	295	294	+ 1
1965 (Accounts)	865	903	− 38
1968 (Accounts)	1,251	1,326	− 75
1970 (Budget)	1,377	1,478	− 101

The main categories of revenues and expenditures, according to the 1968 budget, are shown in Table II.

The 1968 budget also included the following items for the various major functions of the city government.[1]

The budget has to be approved by the provincial government, which can only approve or reject it as a whole. So far, however, the budget of the city of Amsterdam has always been approved.

The budget is not an effective instrument for policy-making as it mainly reflects the financial implications of decisions previously taken by the council. In order to promote more rational financial decision-making, and thus also policy-making, one-year capital investment programmes are drawn up every six months. As these are also inadequate for long-term policy-making, five year capital investment plans and financial plans have been prepared.

Capital investment works are financed through long-term loans and floating loans. The 1963 Act on Capital Investments by Lower Public Authorities (the necessity for which was caused by the general scarcity on the money market and the central government's desire for general control over public investments) submits local governments to considerable restrictions. The

---

[1] Not including internal transfers.

TABLE II

Budget of the City of Amsterdam for the year 1968[1]

Expenditure	Dutch guilders	Income	Dutch guilders
Salaries and wages	198,937,959	Municipal Fund, general grant	312,728,670
Social charges	72,888,152	Municipal Fund, guarantee grant	8,461,600
Interest on long-term loans and amounts written off (not including enterprises)	178,388,409	Municipal Fund, education grant	35,990,262
Interest on short-term loans	69,249,590	Grants from the Exchequer	186,654,628
Material expenses	143,855,174	Provincial grants	807,500
Statutory subsidies and grants	247,080,444	Taxes	70,686,779
Other subsidies and grants	40,999,121	Central government grants for hospitals and asylums	26,742,050
Reimbursement municipal transport (deficit balance on ferries)	5,093,000	Credit balances, enterprises	15,623,578
Deficit balances, enterprises	44,536,639	Repayment of loans	11,133,579
Wage tax	27,000,000	Interest and dividends	45,317,784
Tax refunds	977,868	Interest on capital advances to Loan Fund	59,281,390
Internal transfers	12,862,070	Interest on short-term loans to enterprises	4,581,400
Miscellaneous expenses	687,266	Ground rent	29,851,342
		Wage tax	27,000,000
		Personnel expenses charged but not expended	10,000,000
		Internal transfers	26,944,784
		Miscellaneous receipts	76,650,346
			948,455,692
		Deficit	94,100,000
Total	1,042,555,692	Total	1,042,555,692

[1] The figures given in this table are estimates whereas the total given on the preceding page for 1968 is the amount shown in the final accounts. This explains the discrepancy.

city may only conclude long-term loans with the Central Bank of Municipalities (and then a separate loan has to be contracted for each capital investment work) after gaining the approval of the Ministers of Interior and
Finance. The central government gives such approval within the framework
of a maximum amount determined for all municipalities together. In addition
to these long-term loans, the city concludes floating loans which constitute
the bulk of its annual loan amount.

	(Guilders)
Public security (police, fire brigade etc.)	70,268,934
Public health	116,411,417
Housing	72,386,632
Public works	143,063,393
Education, arts	201,774,232
Social services and social welfare	207,891,499
Economic affairs (harbour, etc.)	46,202,033

As at December 31, 1970, the city's total debts amounted to 4,443 million
guilders, specified as follows: long-term loans ± Guilders 3,491 million;
floating loans ± Guilders 578 million; debit balance municipal transfer
account ± Guilders 374 million. Long-term loans concluded in 1968
amounted to 231 million guilders.

RELATIONSHIPS WITH HIGHER AUTHORITIES

The city government of Amsterdam, in common with all Dutch municipalities, is allowed discretion in executing its autonomous functions within
the limits laid down by the Constitution and the Local Government Act.
However, this freedom has been considerably confined by national legislation
bearing directly or indirectly on municipal activity, that concerning municipal finance being one of the greatest encroachments by central government.
Central government's impact on municipal activities in the field of co-
government is even more pronounced, concerning as it does large sections
of social affairs, education, public health, housing, etc., for which detailed
regulations have been laid down by central government departments, some
of which exercise control by means of inspectorates. In this way, central
government (and to a lesser degree, provincial government) confines and
guides local governments, or even forces their hands with respect to decision-
making.

It has already been made clear that the city government's activities are
strongly influenced by financial limitations imposed at the centre. Not only
are the quantity and quality of municipal services affected, but sometimes

the very freedom of the city government to determine its priorities. Another financial device by which central government can influence municipal decision making is that of subsidies which are granted for the whole or part of certain municipal activities. They can also be granted to private organizations under the condition, or on the understanding, that the municipal government will do likewise. Such subsidies not only induce the city government to undertake certain activities and thus influence its decisions, but may also imply a considerable degree of central government direction or control.

In several cases, representatives of central or provincial government are formally involved in decision-making by the city government, be it directly or indirectly. This is particularly true of physical planning, as will be explained later. Another example is that of the advisory committee to the executive board for the enforcement of the Unemployment Act, on which the Ministry of Social Affairs and the regional branch of the State Labour Exchange are represented. Moreover, an extremely important influence by higher authorities on the city's decision-making stems from the often intensive contacts between officials of the city and of central and provincial governments on matters for which approval by the higher authorities is needed. Ultimate proposals in such matters will generally be drafted in such a way that final approval is almost ensured.

In addition to these various forms of central and provincial influence on the city government's decision-making, higher authorities exercise a whole array of controls under the Local Government and other special Acts. Legally, the most important is the right of the Crown (the Queen and the minister concerned) to suspend or annul decisions taken by the municipal government if they should conflict with the law or the general interest. In the case of Amsterdam this has rarely occurred. General control further includes the Crown's approval of municipal tax by-laws. Moreover, various ministries exercise extensive control, particularly over delegated tasks.

The general control exercised by the provincial government over local governments is, in principle, even stronger. Under the Constitution and the Local Government Act, the provincial government exercises control over legality as well as over possible conflict with the general interest; it may suspend municipal decisions and submit them to the Crown for annulment. This again has been a very rare occurrence in the case of Amsterdam. Furthermore, the provincial government has to watch over the city's financial management; the budget, loans, sales of municipal real estate, etc., first have to be approved by the provincial government. Co-operative arrangements between local authorities also have to be approved by the provincial government. The city government may appeal to the Crown in several cases, if approval is not granted. Nowadays, however, there is a general tendency towards reducing the control exercised by provincial government over the large cities.

As a general rule, the control exercised by provincial government (and to some extent also that by central government) tends to be less stringent in the case of Amsterdam than in that of smaller municipalities. The impact of the control is lessened in the first place by the frequent consultations previously held between city and provincial officials. Secondly, the provincial government is particularly lenient in its control over the city government in cases where the urgency of the matter concerned requires prompt action. Finally, personal contacts between members of the municipal and provincial governments, and simultaneous membership of the two levels of government, can help to harmonize their relationship.

PLANNING AND DEVELOPMENT

Planning and development depend to a great degree on major decisions made by central government, as in the case of that made some time ago that the North Sea Canal should retain its function as a major waterway to and from Amsterdam. This decision, which entailed deepening and widening the North Sea Canal itself, as well as the waterways between Amsterdam and the Rhine, has given new impetus to the economic development of the city. Moreover, it will have far-reaching consequences for the overall development possibilities of the metropolitan area of Amsterdam.

The city government has no system of comprehensive planning nor an integrated long-term policy encompassing all fields of municipal activity, except in so far as such policy is a by-product of physical planning.

Until recently, planning referred essentially to physical planning. Only during the last few years has some systematic attention been given to economic development planning. After the Second World War, this became a matter of urgency since Amsterdam had lost two predominant sections of its trade: the German market had become almost negligible, and trade connections with Indonesia, so vital for Amsterdam, were cut off. In order to inject new life into the economy, the city government encouraged the establishment of new trading centres and industries: in the course of 20 years, a timber trading centre, a large grain transhipment plant, and recently, a container terminal and a petro-chemical industry. During the 'fifties, the city government set up a committee of experts to study the economic structure of Amsterdam. Moreover, in 1962 a section for economic affairs was created in the municipal secretariat and placed under the member of the executive board who is particularly entrusted with the co-ordination of economic affairs. The tasks of this section are indicative of the city government's activities in the field; it advises the board concerning economic policy and development, furthers co-ordination of economic policy and economic research, and prepares economic development plans. The section has been engaged in preparing a series of reports under the title 'Projection of Economic Statistical Data of Amsterdam', some of which have been published, which should provide a basis for the designing of a model for the city's future economic structure. This model could then be used for exploring the various alternative economic development possibilities, and as a tool with which the city government could frame its economic policy.

In addition to the economic field, there is increasing inclination to draw up long-term plans for other functional fields, such as sports, recreational facilities for the youth, public transport and circular road construction.

Physical planning has always been the core of city planning in the Netherlands. The Housing Act of 1901 made it compulsory for cities to draw up extension plans, thus forcing municipal governments to reflect upon their future developments and policies.

The first large-scale plan for southward expansion of Amsterdam, designed by the famous architect and town planner, Berlage, was finished in 1917. However, the Master Plan of 1935, which was an outstanding example of advanced, far-sighted town planning, has been the major basis for the city's future development. This plan envisaged a city of one million inhabitants by the year 2000: space for housing, harbour, trade and industry, and recreation (for which purpose an extensive wood was planned and laid out on the territory of a neighbouring municipality) was scientifically estimated and projected in the plan, whilst the north-eastern part of the city's territory was to remain rural. The plan was of great help for a more guided policy, and also a means by which to counteract land speculation since it entitled the city to expropriate all land. It is noteworthy that the government of Amsterdam (in contrast to most other cities in the country) only rarely sells the land it has acquired for city extensions, but leases most of it on a long-term basis. Within the framework of the master plan, detailed plans were made for eight garden cities on Amsterdam's territory; these have since been constructed. The Master Plan of 1935 has been executed much more quickly than was originally anticipated, and the city's territory which was earmarked for housing and related purposes has been almost fully used in the implementation of the plan, although the population of the city is not yet 900,000. The major reason is that present-day requirements demand more space for schools, hospitals, offices, universities, as well as for traffic and recreation. In 1953 750 square feet of outdoor space were required per dwelling unit for neighbourhood facilities; by 1965 this had increased to 1,000 square feet, and it is expected to be 1,250 square feet by 1980. Moreover, low-cost housing not only became larger, but more dwellings were necessary because of the decrease in the average family size as a result of such demographic factors as increased life expectancy, younger marriages, and the fact that old people no longer live with their children.

The following table shows the changes that have taken place in housing and population density.

Greater Amsterdam (urban area)

	No. of houses per hectare	No. of inhabitants per hectare
1930	38	142
1939/40	32	114
1950	28	105
1960	24	82
1980 (prognosis)	14	45

As the city's surface that was available for building purposes gradually became exhausted, the city government had to find room to expand outside its own boundaries. It needed space for expansion of its industrial area and for housing its population overspill; and this problem was aggravated by the urgent need for slum clearance and development of the city centre; finally, the recreation and sports facilities on the city's territory were quite insufficient.

The city used three methods by which to meet these needs. First, a regional land use plan was drawn up in co-operation with four neighbouring municipalities on the south and south-east fringe of the city, under the auspices of the provincial government. This plan provided for housing, sport and recreation, as well as for industrial development. Secondly, the city of Amsterdam bought a vast area within one of these municipalities for industrial and inland water trade establishments. Finally, two areas were added to the city's territory by annexation or semi-annexation: one to the north where a new city quarter has been developed, and one to the south-east where what could be called the 'new town' of Bijlermeer is under construction.

The town planning section of the public works service of Amsterdam draws up the extension plans and, with the exception of the first stage when the area had not yet been assigned to the city, the plan for Bijlermeer. Before drafting a plan, the section makes exhaustive inquiries among other city departments, provincial authorities, central government agencies, industrial and commercial firms, as well as among voluntary associations and denominational organizations in the city, in order that it may study their wishes regarding space in the area. During the preparatory process, frequent consultations are held with provincial authorities and bureaux so as to sound out their opinions and to ensure proper co-ordination of the plan with extension plans of neighbouring municipalities as well as with the regional plans. After the draft plan is approved by the executive board, it is discussed in the council committees and finally submitted to the council. The plan needs approval by the provincial government; this is generally granted without amendments being made as a result of the previous consultations. Once a plan has been adopted, the city government can expropriate the land and real estate according to regulations which allow a specially speedy procedure. The Physical Planning Act provides for certain procedures concerning the preparation, adoption, approval and revision of extension plans. However, as these legal provisions impose limitations and slow down the planning process, planning as actually practised in Amsterdam deviates from the legal rules in several respects.

Special mention should be made of the fact that, for the planning and plan implementation of the new town referred to above, use is made of network planning with the aid of a computer.

Autonomous city planning is becoming more and more a thing of the past. There is a growing interdependence among municipalities situated in the same region, and this has been acknowledged by the fact that Amsterdam has co-operated closely with some neighbouring municipalities in the field of physical planning and housing. The interrelationship between local, regional, provincial and national planning has become closer as a result of the enlargement of scale, social mobility, urbanization and industrialization.

National physical planning legislation has assigned certain tasks to various levels of government authorities. Moreover, during the present decade, the government's Physical Planning Service has twice drawn up very general suggestions for the physical plan for the country as a whole, and these have to be taken into account by provincial and municipal governments. The provincial government is the pivot in the physical planning set-up. It establishes regional physical plans, which are global land-use plans, for certain areas within the province, and approves local extension plans for which it has a special committee. Under recent legislation, local extension plans have to conform with regional physical plans. Five different regional plans have been drawn up for the area between Amsterdam and the North Sea. A sixth plan, encompassing the area on both sides of the North Sea Canal,[1] which

---

[1] See map on p. 134.

are not incorporated in other regional plans, is now under consideration. This will cut through part of the area of several other regional plans, and therefore causes problems of co-ordination. A main principle of regional planning in the area is that urbanized centres should be separated by green belts. This is in agreement with the established policy of Amsterdam, which is against a massive and uninterrupted expansion of its built-up area. The provincial and central governments also favour a green belt policy.

BOUNDARY PROBLEMS

To an expanding city, as Amsterdam has been for about a century, boundary problems are a permanent source of concern which, until 1921, were solved by annexation (see figures mentioned above). Between 1921 and 1966, no further extension of the city's territory took place (except in very minor cases) owing to the violent opposition by neighbouring municipalities, and to the strong value attached to local autonomy with which annexation was considered to conflict. As considerable urban development took place in the area during this period, and as the city gradually used most of its territory, there was an ever-increasing need for urbanization of the surrounding municipalities.

This urban expansion, resulting in the growing overlap and in many cases conflict of interests between Amsterdam and one or more of its neighbours, caused an increasing need for intermunicipal co-operation. Considerable tension has long been felt between Amsterdam and its neighbouring municipalities, caused partly by the latter's fear of their 'big brother'. Fortunately, this relationship has improved in recent years. The tension perhaps hampered, but did not prevent, co-operation between Amsterdam and the other municipalities in the area; in the course of time, co-operative efforts have been made in several respects, partly under the Intermunicipal Co-operation Act, but for the greater part outside this legal framework. Striking examples of this co-operation can be found in a joint land-use plan for the south-east and eastern fringe region; the co-ordination committee for the implementation of the city's extension plan in the region, including Bijlermeer; the so-called Green Committee, on which a number of municipalities are represented, and whose task it is to study and make proposals regarding the maintenance and development of green space in the metropolitan area. Moreover, there are a few co-operative arrangements for recreational purposes in which municipalities situated some distance from Amsterdam participate. In the field of public utilities, Amsterdam supplies electricity to other municipalities in the region, whilst water is supplied by a limited company in which a number of municipalities participate. Apart from such co-operation in some institutionalized form, there is a growing degree of consultation on varying matters between the executive board members and staff of Amsterdam and of its neighbours.

These dispersed arrangements and efforts towards co-operation, useful as they may be, offer only a partial solution to the metropolitan problems. Amsterdam's housing schemes for its newly acquired territory and adjacent municipalities may satisfactorily solve housing problems and provide some environmental facilities, but many problems remain unsolved as, for example, that of public transport and particularly that of harbour expansion. Within the near future, the area reserved for this purpose in Amsterdam will have been fully used and further expansion will only be able to take place on neighbouring territory. This will bring the harbour under the competence of other municipalities, an arrangement which might entail considerable difficulties. This problem will have to be solved in due course, either by some co-operative arrangement or by the creation of a special harbour authority, or of a metropolitan authority.

The impossibility of solving all metropolitan problems through conventional methods of co-operation and annexation, causes the widespread feeling that municipalities situated in the metropolitan area need some organizational framework for joint policy and action. In 1963, the Provincial Government of North Holland set up a committee to investigate a suitable form of government for the metropolitan area. Urged by Parliament and the central government, this committee drafted a Bill for a Metropolitan Authority for Greater Amsterdam, which would initially comprise ten municipalities; however, the area to be covered by the authority is to be flexible, and it is anticipated that it might later incorporate even more municipalities. Nonetheless, the opinion has been voiced that the metropolitan area under the authority should be considerably larger, and should include either a number of dormitory towns to the north and east of the city, or most or all municipalities situated on both sides of the North Sea Canal. A larger metropolis of Greater Amsterdam, it is claimed, would promote integrated policy-making and spatial planning for the whole area. On the other hand, a large and powerful metropolitan authority would be likely to affect the position of the provincial government.

A working group established by the Minister of Interior in 1969, has prepared a draft bill that deviates considerably from the earlier draft and will probably be submitted to Parliament during 1971. This proposes that the Metropolitan Authority should comprise about 26 municipalities instead of the 10 originally suggested. The Metropolitan Council would have much wider powers: determining the main lines of development of the area; making the necessary provisions for realization of this development; and co-ordinating policy making by the municipalities. As compared with the earlier draft, this shows a pronounced shift from what was primarily a coordinating task towards development planning and implementation. It is proposed that the Authority lay down a development programme containing a kind of spatial plan, other plans in elaboration of the development programme, and a schedule for their implementation. The Authority may assume other tasks at the request of individual municipalities and for their areas, and will have the power to give binding directives to municipalities. The Metropolitan Authority, as envisaged, will be composed of a council directly elected by the population of the area (the area may be divided into electoral districts, an arrangement which will deviate from the present system of elections at large); an executive board consisting of a Crown-appointed chairman and at least six members; and a 'committee for cooperation' consisting of members of the executive board and two representatives of each municipality, to be of an advisory character and to be consulted in all cases of general major importance, thus also enabling the municipalities to voice their opinions.

Anticipating the establishment of the Metropolitan Authority of Greater Amsterdam, informal consultations regularly take place between members of executive boards of all municipalities in the region concerning development plans, public transport, etc. The Burgomaster of Amsterdam presides over these meetings and the Secretariat is located in Amsterdam's City Hall.

FUTURE DEVELOPMENTS

Future developments of the metropolitan area of Amsterdam will be determined by its economic growth as well as by natural population growth and migration flows. Improvement of the city's water connections by the state has laid the foundation for further economic expansion. The establishment of the petro-chemical industry has brought the city into a new phase of its industrial development; further industrial settlements are likely to follow in its train. This new addition to the city's economy, together with the creation of a new container terminal with highly perfected loading and unloading techniques for uniform cargo, mark the development of Amsterdam into a settlement area for processing plants and distribution centres.

This economic expansion will demand space, especially for those industries which need direct access to the waterways. Extensive areas along the North Sea Canal west of Amsterdam, have already been earmarked for this purpose in the draft regional plan for the North Sea Canal region. To the east of the city, more harbour and industrial sites will become available in the future when the inland sea, the IJsselmeer, has been further reclaimed. The main canal in this new polder, programmed to be constructed by 1980, should be large enough to take seagoing vessels of considerable size.

An impressive urban expansion radiating from Amsterdam, as well as from the smaller economic centres in the North Sea Canal area, is anticipated as a result of economic expansion and population growth. The relationship between the various physical planning regions will be intensified, and it is likely that the North Sea Canal strip will develop into one large metropolitan

TABLE III
Demographic Developments

	1.1.1948	1.1.1965	Index 1948 = 100	Natural growth prognosis 1980	Absorption capacity prognosis 1980
Netherlands	9,715,890	12,212,269	126		
North Sea Canal area	1,222,487	1,419,521	130	1,595,000	1,587,300
Metropolitan Area of Amsterdam	845,750	937,734	111	1,045,000	977,300
City of Amsterdam	813,977	866,290	106		
Metropolitan area of Haarlem	215,685	238,805	111	269,000	290,000
IJmond	73,868	130,826	177	151,000	175,000
Zaan	87,184	112,156	129	130,000	145,000

area, although extensive space will be reserved for green belts. This development will strengthen the need for integrated planning for the whole area.

The demographic development of the areas of varying sizes, and a prognosis of future developments, are shown in Table III, from which it is evident that the absorption capacity of the metropolitan area of Amsterdam, in its present boundaries, is not even sufficient to provide for the population increase due to natural growth, to say nothing of migration into the area. Urban expansion of the area outwards is therefore essential.

Whilst expansion in the past took place to the south and south-east of the city, it will now move increasingly in a northerly direction. Road connections between Amsterdam and the northern area have improved, and will continue to do so, thanks to the construction of tunnels under the North Sea Canal. The small town of Purmerend, north of Amsterdam and outside the metropolitan area boundaries, already feels the impact of this development and has drawn up a development plan in consultation with Amsterdam and the provincial government. In the future, Purmerend's population will probably grow to 100,000.

In the more distant future, the new IJsselmeer polders east of Amsterdam will have to provide ample new space for housing. In fact, the most important expansion of the residential space in the Metropolitan region is expected to take place in these areas. The National Physical Planning Office has forecast that the overspill population of Amsterdam in these two areas will be from 500,000 to 1,000,000 by the year 2000. It should be emphasized, however, that estimates of the future population differ considerably. This is understandable since population growth and its distribution over the metropolitan area of Amsterdam and the various near-by urbanized centres will depend very much on economic development, on central governmental policy regarding overall population distribution in the country (which aims at dispersion rather than further concentration in a few large centres in the western part), and on regional physical plans drawn up by the provincial government.

Traffic and transport form an important feature of the future development of the area. Road and rail improvements will be essential, both for the rapidly growing number of commuters from fringe municipalities to the city, and for the steadily increasing stream of tourists, as well as for the transportation of goods and industrial products. Apart from the construction of tunnels under the river IJ and the North Sea Canal, major improvements are planned by the construction of circular roads, enabling much of the traffic to by-pass the central city. The old centre, however, offers almost insurmountable traffic problems. Any major traverse is likely to scar its historic beauty and therefore meet with great opposition. The plans for city centre development provide for improved traffic flows without causing undue damage to historical sites.

The most important traffic improvement, particularly for passenger transport, will be achieved by the construction of a city railway system which will be laid underground within the city and partly on the surface in the outskirts, and which will also serve Bijlermeer and some neighbouring municipalities. Construction of this railway started in 1970 and the first line is to be opened in 1975.

A very difficult problem which faces the city government is the extent to which the centuries-old heart of the city, which constitutes a value in itself, should be preserved or reconstructed. Plans have been developed to maintain the character of the area as much as possible whilst clearing uninhabitable and unhealthy living quarters. The extensive girdle of ninteenth-century buildings surrounding the ancient centre, typical example as it is of deficient town planning and with obsolete housing conditions, will also have to be cleared and redeveloped.

CONCLUSIONS

It is hazardous to try to evaluate the quality and achievements of the city government, or to make suggestions for improvement. An evaluation is particularly difficult with regard to a city which, since the second world war, has been affected by external factors detrimental to its economy and which only gradually showed signs of reversal, and which, moreover, has had to provide for large-scale housing and urban extension. The new garden cities which have so far been constructed prove that Amsterdam has generally been able to maintain a high quality of town planning. Houses have, however, mainly been built in new districts, but a beginning has been made in the fields of urban renewal and slum clearance.

It is not easy to pass judgment on the adequacy of the various municipal activities and provisions since objective yardsticks are usually lacking, so that an evaluation must depend on what is expected from them. It is undoubtedly true that large sections of Amsterdam's population, well known for a very critical attitude, frequently seem to find municipal services to be unsatisfactory.

It is undeniable that several services do not meet the desired quality, nor are they available in sufficient quantity. It has already been noted that severe financial limitations form the principal reason for the lag in municipal services, and also affect their quality. A striking example is offered by the plan for the 'new town', Bijlermeer. It is likely that his imaginative plan will not be fully implemented in the way originally envisaged since central government will only provide financial support for housing projects if expenses are reduced to the standards it has set for low cost housing. As a result, the city government will probably have to resort mainly to traditional patterns of town planning and housing methods.

Another limitation that hampers the city government in drawing up and executing plans is the lack of space. Large-scale slum clearance and urban renewal have been impeded by the fact that no ground was available to the city government for new housing, thus making it impossible to provide houses for people displaced from the clearance areas.

Amsterdam's government has frequently been criticized for being slow and defective in its decision-making and for a lack of dynamism. Such criticisms have been voiced particularly when comparing Amsterdam with Holland's second largest city, Rotterdam, which, although heavily damaged during the

F

war, has since flourished and is now the world's largest port. It is dubious whether such a comparison is really fair since conditions for economic development have been far more favourable in Rotterdam than in Amsterdam. In many respects, particularly with regard to the harbour and the economy, Amsterdam's government has demonstrated an ability in recent years to grasp propitious opportunities for the creation of favourable conditions for economic expansion. It may be true, however, that economic expansion would have been faster and more comprehensive if Amsterdam had been able to benefit from a climate of co-operation between city government and the business world, similar to that for which Rotterdam is well known.

However, certain features in the structure and functioning of Amsterdam's government have an adverse effect on decision-making. First, the comparatively strong political differences, as well as the attitude of opposition characteristic of the 'Amsterdammer', cause the council committees and the council frequently to disagree with proposals made by the executive board. Moreover, policy preparation and execution is likely to be impeded by the rather complicated structure of the municipal apparatus and the inadequate division of tasks among members of the executive board (as a result of political considerations which play an important role therein), which make co-ordination more time-consuming and difficult than is really necessary. Ten years ago, an investigation into the city government's organization was carried out by a private firm of consultants and by the city's O. & M. bureau. The ensuing proposals met with such strong opposition that they had almost no effect whatsoever.

The city's external organization, that is to say, the government of the metropolitan area, also needs review and improvement. Plans for the creation of an organization for Greater Amsterdam are therefore welcome. It is to be hoped that the Metropolitan Authority of Greater Amsterdam, if it is established, will be vested with sufficient decision-making and executive powers to ensure the integrated development of the area. It is essential, therefore, that the governments of the component municipalities realize the need for joint planning and decision making for the area as a whole with regard to physical planning, electricity and water supply, public transport, air pollution, etc. Whether or not sufficient powers will be vested in the Metropolitan Authority will depend partly on whether the decision to transfer such powers is left to the municipalities, which tend to strongly resist the idea of surrendering their functions.

Belgrade

ŽIVORAD KOVAČEVIĆ

ŽIVORAD KOVAČEVIĆ

Born 1930. Graduated at the School of Journalism, Belgrade University. M.A. in political science at the University of California, Berkeley. Until 1963 Director of the Institute of Public Administration and Professor of Local Government at the School of Public Administration, Belgrade University. From 1963 to 1967 Under-Secretary in the Government of the Republic of Serbia. From 1967 Secretary General of the Standing Conference of Yugoslav Towns (Association of municipalities). Editor in chief of the review *Opština* ('Municipality'). Author of numerous articles and papers and several publications in the field of local government, urban problems and public administration.

Belgrade

BELGRADE (Beograd) has an exceptional natural position, both beautiful and significant. Situated on the ridge between two great rivers, the Danube and the Sava, it dominates the vast Panonian plain, one of the richest wheat-bearing plains in the world. The Danube in its lower course divides Middle Europe from the Balkan peninsula and Belgrade lies on its most important fork. These forks are the gates to the Balkan peninsula which, as a bridge, connects three continents of the Old World: Europe, Asia and Africa.

All this made Belgrade of exceptional strategic significance and attracted numerous invaders from the time of the Celts and Romans until our recent past. Long and bloody battles were fought over Belgrade. Conquerors always destroyed everything reminding them of previous masters. Tourist pamphlets speak of 40 destructions of Belgrade during its 2,500 years of turbulent history; historians are sure of 25. Therefore in Belgrade, except for some excavated remnants and a few houses only 150 years old, no remains from the distant past have been saved. Belgrade kept changing not only its masters, but its population, its name, significance and features. It has been an insignificant suburban settlement, one of the largest and pleasantest towns in Europe, subsequently poor and small again and then the key of various situations upon which empires crashed.

Originally Belgrade was a merchant settlement of a nomad tribe, the Singa, which Alexander the Great conquered in 334 B.C. Soon after this, between 284 and 278 B.C., Celts invaded the Balkan peninsula and named it Singidunum, i.e. the town of the Singas, after the ethnic group they found in this settlement. The Romans succeeded the Celts and ruled the town from the first to the fourth century A.D. retaining this name. After the fall of the Roman Empire, Singidunum appears on the world scene as one of the most significant Roman fortifications. During the great migration of peoples Singidunum frequently changed its masters. The Huns under Attila captured it in A.D. 441 and destroyed it to its foundations. This time Singidunum lost its Roman population. The invaders kept succeeding each other. Slav tribes coming from their homeland between the Volga and Dnieper rivers settled on the left bank of the river Danube in the sixth century. During the seventh century they spread through the northern part of the Balkan peninsula to the Adriatic Sea. The Slav tribe of the Serbs settled on the site of Belgrade. It was known as Alba Urbs, Alba Graeca and Alba Bulgarica before receiving

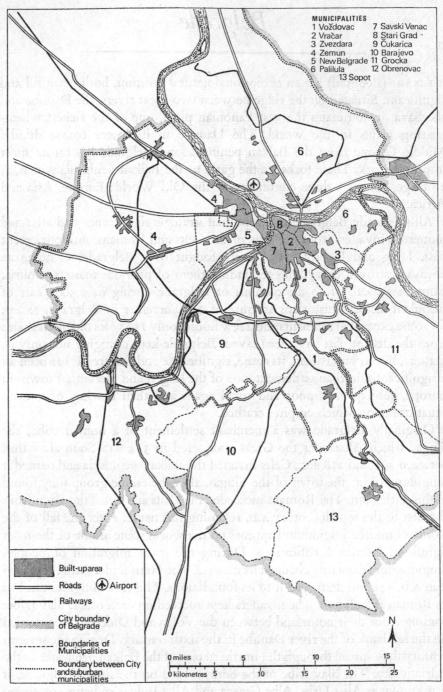

MUNICIPALITIES
1 Voždovac   7 Savski Venac
2 Vračar   8 Stari Grad
3 Zvezdara   9 Čukarica
4 Zemun   10 Barajevo
5 New Belgrade 11 Grocka
6 Palilula   12 Obrenovac
           13 Sopot

Built-up area
Roads   Airport
Railways
City boundary of Belgrade
Boundaries of Municipalities
Boundary between City and suburban municipalities

0 miles   5   10   15

0 kilometres 5   10   15   20   25

N

MAP 2 BELGRADE

its present name of Belgrade (the white city), which was recorded for the first time in 878 in a letter written by Pope John VIII.

In the thirteenth century Belgrade belonged to the State of Serbia, ruled by King Dragutin. It fought off for a long time attacks from Bulgarians, Hungarians and Turks. The Siege of Belgrade in 1456 ended with a great defeat of the Turks, celebrated by the entire Christian world. After a long siege in 1521, the Turks finally captured Belgrade, however, and it remained in their hands with two shorter Austrian conquests until the beginning of the nineteenth century. At the time of the first Serbian uprising (1804–13) Belgrade was again the political, military and cultural centre of the Serbs. After the second uprising in 1815, Belgrade became the centre of the struggle for the complete independence of Serbia, and finally in 1867, after 346 years of Turkish domination, the Turkish commander of the town handed over the keys of the city to the ruler of independent Serbia, Knyaz Mihajlo.

Serbia and Belgrade now entered a trying chapter of their turbulent history. In the First World War in 1914 the Austro-Hungarian Empire attacked Serbia, occupied it and halved its population. In December 1918 Belgrade became the capital of the new united Yugoslav state. In the Second World War the Germans bombed the city; 20,000 inhabitants were killed in one attack. During the German occupation gallows were erected in the centre of the city. Partisans liberated devastated Belgrade on October 20, 1944.

Belgrade is today the capital of the Socialist Federal Republic of Yugoslavia which has 6 republics—Serbia, Croatia, Slovenia, Bosnia and Herzegovina, Macedonia, and Montenegro. Belgrade is also the capital of the Republic of Serbia.

After the war Belgrade grew very quickly. Before the war it had 280,000 inhabitants, in 1946 there were 450,000 inhabitants, in 1956 700,000 and at the end of 1967 there were 1,046,000 inhabitants. These figures refer to the city plus all the suburban areas. Of this total 754,000 inhabitants live in the city area itself and 301,000 in suburban areas. The town extends over an area of 242,000 hectares and the narrower city area, regulated by a town plan, only 21,000 hectares.

During the past few years the rate of increase in the number of inhabitants has fallen (in 1966 it was 3·3 per cent, in 1967 2·0 per cent and in 1968 it was estimated to be 1·7 per cent). The natural rate of growth gradually fell (in 1967 the increase amounted to 6,500); the net inflow from immigration has also decreased although it is still double the natural increase (in 1967 13,900). It is notable, however, that the educational qualifications of newcomers are still unsatisfactory (only 6·2 per cent in 1967 with university education, and the majority with elementary or incomplete elementary education).

Belgrade is the most important political and administrative centre in the country, the seat of the Federal and Republic Assemblies, of the government and various public institutions; it is the scientific centre containing two academies of science and numerous institutes; it is the educational centre containing the university with 60,000 students, and various occupational and professional schools; it is the cultural centre, having 7 permanent theatres, 153 exhibitions in 1967, the Philharmonic Orchestra, museums, etc.; it is the centre for medicine, banking, trade and the like. The industrial structure is, however, quite unfavourable, for there still exists a number of enterprises (textile and similar industries), which employ a great number of unskilled or semi-skilled workers who earn low wages. This is one cause of the basic imbalance of the city: an extensive growth of the town with great pressure on city services combined with inadequate productivity. The economic structure cannot provide sufficiently high personal income to cover steep increases in communal services.

The city assembly, therefore aware that it will be impossible to limit the pressure of immigration by administrative means, has endeavoured through the development programme to stimulate the economic development of highly productive activities and to change the economic structure gradually. During the last few years this policy has achieved its first modest results.

THE ORGANS OF THE METROPOLITAN GOVERNMENT

After the war Belgrade changed its administrative boundaries a few times and reorganized the structure of its local government. A two-level structure of local government has remained constant, however, in the attempt to satisfy two essential demands: to provide a uniform solution of the problems of the whole city (i.e. the metropolitan area) through a metropolitan organ of authority and metropolitan services, and at the same time to avoid the removal of local government from close contact with the citizens, their needs, interests and influence.

While the two-level structure of local government (municipalities and districts) was applied generally in Yugoslavia, the city had the status of a district and the lower-tier units in the city were given the status of a municipality. However, with the process of greater decentralization of functions and their transfer to the municipalities, particularly since 1955, it has been more and more difficult to apply the general scheme of local government organization in Yugoslavia to large towns. According to the Constitution of

Yugoslavia, the municipality is the basic socio-political unit; the general legal assumption of competence is in favour of the municipality, i.e. *all* social functions are carried out by the municipality, *except* those which by the Constitution and other legal regulations are expressly retained for the federation, republic or district. Districts did not represent higher organs of government, hierarchically superior to municipalities, but a kind of federation of municipalities. District assemblies consisted of the representatives delegated by municipalities and the assemblies performed tasks of joint interest for the municipalities. Lower-tier local authorities in Belgrade and in other big cities had the status of municipality and the same rights as all other municipalities in Yugoslavia. They appointed councillors to the city assembly and entrusted the city with tasks of joint interest. Since Belgrade is a community many tasks should be tackled in a unified manner. Certain functions of the city were thus 'ceded' to it by the city municipalities. Also many functions were organized and financed on a unified basis. However, this legal solution created many difficulties in the relations between the municipalities and the city, because the municipalities, particularly the richer ones in which trade and industry were concentrated, were reluctant to relinquish some of their rights and wealth, so that problems facing the city as a whole could be solved on a co-ordinated basis.

When in 1966 the last two republics (Serbia and Croatia) decided to abolish districts, as they had become a hindrance to municipal autonomy, the question arose of the future organization of Belgrade under a single tier of local government. The city assembly had set up a commission (consisting of councillors, deputies, university professors, experts and representatives of vocational organizations) long before this question became urgent, and entrusted it with the task of considering the problem and of submitting proposals for its solution. The commission worked for nearly two years. After six months of discussion the city assembly adopted, in principle, the recommendations of this commission and submitted a proposal to the Assembly of the Republic of Serbia requesting amendments to the Constitution of the Republic so that the position of the city could be regulated accordingly. In spite of the strong resistance of deputies from villages which were against any 'privileged' solution for Belgrade, the proposals were adopted and the amendments to the Constitution came into force on January 1, 1967.

These amendments for the first time recognized and adequately provided for the special conditions and needs of Belgrade. They are the needs of a large city, not those of the capital of Yugoslavia and the Republic of Serbia. Belgrade has never had special legal or financial treatment as the capital.

F*

THE CITY CONSTITUTION

According to new constitutional amendments the city is entrusted with certain rights and responsibilities which are elsewhere in Yugoslavia the responsibility of the municipality; these comprise tasks of joint interest for the municipalities, which were performed previously by the districts and tasks which are the responsibility of the republic, if they are entrusted to the city by legal provisions.

In this way the position of the city is determined in a new and special manner: it has the rights and duties which the city carried out previously in the capacity of a district (although all districts are now abolished) and it is also able to perform certain functions of the municipalities, which the city in fact performed earlier, but in the form of tasks ceded to it by the municipalities.

The Constitution does not directly list the functions of the municipalities in the city, but provides that the municipalities shall have only those rights and duties which are not performed by the city itself.

The Constitution lays down only in principle the nature of the functions to be performed by the city, and the division of responsibilities between the city and the municipalities is to be determined by the city charter. Thus the city charter became the basic Act regulating the functions of the city and the municipalities, their relations and co-operation, the division of income, the organization of the city assembly, and similar matters. This gives the city a high degree of autonomy in shaping its internal structure. The city charter is passed by the city assembly subject to the agreement of at least two-thirds of the members of municipal assemblies.

The new city charter was adopted at the beginning of 1968 after broad public discussions which lasted nearly a year. The charter has ten chapters and 227 articles. All municipal assemblies have also adopted their own charters.

There are in Belgrade 1 city assembly, 13 municipalities (9 city and 4 suburban[1]), and 108 neighbourhood communities. Neighbourhood communities are not local government units but self-governing organizations of citizens set up to consider everyday problems.

The territory of the city of Belgrade incorporates nearly the whole metropolitan area. (The influence of Belgrade extends, of course, considerably

---

[1] The suburban municipalities have more functions than the city municipalities although still less than the average Yugoslav municipality. The suburban municipalities may administer transport, housing construction, slum clearance, public open spaces, public baths, protection of cultural monuments, naming of streets and squares, which are elsewhere the responsibility of the city assembly.

beyond its administrative boundaries.) Such expanse of territory facilitates the planning of the development of the city. It follows the common pattern for a Yugoslav municipality. An average municipality consists of both an urban nucleus and its rural environs; its territory is always considerably larger than the extent of its built-up area. The average Yugoslav municipality has about 40,000 inhabitants and covers a territory of 500 square kilometres. There are no very small municipalities.

The largest municipality in Belgrade is Zemun (with 128,000 inhabitants) and the smallest Barajevo (with 16,400 inhabitants).

FUNCTIONS AND ORGANIZATION

In determining the functions of the city the charter adopted three criteria: first, that these functions should concern the planning, administration and co-ordination of the development of the whole metropolitan area; second, the provision of joint financial, social, cultural and other services needed by citizens; third, tasks which would be more rationally and successfully performed for the city as a whole.

In accordance with the above, the charter provides that the city will perform the following groups of tasks:

(i) the making and adoption of physical, economic and social plans and programmes;
(ii) the regulation of city public transport; the construction, improvement and maintenance of streets and roads; public open and green spaces; public parking lots, public lighting, city cemeteries and crematoria; the supply of water and electricity; drainage; the preparation and lay-out of building sites;
(iii) the provision of secondary and special schools, dormitories, and teacher training institutions;
(iv) the establishment of theatres and operas, museums, galleries and other art institutions; the maintenance and protection of cultural monuments and the preservation of the countryside;
(v) the promotion of sport and recreational centres; together with the municipalities the promotion and development of physical culture;
(vi) the provision of health protection and health institutions, regulations against epidemics, general hygienic and sanitary measures;
(vii) the provision of social welfare services and institutions; together with the municipalities, the analysis of social problems and the undertaking of necessary measures for the prevention or solution of such problems;
(viii) the administration of the city police, traffic safety and fire brigades;

(ix) the making of regulations in the field of civil defence; determining the policy of defence preparations and preparation for protection in case of war and natural catastrophes;

(x) the making of regulations concerning the introduction of local duties, contributions, taxes and other public levies; determining the financial obligations of the public utility services (city transport, water and sewerage, street-cleaning and garbage removal and the like);

(xi) the performance of all kinds of supervisory tasks (sanitary inspection, veterinary, the supervision of markets and the like), except building and construction inspection which is in the charge of the municipalities; surveying, the maintenance of the land registry and all statistical records.

The tasks entrusted to the city are performed by the city assembly. Previously the members of the city assembly were elected from among the members of the municipal assemblies, proportionally to the number of inhabitants. According to the new charter members of the city assembly are elected directly by the citizens.

The city assembly consists of several chambers. This is a characteristic of the organization of government in Yugoslavia in general. All assemblies have several chambers: one general political chamber whose members are elected by all citizens of the area and one or more functional chambers whose members are elected by the employed citizens of each particular branch. The Federal Assembly and assemblies of the republics have five chambers; city assemblies, in general, have two chambers (one political and the other functional), but sometimes they have three, four or five chambers. This is regulated by the city charter.

The city assembly of Belgrade formerly had two chambers; since 1967 it has had five chambers: the city (or general) chamber with 100 councillors, and four functional chambers; the economic chamber (80 representatives), the culture and education chamber (50 councillors), the social and health chamber (50 councillors) and the public services chamber (40 councillors).

The councillors of the general chamber are elected on a ward basis. There are between one and five councillors for each ward according to population. The 100 councillors in the general chamber represent 72 wards. The elections are direct and uniform; every citizen over 18 years of age whose name is entered on the voters' list for the territory of the municipality has a right to vote. And every voter is eligible to stand for councillor.

It is considered very important that as large a number of citizens as possible should be able to take part in the process of nominating candidates. Consequently each ward is divided into several areas for voters' meetings; these must consist of at least one-tenth of the total number of voters in the area. Each voter is entitled to propose one candidate and a separate vote is taken in respect of every name put forward. All candidates who receive a majority vote at a voters' meeting are considered officially nominated. In addition, any fifty voters in a ward may propose a candidate. For the functional chambers, councillors are nominated and elected by voters in their particular fields of activity. Thus, the councillors of the economic chamber are elected by citizens working in industry, agriculture, transport, trade, catering, handicraft, public services, banks and publishing enterprises. The councillors in the chamber for education and culture are elected by those working in elementary and secondary schools, universities, scientific institutions, museums, libraries, theatres, broadcasting stations, films, etc. The councillors of the council for health and social welfare are elected by citizens working in hospitals, health centres, health stations, medical centres, institutions for health protection, apothecaries, social centres, children and adult homes, institutes for social insurance, and the like. Councillors for the chamber for public services are elected by those working in state administration, courts, sociopolitical organizations, the army, and the like.

Nomination of candidates is by meetings of workers. A large enterprise may be divided into several workers' meetings for this nominating process; on the other hand, small enterprises may be grouped together for this purpose (for instance two schools may form one workers' meeting). In Belgrade there are 52 electing units and 756 workers' meetings for the economic chamber, 27 electing units and 127 workers' meetings for the chamber of education and culture, 26 electing units and 80 workers' meetings for the social and health chamber and 24 electing units and 94 workers' meetings for the public services chamber.

The law lays down the principle of incompatibility of functions. An employee of the city administration or the judge of a county or municipal court cannot be at the same time a councillor of the city assembly. Employees of the federal and republic administrations, and Supreme Court judges are, however, eligible for election to the chamber of public services.

Councillors are elected for a term of four years, with half retiring every two years. In this way continuity in the work of the assembly is secured.

The constitutional principle of rotation is applied to councillors. No councillor can be elected twice in succession, i.e. re-elected to the same chamber of the same assembly. This is the general principle applied to all elected offices in Yugoslavia (federal and republican deputies, the President and members of the government, state secretaries, etc.). Councillors may, however, be elected to another chamber of the city or municipal assembly.[1] In the case of the president of the city or municipal assembly this principle is strictly applied; the president cannot be re-elected as president. Although nobody denies the democratic intention of such provisions which prevents bureaucratization of functions, many students of the political system question the justifiability of such a strict principle, particularly in the case of the president of the municipality who devotes much time to mastering his complex functions.

Members of the city assembly perform their functions without any remuneration but are entitled to compensation for loss of earnings while engaged in their official duties.

A councillor has the right to initiate the consideration of certain questions, to submit proposals for certain decisions, to suggest amendments to proposed rules and regulations, to put questions referring to the work of the assembly, its organs and members, or to discuss any other city problem, and to receive an answer at the current or the following session, in verbal or written form. Each service is charged with the duty of keeping the councillor informed about everything that goes on, of helping him in the formulation of regulations proposed by him and the like. The councillor is obliged to keep the voters' meeting in his constituency regularly informed about his work and the work of the assembly, and also to inform the assembly about any demands put forward by his constituents. There were 419 voters' meetings in Belgrade during 1967.

A member of the city assembly is obliged, if required by the municipal assembly in the area of which his constituency lies, to inform the assembly about the attitudes, measures and policy of the city assembly, as well as to inform his chamber about the conclusions and remarks of the municipal assembly.

A councillor of the city assembly enjoys immunity in the performance of his function. If a member of the assembly claims immunity he cannot be arrested in the territory of the city, nor can criminal proceedings be taken against him without the prior consent of the assembly of which he is a member (unless he is caught *flagrante delicto* in a crime punishable by imprisonment or if during investigation of the crime detention is obligatory and there is a risk of his escape).

The city chamber and the competent functional chambers decide jointly upon questions of major importance within the competence of the city

[1] All Yugoslav municipalities have a representative body, the municipal assembly. In a few larger cities which are divided into municipalities the representative body is termed the city assembly.

assembly. This means that questions concerning education, for instance, are considered and decided upon both by the city chamber and the chamber for education and culture. As a rule the chambers debate and vote in separate sessions. If the chambers agree, they may jointly discuss certain questions or hear introductory comment but the vote will be taken at separate sessions. The decision or some other act is considered as adopted when the vote is taken on an identical text in both chambers. If the chambers do not agree on the text a joint commission must be set up to co-ordinate the text. If the commission cannot agree on the text, the disputed draft is submitted for discussion at a joint session of both chambers. If no agreement can be reached, the decision is postponed for a period of three months. There can be another postponement, if necessary. If even after this period no agreement is reached, the disputed issue is decided by a referendum of citizens. No issue has been decided by referendum as yet; indeed the suggestion of a referendum is regarded as a threat, warning councillors that chambers should try to agree on a compromise.

Some issues may be decided upon by three chambers. For instance, the question of vocational education of workers is of equal interest to the city chamber, the economic chamber and the chamber for education and culture. In this case the procedure of decision-making will be the same as in the case of two chambers.

Some issues (such as adopting by-laws and the town plan) as provided for by the charter or by agreement among the chambers, are discussed at a joint session of all the chambers. In this case the decision is passed by a majority of votes of members regardless to what chamber the members belong.

Chambers may also make decisions on some issues individually. There are, first of all, decisions concerning the constitution and work of the chamber itself, election of the organs of the chamber and the like. Also each chamber has its own independent field of activity. The city chamber independently makes decisions and attends to other tasks in the field of national defence, police and other matters pertaining to internal affairs, appoints judges and members of the juries of the county and municipal courts and justices of the peace of the city chamber.

Each functional chamber follows up and considers independently the state of affairs in its own field, co-ordinates the interests of organizations within its field, agrees about various attitudes and undertakes certain measures, and for this purpose passes conclusions and recommendations.

The present practice of the joint working of several chambers has not been in existence long enough to be studied more seriously and to enable definite conclusions to be drawn, but it indicates that the basic concept is correct—

that in a developed self-governing structure each sector should be enabled to constitute and express itself separately. The influence of functional chambers upon the work of the city assembly has made it possible for all issues to be discussed more expertly. For instance, questions of education have been more thoroughly considered since the introduction of the chamber for education and culture. The danger of a partial approach or pressure from narrow professional interests is alleviated by the fact that the city chamber considers and decides on all matters equally, in its capacity as the general political representative body of all citizens. It seems that the most doubtful chamber as far as drafts, content of work and present results are concerned is the 'bureaucratic chamber'—the chamber of public services—the members of which are mostly public officers from federal and republican organs, the army and the like. The basic reason for the setting up of this chamber was not so much the need to consider and decide separately about the issues arising in a certain field, but the fact that the citizens working in this field enjoy also a constitutional right to elect and to be elected. It would be very difficult to include them in any other chamber, especially because in Belgrade, the largest administrative centre, the number of citizens working in this field is very great. It should be said, however, that this chamber has made a more valuable contribution to the discussions about the city charter and the organization of city administration, than to any other issues.

COMMITTEES OF THE ASSEMBLY

The assembly has its own committees, political executive organs for individual fields of activity. The committees consist of councillors and other citizens elected by the city assembly.[1] Each committee has its chairman and 14 members. The members of the committees are elected for a term of two years. No one can be a member of the same committee for more than four years.

The functions of the committees are, first of all, to propose to the assembly and its chambers the policy and the making of various decisions; secondly, to see to the carrying out of the policy and implementation of laws and to pass for this purpose necessary regulations and recommendations; and thirdly, to supervise the work of administrative organs and to give special instructions for their work.

The committees in municipal assemblies in Yugoslavia have a very

---

[1] There is no fixed relationship between councillors and other citizens on committees nor any obligatory quota of councillors from individual chambers on committees. This is left to the discretion of the city assembly.

important role because they are entrusted with the political-executive function. Until 1952 the municipal assemblies had executive bodies, small bodies with a chairman in which real authority was concentrated, so that the representative body frequently found itself in the position of only a voting machine. The committees as broader social organs with a mixed composition have exerted an influence upon the democratization of decision-making and at the same time have enabled discussions and decision-making to be much more knowledgeable and thorough.

There were 20 committees until the reorganization of the city assembly in 1967, while the assembly had only two chambers. With the setting up of the chambers for individual branches there was no need to have committees for the fields in question, and their number was cut down to 5; for internal affairs, national defence, town planning, social planning and finance, and for general administration. Thus committees were set up only in the branches which do not fall within the jurisdiction of existing chambers. In other fields the political-executive tasks were undertaken by the chambers themselves and their organs. Although the present work of functional chambers may be judged positive as a whole, many students of local government consider that the committee is a superior form for carrying out the political-executive function of the city assembly.

For the performance of various tasks, the preparation of drafts or execution of special affairs, the city assembly and its chambers set up permanent or temporary commissions.[1] In 1967 the city assembly and its chambers appointed the following permanent commissions: for elections and appointments, for organizational and political issues, for citizens' complaints and petitions, for orders and medals, for religion and for legal regulations.

The commission for elections and appointments submits proposals to the assembly for the appointment of representatives of the assembly to the management organs (or boards) of educational, cultural, health, social and public institutions which are of significance for the city as a whole. In 1967, the assembly appointed 251 representatives to such bodies. Judges and members of juries in Yugoslavia are also elected by competent assemblies; the assemblies of the federation and republics appoint the judges of the Constitutional and the Supreme Court of the federation and of the republics; municipal assemblies elect the judges of the county and municipal courts. As Belgrade has 5 municipal courts and 13 municipalities, the city assembly elects the judges of both the county and municipal courts in accordance with the provisions of the city charter. The commission receives the candidatures

---

[1] Unlike committees, commissions have no executive powers but merely make recommendations to the assembly.

and proposals for judges. On the recommendation of this commission in 1967, 86 judges of the county and 132 judges of the municipal courts were appointed from 845 candidates. All applications were submitted for public discussion to the collectives of the relevant courts, trade unions and the like.

The commission has a very complicated task in proposing managers and directors of various enterprises and institutions. According to law, in each enterprise or institution a manager is elected every four years. Serving directors are eligible for re-election. The workers' council (a body consisting of the workers themselves, the members of which rotate, which decides on all essential issues in the enterprise, such as the production plan, the distribution of income, personal income and similar matters), determines conditions for the post of director in an open competition. A commission, which consists half of members appointed by the workers' council and half by the city assembly, considers the applications received and selects a proposed candidate. The final decision about the election of the director is taken by the workers' council. The commission for election and appointments of the city assembly submits the proposals to the assembly for the appointments of its representatives to these commissions; in 1967 there were 154 appointed representatives. The commission also proposes and appoints the heads of the organs of city administration.

The commission for organizational and political affairs consists of councillors, public officers, professors and other experts, and deals with questions of the organization and work of the assembly, its bodies and organs of administration, and the functioning of the whole system of self-government in the city. This commission also prepared the draft city charter and arranged the public discussions on it.

The commission for citizens' petitions and complaints considers the complaints and endeavours to provide remedies. It informs competent organs and organizations of its views, informs the city assembly about irregularities in the work of city organs and recommends appropriate measures. In 1967 960 written proposals and complaints and 1,660 verbal petitions were heard by the commission.

The commission for orders and medals submits proposals to the President of the Republic for decorations to be granted to meritorious citizens and organizations. The commission for religion, together with the religious communities, considers requests and submits proposals to the city assembly. The commission for decisions and regulations considers all proposed regulations from the standpoint of their legal validity and, with the statement of the proposer, submits reports to the Assembly.

THE PRESIDENT AND OTHER OFFICERS OF THE ASSEMBLY

The city assembly has its president. The president is elected from among the members of the assembly, as provided for by the charter, from any chamber, but as a rule the president is a member of the city chamber. The president's term of office is four years. He receives a regular monthly remuneration for his work of 4,000 new dinars.[1] His responsibilities are such that he cannot continue, during his term, with his professional activity. Only a few municipal assemblies have presidents who may carry out this duty as an honorary office in addition to their regular employment. The president is the first citizen in the city. He supervises the work of the city assembly and its organs and co-ordinates their activity, convenes and proposes the agenda for the joint sessions of all chambers and presides over the sessions; he supervises the work of secretaries and organs of city administration, co-ordinates the work of the city assembly with the activities of other organs in the city. Co-ordination is his main function.

The president of the city assembly of Belgrade is assisted by two vice-presidents, who are also paid officers and are elected for a period of four years. One vice-president is concerned with educational, cultural, social and health affairs, and the other with housing, communal and organizational matters. Belgrade has an exceptional arrangement whereby the president and vice-presidents of the city assembly are at the same time chairmen of some of the chambers. The president chairs the city chamber, one vice-president is the chairman of the chamber for education and culture and the other of the chamber for public services. The chairmen of the other two chambers execute their duties in an honorary capacity: the chairman of the economic chamber for 1967–68 was the manager of a tractor factory and the chairman of the chamber for social and health welfare was a professor of the university medical faculty.

The city assembly has a secretary. The secretary is not a member of the assembly, and is appointed for a period of four years and, unlike the president and vice-presidents, he may be reappointed to the same post. The secretary is in charge of the work of the organs of city administration. He is usually a lawyer. He is responsible for his work to the city assembly and to the president.

The president, vice-presidents, chairmen of the chambers and the secretary consider questions concerning the work of the city assembly and its organs, intervene in case of disputes between the chambers, and together with the chairmen of the committees, commissions and other organs of the city

[1] U.S. dollar = 12·5 new dinars.

assembly discuss the co-ordination of the work of all these organs, the making of their programmes and their execution. The old statute and the new city charter prescribe certain procedures in order to prevent the transformation of this meeting of the most responsible officers into some sort of presidency or old-style executive council, which could seize the rights of the city assembly and its organs and *de facto* make decisions on a series of issues. Of course, the prevention of the transformation of such a co-ordinating body into an organ with political and executive power does not depend only upon the charter and democratic procedures, but, above all upon real political relations and the power of democratically elected organs. Adequate attention to such relations is paid also by the councillors' club[1] and by socio-political organizations in the city.

In the execution of policy the last word lies with the city assembly, that is the councillors. According to the city charter only the city assembly may decide some questions (e.g. enacting of the charter, passing regulations, the town plan, loans, election of judges and the like). The city assembly may delegate all other issues to individual chambers, committees and administrative organs. By special regulation of the city assembly, individual or all municipalities may be authorized to regulate certain issues which are otherwise in the charge of the city assembly.

THE ROLE OF THE CITIZENS

The initiative for regulations may come from citizens themselves, their associations, neighbourhood communities, socio-political organizations, enterprises and institutions. If the competent organ of the city assembly concludes that such a proposed regulation is necessary, it prepares a draft for the city assembly. If the assembly considers that there is no need for such a measure, the proposer is informed accordingly.

The councillors, committees, commissions and other organs of the city assembly are entitled to submit proposals. The administrative organ prepares the draft of the regulation or assists the proposer in its formulation. The draft is forwarded to relevant organs of the city assembly, municipal assemblies and other organs and organizations. The following documents have to be forwarded to voter's meetings throughout the territory of the city, for their consideration: drafts of economic and social plans and the town plan, decisions concerning the introduction of taxes and levies, and decisions concerning the division of revenue between the city and the municipalities. If

[1] This club is for both social activities and discussions about current questions concerning the city.

two-thirds of the voters at the voters' meeting are against a proposal, the city assembly is obliged to act according to the conclusions of the voters' meeting or a referendum may be held. Proposals concerning an increase of the fares or charges in the city's public transport, for street cleaning, garbage disposal and water supply, which the city assembly must approve, as well as draft decisions concerning the level of rents, must be forwarded to the voters' meetings on the territory of the municipality from the narrower city area (viz. of the nine city municipalities); outside this area the four suburban municipal assemblies fulfil this role. Members of the city assembly are obliged to attend voters' meetings in order to give explanations or answers. The city assembly, in addition, seeks the opinions of voters' meetings on proposals relative to other significant matters, even where it is not compulsory to obtain the views of the citizens.

The final draft of a regulation is determined by the competent committee, commission or board of the assembly, or one of its chambers. The proposer has to inform the city assembly of the views expressed at the public meeting and has to explain why any of them have not been accepted. If the proposal is one in which public consultation is compulsory, the committee of the city assembly, before making a decision, has to state the reasons for the acceptance or rejection of the opinions of the voters' meeting.

Proposals and documents are also forwarded to the city assembly by non-governmental organs. The city assembly considered, in 1967, proposals made by the city chamber of economy, the city employment board, the institution for the protection of monuments, the trade union of educational workers, and other bodies.

The representatives of interested organizations directly participate in the work of the city assembly and its committees and are regularly invited to attend the sessions. For instance, during discussions about delinquent children and young people, representatives of the homes for children and young persons, of the youth club, courts and public prosecutors, the educational board, the board for social welfare, the city committee of the youth organizations and others have taken part in the work of the session. Certain committees hold joint sessions with interested organizations, trade unions and the like whenever considering questions in their particular fields, prior to the formulation of policy.

LOWER TIER AUTHORITIES

The thirteen municipalities in the city have the following functions: first, all tasks and duties which the Yugoslav municipality is in charge of according to the constitutional law which are not executed by the city assembly; secondly, participation in functions which are entrusted to the city assembly.

According to their charters, the municipalities execute the following groups of tasks:

(i) communal problems of lesser importance (side streets, pavements, squares, telephone booths, green spaces within public lots, recreation and play grounds for children, the demolition of dangerous buildings, etc.);

(ii) the organization of basic health protection by the provision of health stations and polyclinics, the implementation of preventive measures (vaccinations, X-rays, etc.), and of measures for the control of contagious diseases;

(iii) the provision of social assistance for children and adults, the accommodation of children without parental supervision in institutions or foster-families, the construction of children's nurseries, crèches, institutions for mental and delinquent children and old persons, the organization of care for the old and the sick in their homes;

(iv) the provision of elementary schools and institutions for the education of adults, the establishment of children's nurseries and part-time nurseries, the promotion of co-ordination between the family and the school, looking after the work of cultural clubs, people's universities and public libraries, the development of artistic recreations, the construction and maintenance of buildings and grounds for physical culture;

(v) the encouragement of supply and service shops (foodshops, handicraft shops, laundries and similar services required by families) by means of land policy (providing sites at a reasonable price) and tax policy; also the creation of the necessary conditions for the work of such shops (for instance by providing credit); the maintenance of hygiene in flats, the care of children during the absence of their parents, and the like.

It can be seen that although all important functions for unified planning of the city development and the execution of common services are performed by the city, the functions of the municipalities are not insignificant. These functions are so formulated that they enable the specific needs and requests of citizens from each part of the city to be satisfied. This is of particular significance because the standard of public utilities and services (sewage, water, transport, streets, etc.) varies greatly between the centre of the city and its suburbs. It is of particular significance that the citizens in any area can bring their influence to bear upon issues in the municipality itself and in that way in the city as a whole. This influence the citizens also exert directly upon the city assembly through voters' meetings, the press and in other ways; but the influence is greater if a municipal assembly stands behind it.

A different distribution of functions between the city and the municipalities, downward or upward transfer, may be provided for only by the city charter. Each change in the charter of the city requires the agreement of at least two-thirds of the municipalities.

The city charter envisages the participation of the municipalities in the execution of the city's own tasks. The most important form of such participation is by approval of certain actions of the city assembly. Without the agreement of two-thirds of the municipalities the following matters cannot be settled: the town plan, the development programmes of certain branches, and the distribution of institutions (in education, culture, health, social protection, public housing); decisions concerning the distribution of revenue between the city and the municipalities, and the regulations concerning the preparation of building sites in the city. Municipal assemblies have to give their opinion about all these matters within one month of their adoption by the city assembly. If the municipal assemblies refuse to agree to certain policies which the city assembly has adopted in conformity with the opinion of the voters' meeting, the city assembly will draw the attention of the municipal assemblies to this fact. If the municipal assemblies refuse their agreement even after this observation, a referendum decides the disputed issue.

A second form of participation by municipalities in the tasks of the city assembly is obligatory prior consultation about certain matters within the competence of the city. These include decisions concerning various taxes and rates, and the city budget. The city assembly is obliged to consider the opinion or proposals of the municipal assembly and to endeavour to amend the provisional decision. In the case of disagreement the city assembly informs the municipal assembly of its reasons. The city assembly also has to consult, before making detailed town plans, all those municipalities whose territory is affected.

A third form of participation by the municipal assemblies is the right to propose regulations within the competence of the city; the city assembly has to include such proposals in the agenda of its session and to decide about them. Municipal assemblies may urge that a referendum be held on a certain question, and if this is demanded by one third of the municipalities, the city assembly is under an obligation to hold one.

The municipal assemblies in Belgrade have two chambers: one general-political and one functional—the so-called chamber of work communities. This second chamber is elected by all citizens employed in various branches of activity, proportionally to the number of citizens employed in each particular branch. Municipal assemblies in Belgrade usually have 50 councillors in each chamber. The procedure for the election of members of the municipal assemblies and their term of office is the same as for the members of the city assembly. The municipal assembly has a president and a vice-president. In some municipalities the president receives a regular monthly remuneration while in others the office is an honorary one. Each municipal assembly has commissions similar to those of the city assembly. In addition to these, the municipal assemblies usually have a commission for neighbourhood communities. Chambers decide equally on most important questions, sometimes in a joint session; in a smaller number of matters each chamber has its own independent field of activity. In comparison with the organization of the city assembly, the municipal assemblies have a larger number of committees (for economics, finance, education and culture, health and social welfare, communal services and housing, national defence, internal affairs and others). At least two members of each committee must be members of the municipal assembly, and at least half of the committee consists of members delegated directly by interested organizations, such as schools, health institutions and the like. Committees play a very important part in the functioning of the municipal assembly, because they are the basic political-executive organs, proposing the policy and overseeing its implementation. The secretary is in charge of the work of the administrative organ.

NEIGHBOURHOOD COMMUNITIES

Neighbourhood communities enjoy a separate place in the socio-political structure of the city. During 1967 there were 108 such communities in Belgrade. The essential characteristic of the neighbourhood community is the direct part it plays in deciding about joint needs, i.e. the encouragement of citizens to concern themselves in matters in which they have a common interest. The neighbourhood community is founded on the basis of the wishes and interests of the citizens; it is not obligatory. Its area is determined by the charter of the municipality after consultation with the citizens.

A neighbourhood community is a legal person (it can own property, sign contracts, etc.), but it is not a local authority and it has no statutory powers. The citizens decide for themselves and the neighbourhood community cannot exert pressure upon them in any way.

The work and activities of neighbourhood communities vary considerably. It has been noted that in the rural and suburban areas the neighbourhood communities are particularly active, as the need for common action is greater than in the central area of the city. The complete list of issues in which the neighbourhood community may take part is very long.

The protection of children is a field of activity in which every neighbourhood community engages. The capacities of the child care institutions set up by the municipalities do not satisfy increasing needs, particularly with the growing employment of women. Neighbourhood communities arrange for the care of children through simpler and cheaper forms, such as the engagement of part-time staff (retired teachers and the like) to look after children, voluntary participation of citizens in this work, the provision of adequate premises in the larger residential buildings, voluntary work by citizens to provide play-grounds, the organization of excursions, summer vacations and the like. Other forms of social welfare, such as the care of old and disabled persons, also evoke similar efforts. Neighbourhood communities frequently make proposals for the allocation of social aid from municipal funds.

In the field of education and culture, neighbourhood communities take part in the organization of courses for the illiterate, in domestic economy and health education. They offer assistance to slow pupils, organize cultural and artistic performances and the like. They endeavour to strengthen and facilitate contact between family and school. They have set up some centres for services, e.g. workshops in which citizens may themselves use equipment for small household repairs or share in the use of household appliances.

The experiences of neighbourhood communities are particularly rich in the construction and maintenance of smaller communal amenities. This is particularly the case with rural municipalities, where the citizens collect financial contributions to provide a local road, a water supply, etc. In the city these amenities usually consist of a local park or sports ground, improving the appearance of the area, planting trees, etc.

All these and other tasks should be performed by the municipality. The initiative of citizens, their financial contributions, and their participation widen the scope of such activities. The municipalities, therefore, support these activities with financial aid. Some municipalities provide in their charters that if citizens through their voluntary contributions or work provide a fixed percentage of resources required by a programme of broader interest, the municipal budget will undertake to cover the balance. The most frequent form of assistance does not consist of a general allocation, but participation in the financing of specific programmes of neighbourhood communities.

The territory of the neighbourhood community is also a basic unit of the town plan. It is a micro-urban entity in which a group of neighbours reside and spend much of their leisure time and in which citizens or households can quickly and easily satisfy their basic needs. This pattern is constantly applied

in the construction of new parts of the city and separate competitions are
announced for particular neighbourhood communities, during the working
out of the detailed town plan. The idea is to create an inner circle in which the
children may reach their school or their playground in a few minutes, their
parents the self-service stores, club or pub, and the old people their favourite
seat in the park or public garden. The results achieved in new residential
settlements are more conspicuous than in the older built-up areas. The
neighbourhood community is a widely accepted town planning concept
which fits into the existing organizational and political structure of the city
and which helps to humanize metropolitan life and to strengthen primary
social relations.

Neighbourhood communities in Belgrade have an average of 6,000 to
12,000 inhabitants. The citizens elect the council of the neighbourhood
community and the committees for various branches of its activities. Many
neighbourhood communities have a paid secretary.

OTHER SELF-GOVERNING AUTHORITIES IN THE METROPOLIS

The federation and the republic have no organs or agencies in Belgrade
which perform functions of significance to, or in the interest of, the city. There
are, however, a whole series of other self-governing authorities in the
city.

In 1967, education, which was formerly a responsibility of local authorities, was transferred to a new form of organization, namely, to educational
districts, which are somewhat similar to American school districts. The
educational district in Belgrade contains 276 elementary and secondary
schools. The city assembly guides the work of the district; half its members
are educational workers and the other half consists of representatives of
competent organizations. The university belongs to another educational
district. The funds for education, which were previously allocated from the
city budget, are now derived from the independent revenue of the district.
This revenue is provided by a separate education tax, the amount of which
is determined by the city assembly. Each school receives its share of the funds,
on the basis of a contract concluded with the district, based on the criteria
which the district has defined in evaluating the needs of the school and the
results of its work. Each school has its own school board consisting of teachers
and citizens.

The education district has a right to submit proposals to the city assembly
on all matters in the field of education and a right to participate in discussions
on these questions, particularly when the amount of the education tax is

determined and the school development programme prepared for the city. The district has to submit reports about its work to the city assembly and to submit for consideration its programmes for the development of the network of schools.

The communal board for social insurance has similar rights and duties in respect of the city assembly. This board covers all kinds of social insurance: health insurance, benefits for the disabled, retirement pensions, children's allowances and employment contributions.

The city assembly has also founded certain independent institutions which are self-financing, have their own managing organs and possess the right to decide their internal organization. These institutions, however, perform tasks of public interest and exercise public power within the limits of the city's competence. One such institution is the city housing enterprise, which manages all residential houses in public ownership, determines rents (with the agreement of the city assembly), maintains residential buildings and constructs new ones. Another body of a similar kind is the direction for the preparation of city building sites, which prepares sites for new housing and other construction, supplying water, electricity and other public utilities. It is financed by payments made for the use of city land by citizens and firms, and by payments by developers for the preparation of building sites. The direction for the construction and reconstruction of streets and roads performs similar functions in relation to streets. The town planning institute for Belgrade prepares the general town plan and makes detailed plans, carries out town planning inspection and issues town planning licences, etc.

All these organizations have their own boards which include representatives of the city assembly, interested organizations and citizens. The city provides additional funds for some of them. Such organizations have to submit to the city assembly annual reports about their work and the use of financial resources allocated from the city budget.

THE ROLE OF SOCIO-POLITICAL ORGANIZATIONS

There are no classical political parties in Yugoslavia. The Socialist Alliance of Working Peoples with about 8 million members is a general political alliance of citizens, a mass socio-political organization in which the citizens discuss social problems, present their opinions, evaluate the work of the assembly and its organs, and exercise public control of its work. A similar role is played by other socio-political organizations, as for instance the Youth Alliance, the Conference for the Social Activities of Women, and others.

The League of Communists of Yugoslavia with 1·2 million members has transformed itself from an old style Communist Party which conducted the national liberation struggle during the war, and organized socialist construction and renewal in the post-war years, into a guiding ideological influence. Today the League of Communists cannot interfere with the work and decision-making of public enterprise, municipalities, republics or the Federation, but it endeavours to throw light on some ideological aspects of social movements and political processes, in furtherance of its goal of self-governing socialism.

Each municipal assembly co-operates with the Socialist Alliance and other socio-political organizations in the preparation of drafts of the more important regulations and plans for public consideration and in the carrying out of elections for members of the assembly. The city assembly and its bodies consider the opinions and proposals of citizens stated by particular branches and other meetings within these organizations.

For example, on the initiative of the Socialist Alliance and other socio-political organizations in 1967, the city assembly considered problems created by the introduction of the five-day working week, the reform of health insurance, protests of citizens concerning the proposal of the city housing enterprise to abolish housekeepers, and other questions.

The city assembly co-operates closely with the economic chamber of the city, which is an association of economic enterprises. On the initiative of the economic chamber in 1967 the construction of additional hotel space was considered, as well as working hours in shops.

The city assembly, in considering certain questions consults numerous other associations of citizens, such as the Association for Child Welfare and Education, the Red Cross, the Association of Organizations for Physical Culture, professional associations of lawyers, economists, doctors, town planning experts and the like. The city assembly may allocate financial aid to such associations.

In view of the structure and activities of the socio-political organizations, party affiliation is not a decisive factor in the nomination of candidates for the assembly. Each person nominated by a voters' meeting and proposed by a group of citizens is considered as a candidate. There are always more candidates than seats, this being encouraged by electoral law, which requires an absolute majority of all registered voters for the election of councillors in cases where the number of candidates is smaller than double the number of seats. The Socialist Alliance engages in the political preparation of elections, without supporting one candidate against another. Therefore, instead of party affiliation, the personality of the candidate is the centre of attention, his career, previous social activity, qualifications for office and the like.

CITY AND MUNICIPAL FUNCTIONS

The functions of the city assembly and the municipalities have already been considered. All basic social functions and services are performed in the city and none is carried out by federal or republican agencies. However, this does not mean that all services are administered by the city assembly and the municipalities. On the contrary, the largest number of functions are performed and financed by independent self-governing organs. They may be economic organizations (in the public housing sector) or independent institutions which have their own sources of finance (education, etc.).

The role of the city and municipal assemblies in the greater part of social activities is to make plans and programmes of development to serve as guide lines, to regulate matters of interest to the city as a whole, to subsidize institutions not able to finance themselves completely, to create institutions to perform tasks of interest to the city or the municipalities, to supervise the legality of the work of self-managing organizations and to provide general supervision through inspection.

In a relatively limited number of fields the city and municipal assemblies themselves directly provide necessary services. These include the maintenance of law and order, traffic regulation, civil defence, protection against fire and natural disasters, statistical records, health and social welfare.

There are a number of independent economic organizations which provide communal services, such as water supply, sewerage, refuse disposal, city public transport, electricity supply, thermal energy, cemeteries, public baths, chimney-cleaning services and others. All these organizations finance themselves from the prices charged for their services. The city assembly approves the prices determined. If an increase in prices is requested, the city assembly must consider the justification for such a demand. If the city assembly is of the opinion that the increase should be approved, such a proposal is put to voters' meetings. The city assembly explains to citizens that the refusal of their agreement would mean stagnation or even a decrease in the quantity or quality of the service in question, or that the deficit would have to be covered by the city budget and that this would unavoidably also affect the citizens.

Capital investment in these undertakings presents a particular problem because the resources needed are only partly covered by the prices charged for the services. The city tries to assist by granting long-term loans with the interest provided partly from the budget, and by allocating subsidies directly from the city's budget. Also industrial enterprises may contribute from their own funds to the capital development of municipal undertakings which directly benefit them. Thus, a factory situated in the suburbs might help to finance the extension into its area of the sewerage system.

In the sphere of the social services (education, culture, health and social welfare, sports) the competent self-managing organizations act directly in administering schools, hospitals, cultural centres, and so forth. In addition to planning, co-ordination, the founding of institutions and supervising the legality of their work, the city directly employs budgetary and other funds for their current and particularly capital costs. This applies to activities which have no fixed sources of revenue or cannot realize sufficient resources from the prices charged for their services.

The city assembly, in its relations with the organizations which directly perform certain municipal functions, takes a more direct part in the direction of their work and provides additional financial resources. Such institutions are, for instance, the town planning institute, city housing enterprise, and various boards and directions for the preparation of building land and sites, the construction of streets, and the like.

AN APPRAISAL OF THE CITY'S SERVICES

The number one problem in the city is housing. In the course of 1967 9,000 flats were constructed. The number of flats constructed per 1,000 inhabitants is 11·4, thus reaching the European average figure. However, housing remains a burning problem. Four factors have played a decisive part in this situation: the very bad state of the inherited housing stock, the great devastation suffered during the war, slow housing construction in the first decade after the war and, finally, a threefold increase in the number of inhabitants. Even the accelerated housing construction programme from 1956 until today has been unable to cope with the problem. Average dwelling space per inhabitant amounts to 11·4 square metres.

The second greatest problem is probably transport. The city public transport system has succeeded by great efforts in satisfying great needs in spite of a huge increase in demand. Even greater problems are created by the increasing number of cars which cannot be solved by partial measures (e.g. one-way streets, introduction of a central 'blue zone', construction of pedestrian under-passes); extensive and expensive reconstruction of city communications is necessary. The city was unprepared, because of its inherited structure and quality of streets, and insufficiently imaginative planning immediately after the war, for the dynamic growth in the number of cars.

The next question, in terms of its gravity and relatively unsuccessful solution is child welfare. The quality of children's institutions is adequate, but their capacity is far from satisfying increasing demands. The activity of neighbourhood communities cannot as yet decisively influence the situation. Ambitious programmes for a more radical solution of this question are therefore in preparation.

Belgrade has three football stadiums, but insufficient attention has been paid to one of the most important aspects of sport, physical culture and its material needs. During the last few years remarkable results have been achieved in equipping schools with adequate facilities for physical culture and some of the municipalities and neighbourhood communities have done a great deal towards solving this problem.

Elementary schools, thanks to the decrease of the natural growth of population no longer present a significant problem, but this difficulty has now moved to secondary and intermediate schools, particularly because a large number of pupils attend the special, vocational schools in Belgrade. A similar situation exists at the university, which is overcrowded despite the existence of three other university centres in Serbia. (In the number of students per 10,000 inhabitants Yugoslavia is among the first in the world.) Health services are mostly at an adequate level. As far as cultural activities are concerned, many of them (theatres, galleries and museums, musical life, etc.) are far better provided in Belgrade than in the majority of other towns of its size.

Protection against fire is fairly inadequate. City police with increasing rapidity and success are adapting themselves to the problems arising from the transformation of Belgrade into a big city.

ADMINISTRATIVE ORGANIZATION AND STAFFING

A secretary is usually in charge of the work of each organ of the city administration. At the head of some of these organs, however, are directors appointed by the city assembly for a period of four years, with the possibility of reappointment. There is in principle no difference between secretaries and directors. The former manage the traditional organs of administration and the latter the more technical units. Both are administrative not political heads and may be reappointed *ad infinitum*. Generally they are recruited from the city's permanent staff but sometimes from experts and managers in other fields (for instance directors of public utilities). As a rule they have a university education. The city has 10 secretariats: for finance, economics, communal services, education and culture, health and social affairs, inspection, national defence, home affairs, general administration and, finally, for expert services of the city assembly. The city assembly also has four city institutes: for social planning, statistics, prices and surveying. Three secretariats are shared by the city and the municipalities: internal affairs, national defence and inspection. The municipal organs of administration have generally a similar pattern of organization, except where the organs are shared with the city.

The staff is recruited by way of open public competition, specifying the necessary conditions in respect of school qualifications and working experience. Working posts are filled according to the classification and complements of posts laid down by the city assembly. The heads of various organs are appointed by the city assembly and other staff by the heads of organs and the staff council.[1] The city assembly has effective control and there does not exist a higher 'public service commission' which could intervene in the question of conditions of recruitment and promotion of staff. The same applies to all municipal assemblies. In the administrative organs various courses for additional professional training of staff are being organized.

Inspection is one of the most important duties of the administrative organs. All the inspectorates are located in one secretariat. Market inspection covers the work of trade enterprises, foodshops, catering, crafts, markets, etc.; for violation of regulations this inspectorate may initiate legal proceedings; the cases are decided by municipal courts. Sanitary inspection covers the control and prevention of contagious diseases, and the work of organizations in the field of communal hygiene, catering, occupational medicine, hygiene in residential buildings, handicraft shops, etc. Veterinary inspection exerts veterinary, sanitary and technical control over slaughterhouses, butchers, dairies, markets, stores, etc. Agricultural and forestry inspection controls the protection of plants and the use of chemicals for plant protection, and the protection of forests, orchards and vineyards. Labour inspection supervises the implementation of regulations concerning safety at work and the conditions and safety of workers. Communal inspection supervises the location and maintenance of parks, squares and lawns, newspaper kiosks, post boxes, telephone booths, car parks, bridges, hydrants and the like. Traffic inspection controls the city public transport, taxi stations, private owners of lorries, etc.

The city administrative organs (without the secretariat for internal affairs which is in charge of the police) employed, at the beginning of 1968, 855 personnel. Of this figure 375 or 49·06 per cent had a university education, 277 or 30·16 per cent secondary education, and 114 or 14·88 per cent only elementary schooling.

---

[1] This is a self-managing staff organ with the power to decide certain matters independently (e.g. annual holidays) and other matters jointly with the head of the organ (e.g. recruitment of new personnel). It is not a trade union but a kind of workers' council.

Municipal administrative organs in Belgrade employed at the beginning of 1968 a total of 1,772 staff.

FINANCE

The law determines the sources of revenue which are available to local authorities. The municipalities decide independently which contributions and municipal taxes, among those prescribed by law, shall be used and decide also their amount. The federal law provides, as an exception, that these rates may, if the economic situation of the country requires, be limited by federal law. The federation fixed in 1968 the upper limit of turnover taxes, but all other taxes are independently determined by the municipalities.

The Constitution of Serbia provides that all municipal revenues are to be treated as joint revenues of the city and the municipalities in Belgrade and are to be distributed according to the procedure prescribed by the city charter. The federation and the republic give no aid to the city, and the city finances jointly with the republic only a few institutions of broad interest (such as certain museums and art galleries). Belgrade enjoys no special financial treatment as the capital of Yugoslavia and Serbia, nor does it receive on this account any additional revenues.

The bulk of the revenue is derived from personal income taxes and the retail sales tax.

Personal income tax is paid as a percentage on all monetary income received in regular employment and is calculated at each payment of the salary. This tax is paid to the municipality in which the citizen resides and not to the one where he works. In this way the differences are reduced between the more developed municipalities and those from which the manpower is recruited.

Personal income tax is also paid by citizens who independently produce commodities (e.g. handicrafts) or perform services. It can be assessed either as an annual fixed amount, or as a percentage of the actual income received, or according to real personal income. Where personal income is received from copyrights, patents and technical improvements a fixed percentage tax is paid in respect of each payment.

The city land-use tax is paid by users of developed or undeveloped city land. All the land in the city proper (viz. excluding the suburban municipalities) was nationalized, or rather municipalized, in 1958. The tax is paid by all those who use this land. This tax can be used only for financing the preparation of city land for building (clearing, levelling, installing services, etc.)

G

The turnover tax is paid with the retail sales tax and charges for services (markets, cinemas, football and boxing matches, etc.).

The rent tax is paid by the owners or users of business and residential buildings. Residential buildings are freed from this tax for a period of 25 years after their construction.

Taxes on property and on property rights are paid by citizens who receive an income from the renting of real and personal property and other property rights.

Production equipment taxes in agriculture are paid by the owners of machines with mechanical power used in agriculture and forestry.

TABLE I

Revenues, 1968 (in new dinars)

No.	Revenue realized from	Amount	%
1.	Personal income tax on regular employment	115,100,000	33·00
2.	Taxes from independent crafts and other activities	11,320,000	3·00
3.	Personal income taxes on copyrights and patents	1,950,000	0·56
4.	Turnover tax	142,185,000	40·40
5.	Administrative taxes	9,940,000	3·00
6.	Court taxes	35,500,000	10·00
7.	City land-use taxes	16,000,000	4·44
8.	Independent revenue of administrative organs and courts	2,100,000	0·60
9.	Balance from the last year budget	17,454,040	5·00
	Total revenue	351,549,040	100%

The municipality also receives some smaller revenues from taxes on additional employees other than family members in handicraft shops and catering, a tax on production tools in agriculture, taxes on lotteries, and others.

The municipality has introduced also various other taxes: for instance, administrative taxes paid in respect of applications made to municipal administrative organs, or communal taxes paid when bringing cases before municipal courts. The scales of these taxes are fixed by the city assembly.

In 1967 the total current revenue in the city amounted to 745,780,000 new dinars. From this amount the educational community received 275,490,000, the city budget 322,960,000 and municipal budgets 147,330,000 new dinars.

The city budget includes all revenue and its distribution. The budget is passed for each calendar year. It should be balanced. The law provides that the budget has to be submitted to voters' meeting for consideration. Conclusions from voters' meetings which are not adopted should be attached to the proposed budget. The secretariat for financial affairs prepares the draft of the budget on the basis of financial results achieved during the period of nine months and the draft is determined by the committee for finance.

The city sets up various funds for the financing of certain social needs, obligations and tasks which require permanent financial provision and special managing organs. The funds are established from the city revenue. Each fund

TABLE II

General Distribution of the Budget Revenue, 1968

No.	Basically devoted to	Amount	%
1.	Education	1,700,000	0·49
2.	Culture (theatres, museums, art galleries, etc.)	41,620,000	12·00
3.	Social welfare	4,850,000	1.30
4.	Health protection	4,800,000	1.35
5.	Communal activities	55,450,000	15·80
6.	The work of administration and courts	139,534,300	39·68
7.	Allocation to citizens' associations	3,288,000	0·90
8.	Investments (current investments and annuity payments)	91,545,540	26·00
9.	Budgetary obligations from previous years	600,000	0·18
10.	Emergency fund	3,161,200	0·90
11.	Undistributed revenue	5,000,000	1·40
	Total expenditure	351,549,000	100%

is a legal person and has its own statute. The representatives of the users of the fund participate in its management together with representatives of the municipal assemblies and of organizations interested in the goals it serves. The city assembly has to confirm most important actions of the fund. The managing organ of the fund has to prepare its draft statute, its programme of work and its financial plan; these are all forwarded to the users of the fund, municipal assemblies and interested organizations for their opinion.

In accordance with a 1968 budget regulation, out of the total revenue, including the balance from the previous year, 10·12 per cent is paid into the city fund for culture, 7·33 per cent into the city fund for the financing of communal activities and 1·83 per cent into the city fund for reconstruction.

By law certain funds *have* to be established, e.g. the road fund; 25 per cent of the revenue obtained from petrol tax is paid into the city road fund together with 20 per cent of the fees for the registration of motor vehicles. The emergency fund is used to cover expenditures incurred as the result of floods, earthquakes, epidemics and the like, for the reorganization of institutions for social services and for the provision of a budgetary reserve in case of a failure by the expected revenue to meet expenditure.

The city is authorized to raise a loan to finance the construction of certain projects and for investments in projects of general significance for the city. In case of temporary imbalance between resources and expenditure, the city may raise a short term loan.

The city charter envisages that the distribution of resources between the city and municipalities should be in accordance with the social needs which are financed within the city, i.e. in accordance with the tasks resulting from the adopted programmes and plans. The distribution should provide for the equalization of conditions, for the fulfilment of the rights of citizens and for the satisfaction of their needs. The decision about the distribution of resources may remain valid for one or more years; it remains in force until the city and the municipalities change it. Such decisions must be agreed by two-thirds of the members of municipal assemblies. The decision determines also the proportions in which the municipalities and the city share certain sources of revenue, and endeavours to leave some resources entirely to the municipalities and others to the city. All special funds are established by the city.

The city and all or some of the municipalities may merge their resources, together with sums obtained from work organizations and neighbourhood communities, to execute certain tasks.

RELATIONS WITH HIGHER AUTHORITIES

The city assembly, like all municipal assemblies, decides independently according to its charter and other regulations all internal relationships, its organization, the size and distribution of its revenue, the manner of execution of various tasks and all other questions of interest to the city.

Federal and republican organs have no hierarchical controls over municipal organs, and their inter-relations are based exclusively on the rights and duties provided for by the Constitution and the law. The federation has no direct relations with the city and the municipalities, and communicates with them through the Republic of Serbia. Governmental organs of the republics have no administrative rights in relation to municipal organs. Executive and administrative organs of the city assembly and municipal assemblies are responsible only to their assemblies. Higher state organs have no control over municipal regulations except that where a regulation is thought to be illegal, they can bring it to the attention of the constitutional court. This body decides its legality. No grant of money is made to Belgrade or its municipalities by the republic or federal governments. As a rule there exist no organs of government administration on the territory of a municipality, except municipal ones.

PLANNING AND DEVELOPMENT

The city passes the programmes and plans of economic and social development, the general town plan and detailed town plans, and town planning regulations, determines which parts of the city and which buildings have to be protected because of their architectural, historical, cultural or other value, and determines urbanistic and technical conditions for construction.

After the Second World War, at the end of 1945, the preparations and first studies for a new general town plan of Belgrade were started. The city assembly adopted this town plan in 1950, which took into consideration the development of the city until 1980. The main conceptions of the general town plan were as follows:

(i) the growth of the city to one million inhabitants was envisaged;

(ii) the greatest provision of new land for development was planned for the left bank of the river Sava, on the area between the old part of Belgrade and Zemun; this is within the city boundaries;

(iii) it was envisaged that the territory of old Belgrade should have about 600,000 inhabitants, New Belgrade 250,000 and the settlement in Zemun, also on the left bank of the Sava, about 150,000;

(iv) the basic structure of the town was to consist of residential zones, work areas and recreational spaces; industrial zones were to be distributed on the periphery of the city and connected with the residential parts by main communications; the creation of a continuous industrial ring around the city was to be avoided; broad green spaces in the form of large parks and spacious water surfaces of rivers and a future lake were to facilitate the penetration of fresh air to the central parts of the city and to offer possibilities of mass recreation;

(v) the network of main traffic communications was to be solved by an orthogonal system, with three bridges over the Sava and the highway connecting the main Zagreb–Skopje highway;

(vi) the river Sava, the old boundary and periphery, on which the city has 'turned its back', was to become the central city motive, and a feature of first-class importance in the general town plan. Economic functions were to be related to the river Danube.

The general town plan has been only partly realized. The greatest construction has taken place in New Belgrade on the left bank of the Sava, making it possible to unite in an unbroken urban entity Zemun, New and Old Belgrade. The volatile development of Belgrade has, however, exceeded greatly the general town plan and the city assembly intends to undertake its revision. General guide lines have been laid down and these indicate that the future town plan should incorporate the whole metropolitan area and plan the city development until the year 2000.

The revision of the plan raises several major questions of policy. Among them is the direction in which the city should grow and the question of new territory. Another important question is the basic conception of the traffic network; traffic conditions were relatively undeveloped at the time of the adoption of the general town plan.

Since 1959 detailed town plans were worked out for municipal areas and nearby suburban settlements within the administrative boundaries of Belgrade. These plans determine the detailed use of each building site, including the density and average height, as well as the internal structure, of the residential zone. These plans also lay down norms for the amenities required in neighbourhood communities and their centres, and the location of the most important buildings. The traffic network is also being determined and all other infrastructural projects.

All town plans and studies are prepared and implemented by the Town Planning Institute of the city. The drafts of the plans are first submitted to broad public discussion. The plans are finally adopted by the city assembly.

Municipal boundaries are established by republic not federal law; municipalities cannot annex territory unilaterally. The last extension of Belgrade's boundaries was provided for by a republic law of 1959. The city proper today has a territory of 21,000 hectares while its administrative area is ten times as great, 242,000 hectares. This territory coincides fairly closely with the metropolitan area and also includes a part of the larger area of influence. There is, therefore, no problem of administrative boundaries in Belgrade. The problems of the joint interests of the city with contiguous areas are dealt with by various forms of cooperation with the neighbouring municipalities.

As all the necessary changes in the structure, functions and organizations of the city organs of Belgrade were carried out in 1967 and 1968, no significant changes are expected in the near future.

Birmingham

Born 1919. Read sociology and law at the University of Birmingham. B.Com.(Social Studies), 1949. Served in Provincial Administration in Eastern Nigeria 1949 to 1963. Returned to conduct research at Oxford University into British humanitarian attitudes to colonial expansion in south and west Africa. D.Phil., 1968.

Member of staff of the Institute of Local Government Studies, Birmingham University since 1968. Seconded to the University of Mauritius as Professor of Local Government Administration, 1969–70.

Birmingham

WITH a population of 1·1 million the city of Birmingham is the second largest town in the British Isles. Close to the geographical centre of England it is part of the West Midland conurbation, an area of urban and industrial development covering 263 square miles[1] and lived in by 2·5 million people. Metal working is the major occupation of the area and in large part it serves the motor-vehicle industry. Rubber, cocoa and chocolate manufacture provide the major variation from the pattern of metal winning and working, but these are small in comparison. The numbers of large and small scale firms are above the national average, but those of middling size fall below it, a factor influencing class structure. Industry in Birmingham tends to be lighter and more sophisticated than in the rest of the conurbation, for no coal or iron is found in it. Die-making and jewellery are important, as is the making of components and accessories for motor cars. Over half the insured population is in manufacturing industry, compared with a national average of 38 per cent, and among the 1,500 trades the proportion of skilled workers is high.

HISTORY

The first clear evidence of occupation is the remains of Metchley Fort, a Roman camp in the south-west of the city. Except that the name Birmingham implies settlement by an Anglo-Saxon clan there is nothing more until the Domesday Book of A.D. 1086, which listed fifteen manors in the shires of Warwick, Worcester and Stafford which are now encompassed within the 52-mile perimeter of the county borough.

Though a movement was afoot in 1716 to gain a municipal charter for Birmingham, this was not granted until 1838, and it was 1851 before the *ad hoc* Street Commission set up under an Improvement Act of 1769 was abolished and the council entrusted with the function of laying out and maintaining streets, as well as maintaining law and order and seeing to public health.

The year 1873 saw the start of Joseph Chamberlain's three-year mayoralty and a decade of accelerated development, the fruits of a period of growing prosperity. In that year private enterprise laid the first tramway, the initial step towards a municipal enterprise which was operating twelve hundred

[1] 680 square kilometres.

Built-up area

Birmingham
City boundary

Railways

Motorway

Main roads

Airport

N

0 miles   5   10   15
0 kilometres   5   10   15   20

MAP 3 BIRMINGHAM

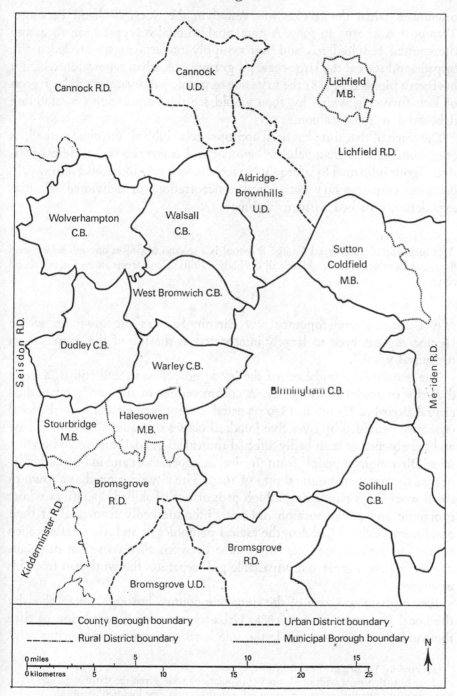

County Borough boundary

Rural District boundary

Urban District boundary

Municipal Borough boundary

0 miles 5 10 15

0 kilometres 5 10 15 20 25

N

MAP 4 BIRMINGHAM—municipal boundaries

omnibuses when the service was vested in the West Midland Passenger Transport Authority in 1969. A municipal hospital was opened in 1874, and the council acquired gas and water supply undertakings, enrolled a fire brigade and started the large-scale programme of urban renewal in which it has been a pioneer. In 1881 the first issue of municipal stock started the process of loan-financing which by 1969 would see the corporation's outstanding debt stand at £388 million.

The spirit of that time has been appropriately dubbed 'the civic gospel', as compounded with material development and enterprise was a radical political vigour informed by a largely Nonconformist religious leadership which, decrying contemporary evangelical concentration on individual religious experience, preached a true urbanism:

A town [wrote the Reverend George Dawson] is a solemn organism through which shall flow, and in which shall be shaped, all the highest, loftiest and truest ends of man's moral nature.[1]

A Unitarian contemporary saw Birmingham as the town 'in which Democracy has been so largely interpreted as the life of the people as an organized whole'.

The economic foundation of the 'civic gospel' was, and still is, a great diversity of trades and industry. A commissioner of the newly established central Board of Health in 1849 reported 'exceptional elasticity' in the local economy provided by over five hundred classes of trade. This diverse base and the absence of such badly affected industries as coal mining and textiles saved Birmingham people from the deeper experiences and industrial bitterness of the great economic slump of 1929. The city developed as a town of small workshops employing a high proportion of skilled operatives whose economic and social position did not differ markedly from that of their employers. Richard Cobden, the radical pamphleteer and Manchester calico printer, remarked 'the freer intercourse between all classes than in (Manchester) where a great and impassable gulf separates the workman from his employer'.

Birmingham was one of the sixty-one county boroughs established by the Local Government Act, 1888. Urban areas with a population of fifty thousand or more[2] were made the sole local government authorities with

---

[1] Quoted in Asa Briggs: *Victorian Cities*, p. 199.

[2] Four historic towns with much smaller populations were given the status as an exception. The minimum population for new county boroughs is now one hundred thousand.

jurisdiction in their areas.[1] The elevation of the county borough a year later to the style and dignity of city did not affect its powers.

As neighbours Birmingham has the administrative counties of Worcestershire, Warwickshire and Staffordshire with two municipal boroughs, two urban and a couple of rural district councils exercising second-tier powers within the counties. The other neighbours are three of the six other county boroughs of the West Midland conurbation. Much of the city's population and 80 square miles[2] of area were gained at the expense of the counties in five major extensions sanctioned since 1891. Her neighbours are vigilant.

THE CITY FATHERS

Of the 156 members of the council, 117 are elected by direct adult suffrage, from among citizens of Great Britain or the Republic of Ireland who are at least 21 years of age, are on the register of voters, and not disqualified, to represent the 39 geographical areas known as wards into which the city is divided. Recent electoral history suggests that nomination by a political party is necessary. After the election in May 1970 there were 109 Conservatives, 39 Labour and 8 Liberal members of the Council.

In general, while Conservatives think in terms of municipal provision where monopoly is reasonable or necessary, the Labour Party is more ready to compete with private enterprise. But nine-tenths of local government business does not properly lend itself to party politics, for sewers and sidewalks are apolitical. Even where innovation based on different policies is desired, the existence of valid contracts and the proper part played in decision-making by professional and technical advice makes for continuity.

Present Liberal representation on the council is in an interesting position. In 1961 the election of a solitary councillor ended nearly thirty years' absence of the party which had once dominated local government in the city. It was the first step in a slow revival of fortunes. Untrammelled by party responsibility for council policy, Liberal councillors and candidates have campaigned vigorously on the grievances and needs of individual citizens, assuming the role of champion of the person against party machines, the citizen against juggernaut bureaucracy.

Though national party politics impinge on local government it does not follow that verdicts in local elections reliably predict what could happen at the centre. The national headquarters of all the parties make much or little of the results depending on how their local branches fare, and a defeat may even be acclaimed a moral victory. If the link between the two levels of

[1] In the other major local government areas, the administrative counties, there are three tiers of councils, each with different functions.

[2] 207 square kilometres.

government were so very close one would expect, as in Sweden or West Germany, to find council membership the most common apprenticeship for parliament, but this is not the case.

An important function of party politics in local government is as safety valve for the party in power at the centre. By staying away from the poll in council elections supporters can pass interim judgment on performance with little risk of unseating the government of their choice. Within four years of Labour forming the central government in 1945 Conservatives ousted them from control of the city council, but only two years after power changed hands again in Westminster, Labour started on a fourteen-year tenancy of power on the council, a period only a little longer than the Conservative hold on the centre. After two years of renewed Labour central government, Conservatives again reigned in the council chamber.

The other 39 members are aldermen elected by councillors either from among their own number or from persons outside the council who are qualified to seek election as councillors if they so choose. The provision in local government law for an indirectly elected element not greater than a quarter of total council membership[1] and serving for six years is intended to give continuity to business and policy. It is not the practice in Birmingham to elect to the aldermanic bench from outside the council.

The most typical member of the council of both main parties at the time of writing is between 45 and 54 years of age if a woman, and between 55 and 60 years if a man. (Liberal representatives are significantly younger on average.) He has served for more than ten years and is of professional or managerial status, with attendant social status, and has received higher education. A member does not have to live in the ward he represents, but Labour members are more likely than Conservatives to do so. On the other hand the latter are more likely to be natives of the city, for some Labour members first came here only in the economic depression after 1929 in search of work. No unskilled manual worker has sat on the council for more than forty years. With 30 women members the council in 1970 has almost twice the national average, their proportionate representation in Labour ranks being almost twice that among Conservatives.[2]

Councillors serve for three years, one of the three from each ward retiring annually to provide continuity and, in theory, to keep councils sensitive to changes in public opinion. No payment is received except for strictly

[1] In the Greater London Council and 32 London boroughs the number is restricted to one-seventh of the council.

[2] Most of the information given about social composition of the council relates to the period 1964–68 and is to be found in *Discussion Papers Series F* by D. S. Morris and K. Newton, Faculty of Commerce and Social Science, University of Birmingham. November 1968–March 1969.

limited out-of-pocket expenses. Where loss of earnings can be proved up to
£4 a day may be claimed.

By convention the office of lord mayor is not reserved to the majority
party, but is occupied by representatives of the several parties with a fre-
quency governed by the proportion of seats each party holds on the council.
The lord mayor is thus not always of the ruling party, and since the war
Conservative lord mayors have presided over Labour-controlled councils for
more than a third of the latter's time in power, while Conservative councils
have had a Labour lord mayor for rather less. Though there is no legal bar to
occupying the office in successive years this has not occurred since 1936, for
the holder is first citizen during his mayoralty and it is considered that the
honour and personal expense—despite an allowance of £3,000—should be
shared. No woman has yet held the office. Though the lord mayor presides
at council meetings his duties are largely representational and social.

THE COMMITTEE SYSTEM

The use of committees is an important feature of British local government
and all parties on the council are represented on them. Birmingham has 26
committees, a reduction of eight since the Second World War and in the
direction of the reorganization recommended by the Maud Committee.[1]
In the same period sub-committees have been reduced from 86 to 52. Since
1929 councils have been able to delegate to committees all powers except the
making of by-laws, levying a rate or raising a loan,[2] but this power has been
enjoyed by Birmingham Corporation since the middle of the nineteenth
century under the provision of Private Acts, and it is used to a greater extent
than in most authorities. It is usual for committees to report what they have
done rather than what they wish to see done, for though under the law of
agency the council retains responsibility for its committee's actions, it is usual
practice for a committee only to seek prior authority in matters of high
policy or of major expenditure not previously sanctioned. Even in the latter
case it may with Finance Committee concurrence in emergency purchase
land costing not more than £100,000 and report action to the next council
meeting.

Some committees are a requirement of Statute and among these in Birmingham are those dealing with public health, welfare, police, education and
children in need of care and protection. A council may set up any other

[1] *Report of the Committee on the Management of Local Government*, H.M.S.O., March 1967,
Vol. I.

[2] Committees of county and parish councils may not precept on a rating authority.

committee it chooses. It is a peculiarity of the law that only the 58 administrative county councils are required to have a finance committee, but like
all other major councils Birmingham has one charged with this responsibility.

Each of the twenty 'spending' committees is responsible for the work of
one or more of the 27 departments which undertake the corporation's
many functions. Except for the finance committee, which must be solely
composed of councillors, committees may co-opt into membership a
limited number of persons from outside the council. This power is used
sparingly in Birmingham, where only six committees use it. The education
committee with its 17 sub-committees[1] and 21 co-optees among 51 members,
is the major exception, to meet the requirements of the 1944 Education Act
for representation of a number of interests including teachers and voluntary
bodies such as trade unions and the religious bodies which maintain schools.
Limited co-option is one reason why most committees are small, 14 having
twelve members or less.

Since 1961 it has been the practice for the chairmanship of all committees
to be held by the controlling party. In that year, when Conservative and
Labour councillors were equal in numbers, but the latter had control through
the aldermanic bench, Conservatives were allotted the chairs of twelve committees including the finance committee. Pressure from Labour members of
the finance committee for the brunt of economies to be borne by Conserva-
tive-chaired committees, when the following year's estimates were under
consideration, convinced the minority party that a share of responsibility
without effective control of policy was an experience not to be repeated.

With two exceptions all committees meet at least bi-monthly and report to
council at least twice a year. The public works committee reports much more
frequently and the general purposes committee, a large co-ordinating body
of considerable power and influence with representation of all other committees, reports at each meeting of council.

THE DEPARTMENTS

It is a basic feature of local government in Great Britain that a council may
not lawfully perform an act for which there is no warrant in statute or sub-
sidiary regulation. An *ultra vires* act from which a council member and, in
some circumstances, a senior official does not positively dissent may render
him liable to meet the cost through surcharge by the auditor or challenge in

[1] Eight, in the usual sense of the word. The other nine include special groups such as governing
bodies of colleges.

the courts by an aggrieved party. As thinking in the nation at large about the frontiers of government function have expanded from the fiscal and merely regulatory to development and welfare, application of the doctrine has become less rigid than the theory. But it still exerts a potent influence in shaping council and national policy. When, in 1953, an aggrieved ratepayer sought and obtained a judicial declaration that Birmingham Corporation had no power to allow old age pensioners to travel free on its omnibuses outside rush hours, Parliament had to legislate before councils could follow a course clearly acceptable to majority public opinion.[1]

Some functions are mandatory, laid upon all or particular classes of local authority, while others are assumed under permissive legislation. Birmingham Corporation must provide primary and secondary schools, employ a children's officer and administer a wide range of public health services, but it is by the council's own choice that it maintains civic restaurants and museums and contributes towards the cost of concerts. Another important source of legal power and one much used by the city is the Private Act. Initially promoted by a local authority for purposes in its area not covered by general legislation, such Acts have pioneered much local government activity. A good example of a Private Act is the Birmingham Corporation Act, 1919, under which the wartime Corporation Savings Bank was established as the Birmingham Municipal Bank, the only local authority enterprise of its kind in Great Britain.

Services provided by the corporation for its citizens may roughly be classified into six groups. The quality of the physical environment is the main concern of those departments which plan the city, build and manage houses and swimming baths, lay out and maintain parks, provide and cleanse streets. Ninety million gallons of water are brought from central Wales and the Severn Valley each day, and 326,000 tons of domestic and industrial waste are removed each year. The collection and disposal of sewage results from co-operation between the council and an *ad hoc* statutory board. The corporation instals and maintains all sewers except the trunk conduits which are owned by the Upper Tame Main Drainage Authority, the body which disposes of 140 million gallons of sewage, storm-water and industrial effluent from the West Midlands each day.

The public health department sees to the purity of foodstuffs and is responsible for most preventive and some curative health services, including maternity welfare and some aspects of that of children of school age and below. Health centres, immunization programmes, convalescent homes and analytical laboratories are among the more obvious means through which the

[1] Prescott *v.* Birmingham Corporation, [1954] 3 All England Reports 698.

department does its work, but catching rats, providing a chiropody service for the aged, and inspecting the premises of those who set up as child-minders for mothers who are out at work are some of its less well-known activities.

The second group of services affords more direct protection through the police force of 2,500 men and women, the fire brigade and ambulance service with its 211 appliances maintained in 17 stations and depots, inspectors of weights and measures, and a civil defence service maintained on a caretaker basis.

Education and cultural activities form the third group, and one which—if recreational facilities provided by the parks department in its 2,000[1] acres of sports fields are excluded—cost almost £41 million, or 56 per cent of net recurrent expenditure in the financial year 1968/9. 183,000 pupils are taught by 9,000 teachers in 355 primary and 138 secondary schools maintained or assisted by the county borough, while 3,000 others attend the 33 special schools run for the handicapped. 103,000 persons take advantage of day or evening classes provided in the corporation's 29 institutes of further education. In addition the council trains 1,400 school teachers in two colleges, one being a day college which organizes its programme to enable housewives to attend while their children are in school.[2] The corporation owns an art gallery and several museums, most notable among the latter being the Museum of Science and Industry. Financial support is given to the City of Birmingham Symphony Orchestra, a repertory theatre and other cultural centres.

The council has responsibilities towards children other than schooling and the provision of play areas. The Children Act, 1948, made county boroughs and administrative counties responsible for seeing that all children and young persons under 18 years of age whose circumstances were below acceptable standards were adequately cared for. Such importance is attached to this function that a local authority may only appoint a children's officer from a short list of candidates submitted to the government for scrutiny. Birmingham Corporation in April 1969 had 2,430 children and young persons in its care. Of these 1,445 were in residential accommodation provided by the council or by voluntary agencies or other local authorities; the rest were placed with foster parents or were being supervised in their own homes. 3,000 others were under supervision in foster homes or on discharge from institutions. The service costs the city about 2·8 per cent of net recurrent expenditure, a percentage which does not seem high until the relatively small number is considered. It is a measure of the quality of the service.

[1] 808 hectares.
[2] The two universities with a total student body of 11,000 are, like all British universities, independent bodies.

The Welfare Department cares for the handicapped and the increasing proportion of the elderly in the population under the provisions of the 1948 National Assistance Act and the Health Services and Public Health Act, 1968. In 1966 the department set out to compile a register of persons of 75 years of age and over, as the first stage in a complete registration of those of pensionable age. It now contains 53,000 names. Two features of particular interest emerged from the inquiry. One was the large measure of independence asserted by the elderly; the other was that chiropody was the largest single need expressed; corns and bunions contribute to the isolation and loneliness of the elderly! The shift in national thinking is towards keeping people with special needs in the community for as long as possible and the corporation, though it accommodates more than 2,000 old people in its own residential accommodation, makes grants of £40,000 a year to voluntary societies largely for clubs, home visiting and such services as the provision of hot meals. More than a thousand volunteer visitors do this work. Another £9,000 a year is paid to voluntary agencies for services to the handicapped. The largest part of this goes to the welfare of the deaf, a statutory obligation of local authorities which in Britain is almost entirely discharged on an agency basis by voluntary societies. The corporation runs the largest workshop for the blind in England.

Voluntary association is an important feature of social organization in Britain. The Birmingham Council of Social Service, the main co-ordinating body for the large number of voluntary agencies at work in the city, has noted no change of attitude towards the voluntary principle with changes of political control in the city council. Co-operation in Birmingham between voluntary societies and central and local government is strong, co-ordination of effort being achieved in formal machinery and by such informal means as officials and councillors serving on the committees of voluntary societies.

There are a number of trading services. The omnibuses have already been mentioned, but there are also an airport, markets, restaurants, and allotment gardens for letting to members of the public. In 1968 450,000 depositors did £145 million-worth of business in seven million transactions at the 71 branches of the Municipal Bank. Water supply is a clear case of a municipal trading service. The corporation once sold electricity and gas but these are now supplied by state-owned regional corporations, and passenger transport has just passed into the ownership of another such non-elected body.[1]

[1] In the West Midlands and several other conurbations, a Passenger Transport Authority (P.T.A.) has been established. The majority of P.T.A. members are appointed by the local authorities in the conurbation (including Birmingham); a minority are government appointees. The P.T.A. is responsible for the broad lines of public transport policy in its area, including fares policy. In accordance with law the P.T.A. has appointed an executive which has taken

Crematoria and cemeteries may be thought macabre areas of commerce, but they also are listed under this heading—municipal trading services.

Finally, there are the administrative departments—the town clerk and his staff, the city treasurer's and establishment departments—which service the council and its committees.

STAFF

There is no unified local government service in Great Britain, nor any local government service commission. All personnel are the employees of the several councils and conditions of service are negotiated between organizations of employing authorities and employees' associations or trade unions. The ordinary application of the common law of employment and industrial negotiation to local government is further modified by statute and administrative practice. The offices of medical officer of health and public health inspector, among a few others, for example, must be established and dismissal from them is impossible without ministerial consent.[1]

The common way to promotion lies through application for higher posts with other councils, and Birmingham as the largest of the county boroughs has provided many chief officers and deputy chief officers of departments in other authorities. Such movement creates and maintains a corpus of nation-wide experience and a network of personal acquaintance producing strong *esprit de corps*.

There is a high degree of security for established employees which constitutes not only fair recompense for restricted right to political activity, but an aid to impartiality. Indifferent performance is rarely sufficient on its own to earn dismissal, a fact contributing to the myth of town-hall mediocrity.

The corporation employs 54,660 people, a number which includes teachers, police, firemen and 1,700 nurses. Ten thousand are in the administrative, professional, technical and clerical grades and there are 28,000 manual workers.

As with other councils, most recruits other than labourers are secondary school leavers. Over a thousand apply each year to the establishment department which sifts their applications for forwarding to departments for selection. The principal form of training is practice in the job, but several

over and now runs all municipal bus undertakings in its area. It is also responsible for preparing a passenger transport plan.

[1] This is not invariably true, but in view of the complexity of the law, it may reasonably be assumed so.

departments have their own training officers and in-service training programmes. This is supplemented in some cases by day and block-release[1] study at colleges and institutes of further education, or by evening classes or correspondence courses. Some in the clerical division pass the Clerical Division Examination and go on to work for the Diploma of Municipal Administration, a nationally awarded in-service qualification.

Of all officials only medical officers must by law have had a university training, but an increasing number of others is entering from the universities or after other post-secondary education. Some of these recruits to the corporation's service are required to undergo further training, often on post-graduate courses at universities. For some, such as librarians, entrance to qualified status is governed by a professional body rather than the corporation's own requirements. The trend is for town planners and engineers to do a five-year 'sandwich' training,[2] of which the fourth year is spent in practical work with the public works department. Planning, at one time largely the preserve of architects and engineers, has in recent years increasingly recruited sociologists, geographers and economists, and a dearth of recruits to the profession has been replaced by a glut. Each department engages its own graduate administrators and arranges their further training in schemes approved by the establishment committee.

It will have been noted that the council does not have a central recruiting and training organization. The establishment committee and department are responsible to the council for negotiating the size, structure and conditions of employment of all departmental staffs and has some other co-ordinating and advisory functions, but recruitment and personnel management are largely decentralized.

Because of the antiquity of the office and the precedence he enjoys on ceremonial occasions the town clerk is popularly believed to be at the pinnacle of a single hierarchy of staff. This he is not; he is head of his own department, a chief officer like the treasurer or city engineer and, like them, he is in separate contractual relationship with the corporation as a department head. In practice the general public appraisal of his pre-eminence is reinforced by administrative arrangements. Co-operation and co-ordination between the several departments in Birmingham is impressive and largely results from a fortnightly meeting of chief officers and much informal contact between them, but the primary co-ordinating task in the submission of business to

[1] Day-release means one or more days each week, block-release is for a longer period of continuous study.
[2] 'Sandwich' courses are made up of alternating periods of full-time class work and practical experience.

council and, less directly, in ensuring that its decisions are implemented, is the clerk's. He conducts correspondence with ministries about policy, or in matters and projects involving more than one department. Like 84 per cent of clerks to councils the Town Clerk of Birmingham is a lawyer, as are his deputy and assistant town clerks.[1] There are another dozen lawyers in administration on the corporation staff in addition to those engaged in law enforcement. The preponderance of lawyers in clerkships is explained by local government having its origins in regulation and the administration of justice.

A reform recommended by both the Maud and Mallaby Committees[2] is provision in local government law for delegation of power and function to officers. Apart from duties imposed on a few by particular statutes no council employee could legally exercise personal authority until the Town and Country Planning Act, 1968, allowed limited delegation. Though reality may be very different, in legal theory when officers take action they are merely assisting council members to perform the act. This reform is likely to be carried out in furtherance of better management.

FINANCE

In the financial year ending March 31, 1969, the council's gross recurrent expenditure was £114·6 million. Of income raised locally £36 million came from a tax on real estate; £15 million in rents from municipal-owned houses and other property; £25·1 million from sales, fees, licences and other charges and £6·5 million from miscellaneous sources. The remaining £32 million, in the form of central government grants, constituted 28 per cent of gross income, but the true measure of local financial dependence on the centre was 35 per cent; trading receipts should be ignored for they are in rough balance with expenditure. The largest element in the Rate Support Grant, the principal source of grant aid, is calculated on factors related to size, age composition and density of population. Grants specific to particular services still form a quarter of central subvention of revenue but, if that made to the housing revenue account is regarded more as aid in servicing the cost of capital development rather than subvention of recurrent expenditure, the contribution of 50 per cent towards approved police costs is the only substantial example.

The recurrent gross cost to the city of its principal services in 1968/9—if,

[1] Nearly half of clerks to councils in Britain received their professional legal training as pupils of local government officers.
[2] See select bibliography.

for the moment, housing revenue account and some of the principal trading activities are excluded—was as follows:

	£ thousands
Administration of justice	488
Airport	511
Allotments and smallholdings	123
Baths	679
Cemeteries and crematoria	270
Central departments (unallocated)	149
Comprehensive redevelopment areas	1,094
Children	2,011
Civil defence	58
Dwelling-house improvement scheme	49
Education	40,888
Fire service	1,458
Flood prevention	168
Green belt	11
Health, local health services	3,209
Health—Other services	897
Highways and bridges	3,355
Highways—Inner ring road	1,372
Housing, certain services	460
Housing—Rate Fund contribution	1,426
Land drainage, river boards	233
Libraries	806
Markets	383
Motor taxation, expenses	126
Municipal buildings and general properties	207
Museum and art gallery	362
Parks and recreation grounds	1,644
Planning	530
Police	6,671
Probation service for offenders	184
Public lavatories	140
Public lighting	681
Refuse collection and disposal	2,949
Registration of births, deaths and marriages	91
Representation of the people (elections)	100
Sewers and sewage disposal	2,060
Weights and measures	41
Welfare services for aged, infirm and handicapped persons	2,009
Miscellaneous services	1,691
	79,584

With grants and the corporation's own miscellaneous income subtracted, the council had to find another £36·1 million to meet costs. This was mainly raised through rating. The main local tax in Great Britain is levied on the value of real estate. Introduced in 1531 for land drainage and made general in 1601 to provide funds for relieving the poor, the system involves a tax at a certain rate for each pound sterling of the estimated rent which the assessed property might command in the open market. The present rateable value of the 400,000 assessed properties in Birmingham is approximately £53 million. 36 per cent of rate income is paid by domestic ratepayers, the rest mainly by commerce and industry. A little comes from public utility corporations like the railways and by way of a Treasury payment-in-lieu of rates on central government properties. In 1969/70 the rate was 79p in the pound.[1]

Critics of the system claim that at best the assessed values are only a rough approximation and that as a tax its regressive character, ignoring as it does capacity to pay, bears hard on the less wealthy. There is limited provision for relief for the poorest ratepayers. The system is not without solid virtues, however, not the least being that it is a source of income reserved to local government and giving a measure of financial independence, for which it provides a stable base for taxation. Because the better-off tend to live in more highly assessed dwellings the rates bear some relation to resources and possibly as much as income tax to benefit enjoyed. It is a cheap tax to collect; in 1968/9 collecting the rate in Birmingham cost 0·76 per cent of the yield whereas the national income tax, despite the fact that much of the cost fell on employers, still cost the Exchequer 1·33 per cent.

In addition to the services listed in the table of expenditure above the corporation in 1968/9 spent £21 million in maintaining existing and providing new municipal housing; it ran its restaurants and omnibus service at a profit, and supplied water to the city and another 115 square miles at a loss of £214,000 which was met from accumulated reserves.

Capital expenditure

In 1968/9 £50·3 million was spent on capital works. The average rate of increase in recent years in local government spending, reflecting public demand for expanded and improved services, has been double the growth of the gross national product. A high rate of interest and a government curb on expansion on the revenue account—from which repayments and interest

---

[1] A Treasury relief element only for domestic ratepayers reduced the rate to 72½p in the pound on dwelling houses.

come—have proved an effective brake on local authority capital development.

Only £1·3 million worth of capital investment in the year was financed from revenue, the rest being met from the £47·4 million raised mainly by mortgages and the issue of local bonds and stock. Total indebtedness stands at £388 million, of which 60 per cent was incurred in providing municipal housing.

The budget

The timetables followed in preparing the revenue and capital sections of the council's budget are different, but both involve the three main stages of preparatory work by officials and consideration by committees and the council.

Five-year rolling programmes are maintained for capital investment. Preparatory work by senior officers of the departments begins in June for a meeting of the priorities (expenditure) committee in November. This committee, meeting infrequently and consisting of a limited number of members representing both main parties and reflecting their respective strengths was set up to make recommendations to the city council on the maximum capital investment in each year and the schemes which should be approved within that total. While recommendations are made on individual schemes where appropriate, it is the normal practice to recommend overall allocations within which spending committees decide their own priorities. In December each year the committee reports to the council.

The result of the committee's work on the capital budget proved sufficiently encouraging for it to be extended to a review of recurrent expenditure. This is an area less susceptible to planning and necessarily less sensitive to changes in prices, for retrenchment of existing services is difficult on several scores, not least the political. In February each year the committee considers trends in expenditure on existing services and the demand for expansion and improvement in the light of the resources likely to be available on revenue account. It fixes a limit of expenditure for each spending committee which then proceeds to prepare detailed estimates within this overall figure, these detailed estimates for all the rate fund services being submitted by the finance committee to the city council for approval at the April meeting. Before then much calculation and negotiating has gone on. Between September and December, departments prepare 'forecasts' of revenue and expenditure. Preliminary figures of government grants are known early in January and on the basis of all this information there follow unofficial consultations among committee chairmen and leading members of the majority party from which an agreed policy emerges.

Audit

Three systems of audit operate. As a borough Birmingham exercises the right to have certain of its accounts examined by private professional auditors. Citizens have no right of appearance and challenge before these and the latter have no power of surcharge. Other accounts must be audited by a central government official known as the district auditor. Members of the public have a right of appearance and challenge before him and he can surcharge those councillors who did not actively dissociate themselves at the time from a decision to incur expenditure not covered by the council's legal powers. In some cases officers may also be surcharged. Complementary to both forms of audit is an internal audit operated continuously by a section of the city treasurer's own staff. So effective is the overall system that there has only been one case involving a defalcation by an official which has resulted in a surcharge being made by the district auditor since the Second World War.

RELATIONS WITH CENTRAL GOVERNMENT

Access to records not available to the public would be needed to discover whether there are exceptional factors influencing the relations of the corporation and the several ministries, and by what permutations of local policy and personalities these have been worked out. Evidence from local and central government officials suggesting that relations are generally amicable and well managed, is not necessarily disinterested, but it is supported by absence so far of dramatic confrontation between the two, though the comprehensive school issue almost provoked one. To discuss the council's relations with the centre to date is, therefore, to describe the general experience of councils.

There is no general inspection of local government. There is a regional representative of assistant secretary rank in Birmingham of the Department of the Environment, but his functions are purely administrative and largely concerned with the development of municipal housing, loan sanction applications and town planning schemes. Three ministries have powers of inspection of specific services.[1] The Home Office inspects police and fire services;

[1] Inspectors of fire brigades, constabulary and schools are direct appointees of the Crown and not of ministers. This could be an important distinction to draw in some circumstances, but in present-day practice they, like the other two sorts of inspector mentioned, virtually report to a minister.

the Department of Education and Science receives reports from H.M. Inspectors of Schools, and the Department of Health and Social Security inspects some welfare services and the work of the children's department. The inspector most heard of by the public is not, in the usual sense, an inspector at all. When development proposals—however limited—under town planning schemes are duly challenged by aggrieved persons the government appoints an officer confusingly called an 'inspector' to hold a public inquiry. In a city the size of Birmingham there is usually at least one such inquiry in progress.

The district auditor is, of course, an inspector whose field of inquiry is peculiarly susceptible to clearcut conclusions of error and shortcoming. It is symptomatic, however, of the changing nature of the local and central relationship, that checking accounts is now a less important part of his work than advising councils on management problems. Recently, for example, he pointed out that the Birmingham Corporation's policy of putting cheaper doors in schools was uneconomical because the breakage rate was high.

If inspection has decreased and changed its nature, and the doctrine of *ultra vires* is interpreted in a more liberal way, the extent and apparatus of central control is still formidable. More than half of the annual recurrent expenditure goes on education, a service subject to professional inspection and the audit of its accounts by the district auditor. 42 per cent of Birmingham householders are tenants in corporation houses and the cost of providing and maintaining their dwellings and the rents they pay as well as government subsidies of new houses appear in accounts which have to be kept separately from the general accounts, and which are subject to central audit.

With the shift in policy from subvention of specific services to the making of block grants, control of recurrent expenditure is exercised mainly by limiting the size of the global sum and is therefore negative in form. Local authorities do not submit their budgets for central approval and provided expenditure is not *ulta vires* the block grant and their own revenue may be spent as councils think fit. Recently, however, national economic factors have enforced economies, and these have been made mostly in education, recreational and cultural amenities. In terms of the real value of money capitation grants for education have declined and such routine maintenance as painting school buildings is undertaken at longer intervals. Road maintenance is suffering and the programme of conversion to dustless garbage collection has had to be slowed down. So has the recruitment of police, and the expansion of the children's department to implement a policy of prevention aimed at keeping problem children out of residential care.

In the field of capital development, central control is at once more positive and potent, forcing local government policy and performance to conform to central social policy and estimates of economic need. Loan sanction is the main device used. Local authorities require ministerial approval in most cases before they borrow money, and here again present restrictions bear most hard in such matters as parks and swimming baths. £400,000 is presently needed by the council for extension of these amenities, but loan sanction extends only to £250,000. The welfare department is another sufferer and experiences in addition conflict between central policies. The Department of Health and Social Security wants large institutions replaced by small residential homes but national economic policy, as mediated by the Department of the Environment, limits approval of council borrowing. The former annual programme of three new sixty-bed homes for the elderly has been cut back and in the next two years only one a year will be built.

The relative merits of conflicting social policies are not our present concern, but the national debate over those respectively of comprehensive and selective secondary education may be paralleled by conflicting legal interpretations when the Department of Education and Science sought to force the former on an authority favouring the latter. The Education Act, 1944, required local education authorities[1] to provide secondary education for all over eleven years of age, but specified no type, form or arrangement. This means that the minister cannot direct a council to introduce or develop a particular kind, and is forced to use powers intended for other purposes if he wishes to prevent development of a form he does not favour. Refusal to approve school building plans is such a method. The omission in the law has not to date been remedied, probably because with present limited resources of all kinds, including teaching capacity, a total programme of comprehensive secondary schools could not be achieved. Department of Education and Science Circular No. 10/1965 couched in a range of tones from plea to virtual order, and not entirely devoid of a note of silken threat, urged local education authorities to make what progress they could in response to a resolution of the House of Commons approving a policy of comprehensive education.[2] The Conservative majority party in the council considered that the corporation had gone some way towards meeting the parliamentary resolution, but wished to retain some present grammar schools,[3] while the former Labour central government held that creaming off academically more advanced pupils to stock grammar schools is harmful to co-existing compre-

[1] Counties and county boroughs. There is provision for some other local authorities to assume the duties.
[2] July 12, 1965.
[3] High school, *lycée* or *gymnasium*.

hensive schools. The corporation asked an eminent lawyer whether the minister had exceeded his powers in refusing to approve a school building programme designed for other than comprehensive schools. Counsel's view was that he was within his powers in respect of new construction, but *ultra vires* in refusing approval for extensions to old schools. The council were prepared to consider asking the High Court to declare whether the minister was acting legally or not, but a change of government and withdrawal of the circular removed the immediate need for such action.

In local as in national politics there is a certain amount of ritual sound and fury and marching and counter-marching in the manoeuvres of pressure group politics. Speeches are made for public consumption and ministers receive deputations of members and officers presenting a case. Sometimes it works by clearing up an important point or creating an impression of greater urgency than letters convey. It is as much the proper task of council members to press local claims and for their officers to support them in doing so, as it is for ministers and their officials to see local claims in the national perspective. Though politicians of all political complexions usually understand one another well enough, at officer level there is considerable understanding of the total problem. Though city officials may complain of inconsistencies in national policies and fret at delays imposed on schemes they are anxious to develop, they are aware of the problem of establishing priorities, and balancing the needs of competing areas.

TOWN PLANNING

Birmingham has been a pioneer in town planning. In 1878 it was the first local authority to apply the provisions of the Artisans and Labourers Dwellings Act, 1875, when slum property was acquired in the congested centre to make way for planned redevelopment. The Quinton, Harborne and Edgbaston town planning scheme, covering newer development and extensions in the south-west of the city in 1913, was the first in the country to be approved under the Town Planning Act, 1909. This permissive measure was the first general act to make planning a local government function. There followed a succession of plans for several areas, and in 1943 the council determined on rebuilding more than twelve thousand acres[1] of property in the centre, almost a quarter of the area of the county borough.

The Town and Country Planning Act, 1947, was intended to seize the opportunities provided by wartime damage and dispersal of population and industry, but it also marked the revolution of rising expectations of a

[1] 4,848 hectares.

redeveloping country. The development plan submitted to the Minister of Housing and Local Government in 1952, was finally approved in December 1960, after the holding in 1954 of a public inquiry lasting four weeks and amendment to meet some of the 447 formal objections and taking further account of national considerations. It incorporated the nine area schemes already operating and provided for all classes of land use for the forthcoming 20 years, including a network of major roads to ease traffic flow and link the city with the new national motorways.

Although the master plan for the whole city was prepared in accordance with the 1947 Act, the major central redevelopment is based on the Town and Country Planning Act passed in 1944 and intended especially for bombed areas, but including also 'areas of bad layout and obsolete development'. Under its terms there were compulsorily acquired 981 acres[1] in which stood about 30,000 houses, nearly 4,000 shops, more than 2,000 factories, workshops and offices and 335 other buildings such as churches, cinemas and taverns. Most of the property had been built before 1914, and much of it was in poor condition.[2] The shortage of houses was too great to permit immediate demolition, and enough repairs and reconditioning were done to make them weatherproof for the further life term expected of them.

At the hub of the area being redeveloped, and on land already in Corporation possession, there is the seven-acre[3] Bull Ring shopping precinct. Markets and a twice-yearly fair have for centuries been held on the site next to the parish church of St. Martin's, and when the holders of market stalls packed up for the night preachers of theological and secular gospels moved in to provide another part of civic life. They do so still. A complex of shops on four floors together with covered and open markets and gardens is completely segregated from the traffic on the new inner ring road which passes through it. An omnibus station under the Bull Ring avoids the need for out-of-town shoppers to cross traffic and a network of walks and underpasses enables pedestrians to reach the shops without crossing roads.

Beyond the immediate centre lie five comprehensive redevelopment areas which contained nearly 25,000 unfit dwellings. Clearance and rebuilding were planned in 20 stages, each to take about a year but the speeding up of slum clearance as a matter of national policy may result in the foreshortening of the period by a year or two. The land lying in the inner of the two residential zones provided for in the city's approved plan, is to have an

[1] 396 hectares.
[2] 55,000 slum houses existed at the end of the war. 21 per cent of the total number of houses in Birmingham in 1948 were condemnable under the Housing Acts.
[3] 3 hectares.

occupation of 90 to 144 rooms to the acre. This lower density and the provision of new open spaces and community facilities means that only 56 per cent of former dwelling space is available and 46,000 people have had to be rehoused elsewhere. The area allocated to industry is almost the same, but schools have been given four times as much land as was previously used for education. Public open space has been increased tenfold and covers 15 per cent of the redeveloped area.

The corporation is under no legal duty to rehouse those displaced by re-development but has accepted the moral obligation to do so for most. There is even less obligation to accommodate disturbed industry, but the council has made some provision for the 1,526 firms which have had to move. Of particular interest are two 'flatted' factories, multi-storeyed blocks of self-contained units with internal loading facilities which only displaced firms may occupy. A disadvantage is that rents are much higher than in the old property.

A central district receiving special treatment is the jewellery quarter. A dilapidated area of 243 acres[1] housing, among others, some 900 firms in the jewellery and ancillary trades, it is the nearest thing in the city to a medieval craft quarter, though this dates back no further than the eighteenth century. A quarter of the businesses are one-man concerns and few employ more than ten. One-fifth of all industrial premises in the county borough are to be found here, but they comprise only 6 per cent of the city's industrial floor space. Meeting the cost of replacing an area of decaying nineteenth-century houses with modern structures capable of housing heavier machinery and disposing safely of acid and other effluents was beyond small firms producing mainly for the cheaper and medium-priced markets. Lack of capital was not the only problem; there is a high degree of interdependency through specialization of process. In redevelopment close proximity was essential and it has been provided in the layout developed since the British Jeweller's Association first approached the city council in 1945. An eight-storey flatted factory is being built on a ten-acre[2] site to accommodate some of those displaced.

Completion of these schemes will not finally have cleared the inner area of obsolescence. According to an estimate made in 1966 there were still 140,000 pre-1914 houses standing. It will be another 15 to 20 years before the present slums are all cleared, but the occupants cannot be expected to go on living with the present low level of amenity, especially when neighbours and friends move to better neighbourhoods. The council's answer to the problem is a bridging period of conservation, when houses represented as

[1] 98 hectares. [2] 4 hectares.

unfit by the medical officer of health[1] are compulsorily acquired and renovated. Additional community facilities are provided. By March 1969 the
council had spent £14 million on such make-do and mend.

The corporation is not only the planning authority responsible for the
physical and, in some measure, the social environments in which the citizens
live; for four out of ten households it is the landlord with a rent roll of £18
million a year. Between the world wars, nearly 52,000 dwelling houses were
built by the corporation for letting and another 72,000 have been put up
since. A third of these dwellings are in blocks of flats, almost all of which are
of post-second world war construction and a reflection of the need to
provide open space in a town chafed by the tight seams of its boundaries.
As a solution it is not very popular, as many prefer to wait six years for an
ordinary house rather than spend only half that time on the housing list
waiting for a flat.

OVERSPILL

That Birmingham's net population decreased by 0·6 per cent between
1951 and 1961 and is expected to contract a little more yet, while the number
of jobs increased by 6 per cent in the same decade and is predicted to rise by
another 73,000 by 1981,[2] suggests that the solution of the city's population and
land-use problems is not a matter for it alone. This has long been recognized,
but the using up of the remaining available building land within its boundaries
and the spur given to 'green-belt' thinking by government circulars in 1955
and 1957[3] have precipitated a crisis in planning, the results of which may pro-
foundly influence land-use policy in the country as a whole. Over all is cast
the shadow of uncertainty as local and central government engage in pro-
tracted debate following the publication of a Royal Commission's proposals
for local government reform.

For two-thirds of its length the City of Birmingham boundary marches
with those of urban neighbours, each with its own development problems.
Some of the Black Country county boroughs need to export population,
while the mainly residential Solihull county borough in the south-east and
municipal borough of Sutton Coldfield[4] in the north-east are rapidly filling

[1] The Housing Act 1957 places a duty on a medical officer of health to make official report to
his employing council if he considers a house unfit for habitation.
[2] *Birmingham Overspill Study*, 1967, p. 17. See Select Bibliography.
[3] Ministry of Housing and Local Government Nos. 42/1955 and 50/1957.
[4] A county borough is the sole local government in its area. A municipal borough though a
separate legal entity shares in the provision of services with the administrative county of which
it is part.

with private commuting migrants from Birmingham in search of a more fashionable environment. To the east and south lie rural parts which in some sectors have grown dangerously thin under the inter-war years thrust of unplanned urban sprawl and the urgency of some planning in the 1960s. Bearing down upon efforts to solve the problems of these several local authorities are national economic and social policies. Like glaciers of varying pressure and rates of movement these give a general direction, but produce buckles of inconsistency and a moraine of piecemeal attempts at adjustment.

Despite the number of studies made since 1945 by official and private agencies the size of the problem is unknown. Estimates of sites needed outside the conurbation for housing its overspill vary from 100,000 to 180,000. One relating to Birmingham alone puts urgent need at 15,000 houses between 1971 and 1975. Decisions crucial to planning may have to be taken on it before its accuracy has been verified.

Formal co-operation in planning started in 1956 when the city and the counties of Staffordshire, Warwickshire and Worcestershire appointed council members to a joint committee on Birmingham overspill. In 1967 expansion of membership occurred at the instigation of Worcestershire, a county particularly vulnerable to Birmingham expansion, and now includes representatives of the five shires in the region and its eleven county boroughs.

INDUSTRIAL RELOCATION[1]

When approving the city of Birmingham development plan the Minister of Housing and Local Government reduced from 24 to 18 per cent the proposed increase in area for industry. The additional acreage was needed for improvements to existing factories to accommodate new machines and processes and provide better working conditions, and not to attract new industry, and the council has been most successful in keeping new developers away. In the ten years since 1956 only three applications from newcomers were approved for new projects and two of these were special factories for the handicapped.

Although in the last year or two the corporation's zeal for exporting industry and population to other areas may have abated somewhat the evidence points to general sustained effort for some years to conform to the national policy of reducing urban congestion. In 1957 this was considered to involve moving from Birmingham 180,000 people and 32,000 jobs for them

---

[1] See: *Industrial Location Working Paper No. 19* by B. Smith, Centre for Urban and Regional Studies, University of Birmingham, for a most detailed examination of this problem.

H

to do elsewhere.[1] As the corporation's housing manager had remarked some months earlier:

if industry does not follow the movement of the population then the City will have to review the position. If it stays it will continue to attract new people and nothing will have been solved.[2]

The four member authorities of the joint committee each set up an industrial bureau to provide inquirers with information about sites and facilities, and Birmingham Corporation's industrial selection scheme registered employers needing labour in a reception area and workers seeking jobs and prepared to move if suitable work could be found for them. At any one time, the number of persons prepared to move has hovered between 6,000 and 7,000. Many of these are fired less by pioneering spirit than by the need for a house and would prefer it to be in present familiar surroundings. A significant minority of those who go come back, some because social adjustment in new, less urbanized surroundings proves too difficult, and others because failure to find work in the new area means the erosion of pocket or health through commuting.

Promotion of overspill areas needs the reinforcement of adequate control of vacated property in Birmingham. Though lacking sufficient powers to do this, councils of both Conservative and Labour complexion have had some success in acquiring vacated industrial property in the open market. Such buying-in has helped, but is inadequate both because strategic sites may be missed and planning permission is not required where use is not changed. Yet a further loophole to effective control is the availability of redundant railway and canal sites which require no industrial development certificate.

There is overall evidence of modest success between 1956 and 1966[3] in moving people and employment to reception areas in the three counties and elsewhere, but since 1962 the pace—never brisk—has declined. Part of the explanation may be found in local inertias, but these have been fostered and in some cases sired by the application of overriding national policies.

When the technical officers' committee was set up to advise the joint committee on Birmingham overspill there were fields solely within the competence of local planning authorities in which it could advise the corporation through its parent committee. In performing its main task, however, it lacked essential freedom. Instructed 'in as close liaison as possible with the Board of Trade' to keep under constant review all matters and measures concerned with moving industry and workers from the city, the function was

[1] *The Times*, October 15, 1957.   [2] *Birmingham Post*, December 10, 1956.
[3] The period for which figures are available.

solely advisory. Failure, however, has not stemmed from this, for the four constituent councils—and now 17—are executive planning authorities. The operation of the doctrine of *ultra vires* has ensured the subjection of these bodies and their work to the Board of Trade[1] which only had—and, indeed, for its own purposes did not even need—observer status on the committee. The brute fact is that whatever the local government authorities considered best for planning in the West Midland region has had to be firmly subordinated to the central government policy of diverting development to designated development areas, where in general industry is in decline and unemployment above the national average.

The principal lever used by central government in effecting its policy is the Industrial Development Certificate. This is required for all development where there is to be change of use, or for total extensions to existing premises of more than 3,000 square feet.[2] Except where there are road or comprehensive redevelopment schemes the advice of the technical officers' committee and decisions of the planning authorities[3] are subordinated to the board's decisions about issue of certificates. In 1960 it refused approval to three Birmingham firms wishing to develop in Staffordshire and, according to the chairman of Daventry development committee, five firms were refused permission to set up in the Northamptonshire town where Birmingham Corporation is building factories and houses for its overspill.[4] 207 of those houses stood empty awaiting occupants who could not come because there was no work,[5] and in Telford, a new town in Shropshire, 300 houses were empty for the same reason.

Though all this was frustrating and inhibited sound planning it had the merit of austere consistency. The grant by the board in 1960 of an industrial development certificate to a major developer was an action of a different sort. In exchange for agreement to put three-quarters of its planned development in Scotland, South Wales and Merseyside, the British Motor Corporation was allowed to extend its Austin works by ten acres[6] and 1,600 jobs. The latter

[1] The equivalent of the Ministry of Commerce in other countries. It is now a part of the Department of Trade and Industry.
[2] 280 square metres. In 1956 it was 5,000 square feet, and in 1965 only 1,000.
[3] In law the city council, but in most matters *de facto* its public works committee through delegation.
[4] Statement made at a meeting of Birmingham City Council, October 1, 1968.
[5] *Birmingham Post*, April 16, 1969. In Daventry the position has improved, partly because large companies have provided employment in warehousing, a type of development exempt from industrial development certificates, and in part because the planners have learned to discount the inflated estimates of housing needs provided by incoming firms. The annual housebuilding rate had been reduced from 800 to 350 by 1971.
[6] 4 hectares.

figure was greater than the total involved in all applications for certificates in Birmingham in most years and virtually wiped out the gains made to date by the technical officers' committee and the board itself. The council was not only frustrated in its efforts to comply with national policy, but was made doubly its victim.

THE MACHINERY OF OVERSPILL

Three Acts of Parliament provide the main machinery, the Housing Subsidies Act, 1967; the New Towns Act, 1965; and the Town Development Act, 1952 but only the latter two play much part in attempts to deal with Birmingham overspill. The 'new' towns of Telford and Redditch were designated under the New Towns Act, 1965.[1] Such new towns usually have an existing urban settlement as a nucleus around which the development corporation established by the government plans and initiates the new development. Existing local authorities within the designated area retain their statutory responsibilities for providing services, but as much of the development corporation's work is financed by central government the burden falling on local government is lightened.

In the 1950s Birmingham City Council pressed the government to designate new towns in the region, but met with no success. The corporation declined to undertake such a project at its own expense, justly maintaining that new towns were part of national policy to deal with a national problem and that the citizens of a single local authority should not be called on to meet such heavy cost alone.

In 1963 Telford, 30 miles west of Birmingham, was designated[2] in an area which includes three Shropshire urban districts with a total population of 54,000. The new town is planned to house more than four times that number. Redditch, a few miles south of Birmingham and traditional centre of small-scale iron and steel industries such as making needles, locks and fish-hooks, was designated a new town a year later and its population is to be expanded from 37,000 to 70,000.

The Town Development Act, 1952, more directly involves areas wishing to export population by agreement between them and the receiving councils. Of the 112 local authorities which have negotiated with Birmingham, 38 have signed such agreements. Not all have borne fruit as some have depended on the arrival of industry touching off a housing programme, while others

[1] This codifies earlier legislation.
[2] Originally as Dawley New Town; the area was considerably extended and the name changed in 1968.

are with authorities in areas too remote to attract firms or workers from Birmingham. Unless government policy concerning the location of industry changes even the more promising of such agreements are likely to remain dormant.

It is usual for the receiving council to build the necessary accommodation, as is happening under the agreement with the Worcestershire borough of Droitwich. Under this Birmingham Corporation will nominate to tenancies of the 2,000 new houses, the building of which they have subsidized, workers who accompany industry which is moving there from the city. With the borough of Daventry there is a different kind of agreement. In the town's growth from 7,000 to 36,000 by 1981, Northamptonshire County Council will provide new schools and other services for which it is responsible in the county, while the borough puts in roads, water and sewerage. Birmingham Corporation, which provides the chairman of the tripartite development committee, is building houses for sale at cost on completion to the Daventry Borough Council. In addition Birmingham matches an annual central government grant of £12 a house for ten years under the provisions of the third statute, the Housing Subsidies Act, 1967, which authorizes the central government to provide financial assistance for overspill housing.

THE MOVING FRONTIER

The term 'overspill' is not the most felicitous for describing the planned, ordered and imaginative redistribution of population and industry envisaged by those Acts. It is more appropriate to the unco-ordinated and usually un-inspired urban encroachment which, starting in the late eighteenth century and accelerating dramatically between the world wars, has disfigured so much of Britain. While planning and co-ordination are no longer absent the temptation towards sprawl is there and in the case of Birmingham is power-fully reinforced by frustration of the grand strategy. During the 1950s Birmingham's housing need backed up behind the dam of Ministry of Housing and Local Government indecision about new towns in the region and Board of Trade inhibition of development under the Town Development Act. In 1964 it spilled over.

The process, still in progress, proves disquieting to many without, and some within, the city council.

When the West Midlands Group considered in 1945 the future of development in the area, its report[1] employed the term 'green setting' for the rural

---

[1] '*Conurbation*', The Architectural Press, 1948. This non-official body included academics, industrialists and persons in local government.

surroundings which the members hoped to see preserved for every town. They preferred not to look upon it as a constricting belt, but as an area developed by its own industries of agriculture and forestry and, incidentally, forming a nearby agreeable setting for urban leisure. They were clear, however, that the objective was unattainable unless a clear line was maintained and expansion of the conurbation's population leap-frogged the green setting to self-contained communities beyond. The idea of a rural *cordon sanitaire* as a ward against continued urban expansion has informed post-war planning thought until recently.

The need for restricted boundaries and a green belt had been recognized by the city council in evidence given in 1938 before the Royal Commission on the Distribution of the Industrial Population,[1] and in proposals submitted in the city development plan in 1952. More telling recognition found expression in the acquisition shortly before the second world war of several large estates to the south of the city for preservation as open spaces. The issue in 1955 and 1957 of circulars by the Ministry of Housing and Local Government[2] led to the three neighbouring counties and the city submitting green-belt proposals which, though not yet approved, provide a guide when individual planning applications are dealt with. The commitment to principle of the city council is tempered with a wish for some flexibility to be retained in the proposals, and in this it has not been discouraged by the ministerial conclusion of January 1963 that it would be premature to give a final decision to Worcestershire's green-belt proposals 'until the full implication of the overspill situation had been explored'.[3] To argue, as city council witnesses have occasionally done at planning inquiries, that there can be no breach of the green belt since it has no legal existence is to indulge in casuistry at the sacrifice of a reputation for integrity of purpose.

There are only about 18 miles of 'open' frontier over which the city could spill and the assault in search of *lebensraum* has been mounted in several sectors. In 1964 it was successful in the east when the minister agreed to 16,000 houses being built at Chelmsley Wood in Warwickshire.

In the south and south-west successful resistance against the encroaching city has been maintained for ten years, sometimes with ministerial support and sometimes with his weight thrown on the other side. In 1959 the city council sought planning permission for housing and industry in 4 square miles of parts of Worcestershire and Warwickshire just beyond its southern boundary. It was claimed that this increase of 5 per cent in the area of the county borough would meet its housing needs for 20 years. After a public

[1] Known as the Barlow Commission after its chairman, Sir Montague Barlow.
[2] Nos. 42/1955 and 50/1957.   [3] *Birmingham Overspill Study*, 1967, p. 48.

inquiry the Minister refused consent.[1] In doing so he recognized the city's problem and agreed that a breach of the green belt might yet be unavoidable. A year later it was he who suggested excision of 600 acres[2] in the same area for Birmingham development, but after an inquiry in October 1961, he decided against all but a negligible part of his own proposal. The next move came from the city council when it asked in 1963 for planning permission on 420 acres and was again frustrated. Though the minister then pointed to the possible damage to Redditch New Town of urban extension towards it, by December 1966 he believed that acceleration in local authority housing programmes at lower densities had made the shortage of building sites so acute that Birmingham could not look for timely relief to planned development at Telford and Redditch. 15,000 more houses were essential between 1971 and 1975. Only to the south-west of Birmingham could the land be found in time.[3] With great reluctance the Worcestershire County Council, with the agreement of the minister and two other local authorities in the county closely concerned, approved proposals in July 1968 which would put 11,000 more houses on 1,700 acres[4] of the green belt, and further compromise the role of Redditch as a new town by adding 4,000 commuter homes to its population.

Of the 1,700 acres some 600[5] are subject to a covenant made in 1937 between the corporation and Cadburys, the well-known cocoa manufacturers, when the latter materially assisted the city to acquire 700 acres as public lands which:

shall not or shall any part thereof at any time hereafter be developed for housing or building purposes.[6]

The company, accepting that problems can change in scope and scale, and realizing that the Lands Tribunal could vary the terms of the covenant if persuaded by an application from the corporation, is seeking a constructive solution. It has proposed compensatory provision elsewhere which, linked to the city's present holdings could form a country park which would attract a government grant under the Countryside Act, 1968, and the minister has ordered a fresh inquiry into the city's planning application.

Though government, however justified it may be by over-riding national considerations, must bear the major blame for Birmingham's failure fully to implement its part in the national policy of urban and industrial dispersal, public and private interests in the city cannot be entirely acquitted. The

[1] Inquiry July 1959. Minister's decision given April 5, 1960.   [2] 242 hectares.
[3] Minister of Housing and Local Government to Chairman, Worcestershire County Council, December 5, 1966. Reproduced in *Birmingham Overspill Study*, 1967.
[4] 687 hectares.   [5] 242 hectares.   [6] Covenant dated September 17, 1937.

effect of national policy is reinforced by local factors. Trade unions note that work may be hard to find in reception areas, and key workers in an industry are often those to whom home-ownership and satisfactory schools for their children are good reasons for staying put. They may not qualify for one of the local authority houses subsidized by their own council. For many families work for wives is important especially where—as at Chelmsley Wood—rents are two or three times higher than in the old terraced streets and when husbands may for the first time face the costs of commuting to work in Birmingham. Firms on the move can more easily leave their un-skilled than their key workers behind, and much industry in the city is part of a web of interdependent processes carried out by many different firms. The considerable traffic of transporter lorries conveying cars in many stages of assembly between works in Birmingham and branch factories elsewhere shows that dispersal may create new problems as well as solve old.

The trade unions mainly support the Labour Party and the interests of industry and commerce are well represented by the Conservatives, the two parties which have alternated in power since 1945. How much of present resources a locally elected body should invest in the long-term solution of a national problem is a proper question to be considered by whatever party is in power. Dispersal could mean the export of rateable value, a matter bound to be considered by a council which year by year is forced to put up the rates even to maintain the standard of services in the face of continuing monetary inflation.

Success in breaching the green belt at Chelmsley Wood and the prospect of doing so again may also have had a muting effect locally on the sense of urgency, especially when civic conscience is eased with predictable declara-tions of last territorial demand. Peripheral expansion, by weakening the return on private and public investment in new towns, is inimical to their success and, ultimately, perhaps to the development areas as well. In an effort to permit expansion without indiscriminately sacrificing the rural surroundings of large towns some planners advocate 'linear' development along main routes from conurbations. Building at Wythall would reduce the gap between the city of Birmingham and Redditch New Town to four and a half miles. Could this be the county borough's first essay in implementing a new planning doctrine, or would it be, perhaps, a planned admission of inability to implement the old?

THE FUTURE

Some internal and external structural change will come to the local government of Birmingham, in common with the rest of England, for both main political parties are committed to reform. The former ought to make services—perhaps control, too—more accessible to the citizens; the latter to recognize the problems and possibilities presented by increased mobility. The two are complementary, for the latter may prove more harmful than helpful if the former fails to assimilate the exercise of power to a sense of identity.

A feature much stressed by the advocates of decentralization is the enhancement of citizen participation nurtured by a maintained or recreated sense of community. Birmingham, where the cores of totally urban and industrialized inner suburbs are still referred to as villages, might seem a suitable place for the development of neighbourhood town halls which involve some measure of political devolution as well as decentralization of services. The Kernan Commission, which blamed all the 1967 riots in the United States on grievances against local authorities, advised the setting up of such local administrative centres.[1] In theory most attractive, the plan poses special social problems where large ethnic concentrations might become the basis of such units. Cultural assimilation could be delayed and the apartheid outlook receive encouragement. In Birmingham, though the 8 per cent of the population which came from overseas[2] is mainly to be found in a few areas, the danger of this happening is less acute than in the United States but it could be reinforced by devolution. On the other hand, decentralization without effective devolution may make for greater efficiency in some services, but is unlikely to foster local pride and corporate identity, especially when the increasing volume and range of the mass media are hard put to it to encourage a sub-culture more local than that of a region.

Since the lord mayor complained in 1963 that the city's departments were too large and remote from the citizens some attempt has been made to decentralize services. The city was divided into twelve areas which were intended as much for economy as administrative decentralization. Land values and building costs in the centre were rising rapidly and it was thought cheaper to set up offices elsewhere. No department has yet completely based its work on these areas, but the children's and welfare departments recognize their boundaries and they may yet be the areas for social service bureaux under a reorganization of health and welfare services based on the Seebohm Committee proposals.[3] The public works department has only five districts while the housing department has six, all of which are housed at the centre. The health department has four family advice centres while the education

[1] The National Advisory Commission on Civil Disorders, U.S.A.
[2] This figure does not include the very large Irish minority.
[3] *The Committee on Local Authority and Allied Personal Social Services*, H.M S.O., July 1968.

H*

department organizes its youth employment service through seven offices, but uses several different 'district' organizations for other functions. This all points to the problem of selecting effective functional boundaries; what is most effective for one service may be inconvenient for another. Birmingham Corporation is already a member of seven joint boards or committees providing common physical services in an area wider than the city.

Most public transport routes in Birmingham lead to the centre and a new pattern of routes would be needed to ensure the accessibility intended by decentralization. This could lead to the loss of the incentive and drama of a visit to lodge a complaint at the council offices combined with the pleasures of a shopping expedition. The experience of the citizens' advice bureaux is instructive. Prior to 1939 there were 33 scattered throughout the city, but now there is only a central one to handle 40,000 inquiries each year. Lack of custom in the others brought about their closure and it is claimed that clients feel better served by the concentration of skills and knowledge centralization is believed to achieve.

Because its size and influence are factors compelling recognition Birmingham would not have suffered major change under the majority proposals of the Royal Commission Report.[1] As one of the seven second-tier metropolitan districts in a metropolitan area covering the present conurbation, it would have lost to the major authority important powers covering transport, police and fire services, general housing policy, major planning and water supply, but education, welfare and health as well as other extensive services, including the building and management of housing, would have been retained. In combining with the county borough of Solihull, the municipal borough of Sutton Coldfield and certain rural parts of Warwickshire, the district would have been half as large again in area and a fifth more in population than the present city.

The minority report's proposals would have vested more powers in a city region of which a slightly smaller Birmingham than the present county borough would have been a district.

Not surprisingly, the minority proposals elicited little comment in Birmingham; equally to be expected was the generally favourable opinion accorded the majority report. With diplomacy all three political parties in the council disclaimed a desire to see reluctant neighbouring boroughs forced into a shot-gun wedding with the city, but none protested against rural areas with potential building land being added. On the contrary, official and council comment welcomed the prospect of easing this particular problem. Comments in other communities in the area were understandably hostile,

[1] *Royal Commission on Local Government 1966–9*, Vol. I, H.M.S.O., 1969.

whether from boroughs resenting 'take-over by Big Brother Birmingham'[1] or from representatives of peripheral rural populations afraid of being reduced to the condition of the 'poor whites of Kentucky'[2].

Though proposals for reform over most of England put forward in the Conservative Government's White Paper reject much of the Royal Commission's radical thinking,[3] the metropolitan area concept not only survives but is extended to other conurbations. Proposals for Birmingham as a metropolitan district, except for some difference in boundaries, are the same in both. The intention in the White Paper of including Coventry as a constituent district of the metropolitan area with boundaries extended to join those of Birmingham alarms protagonists of the Green Belt, since this would seriously increase the risk of continuous urban development for some forty miles.

Both sets of Royal Commission proposals proposed a third, superior tier known as the province to deal with regional planning and development strategies, but as membership would be indirect through lower authorities acting as electoral colleges the provinces were unlikely to become a vital element of popular government representing regional loyalty. It might, therefore, be thought fruitless to consider whether there is a West Midlands region which Birmingham is best placed to lead, but in view of the suspicion which the county borough's size and influence create and the fact that, whatever proposals prevail, it may lose some of its present autonomy and be more closely associated with other local authorities, it is worth asking what bases there might be to validate the city's leadership.

A claim rooted in history is none too strong. Early in the nineteenth century Birmingham was the most prominent town outside London, but lost its pre-eminence to Manchester for some decades, until 1857. Between then and 1876 when Joseph Chamberlain resigned his mayoralty to go into Parliament the borough's justifiably high reputation came from application of the civic gospel—good local housekeeping. It was the exemplar of what a town could do for its own citizens rather than for region or the country at large. The degree of social unity remarked by many observers provided radicalism when it moved from the north with Bright with an electorate prepared to change it from a parliamentary 'mass movement' politics into effective pressure group activity in Parliament. Chartism had been a national struggle for the right to vote for a local representative, but political activity

[1] *Birmingham Evening Mail*, June 18, 1969.   [2] *Birmingham Post*, June 14, 1969.
[3] Local Government in England: Government Proposals for Reorganization. Cmnd. 4584. The Royal Commission proposed to retain two tier organization only in three metropolitan areas; the White Paper retains it throughout the country.

in Birmingham after 1865 was local organization for effective sharing in central administration. When provincial pre-eminence returned to Birmingham better communications and the Reform Act of 1867 called for, and made possible, an interest and participation in national rather than provincial affairs. An article by Chamberlain in the *Fortnightly Review* in 1874 almost constituted the manifesto of change. In it he marked the start of his own vigorous mayoralty with a denunciation of the mid-Victorian creed of self-help and placed the onus of leadership in social and economic change on government. Westminster was to be Birmingham Council House writ large. The London and North Western Railway and the ballot box had made provincialism redundant—temporarily at least—and abolished Birmingham's leadership with it.

The presence of several regional offices of central government departments constitute some claim to regional pre-eminence, but telecommunications, location on the same electric railway serving London and the north, as well as equal ease of access to national motorways, make Wolverhampton an equal, and geographically better-placed, regional centre.

There is a certain administrative convenience—or, at least, geographical tidiness—in describing the five shires and eleven county boroughs as a region, but it is difficult to detect a sense of common identity such as York-shiremen or East Anglians seem to have. The history of local planning shows some affinity of interest between Staffordshire and the conurbation, but there is far less between the other counties and the six industrial county boroughs. Even within the conurbation there is a cultural frontier; the Black Country boroughs, whose fortunes were born and rose with those of Birmingham in the Industrial Revolution, stand as a group. Their own mutual fears and suspicions are but family squabbles to be put aside when facing a brash, outsized upstart outsider whose dialect is considered a mere parody of theirs. Still recovering from the reorganization which in 1966 gave them their present form, they expressed in joint evidence to the Royal Commission the 'desire to be left to get on individually and in close co-operation with each other' in consolidating these changes. Their Five West Midlands County Boroughs' Joint Committee has never invited Birmingham to join nor been approached by the city for inclusion. The other councils suspect that, while Birmingham has no wish to dominate, it would be surprised if its leadership were questioned.

In its own evidence to the Royal Commission, the council was at one with its neighbours in resisting structural change. Satisfied that its size made for efficiency without remoteness from the citizens, and well able to play its part in central government's regional plans without an intermediate level of government intervening, all the improvement the Council needed was relaxation of the *ultra vires* rule.

In a report in 1961 the Local Government Commission[1] said: 'Birmingham is, in a legal phrase, *sui generis*'. Its neighbours would be glad to see it continue alone and one suspects that, given easier access to potential building land on its borders, that would also be the option of the council and citizens.

[1] A standing commission now defunct, and not to be confused with the Royal Commission. *Local Government Commission Report No. 1*, H.M.S.O., 1961.

Buenos Aires

CARLOS MOUCHET

CARLOS MOUCHET

Born 1906. Graduate in Law of the University of Buenos Aires. Former Professor of the University of Buenos Aires in the School of Law and in the Department of Economics. Former Member of the Council of Management of the Regulatory Planning Office of the City of Buenos Aires. Former Chief of the Legal Office of the Municipality of Buenos Aires. Director of the Study Group of Buenos Aires in the Metropolitan Problems Seminar, Toronto, Canada, 1967. Adviser to private groups of Planning Consultants.

Author of (Books and Papers): *Las ideas sobre el Municipio en la Argentina* (Doctoral Thesis); *Pasado y Restauración del Régimen Municipal; Tendencias actuales de las instituciones municipales en América; El Municipio y la Constitución; Los aspectos jurídicos del Planeamiento urbano, metropolitano y Regional en los Estados Unidos; Bases y Criterios Legales para el ordenamiento urbano de la ciudad de Buenos Aires y de su area metropolitana; Introducción a los aspectos institucionales y legales del desarrollo económico y social en la Argentina; La legalidad en el Municipio; Planificación urbana y saneamiento; El financiamiento municipal en América Latina; Los derechos de los escritores y artistas; Las competencias gubernamentales y administrativas en las areas metropolitanas; Derecho Hispánico y Common law en Puerto Rico.*

Buenos Aires

BUENOS AIRES has been likened to the enormous head of a giant with feet of clay. Buenos Aires, as a municipality and as a federal district of the Argentine Republic, has around 3,000,000 inhabitants; as a metropolitan area it has a population of 6,800,000 against a figure of 21,000,000 for the whole of the country according to the 1960 census.[1]

Founded for the first time by Pedro de Mendoza in 1536 in the name of the Kings of Spain, the city remained abandoned until its second and final foundation in 1580 by Juan de Garay. Its original lay-out followed the lines laid down by the Laws of the Indies (*Leyes de Indias*) for the founding of cities. In 1880 it had a population of 256,000 out of a total of 2,500,000 for the whole country. Although it was already the most important township of the Republic this relationship of one to ten signified some degree of equilibrium which, a little while later, began to disappear as the rapid and disproportionate development of Buenos Aires took place.

The Argentine federalist crisis is largely the consequence of this imbalance between the various regions of the country arising out of the predominance of Buenos Aires.[2]

The city of Buenos Aires is, at one and the same time, a federal district which is the seat of the national government, and a municipality with power to administer local services. Its federal status dates from 1880. Up to that time it was the capital of the province of Buenos Aires which then found itself obliged to create shortly afterwards a new city, La Plata, for its capital.

The National Constitution of 1853 states in Art. 3 that 'the organs of the Federal Government will reside in the city declared to be the Capital of the Republic by Law of Congress upon the cession, by one or more provincial legislatures, of the territory to be federalized'. The territory of the city of Buenos Aires ceded by the province of that name to the federal government in 1880 was subsequently enlarged by the annexation in 1884 and 1887 of the neighbouring municipalities of Flores and Belgrano.

The city of Buenos Aires has developed on the basis of the original draught-board lay-out of colonial times. It has no natural surroundings of great splendour to add to its attractions like some other cities such as Rio de Janeiro and it has not known how to exploit to the full its privileged position

---

[1] It is estimated that for 1968 the country's population is some 23,000,000.

[2] See: Ricardo Zorraquin Becú: *El Federalismo Argentino*, 2nd edition, La Facultad, Buenos Aires, 1953, pp. 175 ff.

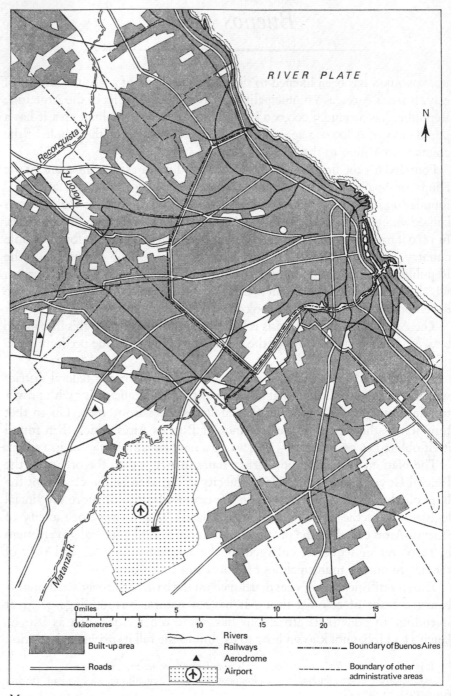

RIVER PLATE

Reconquista R.

Moron R.

Matanza R.

N

0 miles		5		10		15
0 kilometres	5	10	15	20		

Built-up area		Rivers		Boundary of Buenos Aires
Roads		Railways		
	▲	Aerodrome		Boundary of other
	Airport			administrative areas

MAP 5 BUENOS AIRES

on the broadest river in the world. In spite of the pervading monotony of the landscape, Buenos Aires has become a great, lively and attractive city, having fine parks and residential areas, and business and shopping districts showing refinement and good taste. Its high reputation as a cultural centre is well known. By contrast there are the shanty towns known as *villas miserias* within and on the borders of the city, which harbour some 700,000 people and for the eradication of which plans are now being made.

Although the techniques of the science of urban planning are of recent date, Buenos Aires has been fortunate in having had, in the past and from time to time, capable municipal governors—intuitive planners—who carried out important works for beautifying and transforming the city. At the turn of the century the city was, in many ways, an expression of the urbanistic culture of Paris (avenues, parks, large private residences). It had, moreover, the fame, for many years, of being one of the cleanest cities in the world.

The growth and expanding influence of Buenos Aires as the most important city of the Republic has been the result of a combination of physical, historical, economic, cultural and political factors. Its legal capital status dates from Spanish times as the first seat of the government of Buenos Aires and as the headquarters of the Viceroy of the River Plate. Since independence it has always been, except for short intervals, either legally or in fact, the seat of successive national governments until this day. With its federalization, at the expense of the province of Buenos Aires, the so-called 'Capital question' between the national and provincial governments which reached such heights that it gave rise to civil war, finally came to an end.

To its exceptional geographic situation and its almost permanent status as the seat of government have to be added centralizing port, railway, road, economic and other policies which have stimulated the dominant position of Buenos Aires in relation to the rest of the country.

Through its port, 80 per cent of the country's imports are channelled. It has received internal and external immigration in preference to other regions of the country. European immigration ceased after the 1914–18 war but this was replaced by inflows from neighbouring countries, e.g. Bolivia, Chile and Paraguay.

The growth of the capital has spread beyond the political-administrative limits of the Buenos Aires Municipality to the extent that it now constitutes, with the neighbouring municipalities, a zone having all the typical aspects of a metropolitan area.

The city of Buenos Aires has an area of 200 square kilometres (80 square miles). With respect to the size of the metropolitan area, no two estimates agree. According to the studies made by the Regulatory Planning Office of the Buenos Aires Municipality the metropolitan area comprises, in addition to the city of Buenos Aires itself, 22 other municipalities covering in all a total area of 4,000 square kilometres (1600 square miles). On the other hand, the National Development Council considers the metropolitan area as comprising an area of 6,461 square kilometres (4,000 square miles). It includes 15 municipalities and also an extensive rural zone. Here obviously there is a disparity of criteria.

The expansion bringing about the transformation into a metropolitan area and the absence of any joint long-range measures to meet it, has resulted in the growth being in many ways chaotic, especially on the borders. Proper road accesses are still lacking; the use of the land has been irrational and natural amenities and resources have been destroyed. Shanty towns, as stated earlier, have made their appearance particularly on the outskirts of the capital itself.

THE ORGANS OF METROPOLITAN GOVERNMENT

We have already pointed out that in the metropolitan area[1] of the city of Buenos Aires, there are another 22 municipalities situated in the neighbouring territory of the province of Buenos Aires. The municipality of the capital is ruled by special legislation laid down by the national government whilst the rest are governed by the Municipality Charter Law of the Province of Buenos Aires. The whole area also comes under national jurisdiction in federal matters as, for example, commerce and interstate transit.

It has to be borne in mind that the National Constitution of 1953 obliges the provinces to establish a Constitution which *fully guarantees the municipal regime* (Art. 5). On the other hand there is no express reference to the municipal regime for the federal capital. According to the same Constitution, the national congress has the power of enacting legislation exclusive to the territory of the federal capital (Art. 67, Clause 27), whilst the President has, amongst other attributions, that of being 'the immediate and local head of the Federal Capital'. These provisions have given rise to great discussions. It is generally understood that the powers of the national government within the capital refer to its legislative authority leaving local administration in the charge of the municipality.[2]

Legislation regarding municipalities both for the federal capital and the

---

[1] As defined by the Regulatory Planning Office of the Municipality of Buenos Aires.

[2] This is the criterion upheld by Professor Rafael Bielsa in his chapter on Buenos Aires in the previous edition of this work. See also: Borrajo, Elguera, Mouchet, Tibiletti, Vinelli y Weiss, *El Régimen Municipal en la Constitución*, Buenos Aires, 1959, pp. 55 ff.

province of Buenos Aires is based on the North-American system of the two branches of government, i.e., a deliberative and legislative organ of popular origin and an executive, which may or may not be elected by popular vote, reproducing the system of federal government.[1]

As a consequence of the revolutionary movement of June 28, 1966, both the city council of Buenos Aires and those of the municipalities in the province of Buenos Aires were dissolved by the revolutionary junta, and this situation prevails up to the present day. It should be added that this measure covered all the legislative bodies of the country as well as the political parties.[2]

In effect, today only the executive bodies of the municipalities are functioning. The powers of the legislative branch have been partly transferred to the executive, and the most important of them to higher levels of government. In the case of the Buenos Aires Municipality, these now reside in the President of the Republic, and in that of the municipalities of the province of Buenos Aires, they are in the hands of the provincial governor, who is appointed in his turn by the President.

The dissolved city council of Buenos Aires was made up of 30 members elected by popular vote who remained four years in office. For a long time these duties were honorary, being considered as a public duty in accordance with Law No. 1260 of 1882. Later by Law No. 11740 of 1933 it was laid down that members of the city council could be given a stipend which would be assigned to them in the municipal budget.[3] Foreigners could participate in the elections and be elected to the council provided they had had at least four years' residence in the district immediately previous to the elections.

Since the revolution of June 28, 1966, the city of Buenos Aires is being governed in accordance with a legal system which comprises, on the one hand, all those provisions of the Municipal Charter Law No. 1260 of the year 1882 which grant powers to the municipality and on the other, Law No. 16987 of July 7, 1966, which distributes between the municipal executive branch and the President of the nation the functions of the dissolved deliberative body.

By virtue of the 1966 law, the President has reserved to himself many important powers previously belonging to the city council. These are:

[1] For the evolution of the municipality in Argentina see: Carlos Mouchet, 'Las ideas sobre el Municipio en la Argentina hasta 1853' in *Evolución institucional del Municipio de la Ciudad de Buenos Aires* published by the *Concejo deliberante* (city council), Buenos Aires, 1963.

[2] Act of the 'Revolución Argentina' Art. 2.

[3] This stipend was equivalent to the highest salary paid to any member of the Executive, that is, the secretary of the municipality.

1. The approval or modification of ordinances relating to rates and taxes.
2. The approval of the annual expenditure budget or any modifications thereof which involve increases.
3. Adjudication on payment orders the approval of which is questioned by the government audit department.
4. The approval or amendment of contracting regulations including those applicable to the public works contracts.
5. The examination, approval or rejection of the expenditure accounts of the municipal budget.
6. The contracting of loans.
7. The approval or amendment of the general working conditions for municipal staff covering stability of employment, rights and obligations, disciplinary measures, rates of pay, pensions and fringe benefits.
8. Granting of concessions for municipal public services, unless made by public tender.

From this it will be seen that at the moment there is no direct participation by the inhabitants of the city in municipal government. There remains only the influence of the press in shaping decisions, and likewise the opinions expressed by professional and civic organizations. However, the general opinion, both in the city and in the rest of the country, is that at a time which cannot yet be gauged, there will be a return to a system of municipal government allowing for democratic popular participation, but with reforms ensuring greater technical efficiency.

Both before and after the revolution of June 28, 1966, the executive branch has been in charge of an official known as the *intendente municipal*, equivalent to the mayor, appointed by the President of the Republic. Previously the agreement of the National Senate (now dissolved) was required as laid down in Law No. 1260, Art. No. 53.

However, the real government of the city is not the municipal authorities alone. Firstly, the jurisdiction of the national government must be borne in mind. Secondly, many services, which in other countries are run by the municipalities, are here in the hands of state undertakings and agencies at the national level, or at least subject to national jurisdiction (water and sewerage, gas, electric power, slaughterhouses, etc.). The services of these national bodies extend to the remainder of the metropolitan area. We shall refer to this later on in greater detail.

The position of *intendente municipal* (mayor) has never been an elective one. Some political groups have advocated this. But no government has so far plumped for this solution. The fear has always existed that an *intendente municipal* belonging to a different political party from the President could cause him difficulties within his federal seat.[1] Nor has an elective *intendente* been favoured generally in the capital cities of the provinces although this is the case in the remainder of the municipalities.

The relations between the *intendente municipal* and the city council have not always been easy, particularly when the make-up of the elected body showed strong political divergence from the party leanings of the mayor appointed by the President of the nation. In this regard, grave situations arose due to obstructionist tactics in the municipal government immediately prior to the revolution of June 28, 1966.

It should be added that all the judges in the federal capital, whatever the courts, are appointees of the national government. There exists, however, the municipal *tribunal de Faltas*, the members of which are nominated by the *intendente* and are responsible for enforcing the municipal ordinances. But it is considered that these officials are not really judges in the constitutional sense, but rather municipal officers having judicial functions.

From the point of view of the government of the city there are no administrative territorial subdivisions into zonal or district authorities. There is only a division into circumscriptions for certain purposes such as electoral rolls, the civil registry, municipal inspection, as likewise, religious parishes. This lack of decentralization has been adversely commented on by Professor Bielsa. Given the size of the city some decentralization would appear to be desirable; it would enable the different localities to capture the community spirit now lost in the huge metropolis.

A negative factor during the last 30 years has been the frequent changes of *intendente*, mostly men with a political background and some without the capacity or training for heading the government of a large and complex city. It was often the practice to reverse or ignore what had been done by their predecessors, thereby destroying any possible continuity of policy. The writer was a technical officer of the municipality for more than 30 years (until 1966), first as secretary to the tax office, later as a legal adviser, and finally as a member of the management team of the Regulatory Planning Office. During this period no less than 24 *intendentes* took office, that is, an average of one every 18 months, although there were some whose term lasted less than a year. The majority of them had no basic long-range plans, showing a preference principally for immediate solutions of a sensational character, at times quite improvised, despite the existence of an effective and

[1] This recalls the 1862 episode under President Sarmiento, when the municipality turned down the request to grant the use of the principal chamber of the Cabildo (which housed the municipal organ abolished in 1821) from which to review troops. See Carlos Mouchet: *Pasado y Restauración del régimen Municipal*, ed. Perrot, Buenos Aires, 1957, p. 52.

mostly stable bureaucracy as a guarantee for steadfast and continuous action.

No government exists for the metropolitan area. Instead a new type of authority has recently made its appearance for the purpose of national and regional planning within the so-called *Sistema Nacional de Planeamiento y Acción para el Desarrollo* (National System of Planning and Action for Development) Law No. 16984 of 1966, Art. 15. In each regional development area a junta of governors has been constituted formed by 'the governors of the provinces comprised totally or partially within the region, who will be jointly responsible for formulating the regional policies and strategies for development and, individually, for carrying out within their jurisdictions the plans and programmes for development'.

Decree 1907 of March 21, 1967, set up eight regions within the Republic. One of them, the eighth, is named the metropolitan area, which comprises not only the territory which technically possesses all the typical attributes of a metropolitan area but also a zone with rural characteristics—the Entrerrian Delta, which forms part of the neighbouring province of Entre Rios across the Paraná river.

It is worthy of notice that for the purposes of 8th region planning, the position of the *intendente municipal* of Buenos Aires City is equivalent to that of a provincial governor and forms part of the governors' junta for that area, together with the governors of the provinces of Buenos Aires and Entre Rios.

The 8th region contains the most important urban area in the country. This makes it necessary, in my opinion, for the national government to distinguish between its action in the process of economic and social development and in the field of urban development, which could be more conveniently handled in co-ordinated fashion by the municipal governments of the area. This does not deny the need for a national policy in the matter of city development, the more so seeing that a city like Buenos Aires constitutes so outstanding and decisive a factor in the life of the country.

By Decree No. 3880 of November 4, 1967, the province of Buenos Aires created the *Sistema Provincial de Planeamiento y Acción para el Desarrollo* (COPRODE) (System of Planning and Action for Development) which gives policy direction and technical advice on development to the municipal offices. In addition, studies are under way for establishing uniform rules regarding the use of land.

The panorama of government action with respect to the city of Buenos Aires and the metropolitan area has been complicated by the creation by Law No. 16765 of 1965 of the *Secretaría de Estado de Vivienda* (Ministry of Housing). It could also have been a ministry for urban planning at the national level but it was left incomplete. The problem of housing, no matter how tremendous and urgent it may be, cannot be tackled separately but should form part of a general policy for the development of cities and be closely co-ordinated with the economic programme which demands new industrial centres which, in their turn, have their impact on urban development. The law mentioned is concerned with housing and only in a very limited and secondary way with planning by including it among the functions of the ministry in the following manner: 'To co-ordinate the action of the National Government, the Provinces and the Municipalities in all that may concern the application of housing plans and urban planning (Art. 3, Clause a).'[1]

Worthy of mention also is the formation of a corporation known as the *Corporación del Mercado Central de Buenos Aires* (Buenos Aires Central Market Corporation) to fulfil certain economic objectives in the metropolitan area. This interstate entity was formed under an agreement between the National Government, the governor of the province of Buenos Aires and the *intendente* of the city, which was ratified by Law No. 17422. It is financed jointly by the municipality, the province and the national government, who also participate in its direction. Its twin objectives are to rationalize trading in the metropolis and at the same time ease the congestion due to vehicles using the market. It is situated outside the city boundaries but within the metropolitan area.

POLITICAL PARTIES

The citizenry show interest in the governing of the city although there may be a tendency to expect everything from the authorities. This interest is expressed not only in the former participation of political parties in municipal affairs but also in the formation of local neighbourhood improvement associations, the activities of institutions for study such as the *Amigos de la Ciudad* (Friends of the City), in the co-operation of professional associations of architects, and in the constant concern of the press, etc.

As we have already stated, the government arising from the revolution of June 28, 1966, dissolved the political parties as well as the national, provincial and municipal legislative assemblies. The 'Revolutionary Act' contains no reference to their re-establishment, neither have any government plans with regard thereto appeared subsequently, so that in this regard all is still a matter for conjecture. Nevertheless in the opinion of the writer, democratic life based on the free play of political forces will be re-established at all levels

[1] See Raul C. Basaldua: 'La Ley de la creación de la Secretaría de Vivienda de la Nación', in *La Ley*, Buenos Aires, 1966, Vol. 123, pp. 1128 ff.

after a period devoted to the renewal and readjustment of the outworn political organizations. As far as the municipal regime is concerned it is reasonable to believe that a system of government and administration with popular participation will be re-established, taking care, however, to adopt norms and precautions which will ensure the necessary technical efficiency for solving the diverse problems of urban agglomerations.

All that can be said here, therefore, regarding the action of the political parties in municipal government will relate to their recent history.

In the great electoral contests the population of the city of Buenos Aires has generally reflected the predominant political tendencies of the whole country. Nevertheless there have been cases such as that of 1928 when a political party (the Independent Socialists), having a following only in the federal capital, soundly defeated the national governing party (the Irigoyenist Radicals) for the local seats. Parties have also been formed *ad hoc* for the municipal elections as for example, *de los contribuyentes* (taxpayers), *gente del teatro* (stage interests), *salud pública* (public health), etc., which have generally failed to reappear at subsequent polls.

In the chapter on Buenos Aires written by Professor R. Bielsa for the previous edition of this work, he pointed out the defects and corruption which during some periods plagued the elective branch of the municipal government.

A distinction must be made between the criticisms which the municipal corporation has merited during certain periods due to the corruption of some of its members, and those directed against the very structure of the institution. I stated in 1956 when the *Concejo deliberante* (city council) was about to be re-established after one of its many dissolutions ... 'acting as a miniature parliament the City Council had gone so far as to concern itself in some cases with matters outside its sphere for general political ends, to the detriment of the pre-eminently administrative character of its preoccupation with communal functions. But it is evident that these circumstantial excesses are not sufficient to deny the need for, and the advantages of, the institution. We believe, furthermore, that to avoid new crises in the future in the Buenos Aires municipal regime, the re-establishment of the popular elective body must be made so as to approximate it as closely as possible to an *Administrative Council* which, without losing its elective character will respond to the idea of greater governing and technical efficiency'.[1]

Recent history of the intervention of the political parties in municipal life has revealed an almost constant decline in the quality and competence of their

[1] Carlos Mouchet: *Pasado y Restauración del Régimen Municipal*, Buenos Aires (ed. Perrot), 1957.

representatives in the muncipal corporation. By their authority and competence some council members have shown themselves to be honourable exceptions. Nevertheless, to the credit of the city council must be placed its value as a control over the acts of the executive branch of the municipal government.

The participation of the political parties in the government of the city has had an influence on some aspects of municipal activity. Thus the parties of socialistic tendencies (Socialists, Peronists) with strong representation in the city council have exercised their influence in labour and welfare matters affecting the municipal personnel, social assistance, and the wellbeing of the lower-class neighbourhoods of the city. These sectors for example always strove for totally free treatment in the hospitals, and for higher scales of taxation for those groups best able to stand them. In this regard it is significant that until recently the important trade union, grouping municipal employees and workers, was virtually controlled by leaders of the Socialist Party.

In general, the political parties which have intervened in municipal government have shown themselves in favour of an increase in 'municipal autonomy' meaning by this, the election of the *intendente*, the granting of real and not merely delegated powers of taxation, etc. These points of view have led to projects for reform of the municipal charter law.

In various declarations made by the present revolutionary government the significance of community organization has been extolled as a base for social organization. Realizing that this is not possible without some participation of the community in municipal government, advisory committees to the local authorities have been formed in a number of municipalities in the interior of the country, composed of representatives of cultural and local improvement associations, sports clubs, etc. etc. Moreover, there exists a strong tendency to improve municipal government technically.

The present *Intendente* of Buenos Aires, General Manuel Iricibar, laid down a fundamental directive in the governing of the city when he declared, in one of his speeches, that city government should serve above all for the defence of man himself. 'The most valuable thing we have in the city', he said, 'is human existence to which we must give the framework necessary to make it safe, dignified, healthy and satisfying' (September 1967). 'The city cannot be looked upon as nothing but a physical conglomeration but rather as an organization dedicated to the human being with all his physical and spiritual attributes.' Words like these are most opportune at a time in which the city appears to be turning against man in becoming uncomfortable and unhealthy.

MUNICIPAL POWERS AND FUNCTIONS

Municipal powers mainly cover the fields of police and public order, taxation and the regulation and administration of the public domain.

In Argentina the powers of police and public order have come to signify '. . . the regulatory faculty which has as its objective to safeguard not only public security, health and morals, but also generally, the welfare of society'.[1]

By virtue of the Municipal Charter Law No. 1260 of 1882 the municipality has the basic function of determining the lay-out of the city (Art. 45, Clause I). The basic powers in the fields of building and the use of land established by this law were amplified in 1944 by Decree Law No. 9434 which allows restrictions to be imposed on private property in the matter of building, zoning, and the sub-division of real estate. Other powers are exercised in the spheres of security, public health and morals, weights and measures, etc.

For the exercise of its urban development policy the municipality has limited powers of expropriation.

The municipality may only expropriate for the opening, widening, or realignment of streets. In all other cases it must request the national government for the necessary legislative authority. Thus it cannot, by itself, expropriate land for works of such public utility as a square (*plaza*), a cemetery, a market or a hospital. An extension of its powers in these directions has been repeatedly urged but never approved by the national congress.

The municipality controls the safety and hygiene of both public buildings or those to which the public has access, and those which are private property whether they are used as dwellings or for commercial or industrial purposes.

Up to 1966 it was the municipality's responsibility to pass the ordinances governing street traffic, and also to watch over their enforcement (Law 1260, Art. 8). On October 14, 1966, Law No. 16979 was promulgated by which there passed into the 'exclusive province' of the federal police . . . 'the function of regulating and directing urban traffic in the city of Buenos Aires', this force, dependent on the national government, acting as 'the authority for the application, control and verification of infractions of the pertinent municipal ordinances and prevailing rules' (Art. 1).

Possibly this transfer of power was based on the idea that the federal police had greater resources and authority for regulating traffic as dangerous and difficult as that of Buenos Aires; but from another standpoint it constitutes an error as it deals with a function which is eminently local. Instead of taking away the function from the municipality, it should have been improved.

[1] Alberto Elguera: *Policía Municipal*, Buenos Aires, ed. Depalma, 1963, p. 6.

Punishment for breaches of traffic regulations is still in the hands of the *tribunal municipal de faltas* (municipal court for infractions).

The policing of the morality of public spectacles and of publications is of considerable importance in a metropolis like Buenos Aires upon which all the latest expressions of art and literature from all over the world converge. There was considerable public discussion over the prohibition on the sale of a book like *Lolita* or to present an opera like *Bomarzo* or to exhibit certain films. In my opinion the prohibition of certain works which appeal to a very limited public is liable to produce the contrary result by arousing the curiosity and attention of the people at large to them. This power should be handled with great prudence and by highly cultured officials.

Compared with the authorities of other cities of the world, the municipality of the city of Buenos Aires provides or controls relatively few public services of an urban character, notwithstanding its imposing administrative organization. This is due in great part to centralizing tendencies and likewise to technical and financial considerations which, in other times, carried some weight. These centralizing tendencies have not only affected the municipal regime but also the federal system of the country as a whole. In general terms, the position of the neighbouring municipalities to Buenos Aires is more or less the same, although some of them have services which the Buenos Aires Municipality does not control, such as fire-fighting, slaughterhouses, etc.

Some of the Buenos Aires city services have been national since the outset, such as sewage disposal and water supply, for the reason that at the time the municipality had not the financial capacity to instal the systems. Some services which were originally under municipal jurisdiction such as gas and electricity, were afterwards transferred to the national government on being incorporated for technical and financial reasons into vaster systems extending beyond the municipal limits of Buenos Aires City. The municipality had installed and owned an important slaughterhouse and freezing establishment, but this was nationalized on the ground that it not only served the city but was also an instrument of foreign trade subject to federal jurisdiction.

Sewage disposal and water supply are handled efficiently by *Obras Sanitarias de la Nación* (National Water Board) which is a national agency of self-sufficient character whose board of directors is appointed by the President of the nation. The gas supply, also very efficient, is provided by a state corporation *Gas del Estado*, which has connections with the government petroleum concern *Yacimientos Petrolíferos Fiscales*. In so far as electric light and power is concerned, this is mainly supplied in the metropolitan area by a limited liability company, with the state as the only shareholder, known as

Servicios Eléctricos del Gran Buenos Aires (S.E.G.B.A.). This source is comple-
mented by the *Compañía Italo Argentina de Electricidad* (C.I.A.E.) which operates
under a concession and comes under national jurisdiction. The inhabitants
of the city have no say whatever in the management and control of these
services.[1]

The city underground railway system of 31 kilometres (19 miles) in extent
is operated by a state enterprise, *Transportes de Buenos Aires* (T.B.A.). The bus
services throughout the metropolitan area are in the hands of private concerns
but work under national concessions. As for the railways which provide
urban and suburban services, these also come under national jurisdiction and
form part of the state railways system. Telephone services are also in the
hands of a state concern known as the *Empresa Nacional de Telecomunicaciones*
(E.N.T.E.L.). The busy airport for local services situated near the centre of
the city is operated by the Air Ministry.

In contrast to other cities of the world, the Buenos Aires Municipality
has no hand in public education at any of its levels, with the exception of
technical training on a very limited scale.

After reading the foregoing list, the reader may well ask, what does the
municipality of Buenos Aires occupy itself with, other than exercising its
powers of public order?

Among the important services which have remained so far exclusively
within the municipal orbit are the following: refuse collection, street
cleaning, public lighting, hospitals, food supply through municipal markets
and street stalls, cemeteries, the civil registry, the care of squares, parks and
gardens, social assistance of children and old people, cultural services (municipal theatres, libraries, museums, a planetarium, schools of music and allied
arts, a radio station, publications), street paving, construction of dwellings
of social interest, legal aid for low income groups, etc. To these should be
added municipal building projects.

The street cleaning and refuse collection services went from bad to worse
in recent years due to the insufficiency of cleaning and collection vehicles,
and also, at times, due to the indiscipline of the workers assigned to these
tasks. Today a visible improvement is taking place.

The city does not have a sufficient number of covered markets for the
supply of essential foodstuffs. For this reason, for many years past open air
municipal markets were installed in certain streets, which is an objectionable
system from the hygienic and amenity standpoints. The present authorities
have recommenced the intelligent policy of placing the markets in enclosures

[1] The National Water Board and State Gas Corporation as their name suggests are national
concerns, but S.E.G.B.A's jurisdiction is limited to the metropolitan area.

under cover, which was initiated in 1953 by the competent *intendente* Architect Sabaté.

As for the parks and squares of the city, there are splendid ones such as the Recoleta, Palermo, Tres de Febrero, but the area of green spaces is not properly related to the size of the city, being lower than the proportions ruling in other cities of the world.

The free services given in hospitals and dispensaries are efficient although they place a heavy burden on the municipality because they provide assistance for the whole of the metropolitan area, and even to many of the sick from the interior of the country.

ORGANIZATION AND MANAGEMENT

From the outset the executive branch of the municipality was divided, for the despatch of business, into secretariats, that is to say, large departments in charge of officers with the title of secretary appointed direct by the *intendente*.

At the present time, the secretariats are the following: (1) finance and administration; (2) public works and urbanism; (3) public health; (4) supply, municipal policing and public order; (5) culture and social services. In addition and reporting directly to the *intendente* is the general secretariat whose functions are: (*a*) to centralize, co-ordinate and prepare the overall plan; (*b*) to centralize, co-ordinate and keep up to date the general and special structures and procedures for the ruling and governing of the administration; (*c*) to maintain official relations with other official and private bodies and co-ordinate municipal policy with that of other entities.

Within the above-mentioned secretariats are the following directorates and offices:

General Secretariat Consultants, Public Relations, Vigilance and Security, Organization and Methods, and Development Plan.

Secretariat of Finance and Administration General Accounting, Treasury, Finance, Legal Matters, Civil Registry, Cemeteries, Real Estate and Concessions, Official Inquiries, Social Assistance, Receiving Office and Archives, General Caretaking.

Secretariat of Public Works and Urbanism Architecture and Urbanism, Surveying and Public Highways, Private Construction, Public Services, Parks and Gardens, Building Code Committee, Street Traffic and the Zoological Gardens.

Secretariat of Public Health Administration, Hygiene Techniques, Food and Drug Control, Municipal Institute of Re-education, Municipal Radiological and Physiotherapy Institute, Municipal Institute of Children's

Dentistry, Municipal Institute of Odontology, 20 hospitals, School of Nursing, Municipal Institute for Burn Sufferers and Plastic Surgery, Municipal Directorate for Public Assistance (First Aid), Municipal Maternity Institute.

Secretariat of Supply, Policing and Public Order Supply, Refuse Collection and Street Cleaning, General Inspectorate, Public Spectacles and Entertainments.

Secretariat of Culture and Social Services Cultural activity, Welfare Services, Physical Training and Sports, Public Libraries, Vocational Institute of Children's Art, Municipal Conservatory, Technical Schools, Municipal Symphony Orchestra, Historical Institute of the City of Buenos Aires, six Museums, the Colón Opera House, the San Martín Theatre, the Municipal Radio Station and the Planetarium.

A proposal is at present under examination to change the structure of the secretariats into the following six: government, economy, public health, public works, utilities, culture.

The municipal budget for the year 1967 made provision for the salaries and wages of approximately 69,000 employees and workmen but at the same time the municipality planned to effect a reduction of more than 8,000 employees, principally by means of not filling vacancies.

There is a stability of employment statute for municipal personnel which dates from the year 1958 and regulates the conditions of entry, qualifications, duties, rights, obligations and discipline of the staff.

For the purpose of the budget the municipal personnel is divided into various categories: (1) classified personnel; (2) senior personnel; (3) executive personnel; (4) technical personnel; (5) skilled artisans; (6) specialized workers (7) unskilled workers.

Officers not considered as classified and within the wage scales (*escalafón*) are the *intendente*, secretaries of the *intendencia*, members of the *tribunal de faltas* (tribunal for infractions), the administrative director of this tribunal and the secretary of the city council.

The municipal officers and employees are appointed by the *intendente*. Whilst the city council was functioning its agreement was necessary for the appointment of technical assistants to the municipality, of the general accountant, and of the members of the board of the *Banco Municipal* (Municipal Bank of the City of Buenos Aires) (Law No. 5098, Art. 8 and Decree Law 4028/958).

The Municipal Bank of the City of Buenos Aires and the *Comisión Municipal de la Vivienda* (Municipal Housing Commission) merit separate consideration due to their special position within the municipal structure. They are two organs which by law have an autonomous status, that is to say, although they form part of the municipality they are juridical entities separate from the municipality itself and they fulfil certain defined objectives.

The municipal bank was organized originally as a pawnshop for charitable ends, having a monopoly of this business in the city and so avoiding usury. Later on its functions were broadened to cover those of financial agent to the municipality and it was also authorized to carry out operations similar to those of the commercial banks. It enjoys exclusive rights as the receiving bank for deposits made in connection with all lawsuits disputed in the courts of the federal capital, and also for the carrying out of auctions by judicial order or for account of organs of the national government.

With regard to the Municipal Housing commission this, as was mentioned, is an independent entity which was created by Law No. 17174 of February 17, 1967, and which has for its objective 'the promotion of housing for low income families inhabiting the city of Buenos Aires and those districts forming the Greater Buenos Aires area, in accordance with the housing policy formulated in this regard by the National Government and whose realization may be agreed upon with the Buenos Aires Municipality' (Art. 3). The singularity of this organ is that despite the fact that it forms part of the Buenos Aires Municipality it may extend its action beyond its boundaries into the remainder of the metropolitan area. It is presided over by the *intendente* of Buenos Aires.

Generally speaking the personnel comprising the municipal civil service may be classed as good. Its supervisory and technical staff is considered to be among the best in the country. It has evinced a municipal spirit in the sense of defending the functions and interests of the municipality *vis-à-vis* other state organs. Within certain limits the career officers may aspire to the topmost posts.

The personnel is subject to administrative hierarchical control. The municipality also possesses a claims and complaints office which handles public complaints received from inhabitants of the city. There is an office of inquiries which has, as its principal task, the inquiry into the conduct of officers and employees when, through official channels or through information laid by outsiders, irregularities in the carrying out of their duties are brought to light. When the city council was functioning, from time to time it exercised its power of '... naming investigating committees from amongst its members to inquire into the working of certain aspects of the administration' (Law No. 1260, Art. 42, Clause 4).

Law No. 5098 of 1947 provided for a species of arraignment of the *intendente* with the intervention of the city council, judicial officers and a

I

jury of tax-payers for the purpose of his removal in the case of misconduct or grave negligence in the discharge of his duties.

At the present time the *intendente* is subject to civil and penal law with respect to his responsibilities, and he also has a responsibility of a political nature towards the President of the nation who may remove him from his post.

FINANCE

The structure of municipal finance is based on the municipal charter law No. 1260 of 1882 and on various complementary laws of a financial nature. The national laws relating to accounting and public works are also partly applied.[1]

The characteristic of this regime resides in the fact that the powers of the municipality are limited by law. Thus it cannot, in principle, levy taxes other than those authorized. A certain elasticity exists only in the rates charged for services rendered. The municipality also has the power to establish the amount of the tax and likewise concerns itself with the determination, verification and collection of the taxes and other imposts established by law.

The legislation lays down the basic sources of municipal income, viz: (*a*) rates, taxes, and contributions for improvements; (*b*) borrowing; (*c*) payments received for the use of the public domain; (*d*) rents from municipal properties; (*e*) participation in national taxes; (*f*) miscellaneous income (the economic and industrial activity of the municipality).

The original tax regime laid down by Law No. 1260 was modified and radically broadened by Laws Nos. 12704 and 13407. The most important aspect was the creation of the tax on profitable activities which replaced a variety of small taxes and charges for inspection which were difficult and costly to collect and control. This is the most important source of municipal income. It is a tax levied on the gross income of a profitable activity. In accordance with the fiscal ordinance, personal work as an employee on a fixed or variable wage or as a public servant is not considered as profitable income subject to tax under the law. Following in importance are the lighting and cleaning tax,[2] the taxes levied on motor cars, on the consumption of gas and electricity, on the light and power companies, on offices, on sports events, on constructions, and on the occupation of public land, etc. In 1968

[1] See Carlos Mouchet: 'Estudio sobre Financiamiento Municipal en América Latina' in *Reunión sobre Financiamiento Municipal en Latino-América*, Washington, January 1966, Banco Interamericano de Desarrollo, Vol. II, pp. 27 ff.

[2] This is related to the lighting and cleaning of highways and is levied on the owners of real estate with access to the highways, on the basis of the value of the property.

a new paving tax was levied on all property-owners within the capital.

There are some restrictions on municipal taxing activity such as those coming under Law No. 10341 which prohibit any levy on articles of consumption, and under Law No. 12704 which lay down that the product of certain taxes must be devoted exclusively to meeting the cost of all the city's first aid services, which are free for all with the exception of injured persons covered by insurance.

There are legal restrictions on the use of credit. Law No. 12704 allows the municipality to contract loans with the limitation that their annual servicing together with that of the consolidated debt does not exceed 20 per cent of the total income of the city. When it exceeds this amount the municipality has to obtain the authorization of the national congress. Professor Bielsa in his work *Principios de régimen municipal* justifies the need for this national authorization by the fact that '. . . the degree of compliance with obligations emerging from loans may affect the credit of the state' and also in that . . . 'the discredit or the insolvency of an Argentine municipality, especially if it is an important one, has repercussions on the credit of the Nation'.

Until recently the municipality of the city of Buenos Aires had made very little use of credit, principally due to a national policy of limitation of the use of this source of funds on the part of the municipalities. The situation has changed on the obtaining from the Banco Interamericano de Desarrollo (B.I.D.) of a loan of U.S. $19,200,000 for the construction of dwellings in a previously cleaned-up area, Parque Almirante Brown.

It is obvious that expenditures on public works, housing and urban programmes in general, must, as a matter of principle, be based on long-term financing and not fall only upon the present-day tax-payer through current taxation.

What we have said so far refers to the municipality's resources proper which are no longer able to cover the increasing expenditures incurred in its administration. This has resulted in its being granted a participation in the income received from a number of national taxes: income tax, sales tax, racecourse tax, excess profits tax, and capital gains tax, thereby placing it, in this respect, on a par with the provinces. Actually this contribution from national imposts is not a subsidy as it is really a refund of part of the wealth created by the city.

Up to the year 1967 the municipal participation in the product of national taxes represented 16 per cent of municipal income. In 1968 the national government reduced this participation by 50 per cent. This step may be ascribed, in addition to the national treasury's own need of funds, to the fact that the municipality showed a surplus in 1966 and again in 1967, after several difficult years, due to efficient work in this field. This reduction which will mean some 9,000 million Argentine pesos or some U.S. $25,000,000 less in the coffers of the municipality, will seriously affect its urban improvement programmes.

Below is a classification of the sources of income of the municipality for the year 1967:

	Argentine pesos *Millions*
1. *Ordinary income*	
Fiscal ordinances	35,198
Share in national taxes	10,873
Miscellaneous receipts	514
Decentralized departments	1,000
	47,585
2. *Special Accounts Income* (from certain semi-autonomous municipal institutions e.g. theatres)	655
3. *Extraordinary Income* (basically loans)	930
Total	49,170

Note: 350 Argentine pesos = 1 U.S. dollar 1967.

The corresponding breakdown of expenditure for 1967 is as follows:

	Argentine pesos *Millions*
Ordinary Account	
City council[1]	286
Executive branch	30,945
Decentralized departments	9,126
	40,357
Special Accounts	
Executive branch	1,158
Decentralized departments	326
	1,484
Extraordinary Expenditure	
Public works, acquisitions and other investment	7,330
Total	49,171

[1] Although the elective corporation has been dissolved, the departments of the former city council are still operating and hence incurring expenditure.

Nearly half the income for 1967 was applied to the payment of salaries and wages, one-seventh to public works, purchases and other investments, and the rest to miscellaneous expenses. The service of the public debt represented only 194 million pesos.

Up to the revolution of June 28, 1966, the norms set out in Laws Nos. 1260 and 5098 were followed in the process of approving the annual budget of expenditure and incomes, and of the accompanying tax ordinance. The initiative was entirely in the hands of the *intendente*, and the city council could not create jobs, or increase salaries (Law No. 5098, Art. 11). Moreover, the city council could not close its sessions for each year without having approved the taxes and budget for the forthcoming period. On the dissolution of the city council the approval of the budget, or any modifications thereto which entail an increase in expenditure, is in the hands of the President of the nation (Law No. 16987, Art. 1). The execution of the budget is the responsibility of the *intendente*.

RELATIONS WITH HIGHER AUTHORITIES

Although the geographical seat of the municipality of the city of Buenos Aires is superimposed upon that of the federal capital as the seat of the national government, there is no overlapping of the two organisms. The municipality has its own institutional and administrative personality with a series of attributions laid down by law. Within this framework it acts with a certain degree of liberty.[1]

It is true that it maintains contact with the federal government in various ways. We have already said that the *intendente* is an appointee of the President of the nation to whom he has a certain political responsibility. Besides, this official represents the municipality in its relations with the national government. These relations are exercised, in so far as the conduct of administrative business is concerned, through the Ministry of the Interior.

The autarchy of the municipality allows it to make agreements with the national government and with other provinces and municipalities. In this manner covenants have been made to solve problems of double taxation with various provinces, and also in connection with public works involving certain national organs such as *Obras Sanitarias* (Water Board), *Vialidad Nacional* (Highways Board), etc.

Although on occasion, and particularly during periods of *de facto* governments, the national administration has endeavoured to invade the sphere of

---

[1] See: Máximo Gomez Forgues: *La Municipalidad de la Ciudad de Buenos Aires y la Reforma Constitucional de 1949*, Buenos Aires, ed. Perrot, 1952.

the municipality, judicial decisions have declared that it is not a department of the national government. After the 1955 revolution, Decree Law No. 15374/956 reaffirmed the institutional personality of the municipality by declaring that it could not 'be confused with a simple administrative department' and that it was 'the fundamental intention of the Provisional Government to fortify municipal autonomy and to favour administrative decentralization'.

The influence and impact of national government policy upon the development of the city, aside from the decisions of the municipal authorities themselves, has shown itself clearly through the powers wielded by the central government in the spheres of railways and docks and through its taking direct charge of, or controlling, important public services which, in other countries, come within the orbit of the municipalities.

It is obvious that the dependence of the municipality upon the national government has been notably accentuated by the suppression of the city council and by the transfer to the President of the nation of the most important of the functions which previously pertained to it. Among these figure the examination, approval or rejection of the expenditure accounts of the municipal budget. The authorization to effect expropriation, in all cases in which the municipality has no powers to act, must now also come from the President.

It should be added that there is a remedy of a judicial character against decisions of the *intendente* in matters relating to administrative law. The appeal may be made directly to the civil court of appeal of the federal capital. According to the jurisprudence, matters subject to such action are limited to questions arising out of the exercise of municipal powers in the fields of order, hygiene and morals. In the remainder of the cases as, for example, taxation, private individuals must proceed through the ordinary judicial channels.

In contrast with other countries, there is no organ at the national level specifically dedicated to giving technical advice to the municipalities. Nevertheless, mention may be made of the technical assistance which in the matter of administrative rationalization had commenced to be given to the Buenos Aires Municipality by an interprovincial body such as the *Consejo Federal de Inversiones* (Federal Investment Council) which has recently been incorporated into the *Consejo Nacional de Desarrollo* (National Development Council).

The creation in 1966 of the *Sistema Nacional de Planeamiento para el Desarrollo y la Acción* (National System of Planning and Action for Development) and the fact that the city of Buenos Aires forms part of a specific development region subject to the directives, strategies and plans which may be applied by the national government through the *Consejo Nacional de Desarrollo* (National Development Council) and the *Junta de Gobernadores* (Governors' Junta) of the Metropolitan Region, will accentuate the situation of dependence of the municipality in a number of spheres, particularly those of economic, territorial and urban planning.

PLANNING AND DEVELOPMENT

Argentina is receiving, although slowly, the influence of the world-wide movement tending towards an orderly and farseeing development of cities through urban planning. Organs for this purpose are already being formed in several of the country's municipalities. This movement will probably be accelerated by the impact of the National System of Planning and Action for Development.

Up to 1934 the development of the city of Buenos Aires was largely left to private initiative and to the dispersed and uncoordinated activity of state entities, above all, in matters relating to the use of land.

In the year mentioned, Decree Law No. 9434, to which we have referred earlier, was issued, which authorized the municipality to place restrictions on private property. Due to this, the Building Code was able to come into being which, in addition to policing construction proper, introduced two new important factors in urban planning, namely, zoning and control over the subdivision of the land. But this is not sufficient, as it represents merely passive planning. What is required is a system with drive and the creation of a technical body which would actively direct the development and renovation of the city.[1]

After some unsuccessful attempts which, due to lack of understanding, went as far as the breaking up of an incipient planning office, the municipality created in 1959 the *Organización del Plan Regulador de la Ciudad de Buenos Aires* (Regulatory Planning Office of the City of Buenos Aires) under the government of a first-class *intendente*, Hernan Giralt, who gave it his decisive support.

A phenomenon worthy of mention from which the municipality did not escape and which is very common in Latin America, is that in the initial stages of planning organs, many stumbling blocks due to lack of understanding and hostility were encountered in the rest of the administration, which

[1] See Carlos Mouchet: 'Criterios y bases legales para el desarrollo urbanístico de la ciudad de Buenos Aires y de su area metropolitana' in *La Ley*, Buenos Aires, Vol. 109, January–March 1963, pp. 1039 ff.

was disturbed by and suspicious of the possibile ascendency of organizations of this type.

The regulatory planning office was assigned, as its principal function, the task of preparing the master plan for the city, and also of putting forward the provisions and proposals needed to get it under way. The master plan, in its first stage, was approved by a decree-ordinance in 1960.

The regulatory planning office formed part at the outset of the secretariat of public works and urbanism, but in 1967 it was raised to *intendente* level and placed in the general secretariat, which, in principle, was a good move.

The work of the regulatory planning office has not been confined to the city alone, which has been considered as forming part of the metropolitan area and of a region, the studies being in consequence extended to comprise the entire conurbation.

The master plan and its complements are of a preliminary character and, for the time being, constitute a guide and orientation for the elaboration and execution of urban development projects in the city. The complementary documentation includes a draft law for the physical planning of the city of Buenos Aires, in which the broadening of the municipality's powers is foreseen, especially in the use of the land. Also provided for is the legal entrenchment of the planning organ so that its future existence may not depend on the whims of some erstwhile authority. The revision and adjustment of the master plan is left in the hands of the master plan organization itself.

A start has been made with certain aspects of the plan such as those relating to urban renewal, the formation of land reserves, circulatory highways, etc. For example, the cleaning up and development of an extensive zone of 1,400 hectares (3,500 acres) called Almirante Brown Park has been destined for parks, housing, and to some extent for the relocation of industries badly situated in other parts of the city; a coastal motorway to decentralize traffic circulation within the capital is contemplated; as also the construction of a new airport out in the Río Paraná to take the place of that now operating practically in the centre of the city.

The implementation or execution of the master plan is realized through various municipal dependencies, such as the municipal housing committee, the directorate of architecture and urbanism, and the autonomous municipal works directorate, etc. Likewise many state entities which operate within the capital nearly always consult the municipality as and when the occasion arises, although under no obligation to do so as the master plan is the outcome of a municipal ordinance and not a law.

Not all of the aspects of municipal activity have as yet been gathered into a homogeneous policy of urban planning. Thus it may be noticed that, as occurs in other countries, endeavours are made to solve the traffic problem in isolation by taking steps to facilitate the movement of motor vehicles when it should be approached in conjunction with a policy for the regulation of the use of land in the matter of building construction and the mass movement of passengers by underground and surface railways. Moreover, the traffic problem also points to the need for reconsidering the structure of the city which was based on concepts prevailing before the motor-car era.[1]

The acute scarcity of housing which is a national problem, is also nowhere near to being solved. Shanty towns and slums exist within and on the out-skirts of the city. National and municipal plans are in hand to tackle this situation.

Vast sectors of the city, such as the Barrio Sud, require programmes of urban renewal. Traffic flow must be improved by means of the projected construction of the coastal motorway and the transversal avenues running from north to south. It is necessary, as is done in other countries, to build up municipal ownership of real estate and to establish reserved zones for future urban development plans. The means of mass transport must be improved by the extension of the underground railway network and a start is about to be made on the execution of plans in this direction.

Another problem which is being tackled by certain measures but which still has to be solved, is that of air pollution by fumes from factories and motor car exhausts. The greater part of the omnibuses and lorries which circulate in the metropolitan area of Buenos Aires are defective in this respect.

As far as planning in the metropolitan area is concerned, I refer to what has already been stated previously when dealing with the government of that area.

BOUNDARY PROBLEMS AND JURISDICTIONAL CONFLICTS

Concurrent jurisdiction of the federal and municipal authorities exists in certain zones of the city such as the railways and docks, each exercising its powers in its own particular sphere. But in practice it has not always been easy for the municipality fully to exercise its authority in such zones as, for example, in relation to matters like public order, building and hygiene.

[1] Submission to the motor-car 'invasion' has meant a reduction in the width of the pavements, the removal of the avenues of trees and the central islands for pedestrians in the avenues, and even the closing in of squares to provide parking spaces. Furthermore, precipitate authorization has been given to the building of skyscrapers in the central area of the city which has narrow streets, generating thereby more traffic where congestion already exists.

I*

The administrative boundaries of the city of Buenos Aires as a municipality no longer coincide with its real limits since its physical, social and economic life overflows into the metropolitan area.

The neighbouring municipalities have become in many respects districts of Buenos Aires. There is no interruption in the continuity of the built-up area, and they are to a large extent dormitory towns, although not totally, since they contain the most important industrial zone of the country.

After the annexation in the last century of the municipalities of Flores and Belgrano there have been no further attempts to enlarge the municipality of Buenos Aires at the expense of neighbouring townships. It is easy to see that this would meet with lively resistance from the province of Buenos Aires. At the moment there are no jurisdictional problems with the neighbouring municipalities.

In my opinion the solution of the problems of the metropolitan area does not lie in fusion, through annexation, with the townships of the province of Buenos Aires, but rather by respecting the present limits and creating a metropolitan authority for the planning of the area.

No count has been made of the various authorities which operate in the metropolitan area but it is worthy of mention that there are national, provincial and municipal organs, and of these the most important alone exceed 50 in number.

We have already referred earlier to the junta of governors of the metropolitan region so that there is no need here to return to the subject.

PROBABLE FUTURE DEVELOPMENTS

After registering a striking increase between the years 1947 and 1952 the population of the Buenos Aires Municipality (federal capital) has tended to stabilize itself and even decrease slightly, whilst on the other hand its suburbs, as part of the metropolitan area, have shown continuous growth which can only be counteracted by national plans for industrial decentralization and equilibrium between the various regions of the country.

Within the city of Buenos Aires only a few vacant areas of any size remain to be developed, amongst which may be mentioned the Almirante Brown Park, zones occupied by railway installations and some others. In consequence the growth in building construction is taking place more and more vertically. According to studies made by the regulatory planning office, it is indispensable to reduce the present indices of land occupancy allowed under the Building Code as otherwise these will lead to an excessive density in the population of the city.

Theoretically, the growth of the metropolitan area can continue indefinitely as there is an abundance of land for development within its conurbation. It is also easy to foresee an increase in the means of transportation within the area. But this development may encounter limitations due to internal impediments created by excessive growth and from the barriers which may be set up by a national development policy which contemplates the interests of other regions of the country, without prejudice, of course, to such local measures as the control of building densities and coefficients of occupation.

For the years 1970 and 1980 the following increases in population are foreseen compared with the figures given by the National Census of 1960.

	1960	1970	1980
1. Whole country	21,000,000	24,050,000	29,000,000
2. City of Buenos Aires	3,000,000	3,100,000	3,200,000
3. Metropolitan area	6,800,000	8,000,000	9,000,000

The incidence of international immigration should be noted. This gave a favourable balance of 1,047,000 for the whole country during the period 1947 to 1960. Of this number 345,000 persons were attributed to the city of Buenos Aires and 343,000 to the rest of the metropolitan area which adds up to a total of 688,000 persons for the urban agglomeration of Buenos Aires.

CONCLUSIONS

At some time in the future it will be necessary to decide, with respect to the municipal regime for the city of Buenos Aires, whether there will be a return to the traditional system of local government which prevailed up to June 28, 1966, or if it will be necessary to think of introducing reforms so that the municipal government may be more adequately constituted to manage successfully the interests in its charge.

Above all, thought is being given to the need for constitutional reform which will afford guarantees to the municipalities of Argentina which they do not enjoy at present, without forgetting that the concept of 'municipal autonomy' must link itself with the new concepts of metropolitan areas (whose existence has gained recognition and standing in the 1967 reforms to the Federal Constitution of Brazil). In any such reform the Buenos Aires Municipality must be given once and for all a definitive status.

Another fundamental premise in this matter consists of the recognition of the need for the participation of the citizenry in the government of the city. This should not be taken as an obstacle to studies on the advantage of reforming the structure and functioning of the deliberative branch of the municipal government, whose action in a great city like Buenos Aires may degenerate easily into a form of parliamentary stagnation. The solution lies in the establishment of an executive council with a small membership possessing technical ability, similar to the board of directors of a large enterprise. This would coexist with a larger municipal assembly for determining major policy issues and other matters of great importance. Alongside the *intendente* or mayor it would be necessary, following highly successful examples in the United States and Canada, to have a city manager. In this way, the *intendente* would concern himself with political and representative affairs whilst the manager, who would be a specialized professional, would have responsibility for the technical running of the municipality.

At present nothing is known of any official study or recommendation regarding the future municipal regime for the city of Buenos Aires.

Much has been said of installing the federal government in some other place in the country (in another city or creating a new city), in the belief that this could be one of the remedies to restrain the growth of Buenos Aires. Without mentioning the difficulties of transferring the vast administrative machine installed in the city of Buenos Aires to another city or a new city and the enormous cost that this would entail, I think that such a solution would not neutralize by itself the combination of factors which result in the growth of Buenos Aires.

To be able to tackle this problem with better chance of success a policy should be followed which, amongst other measures, would do the following:

(*a*) Bring up to date the legislation which grants powers to the municipality and which is archaic in many aspects notwithstanding its capacity for adapting itself to change. It must contain the institutionalization of urban planning, so that this would be obligatory for the municipal authorities.

(*b*) Give a new structure to the municipal government in its executive and deliberative branches, improving its technical efficiency but without eliminating democratic participation.

(*c*) Without prejudice to the integral planning of the metropolitan area, reach agreement with the other authorities in that area for the urgent co-ordinated solution of problems such as hospital services, air purification and removal of refuse.

(*d*) Rationalize the municipal services so as to absorb a greater load without increasing expenses.

(*e*) Achieve continuity in administrative action by medium- and long-range planning.

(*f*) Create an autonomous entity to attend to the financial aspects of urban development, whose funds could not be used for other ends. A fixed sum out of the resources of the municipality should be set aside for this organism.

The political parties which have taken part in the government of the city of Buenos Aires have presented projects for the reform of the municipal regime, but these are nothing more than retouches and amplifications of the traditional regime, although they have gone to the length of proposing the election of the *intendente*. Many politicians hold fast to the theory of 'municipal autonomy' as though it had a value which, by itself, would solve everything, without comprehending that the municipal administration inexorably deteriorates, however autonomous it may be, if it does not efficiently meet the growing needs of the city. Furthermore, this autonomy is a very relative value within the modern state.[1]

In so far as public opinion is concerned, although it desires a change and improvement in the municipal government and administration, it has no clear idea of the nature of this change. Some think that the suppression of the deliberative branch of elective origin will solve everything. Others believe that, on the contrary, the solution lies in giving more powers to that branch.

The solution must be given at the proper time by means of a study in depth with the participation of all interested groups and sectors which, without leaving on one side the national tradition and mentality, accepts the existence of the causes through which the municipality has deteriorated. The experience of other countries in the field must be gathered and a municipal government and administration organized, with the necessary autonomy within the state, which harmonizes the needs of efficiency with due respect for the participation of the citizenry in their local government.

[1] See Carlos Mouchet: *La legalidad en el municipio*, pp. 63 ff.

Cairo

FOUAD D. ABDEL-TAWAB

FOUAD DIAB ABDEL-TAWAB

Born 1921 at Al-Rahmniya, Dakahleva, Egypt. B.A. (Sociology), Cairo University, 1948; B.A. (Social Work), Cairo School of Social Work, 1953; M.A. (Social Psychology), Cairo University, 1960; Ph.D. (Public Administration), New York University, 1967—thesis title *Opinion Research and Administration in the U.A.R.*

Teacher Saideya High School, Cairo, 1948–51; Supervisor, Social Case Work Section, 1951–53; Inspector of Information Centres, Ministry of National Guidance, 1954–55; Deputy Director, Public Opinion Analysis Section, 1956–57; Press Attaché, Egyptian Embassy, Rabat, Morocco, 1957–59; Director of Information Centres and Institute of Public Opinion, 1960–63; Information Officer, U.A.R. Mission to United Nations, 1963–64; Senior Case Worker, Guardian Society, Diocese of Brooklyn, New York, 1965–67. 1967–70 Technical Member for the Executive Conference Programme for top U.A.R. Executives and Assistant Professor, Department of Economics and Political Science, American University in Cairo. At present Research and Training Consultant, Guardian Society, Diocese of Brooklyn, and Associate Professor, Division of Social Studies, St. Francis College, Brooklyn, New York.

Author of: *Morocco: A Political Study* (in Arabic), Cairo, 1960; and *How to Measure Public Opinion* (in Arabic), Cairo, 1963; *A Study of the Problem of the Congestion of Goods and Ship Cargoes at Alexandria Port*, 1967; *The Developing of the U.A.R. Local Administration System: A Field Study*, Fayoum, 1967; headed Egyptian team for UNITAR Research Project: *The Use by Mass Media of Information on the United Nations*; *Use of Time by Casework Staff*, New York, 1969.

Cairo

SEVERAL centuries before Cairo's birth, its location (at the point where the Nile's long narrow valley to the south meets with the fan-shaped delta to the north) was chosen several times to be the site of the Egyptian capital. Such examples in ancient times include Memphis, Heliopolis and the later fortress of Babylon.

The origin of contemporary Cairo was laid down in the seventh century shortly after the Arab conquest of Egypt. The Fustat, as it was called at the time, was built on the eastern bank of the Nile on a narrow strip protected by a line of hills (Mukattam) to the east bordering the vast desert beyond.

The city then grew northward by additional separate settlements which were connected three centuries later (A.D. 969) into one city to be called Cairo, which constitutes the Old Cairo section to the south of the present city.

The city's site, which greatly influenced its growth and form, is a triangular plane opening northward and surrounded by vast deserts on its eastern and western sides. It is located some 200 kilometres south of the Mediterranean up the Nile river which divides the city in half.

Historically, prior to the construction of the Suez Canal, the strategic location of Cairo en route between Alexandria on the Mediterranean (220 kilometres north-west) and Suez (120 kilometres east) gave it its importance as an international centre for commerce. Likewise, its intermediate location as link between upper and lower Egypt gave it its national importance as a centre for both communication and politics. No wonder, therefore, that Cairo has always spread its dominance all over the country through history. Such dominance has never ceased through the ages.

Cairo has always been the seat of the central government and has witnessed successive civilizations. The gigantic Pyramids of Giza, the impressive Sphinx and the treasures of the Egyptian museum are impressive evidence. The coptic churches and museum tell the story of the Egyptian Coptic Orthodox Church while the numerous mosques relate the story of the living history of Egypt under the rule of different Moslem dynasties. Al-Azhar, founded in 979, now the world's most important orthodox Moslem university, accommodates over 10,000 students from all parts of the world.

Not only is Cairo famous for its ancient history but also for its cultural, financial and commercial activities today, as it plays a leading role in the development of the Arab world. It advocates Arab union which is an age-old

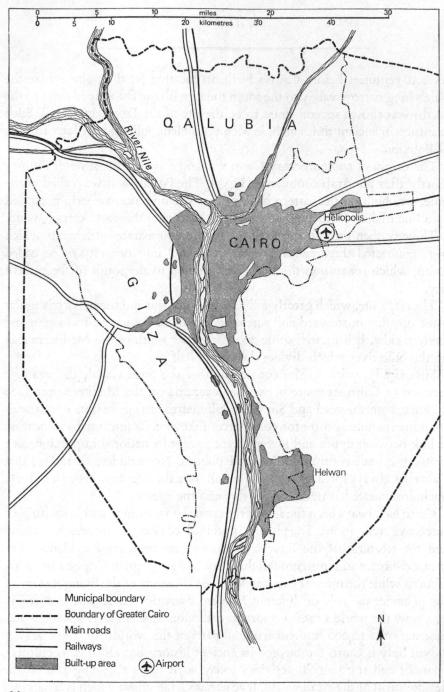

MAP 6 CAIRO

desire throughout the whole region. It is the seat of the Arab League. Cairo is considered the gateway to the Near East, Africa and Asia. It has accommodated several regional and international conferences.

Cairo metropolitan area is rich in its historic sites of different eras and in its beautiful weather. Excellent facilities have been introduced to make Cairo an outstanding tourist attraction. Many new hotels have been built recently while others are under construction. Furthermore, good roads as well as comfortable rest houses link the city with the historic sites.

In addition, as the primary city of an economic system which is at the peak of its transition, Cairo handles 27 per cent of the total national industry, consumes 48 per cent of the electric power, has 48 per cent of banking activities, 49 per cent of social welfare societies, 35 per cent of business and 36 per cent of the labour force and civil servants in the U.A.R. About 25 per cent of national production is contributed by the capital city.

Consequently, Cairo has become the main concentration of the country's urban population and activities. Cairo alone, among sixty-two urban communities, accounts for over 40 per cent of the country's urban population, 60 per cent of its registered motor vehicles and about 30 per cent of the employment in the six leading industries. Furthermore, the increase in population has been sixfold within 60 years. With a population of about 5 million, Cairo has 18 per cent of the total population in the U.A.R.

Planning authorities are thus faced with the massive problems, like several capitals of developing nations, of unwarranted rapid population growth and overconcentration of activities. The Greater Cairo area is expected to reach the 10 million mark by 1980 if the present rate of growth is maintained.

The Greater Cairo planning region covers an area of 200 thousand acres of which the city of Cairo covers one-fourth (see map). The city of Cairo reached 4·2 million in population in 1967 with densities up to 630 persons per acre in some parts. The pressing need is to overcome problems arising from this rapid increase.

THE ORGANS OF THE METROPOLITAN GOVERNORATE

In the U.A.R. the law No. 124 of 1960 and amendments contained in Law No. 151 of 1961 illustrate some modern trends in local government legislation enacted in such nations as Pakistan, Yugoslavia and Sudan. It retains much of the French system which Egypt was the first to adopt in the Near East early in the nineteenth century; it has also some provisions that stem from the English practice in their African colonies.

Accordingly, the U.A.R. is divided into administrative districts, namely:

governorates, towns and villages, each of which is endowed with a juristic personality. Those administrative districts have characteristics both of units of local administration of the national government and of units of local self-government. For example, the chief executives are appointed by national authorities and are mainly responsible to them while the councils are partly elected, partly appointed, and partly *ex officio*. These councils, moreover, while given broad powers of legislation are currently required to follow the national plan.

The boundaries of governorates are defined by presidential decree, those of towns by ministerial decision, and those of villages by decision of the governor. A governorate may be confined to a single town and this is the case at present in Cairo which is divided into districts. The following table shows area and population of the Greater Cairo districts:

TABLE I

Greater Cairo Districts

District	Population 1966	Area (sq. km)	Area (acres)
North Cairo	1,072,215	16	3,834·54
East Cairo	973,314	120	28,617·23
Middle Cairo	680,438	20	4,686·66
South Cairo	598,344	41	9,870·39
West Cairo	681,437	15	3,692·52
City of Cairo	4,219,835	212	50,701·34
Shubra-el-Kheima (governorate of Qalubia)	172,902	30	7,007·32
Giza (governorate of Giza)	572,259	74	17,514·54
Greater Cairo	4,965,514	316	24,521·86

It will be noted that the Greater Cairo area is divided geographically and administeratively among three local jurisdictions: city of Cairo, governorate of Qalubia and governorate of Giza. The city of Cairo is the largest governorate within the nation. It illustrates the general organization of an urban governorate.

The governor

The governor (*muhafez*) is the chief of administration. He is appointed by and can be removed by presidential decree, and has the status of a deputy minister as to salary, pension and fringe benefits, but as to other matters has the rank of an under-secretary of state. He represents the executive authority of the state within his jurisdiction and is in administrative control of all government personnel in the governorate, except judges. He reports to the Minister of Interior on matters of security and to the Minister of State for Local Administration on matters relating to local government. Other national ministers may confer some of their powers on him, thus making him in direct charge of the execution of their projects and activities within the governorate. Besides this, he presides over the governorate council, inspects the reports of the five district councils within his jurisdiction, and must approve certain decisions they adopt. In short, the governor is both an agent of the state and the chief executive of the governorate and its local units.

In the political field the governor's role in taking decisions in controversial matters of public importance is one of the landmarks of success of local government administration. In the Cairo area decisions have been taken in matters of supplies, prices, housing rents, development of private schools, social services and black market dealings. The decisions are of such a nature that they helped to a great extent in solving a number of irritating problems for the masses.

The governorate council

Cairo Governorate Council is composed of:
(a) The governor as chairman (the assistant governor replaces the governor in his absence, and he is appointed by presidential decision).
(b) Twenty-four *ex-officio* members representing the ministries with personnel in the governorate.
(c) Sixteen selected members from leading posts in the regional services, who must be active members of the Arab Socialist Union (they may be either civil servants or ordinary citizens).
(d) Forty-four elected members who are members of the committees of the Arab Socialist Union in the administrative subdivisions of the governorate, each of which is represented by two members.

The elected members always constitute the majority. The national charter of the U.A.R. declares that at least half the membership should consist of farmers and workers. The composition of the council thus assures the predominance of members of the Arab Socialist Union, and the guidance of the technical personnel representing national ministries. It forms a solid basis on which to integrate democracy and national policy.

Elected members of the council should reside within the governorate, be not less than 25 years of age, be willing to be a council member, and be literate. Persons not eligible for council membership include those condemned for crime, those dismissed from public service for dishonesty, insane persons, those deprived of their civil and political rights, and those declared to be bankrupt. The council may declare a membership forfeited if legal incapacity is proved, or if there is a loss of active membership in the A.S.U. or of membership on the executive committee of the A.S.U. The governor must call a meeting of the council within a month of the date of its establishment. Resignation of council membership is submitted to the chairman, who then presents it to the council whose decision is final. Vacancies in the offices of elected and appointed members must be filled within two months from the date of the vacancy, and the new member shall complete the term of his predecessor. The council may ask the ministries to delegate an official to attend its meetings or its committee meetings if the subjects under consideration make this advisable. These delegates may take part in the discussion without any right to vote.

The term of council membership is four years, half of the number of elected and appointed members being replaced every two years. At the end of the first two years, half of the elected and appointed members, chosen by lot, resign. The membership of the second half end at the close of the four-year period. Membership may be renewed.

Jurisdiction of the governorate council

The governorate council may undertake, within the limits of the state's general policies, to establish and manage the different local services and works which are for the welfare of the governorate. It carries on educational, sanitary and social affairs as defined by executive regulations; promotes the exploitation of local resources of wealth and the increase of agricultural, animal and industrial production in the governorate; stimulates co-operation among citizens of the governorate; erects exhibitions in various places within the governorate; provides work for the unemployed; protects motherhood and childhood; assists the disabled and the aged; submits suggestions for the maintenance of local security; manages governmental services and enterprises as the government directs; improves local communications as defined by executive regulations:[1] and supports libraries, museums and centres for popular culture and education of all kinds, including military training.

The governorate council may carry on enterprises of a local character

---

[1] These regulations are set out in Presidential Decree No. 1513 of 1960 as provided for in law No. 124 of 1960.

which the district councils cannot manage. The council may provide various benevolent or social groups with administrative, technical or financial assistance, and may furnish co-operative associations with loans, and administrative and financial assistance. The council may participate with other governorates to establish and carry on public services and works for regions they represent under provisions laid down by executive regulations.

Executive regulations determine matters to be submitted for council opinion and define matters to be approved in advance by the council that fall within the competence of the ministries. Every minister as well as the governor may take the advice of the council in any matter. The council may also reveal to the President of the Republic and to any minister its desires regarding the general needs of the governorate. The council may dispose of any of its movable or immovable estates or property free, or lease them for a nominal rent to any person or corporate body with the intent that they be used for public purposes, up to 5,000 Egyptian pounds in one fiscal year, subject to the approval of the competent minister. Cases exceeding this amount are subject to presidential decision.

The governorate council may contract within the following limits: (*a*) 10 per cent of the budget of the council subject to the approval of the competent minister; (*b*) more than 10 per cent and up to 20 per cent by decision of the Regional Committee for Local Administration; (*c*) more than 20 per cent by presidential decision. The council should not commit itself to a capital investment programme which lasts for more than one fiscal year, unless the gross capital cost is authorized by the competent ministry, and there is a prior agreement to allocate the funds in the council's annual budget. The council may not accept gifts with a restrictive clause the execution of which is beyond the power of the council, nor change its purposes without the approval of the competent minister. Gifts and assistance offered by foreign persons or associations are subject to the approval of the President of the Republic.

As already mentioned, technocrats are members of the governorate council together with representatives of the local population. Decisions are reached in the governorate council through deliberations and require the approval of a majority. Administrative and technical advice has, however, a certain weight in the council, and the *ex officio* members of the council play the leading role in decision-making.

The district councils

As previously mentioned the city of Cairo is divided into five districts:

North, East, Middle, South and West. Each district has its own council which
is composed of:

(*a*) The chairman of the district, who presides over the council (the deputy
    chairman replaces the chairman in his absence, and he is chosen by the
    council from the elected members).
(*b*) *Ex officio* members representing the ministries which are designated by
    the Minister of Local Administration, and the governor may add some
    representatives of the public organizations.
(*c*) Five selected members who are from leading posts in the district
    services. They must be active members of the A.S.U.
(*d*) Twenty elected members who are members of the committees of the
    A.S.U. The elected members must always constitute a majority.

The chairman of the district council is appointed by the Minister of Local
Administration on the basis of the governor's recommendation.

The district council may undertake, within the limits of the state's general
policies and under the supervision of the chairman of the governorate council,
to establish and manage local services which are for the welfare of the
district. It carries out the various functions undertaken by the governorate
council within the districts. It has also the right to submit recommendations
and communicate public demands in order that these may be discussed by
the governorate council which decides the projects and services needed for
the district, and its finance. The governor is competent to settle disputes that
may take place among the districts.

Cairo, therefore, follows the two-tier structure, as it would be difficult for
one council to maintain a close contact with citizens. The lower tier of
secondary councils is a method of decentralizing power in respect of purely
local matters. These district organs are in a position to know more than the
city council about their own districts, and they should be able to keep in
close and intimate touch with their local affairs.

Metropolitan authorities

Although the Greater Cairo area is suffering from the almost universal
phenomenon of metropolitan fragmentation, its problem is far less acute
than that of several other metropolitan areas. The area is divided geographically and administratively among three local jurisdictions (parts of three
governorates) which have, traditionally, been subordinate to a strong central
government. Consequently, some of the most important metropolitan
functions like housing and education are still central government functions.

However, the problems of co-ordination among the several central and local administrative units should not be understated. They led, eventually, to the creation of special-purpose metropolitan authorities. The Greater Cairo Public Transit Authority is responsible for most of public transportation in the area. Two suburban railway lines are operated by the Railway Transportation Authority of the U.A.R. and a partial network of metro lines is operated by the Heliopolis Housing and Development Company. Other metropolitan-wide authorities include the Greater Cairo Water Corporation and the Cairo–Giza Sewage Disposal Establishment. Last, and probably most important, is the newly created Greater Cairo Planning Commission responsible for planning and co-ordination. The members of these bodies are appointed either by presidential decree or ministerial order according to the legal requirements.

PARTY POLITICAL CONSIDERATIONS

A non-partisan system is followed in the U.A.R. and political parties are not allowed in national or in local politics.

The Arab Socialist Union, however, was established in 1963 to mobilize the people in the drive to ensure the achievement of the objectives of the 1952 revolution as laid down in the national charter. The Arab Socialist Union forms the political structure for national action. Its structure embraces all elements of the people, i.e. farmers, workers, soldiers, intellectuals and holders of national capital—who bind themselves to co-operative action in close solidarity.

Membership in the Union is open to every U.A.R. citizen of not less than 18 years old. There are two kinds of membership:
(a) active, comprising those who are eligible as candidates for membership of the various organs of the union;
(b) associate, comprising those who have the right to elect the members of the organs of the Union but are not entitled to be candidates for membership of these organs.

The structure of the Union is based on a hierarchical pattern of leadership with the aim of binding the various groups on different levels. Therefore, we find in Cairo governorate basic units, represented by 'group leaderships' that are considered a link between the popular base and the executive bureau of the district. Such a bureau comprises a number of basic units and, in its turn, is considered a link between the districts and the governorate executive bureau that represents the various districts.

The philosophy of action of the A.S.U. is to intermingle with the masses;

to hold free discussions; to gauge the people's sentiments and to exert all efforts in solving their problems.

Accordingly, the A.S.U. has been able to get into close contact not only with the masses but also with the administrative organs. They have co-operated, through the meetings that have taken place since March 1966, in solving various problems in the city of Cairo of which we may mention:

(*a*) Nasser's project for housing that was successfully carried out as a result of effective co-operation between the governorate authorities and the A.S.U. representatives. The project aims at providing low income families with proper accommodation.

(*b*) Cleaning Cairo's districts. When the governorate authorities faced this problem because of the shortage of the labour force, political organs stepped in and a decision was taken to launch cleaning campaigns. Each campaign continued for a week in every district, and municipal capacities were reinforced by popular efforts to solve the problem and put an end to the popular complaint.

(*c*) Establishment of co-operative societies for artisans and small traders. The A.S.U. sponsors have come to an agreement with the governorate authorities to establish co-operative societies in order to help artisans to get the materials needed for their handicrafts and for small traders to continue their activity.

(*d*) Participation in educational activity. The A.S.U. has played an important role in solving educational problems. Volunteers among its members have exerted great efforts to teach adults in order to wipe out illiteracy. Also when the number of students exceeded the capacity of schools, the executive bureaux of the districts intervened and opened what have been called 'Socialist Union Classes'.

(*e*) National guidance. Conferences and meetings that are held for national guidance assert the co-operation that exists between the political organs and the governorate authorities. These conferences and meetings are usually attended by representatives of the A.S.U. and the governorate.

MUNICIPAL POWERS AND FUNCTIONS

The city of Cairo used to suffer from the strains of rapid population growth combined with slow progress in the various activities such as housing, transportation, schools, recreation and open spaces, lighting, social and health services, sport and youth welfare, and neglect in preserving historic sites.

The city officials began to exert tremendous efforts to remedy such short-comings. They succeeded in carrying out various projects in different fields, some of which are discussed below.

Replanning of old districts

The replanning of old quarters was made to ensure a better distribution of social services and public utilities. Old slum districts were demolished and new popular dwellings were constructed in their place. This work is continuously going on. The Fawala district was completed in 1956. Currently the Maarouf district near the business centre of Cairo is being reconstructed. Many of the historic quarters such as Al Azahar, El Hussein and El Gamaliah are being reconstructed with Arab-style buildings with oriental restaurants, public centres and handicraft centres contributing to the atmosphere of the Khan El Khalili bazaar.

Other districts are being replanned for better communications and sanitary facilities.

Housing

Before the revolution, vast areas of agricultural land were turned into residential quarters, ignoring the desert land east of the city, to the north and south.

The planning commissions formed a scheme to exploit desert land. Thus the waste areas of Zeinhom and Ein El Sirra were turned into a habitable residential district, including youth welfare centres, hospitals and other social institutions. About 1,034 popular housing units were constructed in Zeinhom, 3,576 in Ein El Sirra and 200 in El Darassa.

The area which was formerly occupied by British barracks between Ein Shams and Heliopolis has been turned into a flourishing residential area—El Nasr City. Now included in its newly constructed residential district are public gardens, magnificent buildings, modern luxurious flats and a modern road network. At the centre of El Nasr City stands Cairo Stadium with a seating capacity of 130,000 persons. This stadium forms the nucleus of an Olympic city. It is planned to move all organs of public administration and ministries to the new city. Work is now under way to plan a centre in the capital for all embassies and legations.

The Mokattam hills overlooking Cairo at an altitude of some 200 metres is the location chosen for Mokattam City. With the addition of paved roads and communications, this residential area is rapidly expanding with the building of flats and villas.

In the areas where popular housing units were constructed the buildings are divided into small blocs, each being provided with social, cultural and hygienic centres, a market, a place of worship, a public garden or child welfare centre, a maternity clinic, a kindergarten, co-operative societies and other public institutions.

Gardens and forestation

Experts believe that public gardens or parks amounting to a minimum of 4 *feddans*[1] per thousand inhabitants should be maintained to safeguard public health. The ratio before the revolution was only 0·15 *feddan* per thousand inhabitants. Thus the total area occupied by public gardens during the past ten years has been raised from 270 to 1,096 *feddans*, not including gardens attached to schools and sports clubs. These new gardens were built in popular centres and districts to balance the geographical distribution of greenery among the various sectors of the city. Also the extensive gardens of the former King Farouk were opened to the public.

In order to reduce the dust descending upon the city from the barren desert hills, an afforestation programme was been inaugurated which will eventually screen the city with a wide fringe of trees.

Lighting

Gas lights which prevailed in many densely populated districts were replaced by electricity. Cairo is now illuminated by mercury vapour lamps mounted on steel posts. An extensive low-voltage cable network is used for the supply of the lamp posts. Around 50,000 posts are installed in Cairo and the yearly consumption amounts to 35 million kilowatts.

Transportation

Public transport serving the Greater Cairo area is supervised by three different organizations, namely:

(*a*) Public Transit Organization of Cairo, which operates a network of buses, trolley-buses and street cars.

(*b*) Railway Transportation Authority of U.A.R. which operates two suburban rail lines.

(*c*) Heliopolis Housing and Development Company which operates a

[1] One *feddan* = 1·038 acres.

network of street-cars connecting the suburb of Heliopolis with the central district of Cairo.

Mass transit in Cairo has special importance. The incomes of most of the people do not permit the use of private cars. The transit lines, once short, serving reasonable areas and populations were adequate. Because of the extension of these lines to serve outlying areas of metropolitan Cairo, they suffer from inefficiency and from losses through undercapacity. As both the number of lines and the number of buses in each line are increasing, and they are all passing at the same time in the core, this results in high volumes of traffic. Moreover high rates of population increase together with increase of per capita income create large shifts in transportation demand.

Thus a complete reorganization of the city's public transport network has been initiated. New modern buses have been introduced. New express lines have been created to link the business centre with all quarters and suburbs of the city. Despite the steadily increasing number of buses in service, the problem remains acute.

Health and social services

Public hospitals administered by the city are numerous and treatment may be received in any of these free of charge. Private hospitals are also available for those who prefer them. Specialists from abroad are invited to give lectures and handle special cases. Many of our local doctors have received their specialized training abroad, but our universities are now incorporating high standards within their curriculum to train more doctors to meet the needs of the expanding population.

Social services enable the youth of the country to have a better chance to meet the needs of the future. Other services for the blind, tubercular, etc., are provided by voluntary bodies with subsidies from the city which also pays part of the salaries of their officials.

The city is responsible for establishing and maintaining youth centres and for supervising all private organizations engaged in sporting activities. Sports clubs and youth welfare centres have increased during the past ten years from 79 to 142. Among the most important are the well-known Gezira Sporting Club, Zamalek Club, the National Sporting Club and Heliopolis Sporting Club. They usually win all the trophies of the U.A.R. and many African championships and tournaments.

The Supreme Council for Youth Welfare is establishing a large number of popular playgrounds and summer work camps as well as organizing excursions and trips at nominal cost.

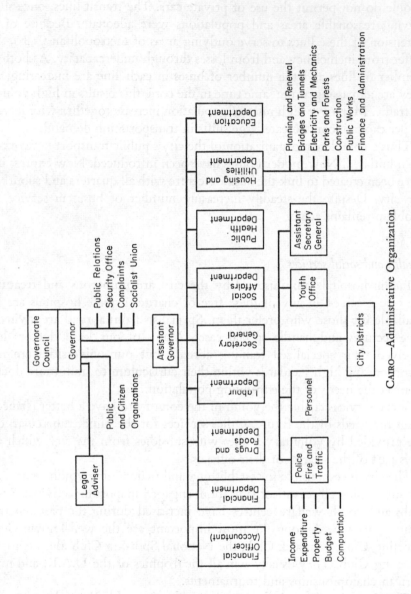

CAIRO—Administrative Organization

ADMINISTRATIVE ORGANIZATION AND STAFFING

The governorate is headed by the governor helped by an assistant. Under the governor are the main departments headed either by an under-secretary or by a director-general. These departments are; education, housing and public utilities, social affairs, public health, labour, drugs and food supplies, and financial affairs (see chart).

The governor's chief staff officers include a legal adviser and various officers for public relations, security, complaints, Socialist Union, and public and citizen organizations. Within the financial department, there are five offices: income, expenditure, property, budget and computation. The secretary-general heads the following offices: police, fire and traffic, personnel, youth and administrative affairs. He also supervises the heads of the five city districts.

Within the governorate there are a total of 12,755 officials and employees of various classifications and within seven grades. They include the following: 386 engineers, 910 physicians, 67 dentists, 80 pharmacists, 61 veterinarians, 5 chemists, 165 public health intermediate, 9,484 teachers, 257 social workers, 51 youth welfare workers, 18 supply inspectors, 264 labour specialists and 978 administrators.

It should be noted that the personnel in the governorate are designated or seconded by the relevant ministers, but they are supervised by the governor, i.e. personnel are controlled by the ministers in such matters as appointment, promotion, transfer and retirement as provided by the national civil service law. The governor appoints all personnel within the governorate who are not higher than the ninth grade (the administrative scale in the U.A.R. begins at the bottom with twelfth grade). Ministers should consult with him on questions of promotion and transfer, and the governor may request the transfer of any employee if his presence appears to be contrary to the general good. If the minister refuses, the governor may present his case to the Minister of Local Government. However, it is the ministers who actually discipline any such employees. These rules are applicable both to employees of ministries who have been transferred to the local councils and to those (such as police and tax administration personnel) who have not been so transferred.

FINANCE

The estimated revenues of Cairo governorate for the fiscal year 1966/7 amounted to 34,967,285 Egyptian pounds. Of this, £E11,967,200 were collected by the governorate and £E23,000,085 were grants from the central government.

This table shows that the central government grants-in-aid amount to about two-thirds of the governorate's total budget. As for other resources of the governorate, they are of two kinds: (a) those revenues in common with other governorates and (b) revenues peculiar to the Cairo governorate. In the first category are; (1) the quota of the governorate from additional export and import duty. The rate of this duty is fixed by the President of the Republic not to exceed 3 per cent of the original customs duty, and the coun-

TABLE III

Governorate Income 1966/7

Item	Amounts (Egyptian pounds)
Taxes on buildings and agricultural land	1,762,200
Taxes on entertainment	650,000
Licence fees on transport vehicles	3,280,000
Share of the supplementary import and export duties	216,000
Supplementary duties on movable wealth[1]	944,000
Rents of municipal buildings	500,000
Charges on public services	664,000
Net surplus of electricity consumption	1,450,000
Taxes on hotel occupancy	60,000
Taxes on properties benefited from public projects	100,000
Taxes on ferry boats and floating houses	20,000
Net markets revenue	6,000
Additional taxes on rental value of buildings	210,000
Quarries and mine licences	150,000
Sale price of buildings and vacant lands	150,000
Miscellaneous	1,805,000
Central government grants-in-aid	23,000,085
Total	34,967,285

cil of the governorate which collects this duty is allowed to keep one-half of the proceeds and to dispose of the other half to a common fund to be divided among other governorates; and (2) the quota of the governorate from the additional duty on movable wealth (interest on loans, revenue from stocks and bonds, etc.) the rate of which is to be fixed by the governorate council if no more than 5 per cent of the original duty; by a decision of the competent minister and approved the Vice-President for Local Administration if

[1] Movable wealth includes interest on loans or deposits, revenue from stocks and bonds, etc. It excludes real estate.

it is more than 5 per cent and less than 10 per cent; and by a decision of the President of the Republic after agreement between the competent minister and the Minister of Public Treasury if more than 10 per cent and not more than 15 per cent. The governorate retains one-half of the revenue from this additional duty and disposes of the other half to a common fund to be divided among other governorates. The common fund resulting from these two sources is distributed among the governorates by the Regional Committee of Local Administration as proposed by the competent minister.

In the second category are: (1) one-fourth of the revenue of the original tax imposed upon agricultural land within the governorate, as well as one-fourth of the revenue of the additional duty on such land, the rate of such additional duty being fixed by the council when it does not exceed 5 per cent of the original duty, and up to 10 and 15 per cent after approval by various central authorities; (2) fees on transport vehicles licensed by the governorate; (3) one-half the sale price of buildings and vacant lands owned by the government within the town borders; (4) the revenue from the council's assets and property, and from the public services it undertakes; (5) governmental subsidies and non-government donations; (6) other charges and fees of a local character imposed for the profit of the governorate; and (7) loans contracted by the governorate council.

The law empowers local authorities to borrow money under the following conditions: loans up to 10 per cent of the council's ordinary revenue require the sanction of the Minister of Local Administration; loans between 10 and 20 per cent of the council's revenue requires the sanction of the Vice-President for Local Administration; above 20 per cent requires the approval of the President of the Republic

Cairo governorate expenditure for the fiscal year 1966/7 totalled 34,967,285 Egyptian pounds.

TABLE IV

Cairo Governorate Budget
Fiscal Year 1966/7

Item	Egyptian pounds
Salaries	19,165,090
Current funds	8,348,040
Capital funds	4,345,852
Transferring funds	3,108,303
(aids to voluntary, social, health, educational, and recreational organizations)	
Total	34,967,285

K

The capital investment was allocated to establish the following new projects:

Item	Amount
Electricity	25,000
Bridges	850,000
Streets	350,000
Drainage	1,745,000
Planning and public works	160,000
Municipal buildings	20,000
Educational projects	237,782
General projects	49,000
Buildings for educational purposes	353,070
Mental hospital	410,000
Social units	146,000
Total	4,345,852

RELATIONS WITH HIGHER AUTHORITIES

Central control is exercised by some of the top level national government officials. The President of the Republic promulgates basic laws, amendments and executive regulations concerning local government. He also appoints the governor of the city council and defines the administrative boundaries of the governorate. His final approval is needed for loans made by the city council which exceed 20 per cent of the annual budget.

The Minister of Local Government acts as the co-ordinator of local government with other ministries and the governor confers with him on budget, personnel and other problems as they arise. He also approves the governorate council decisions and budget. The Minister of the Interior is in charge of public security and the governor reports to him and takes his orders in such matters. The Minister of the Treasury appoints an auditor to audit the financial accounts of each local council, while the Central Authority for Accounts[1] may undertake the inspection of council financial accounts. The Court of Administrative Justice hears appeals of councillors whose membership has been revoked by the council, and from dismissed council officials.

Then, too, the major ministers that have personnel in the governorate have a certain jurisdiction in the governorate affairs. The ministers confer with the governor on personnel, budget and the projects with which each is

[1] This body audits the accounts of both local councils and central agencies before their approval by the National Assembly and checks the legality and regularity of expenditures and appropriations.

concerned, for both personnel and money for the service activities of the governorate came from the ministries, and only the ministers make the final decisions. Ministry inspectors watch local administration, and ministry personnel may participate in local council activities and projects.

PLANNING AND DEVELOPMENT

The first comprehensive master plan for the Greater Cairo area was formulated in 1956/7 by the Cairo Municipal Planning Department. Essentially, the plan centered around the physical layout of the street network which was partially executed during the past ten years. The plan, though for the metropolitan area, was made by the city of Cairo and did not have enough power of enforcement.

In 1965, the Greater Cairo Planning Commission was created for the purpose of planning and co-ordination within the area. The commission consists of the ministers of the relevant central government departments plus the three district governors (for Cairo, Qalubia and Giza), municipal heads and a number of planning officials and educators. It is entrusted with a fourfold function:

First: The preparation of an area-wide comprehensive general plan without regard to jurisdictional boundaries, which includes the services and utilities.

Second: The preparation of detailed projects deemed necessary for implementing the plan.

Third: The preparation of the project development programme, and

Fourth: Supervising the execution of the prepared programme and ensuring co-ordination and co-operation among the various authorities and local administration units in the area. The commission has a planning and supervising technical office to discharge its above mentioned functions.

The G.C.P.C. has the power to co-ordinate interdepartmental and intergovernmental activities in the Greater Cairo area both by review and by direct action. Its decisions concerning the area, once sanctioned by the Prime Minister, are binding on all departments, public corporations, public authorities and local administration units.

The execution of the plan is the responsibility of the various governments, corporations and authorities each within its jurisdiction under supervision of the G.C.P.C. The G.C.P.C. can and does take the initiative in assisting urgently needed projects hampered by financial or administrative problems at the local level. Its budget includes provisions for such projects.

BOUNDARY PROBLEMS

The creation of the G.C.P.C. and the above mentioned metropolitan authorities was a reaction to the ill-defined city boundaries as well as the multiplicity of jurisdictions. Cairo's influence in effect extends far beyond its limits. Daily commuters to and from Cairo, although in small numbers, reach as far as Tanta 40 miles away. The city's dominance in the political, economic and social spheres extends over the whole country and, in some respects, even beyond. The urban area already extends beyond the city limit.

LIKELY FUTURE DEVELOPMENT

No doubt the most pressing problem facing the Greater Cairo metropolitan area is its rapid population growth and over concentration of function and activities. Therefore, the Greater Cairo Planning Commission is currently engaged in the preparation of a general plan for 1990. Although the plan is still in its preliminary stages of formulation, its main policies are more or less established. It aims at discouraging migration into the area. The question of maintaining physical and functional order in the capital city, and of regional balance and spatial distribution of activities have promoted investigation of the possibilities of curbing Cairo's growth and diverting rural-urban migration into other local or regional centers. Of all the possible ways of achieving such an end, regional planning and redistribution of economic activity seems to be the only effective and feasible means. As such, regional planning and semi-autonomous local administration have gained the recogtion and consensus of policy-makers. Until regional plans are prepared, however, central departments have considered redistribution of their functions and activities (decentralization and deconcentration) as one of the goals to be achieved by their respective plans.

As for public transportation, the city is planning to establish a net of rail, and express subways in conjunction with a net of buses, trolley-buses, and rapid tramways to meet the requirements for future travelling, which will reach seven million passengers per day in 1980.

CONCLUSION

Cairo had been centrally governed till the Local Government Law was promulgated in 1960. The governorate council has undertaken the responsibility of establishing and managing the different local services as well as the district councils which carry on local affairs aiming at the welfare of the citizens. Through the two-tier structure, the inhabitants of the city have the chance to make known their wishes and wants, for the lower tier is in a position to know more about the people's needs. Such a system has increased the people's participation. Now they play a positive role in carrying out the resolutions decided by the councils.

The new system has been faced with accumulated problems, particularly the rapid growth of population. Despite the great efforts exerted by the city to provide the citizens with necessary services these are still inadequate. There is a shortage of housing, although thousands of low cost dwellings were erected. Transportation, though the streets are crowded with various means of transport, is inadequate.

Cairo has succeeded not only in providing its unemployed citizens with proper jobs, but also has done its best to train the unskilled in its various training centres. Such efforts have increased production and decreased social ailments.

It is expected that the current problems facing the city will be solved through regional planning which is applied and enforced in some parts of the country, namely, the Aswan area. Regional planning will help in the distribution of functions and activities all over the country. In consequence, Cairo will be relieved of some of its burdens especially those caused by its rapid population growth.

Calcutta

ALI ASHRAF

LESLIE GREEN

ALI ASHRAF

Born 1930. B.A.(Hons.), Patna University; M.A., Patna University; Ph.D., Cornell University. Lecturer, Rajendra College, Bihar University, 1954–60; Fulbright Scholar, Cornell University, 1960–61; Teaching Assistant Cornell University, 1961–63; Research Fellow in Urban Studies, Institute of Public Administration, New York (Calcutta Branch), 1963–65; Research Associate, International Project on *Study of Values in Politics*, 1965–67; Joint Director, Project on the *Functioning of Bureaucracy with special reference to Development* under the auspices of the Research Programmes Committee, Planning Commission, Government of India, and Assistant Professor at the Indian Institute of Technology, Kanpur, 1968.

Author of *The City Government of Calcutta: A Study of Inertia*, The Asia Publishing House, 1966.

LESLIE GREEN

(see page 437)

Calcutta

THE history of Calcutta begins at the end of the seventeenth century, when an Englishman established a trading post there amidst a cluster of villages surrounded by the greenery of low-lying rice fields and bamboo groves. From this unpretentious foundation, the city grew in less than a century to become the second largest in the far-flung British Empire and the capital of British India until 1912, when Delhi superseded it. Despite its uncongenial surroundings, Calcutta's growth was phenomenal. Today, the city forms the heart of a great industrial conurbation, it is a most important centre of finance, and it is a major hub of national and international commerce. It remains the capital of West Bengal. But the Calcutta which once illuminated the cultural and political life of India has become the 'cesspool of Asia'. The reasons for this paradox are not far to seek. With the growth of the city, its problems grew too, in proportions which at first challenged and then overwhelmed its institutions of local government—institutions which, in this century at least, have never been viable or effective organs of administration. And the local government of the rest of the conurbation is a lamentable reflection of the mother city's lamentable example.

The muddy waters of the Hooghly river bisect the heart of the Calcutta conurbation. The city proper is situated on its eastern bank; on its western bank lies the town of Howrah. While administratively a separate unit, Howrah is in fact integrated with the city both socially and economically. It is joined to Calcutta by the Howrah bridge, which also shelters some of the latter's pavement dwellers; and though the railway terminus linking Calcutta with the major industrial and mining centres of eastern India lies in Howrah, the port providing an access for sea-going vessels has been developed on the eastern bank at Kidderpore and Garden Reach. Howrah bridge thus carries a continuous stream of heavy traffic between these vital points in the composite city's commercial life.

In the main, the growth of Calcutta has been a response to the mounting requirements of commerce and industry over a vast hinterland. It commands the gateway to the resources of the whole of eastern India—from Assam in the north-east to Uttar Pradesh in the west—rich both in agricultural

With the kind permission of the Institute of Public Administration, New York, this study makes use of much material appearing in, *The City Government of Calcutta: A Study of Inertia*, by A. Ashraf, Calcutta Research Studies, No. 9, Asia Publishing House for Institute of Public Administration, New York, Bombay, 1966.

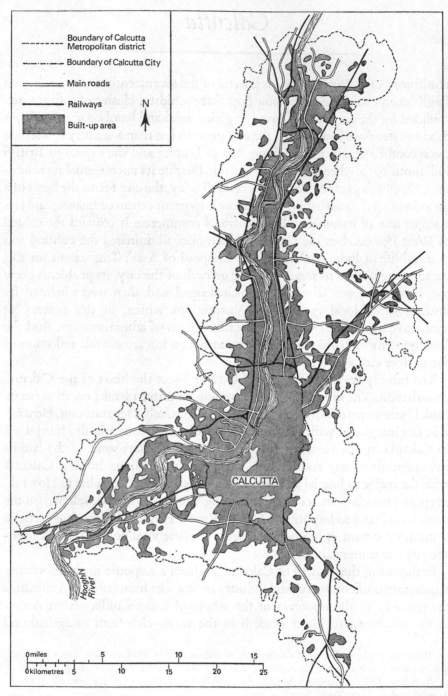

Boundary of Calcutta
Metropolitan district

Boundary of Calcutta City

Main roads

Railways

Built-up area

N

CALCUTTA

Hoogly River

0 miles   5   10   15
0 kilometres 5   10   15   20   25

MAP 7 CALCUTTA

produce such as jute, tea and rice, and in mineral deposits of coal, iron, copper, limestone, mica and manganese. These resources have helped to make Greater Calcutta the largest commercial and manufacturing complex in the country. Thus, its port handles about 42 per cent of India's total export tonnage and receives 25 per cent of her imports; it shares with Bombay the nation's most organized financial markets and active stock exchanges; and it houses the head offices of leading national and international banks. The fact that almost half of the people inhabiting the complex originate from outside its boundaries bears testimony to the close interdependence between the city and its hinterland. Undoubtedly, the commercial and industrial future of eastern India is intimately bound up with the success or failure of Calcutta as its economic nucleus.

It is of more than local moment, therefore, that Calcutta itself has begun to stagnate. In an admirable analysis of the city's problems, a former Registrar-General of India states:

It seems incredible that, while West Bengal's population grew by 33 per cent in the last decade, Calcutta's should have grown by only 8 per cent. In the same period Greater Bombay grew by about 39 per cent . . . The truth of the matter is indeed a paradox; that in spite of the squalor, the crowds, the swarming streets and pathways, the *bustees* [slums] bursting and spilling around, Calcutta is not growing fast enough.[1]

In other words Mitra is citing the slow rate of population growth compared to other Indian cities as evidence of Calcutta's economic stagnation. Population trends are not a satisfactory index of economic prosperity. Nevertheless there is other evidence of economic difficulty: the steady decline in the jute industry (over which Calcutta had a monopoly before partition), the fall in exports routed through Calcutta and, in recent years, the flight of capital from Calcutta to areas like Bombay and Mysore which are more stable politically.

Part of the reason for the tendency to economic stagnation lies in the city's physical setting. Almost the whole of the land covered by the conurbation forms a low-lying area with very poor natural drainage. Much of it is in fact waterlogged. Moreover, for at least the last two centuries, the Hooghly has been receiving a continually decreasing supply of water from the mainstream of the river Ganges, and has consequently been silting up. Since the Hooghly is the principal source of potable water for the whole of the conurbation, this silting, which is accompanied by a high and rising degree of salinity, causes perennial and increasingly serious problems. It also makes the maintenance of the port increasingly expensive, and contributes to the silting of the main outfall rivers on the eastern side of the city beyond its salt lakes.

[1] Asok Mitra: *Calcutta—India's City*, Calcutta: New Age, 1966. The 8 per cent refers to Calcutta City.

Particularly during the heavy monsoon rains, choked drains, open manholes and flooded streets are recurrent reminders to its citizens that, in default of human enterprise and ingenuity, unfavourable natural factors have by now made life in Calcutta well-nigh unbearable for the mass of the people.

Geography is not the only adverse factor preventing Calcutta from fulfilling its proper role in the regional economy. Man himself is equally responsible. For many years, there has been an abject failure to discharge elementary duties of government. As a result: 'There is hardly any aspect of community development that is keeping pace with the growth of Calcutta's population or with the requirements of its hinterland. Overcrowding, degradation of housing, health hazards, primitive water supplies, lack of space for new industries, traffic bottlenecks, power shortages, a still unsolved refugee problem—all are increasing the cost of moving goods and of providing the many services that a growing industrial region demands of its metropolis.'[1] Inertia has been the chief characteristic of the city's administration for at least forty years.[2]

The causes of this inertia are sociological, political, economic and cultural. It has been estimated that one-half of the conurbation's working population is migrant. The overwhelming majority of the migrant people originate from outside West Bengal—from Bihar, Orissa, Uttar Pradesh and even the Punjab, Rajasthan, Madras and Kerala—or as refugees from East Pakistan. Socially, culturally and linguistically they are exceedingly heterogeneous. They represent all religions and all castes. Furthermore, they mostly consist of single, male workers, who flock to Calcutta and its satellites to earn a living, and leave their families in their native towns and villages. They maintain deep and abiding attachments to their real homes, develop no stable family life in the city and its suburbs, do not regard themselves as its citizens, and skimp on necessities of life in order to maximize their savings, which they regularly despatch to their families. Thus, a very large segment of Greater Calcutta's population has little interest in improving its housing, health facilities, water supplies, power network, traffic conditions and general administration. It is more concerned to deny to the city and its satellites the money they need to undertake such improvements, and it is willing to accept standards of living intolerable to the true Calcuttan. In social and political terms there is a sharp and basic cleavage between the city's native Bengali population—which controls the state and local governments—and the

[1] The International Bank for Reconstruction and Development, *Mission Report*, U.S.A., 1960.
[2] Subhas Chandra Bose called on the Calcutta Corporation to 'shake off its inertia' in 1928 (see A. Ashraf: *The City Government of Calcutta*, p. vi).

majority of its migrant elements who desire little or no part in that government. There is a parallel economic cleavage, inasmuch as the Bengalis are engaged mainly in education, the civil service and the professions, while the immigrants are employed in commerce and industry, which they also control.

Nevertheless, in spite of these factors which, in recent years, have increasingly retarded the city's growth, and in spite of antiquated and fragmented administrative machinery that has for long needed a complete overhaul, the recently defined Calcutta Metropolitan District extends over nearly 490 square miles and contains a population of 7,500,000.[1] Within the district, Calcutta City, which is the area falling under the jurisdiction of the Calcutta Municipal Corporation and the principal subject of this study, extends over some 37 square miles and contains above 3 million people. There are also thirty-four other municipal towns, as many non-municipal towns and well over a hundred villages recognized for administrative purposes.[2] Most of these coalesce to form the continuous built-up area of the conurbation, stretching along both sides of the Hooghly for over twenty miles north and up to fifteen miles south of Calcutta and Howrah.[3] Areas of closely settled villages, isolated towns and interstitial and peripheral urban development also fall within the metropolitan district, as defined by the Calcutta Metropolitan Planning Organization.[4]

Reference is often made to the wealth of this vast complex.[5] Paradoxically, most of its inhabitants are very poor. For 1962–63, a reasonable estimate suggests a metropolitan net income of Rs. 5,300 million, or about one-third of the net income of the entire State of West Bengal. But this amounts to no more than Rs. 815 per head of the metropolitan population, and the great majority exists on far less. Indeed, the average income per head of the Calcutta hinterland (including the metropolitan district) has been estimated at only Rs. 306 for 1960–61.[6] Abject poverty is an important key to the understanding of the fundamental development problems of eastern India as a whole, and of Calcutta in particular.

[1] For 1966: see Calcutta Metropolitan Planning Organization, *Basic Development Plan or the Calcutta Metropolitan District 1966–1986*: Development and Planning (T & CP) Department, Government of West Bengal, Calcutta, 1966, p. 1.

[2] *Ibid.*, pp. 135–7 and M. Bhattarchya: *Rural Self-Government in Metropolitan Calcutta*, Calcutta Research Studies No. 5, Asia Publishing House for Institute of Public Administration, New York, Bombay, 1965, ch. 8.

[3] M. Bhattacharya: *op. cit.*, pp. 84–5.   [4] *Basic Development Plan*, map 5.

[5] For example, *ibid.*, p. 3.

[6] For all these estimates, see L. Green: *The Economic Hinterland of Calcutta*, Calcutta Research Studies, No. 7, Asia Publishing House for Institute of Public Adimnistration, New York, Bombay, 1968: Table 20 and Ch. 5. The *Basic Development Plan*, estimates the *per capita* income of the Calcutta Metropolitan District at Rs. 811 for 1961–2 (Table 23).

Such poverty is a direct result of pressure of population upon natural resources. In 1961, 13·5 million people lived in the four magisterial districts of which the metropolitan district forms the heartland. Since the area of cultivated land amounted to 5,060 square miles, the density of population averaged 2,664 per square mile of such land.[1] The soil is fertile, water abundant and rice-growing ubiquitous; but at this density the people cannot hope to feed themselves properly, especially by subsistence farming. Moreover, beneath the surface lie no mineral deposits. In consequence, metropolitan Calcutta is heavily dependent on its hinterland not only for food, but for the raw materials needed by the industries which have sprung up on the basis of its original *entrepôt* function. In 1962–63, the value of its foreign imports and exports possibly represented 43 per cent of the total value of commodities carried between the metropolitan district and the rest of India.[2] The remainder was accounted for by indigenous foodstuffs, jute, tea, minerals such as coal, and manufactures. Metropolitan Calcutta has for long been renowned for its tea trade and jute factories. But, besides producing 95 per cent of India's jute manufactures in 1963 it was also responsible for 92 per cent of her electric fans, 80 per cent of her sewing machines, 78 per cent of her railway wagons, 74 per cent of her rubber footwear, 70 per cent of her enamelware, 56 per cent of her electric lamps, 50 per cent of her crockery, 49 per cent of her paints and varnishes, 31 per cent of her radio receivers, 31 per cent of her soaps, 30 per cent of her finished steel and 21·5 per cent of her paper and paper-board.[3]

Today, the metropolis is thus much more than the major port and distribution centre for eastern India, with its huge iron and steel complexes of Asansol, Durgapur, Jamshedpur, Ranchi, Rourkela and Bhilai, its vast mineral fields of Chota Nagpur, Jharia and Ranigunj, its rice fields, jute and tea plantations and its teeming population. Calcutta is thus a major manufacturing centre in its own right, but its problems of development are of even greater magnitude. Despite its wealth, it is 'rapidly approaching the point of breakdown in terms of its economy, housing, sanitation, transport and the essential humanities of life'.[4]

THE STRUCTURE OF GOVERNMENT

A metropolitan approach to Calcutta's multiplying difficulties is a very

[1] Leslie Green: *op. cit.*, Table 18.   [2] *Ibid.*, Ch. 2.
[3] *Ibid.*, Ch. 2, quoting from the *Eastern Economist*, New Delhi, Vol. 44, No. 24, June 11, 1965.
[4] Concluding Statement, *International Planning Seminar on Calcutta Metropolitan Plan*, Calcutta, January 8–15, 1967.

recent one. It is only during the last decade that awareness has grown of the need to treat the industrial conurbation centred on Calcutta and Howrah as a single unit for purposes of overall urban administration and planning. In this respect, the creation of the Calcutta Metropolitan Planning Organization (with a jurisdiction embracing the whole Calcutta Metropolitan District) was a landmark; but it has always been concerned solely with the preparation of plans, and it is only very recently that the State Government of West Bengal has introduced legislation to establish a single water supply and sanitation authority for the metropolitan district. Aside from these developments, which will be discussed below, the industrial complex growing along both banks of the Hooghly continues to present a picture of an entirely fragmented system of urban local bodies, each responsible for the administration of a separate and limited area. The more extensive complex now defined as the Calcutta Metropolitan District comprises an extremely large number of rural local bodies, too, and the web of government includes many special agencies. As already mentioned very briefly, there are in all thirty-five municipal authorities, which are local self-governing institutions constituted for urban areas and having jurisdiction over 85 per cent of the metropolitan district's population in about 40 per cent of its area. The remaining 60 per cent of the district's area is covered by rural institutions, which are thus responsible for the local government of 15 per cent of its population.

The urban local authorities comprise the three municipal corporations of Calcutta, Howrah and Chandernagore, the Cantonment of Barrackpore, the Notified Area Authority of Kalyani and thirty-one municipalities. The rural local authorities consist of the four *Zilla Parishads* of the magisterial districts of Howrah, Hooghly, Nadia and Parganas, and their constituent *Anchalik Parishads, Anchal Panchayats* and *Gram Panchayats*. Together with the urban authorities, they form a mosaic of some five hundred local bodies, which is well portrayed by Bhattacharya.[1] But this is not all. There are over thirty special agencies, twenty-eight state government departments and twenty union government ministries directly involved, one way or another, in the administration of the metropolitan district.[2] The planned development of this

---

[1] M. Bhattacharya: *op. cit.*, and especially p. (x), Fig. 3, which shows the intricate maze in 1964 *before* the introduction of *zilla parishads, anchalik parishads, anchal panchayats* and *gram panchayats* in the place of district boards and union boards. The maze is now a labyrinth in which every tiny village (*gram*) has two organs of local government, a twice-yearly village meeting (*gram sabha*) which elects a village executive or *gram panchayat*. These in turn elect members of *anchal panchayats* which have replaced the old union boards having jurisdiction over a number of villages. The *anchal panchayats* elect members of *anchalik parishads*, which are similar to subdivisional councils; and the *anchalik parishads* in turn elect members of *zilla parishads* which have replaced the old district councils and have jurisdiction over the magisterial districts.

[2] For a detailed analysis of all government agencies concerned with the administration of

district does not concern merely thirty-five municipal authorities, as is some-times suggested,[1] but a labyrinth of over 570 different arms of government—local, regional, national and special—some 180 of which operate in Calcutta City itself.

The following study of the city government of Calcutta must be no more than partial, therefore, in so far as it cannot possibly describe and analyse the whole web of government which caters to Calcutta's administrative needs. Indeed, it must be remembered throughout that, in focusing upon the Calcutta Municipal Corporation, the study abstracts from the total web of government but a single authority which, as will become only too apparent, on its own unfettered responsibility in reality undertakes no major govern-mental service at all. As for metropolitan Calcutta, while the emergence of the urban and industrial complex of Hooghlyside has at last been recognized by the delineation of the Calcutta Metropolitan District and establishment of the Calcutta Metropolitan Planning Organization, apparently the fact that the government of this district is not primarily the responsibility of its local authorities has yet to be grasped. The truth is that no agency or class of agencies is primarily responsible.

THE CALCUTTA MUNICIPAL CORPORATION

The Calcutta Municipal Act of 1923 laid the foundations of the first autonomous local government institution in Calcutta. It ushered in important changes in the organization of the existing municipal corporation, which had consisted of three co-ordinate authorities, namely, the corporation itself, a general committee and a chairman. The latter had been appointed by the provincial government to exercise the triple functions of the chief executive officer, chairman of the general committee and chairman of the corporation. The Act of 1923 largely abandoned this tripartite division, and nearly all powers and authority were vested in the corporation itself, consisting of ninety councillors. This corporation was to elect its own mayor and five aldermen; and, subject to the approval of the provincial government, it was to appoint its own chief executive officer, who was to be answerable to the corporation for the conduct of its affairs. The Act also provided for standing

metropolitan Calcutta in 1963, see M. Bhattacharya, M. M. Singh, and F. J. Tysen: *Government in Metropolitan Calcutta—A Manual*, Calcutta Research Studies, No. 1, Asia Publishing House for Institute of Public Administration, New York, Bombay, 1965.

[1] Cf. F. Smallwood: *Government, Administration and the Political Process*, Paper No. 4, Centen-nial Study and Training Programme on Metropolitan Problems, Toronto Bureau of Municipal Research, 1967.

committees, district (now borough) committees and *ad hoc* committees. Thus, it gave great authority and autonomy to the new corporation, which was to be the supreme body for the municipal administration of the city. The exercise of any power by the chief executive officer was made subject to the general control and supervision of the corporation, and to such conditions as might be prescribed by it, except when in delegating its authority it provided that his decision should be final. Likewise, all the proceedings of the standing committees were subject to confirmation and revision by the corporation, except when the delegation of powers made their decisions final. The corporation was authorized to elect and dissolve all such committees, and to assign to them whatever functions it deemed fit.

At the time, this constitution was thought to herald a new, constructive era in the chequered history of the city's local administration, which dated back to the middle of the nineteenth century. Moreover, for the first time, it founded that administration on popular representation, in so far as the vote was given to persons paying certain minimum licence fees, rents or rates, and to women as well as men. But, twenty years later, the corporation was suspended by the newly independent State Government of West Bengal on grounds of corruption, maladministration and financial mismanagement. In the opinion of the Biswas Commission of Investigation set up in 1948 to inquire into the corporation's affairs, the root cause of the malady lay in the baneful influence exercised by the elected councillors over the appointed executive.[1] The commission's conclusions were that the primary defects lay in a too restricted electorate and an insufficient separation between the legislative and executive functions of the corporation. Its recommendations, accordingly, were for the broadening of the franchise, with a view to facilitating the election of better councillors, and for a separation between the legislative and the executive functions, with a view to making the executive independent of the councillors.

The result of the Biswas Commission's recommendations was a new Calcutta Municipal Act of 1951 under which the corporation has operated since 1952. The new legislation embodied the principle of separation of powers and instituted a limited extension of the franchise. In that Calcutta did not at first enjoy full adult suffrage it differed conspicuously from all other elected political institutions in India. After the achievement of independence in 1947, adult franchise was accepted as the basis of elections to the national Parliament and all state assemblies; and by that time all other municipal

---

[1] West Bengal, Local Self-Government Department, *Report of the Calcutta Corporation Investigation Commission, 1950*, Vol. 1, Part I (*Interim Report, 1950*). Alipore, West Bengal Government Press, 1950–51.

corporations had adopted this principle. By contrast, Calcutta's new municipal franchise was limited to persons who paid a rate, a rent or licence fees—as under the 1923 Act—or held a high school certificate or technical diploma. It has been estimated that the new legislation thus enfranchised no more than 10 per cent of the voters eligible for assembly and Parliamentary elections. Without going into the philosophical aspects of this restriction, it can at least be observed that it helped to consolidate power into the hands of a *rentie* class, whose parochial and sectional interests seriously reduced the corporation's effectiveness as an agency for the development of the city. The Biswas Commission had already remarked on the part played by a restricted franchise in helping to make a constituency the close preserve of its councillor, and in exposing elections to manipulation by councillors, especially when they operated hand in glove with the municipal executive. The new franchise did not eliminate these evils, and the disinterested attitude of the immigrant population enhanced the possibilities of improper practices.

Paradoxically enough, the main innovation of 1951 was thus to revert to the pre-1923 situation, in which municipal government was carried on by three co-ordinate authorities. The new Act elaborately separated the powers of the corporation (i.e. the city council) from those of the standing committees and the chief executive officer (now called the commissioner). In addition, important changes were made in the statutory position and powers of each of these authorities, and in the recruitment of the commissioner and other senior municipal officers.

The Corporation

As regards the new corporation, it initially consisted of eighty-one councillors, of whom eighty were to be elected for four years by single-member city wards, and one was to be *ex officio* the Chairman of the Calcutta Improvement Trust. In addition, five aldermen were to be elected by the councillors from outside persons after every general municipal election. Two changes were introduced in 1964, however, because of criticisms of the functioning of the new council. The restricted franchise was replaced by universal adult suffrage and the number of elected councillors and wards was increased to one hundred. The first municipal elections under adult suffrage were held in March 1965, and the total strength of the corporation is now one hundred and seven. Under the present system, any person who resides in a ward, and whose name is included in the electoral roll for the West Bengal Legislative Assembly from an area that includes such ward, is qualified as a municipal voter in the ward. The result of at last rendering the corporation a potentially representative and responsible institution has yet fully to manifest itself, however, as the 1965 elections did not fundamentally alter the balance of power.[1] The majority of councillors continued to represent the same class of person as before, and the immigrant population apparently remained disinterested in civic politics.

The corporation is required to meet once a month, but actually it meets for two hours every Friday evening. Its chief statutory responsibility is to take decisions on municipal policy, but the actual functions it performs may be classified as follows:

(a) the laying down of municipal policy by way of resolutions in fields reserved to the corporation for decision;

(b) the broad supervision of municipal administration; and

(c) the ventilation of grievances.

As regards the laying down of municipal policy, the corporation is empowered to take all decisions on major financial and administrative matters. It alone has the power of approving the annual budget prepared by the commissioner and presented to it by the standing finance and establishment committee. It is responsible for all decisions involving large financial commitments and contracts, and the appointment of senior staff (other than the commissioner and finance officer and chief accountant). It confirms or rejects decisions of the standing committees in matters referred to them.

As regards the broad supervision of municipal administration, the corporation has the right to require the commissioner to produce any necessary records, documents and reports, and every councillor and alderman may interpellate the mayor on matters connected with the city's administration. Similarly, with regard to the ventilation of grievances, any councillor or alderman has the right to call the attention of the commissioner to any neglect in the execution of municipal work, to any waste of municipal property or to the needs of any locality, and to make suggestions for improvement.

In practice, the exercise of these powers has become notorious for acrimony, disorder and staged walk-outs by the opposition councillors. The calm, deliberate formulation of municipal policy is rarely apparent, and the general public has come to expect bedlam at the weekly meetings. The mayor is not the head of the city's administration and, when interpellated, can only promise to look into the matter raised, or dismiss it as beyond the competence of the corporation to deal with (since the commissioner is responsible for the working of the executive machinery of city government). Because of

[1] The above gave the position as at November 1967. The municipal election in 1969 resulted in a majority for the Communist Party on the Calcutta Municipal Corporation.

the separation of powers, the corporation in any case has difficulty in broadly supervising such machinery. It is effective only as a forum for the ventilation of grievances, which more often than not means the ventilation of some councillor's spleen at the expense of the commissioner, who cannot answer back. In aggregate, the performance of the corporation as a council of elected representatives is characterized by a great deal of sound and fury, but little constructive effort and no discernible civic leadership.

The standing committees

While the corporation is intended to be a large body of persons engaged mostly in dignified debate and the passing of well-discussed resolutions on matters of broad civic policy, the standing committees are intended to be centres of decision-making in connection with specific functional matters. They are also intended to keep a close watch on the implementation of corporation and committee decisions. Their powers are thus considerable in scope, both legislative and executive, sometimes quasi-judicial, and final when delegated by the corporation. Moreover, although referred powers must be exercised subject to the approval of the corporation, since the standing committees are composed almost entirely of members of the majority party, in practice their recommendations generally receive automatic approval in spite of any opposition criticism.

The standing committees are statutory and not permissive. At its first meeting after a general municipal election, the corporation has no option but to appoint committees for each of the following subjects: finance and establishment; education; health and *bustee* improvement; water supply, drainage and sewage disposal; and works and town planning. Under an amendment of 1964, these committees replace former ones dealing respectively with the following functions: education; accounts; taxation and finance; health; town planning and improvement; public works; buildings; public utilities and markets and water supply (of which only accounts, and taxation and finance were mandatory committee subjects). The rigidity thus introduced into the corporation's committee system is undoubtedly a reaction against its mismanagement since 1952. As such, it seems to be a reaction of either despair or bureaucratic insensitivity to organizational realities. The great administrative advantage of a municipal committee system is surely its flexibility, and consequent capacity to respond to the changing needs of government. The powers of the standing committees are now laid down by Ministerial regulations and the Corporation no longer has any control over the nature and extent of these powers.

Since 1965, the standing committees have continued to be composed, as before, of members of the majority party. But there is now a provision for the nomination of members by the state government, and each committee in fact has two such members associated with it for a period of two years. In spite of this innovation breaking the monopoly of the majority party, committee meetings, which are held in private, continue to be suspect in the eyes of the public, who generally believe members to be concerned only with their own vested interests. Certainly, under the old committee system, judicial comment had held some councillors guilty of adopting dishonest tactics under the pressure of questionable influences, and of otherwise neglecting their duties of acting as the careful watchdog of the corporation over departmental activities.[1] If there is any substance in the widespread criticism of the corporation's government, it is in large part a serious reflection of the working of its standing committees, as they must be held responsible for most of its acts of omission and commission. They have certainly failed to provide any form of worthwhile leadership in municipal affairs. And it cannot be said that the borough committees described below have been exceptions to these general strictures.

The Commissioner

The 1951 Act vests in the commissioner the main executive responsibility for carrying out its provisions. To discharge this responsibility, he is made the chief executive officer of the corporation, all other officers and employees being responsible to him alone. His duties are thus wide ranging. He is required to give effect to every resolution passed by the corporation, unless it has been annulled by the state government. He exercises supervision and control over all other officers and employees, and has the authority to prescribe their duties. He is responsible for the custody of all records, including documents connected with the minutes of the proceedings of the corporation, its standing committees and borough and other committees. He is required to prepare and submit the annual budget estimates, which he must present to the finance and establishment committee by a certain date in the year. While he is responsible for implementing corporation and delegated committee decisions, in an emergency he may himself take a decision and direct the execution of any work which ordinarily requires the approval or sanction of the corporation or a committee. And, unless the state government directs otherwise, he may make an annual valuation of houses and land in order to

[1] Special Judge Bagchi's judgment, *State of West Bengal v. R.C. Roy et al.*, Calcutta Corporation Tubewell Case, Additional Special Court, Calcutta, Case No. 1 of 1957.

fix the municipal rate, and make an annual valuation of any *bustee*, subject to the approval of the finance and establishment committee. Written objections to the valuation are heard by the commissioner or his deputy, appeals from whose orders lie to the courts. The commissioner is appointed for a renewable term of five years by the state government on the recommendation of the State Public Service Commission, or in its own discretion if it deems it necessary to do so. Three of the seven commissioners have been members of the Indian Administrative Service. Neither *de jure* nor *de facto* does the corporation play any part in his appointment. If he does not himself resign before the expiry of his term of office, the state government can dismiss him on its own initiative, and it must do so on the initiative of a resolution passed by an absolute majority of all councillors.

The institution of such an independent and separate executive authority was a reversion to the position obtaining before the passage of the Act of 1923, and a radical departure from that Act in so far as, under its provisions, the corporation was given the power to appoint a chief executive officer who was entirely responsible to it. This radical change was presumably made in the hope that such an independent, separate officer would be rendered immune to the influences and pressures of the councillors. But, in the first place, the division of powers could not be complete. A perusal of the statutory functions and powers of the corporation, its standing committees and the commissioner, makes this abundantly clear. In important matters, such as the appointment of staff and the preparation of the annual budget, all three authorities are necessarily involved; and the separation of powers which has in fact been provided for in the law, tends to disappear in practice. After all, in many cases a clear-cut distinction between policy and administration cannot be drawn. For example, the commissioner makes the initial budget estimates, and thus obviously and inevitably lays down the framework of the city's annual expenditure. By virtue of their powers over appointments, contracts and expenditures, the corporation and standing committees have opportunities to exercise a significant control over the city's administration, whatever may be the theory about the final responsibility placed in the commissioner's hands.

In the second place, the major consequence of the attempted separation of legislative and executive functions seems to be perpetual conflict and deadlock between the commissioner and the councillors. No commissioner has found it possible to hold on to his office for the full term. Pressures from councillors have continued to harass the succession of commissioners, who have come and gone without making any significant impression on the normal tenor of civic administration. The reasons are not far to seek. The statutory authority and political influence enjoyed by the councillors still give them considerable power, which they still seek to use for the promotion of their own sectional and party interests. The commissioner finds it beyond his statutory authority and personal strength to provide an effective check against this misuse of power. When he attempts to do so, he inevitably runs into conflict with the councillors; and, so far, he has found himself no match for them. Indeed far from successfully contending with their machinations, the commissioner even has difficulty in controlling his own supervisory staff, the members of which are appointed by the councillors. Lacking any political base, not only is he unable to meet pressure with pressure, but he can provide no positive leadership to develop sources of revenue, effectively undertake new projects or revitalize the normally apathetic routine of administration.

The conclusion is thus inescapable that the commissioner can at best succeed in providing merely a negative check on the illegitimate interference of councillors in the municipal administration; and that in practice he has failed to achieve even this limited objective. As for providing a positive element of leadership, he is incapable of leading because he does not possess the requisite political support. It thus appears that the ineffectiveness of Calcutta's city government is partly to be traced to constitutional machinery which is ill-designed to produce unanimity amongst its separate, co-ordinate authorities. Divided against itself, that government has conspicuously failed to provide the leadership the city so desperately needs. But failure is not solely to be attributed to the machinery of government. In the final analysis, it is the people themselves who are to blame—the migrant elements who are not sufficiently interested to act as citizens of Calcutta, and the indigenous professional and *rentier* class who, instead of working for the good of the city as a whole, are concerned primarily to achieve their own narrow and selfish ends.

Lower-tier authorities

There is a rudimentary system of lower-tier authorities in the city which originated in the 1923 Act. These are the twenty borough committees, mandatory bodies consisting of five ward councillors and three persons elected by them. Their functions are confined to street naming, refuse collection, the registration of births and deaths, tree-planting, the provision of wash places, and making progress reports on public works. Due to financial weakness and general incompetence these borough committees are of little real consequence.

Other authorities

The local government of the Calcutta Metropolitan District is characterized by extensive fragmentation of authority. The lack of a single metropolitan body catering to the needs of the metropolitan district as a whole, has already been noted. Government in fact is splintered on the basis of both area and function.

The geographic splintering amongst hundreds of urban and rural bodies renders it well-nigh impossible to undertake the planning and administration of civic services for the entire district without new governmental machinery. For example, for the purposes of water supply, drainage and sewerage throughout Hooghlyside, a World Health Organization team[1] pointed out in 1960 that the time had passed when these functions could be dealt with successfully by the many separate local governments of Greater Calcutta, either individually or by any conceivable voluntary agreement. The team thus proposed a metropolitan water, sewerage and drainage authority which, endorsed by the Calcutta Metropolitan Planning Organization and technically planned by W.H.O. engineers, has recently been created under the Calcutta Metropolitan Water and Sanitation Authority Act of 1966. So far, its success has been limited by a failure to confine the authority's governing body to a few capable heads, and by the implacable opposition of the representatives of the Calcutta Municipal Corporation. The principle of the authority is no doubt a correct one, but steps should certainly be taken to eliminate the defects in its constitution.

The functional splintering of local government, especially in the city and suburbs of Calcutta and Howrah, creates just as serious problems for civic administration. In matters such as health and housing, state government departments share powers and functions with both local authorities and special agencies. In addition, there are many separate authorities established for specific functions. These various authorities may be grouped into three functional categories, namely, public utilities, public improvements and urban planning.[2] As regards public utilities, the agencies concerned are the Calcutta Tramways Company, the Calcutta State Transport Corporation, the Calcutta Electric Supply Corporation and the Oriental Gas Company. Until 1967, the Calcutta Tramways were owned and operated by a joint stock company registered in Great Britain, but they have now been brought

[1] A. Wolman, H. F. Cronin, L. Gulick and R. Pollitzer: *Assignment Report on Water Supply and Sewage Disposal, Greater Calcutta*, W.H.O. Project, India 170 (World Health Organization, Regional Office for S.E. Asia), New Delhi, 1960.
[2] For a full analysis of the functions and organization of all these authorities, see M. Bhattacharya, M. M. Singh and F. J. Tysen: *op. cit.*

under the management of the state government, and they will be nationalized in 1972.[1] The Calcutta Electric Supply Corporation, likewise registered in Great Britian, functions in the city and its suburbs under the general supervision of the state government's Directorate of Electricity; and the Oriental Gas Company is also a private undertaking, though placed under state management, which is authorized to produce and supply gas to industrial undertakings, hospitals and other institutions (including local authorities) in much the same area. The Calcutta State Transport Corporation, on the other hand, is a public corporation. It is empowered to operate road transport services in and around Calcutta City, subject to financial and administrative control exercised by the state government, and it could in fact operate the tramways upon their nationalization.[2]

As regards public improvements, the Calcutta Improvement Trust was set up in 1911 under the Calcutta Improvement Act, with responsibility for the formulation and implementation of schemes for the general improvement of the city, for the construction and realignment of streets, and for public housing purposes.[3] The trust is supervised by a board of trustees whose chairman is a senior civil servant of the state government, and the state finance department exercises control over its head officers. In spite of effecting some fine achievements in the redevelopment of major roads and contiguous areas, and in the building of certain housing estates, the trust suffers from various handicaps. Its financial resources have always been meagre and inelastic, its powers are not adequate for its tasks today, and its relatively few existing schemes are not broad enough to extend to comprehensive town planning, including urban renewal, slum clearance, housing, land-use planning and economic development. Moreover, for much of its finance the trust is dependent upon the Calcutta Corporation, which is also authorized to make road, drainage and slum improvements. This division of authority for carrying out city improvements renders co-ordination difficult and diffuses responsibility; and its effects are exacerbated by the undeniably hostile attitude of the corporation towards the trust.

A similar improvement trust for the area of the Howrah Municipal Corporation was set up in 1956, and has likewise suffered from inadequate finances and powers. Indeed, a close study of both trusts concludes that they are basically colonial, *laissez-faire* anachronisms in an era of nationalism, socialism, five-year planning, and the social and economic uplift of the mass

---

[1] For a detailed study of the Calcutta Tramways see L. Green and A. Datta: *Special Agencies in Metropolitan Calcutta: A Comparative Study*, Calcutta Research Studies, No. 8, Asia Publishing House for Institute of Public Administration, New York, Bombay, 1967: Part II.
[2] *Ibid.*, Part II. [3] *Ibid.*, Part I.

of the people.[1] They are in fact local and not state authoriites, and only the state can wield the powers needed.

As regards physical planning, the establishment of the Calcutta Metropolitan Planning Organization in June 1961, marked a turning-point in the history of regional and town planning in India, let alone West Bengal.[2] It was created by executive order on the initiative of the chief minister, Dr. B. C. Roy, to secure and promote the development of Greater Calcutta according to plan, and it has recently produced a massive basic development plan for the entire metropolitan district.[3] But the organization is merely a planning agency and has no executive authority to carry out the improvements which are so urgently needed. Only the trusts and special agencies such as the Salt Lakes Reclamation and Development Board are empowered to implement development projects, and, so far, none has provided a satisfactory answer to the metropolitan problems, which are so overwhelming in their magnitude. Possibly, what is really required may be a small number of multi-specialist departmental units created by the state to undertake specific but comprehensive development projects in limited areas, planned and programmed within the framework of the five-year plans by the Calcutta Metropolitan Planning Organization.[4] For such units could be endowed with state powers, and state resources of men and money, which alone are capable of coping with Calcutta's situation. Alternatively, as suggested below under *Planning and Development*, if consolidated and reformed municipal authorities were to be given development powers, one large-scale state authority could undertake major development projects throughout the metropolitan district which were beyond their individual capacities.

PARTY POLITICS

The Biswas Commission of 1948 made the following observation in its interim report:

By the Act of 1923 Sir Surendranath Banerjee had no doubt intended to establish in this great city the essential principles of democracy.... Unfortunately, however, the actual working of the Corporation has belied all his hopes and expectations, and those with whom it lay to build up a truly nationalist institution which was to be a 'citadel of civic power' in the hands of Calcutta's citizens succeeded in reducing the Corporation to such a deplorable condition that, when the Government took the extreme step of superseding the premier self-governing body in the province, not a word of protest was heard in any quarter and the appointment of an investigation Commission was in fact warmly welcomed.

[1] L. Green and A. Datta, *op. cit.*, Ch. 5. [2] *Ibid.*, Part I. [3] *Basic Development Plan.*
[4] L. Green and A. Datta: *op. cit.*, Ch. 5. In which case, the C.M.P.O. would have to be clearly integrated into the state's governmental machinery at the highest possible level. Otherwise, no departmental or inter-departmental unit would accept its authority to be over-riding.

The Corporation executive must no doubt also bear its share of responsibility for what has happened, but the root cause of the malady afflicting the Corporation must ... be ultimately traced to the Councillors who in fact exercised a most baneful influence over the executive.[1]

Although there is a good deal of truth in this indictment, it needs to be put in correct perspective. The twenty-five years preceding supersession marked a period of great national unrest, and when the corporation was made an autonomous body in 1923, it immediately came under the influence of nationalist politics. The corporation's entire orientation was towards the objectives and tactics of a movement led by the Indian National Congress, whose sights were set far higher than city government. Right from its inception to the day of supersession, Congress maintained a majority in the corporation, and the councillors nominated by the provincial government and other organizations, such as the Calcutta Chamber of Commerce, were mostly British and in opposition. Moreover not only did the last decade before supersession witness a great deal of political confusion, but the partition of Bengal in 1947 resulted in riots, arson, bloodshed and a vast influx of refugees into the city and its suburbs.

The history of the new corporation called into being in 1952 has been politically characterized by three major events, viz.: the emergence of a left-wing organization called the United Citizens' Committee; the rise to dominance of a Congress Party 'boss', Mr. Atulya Ghosh, in his capacity as the President of the Congress Municipal Association in Calcutta; and the introduction of adult suffrage.

The United Citizens' Committee (U.C.C.), which has developed as the main opposition to the ruling Congress Party, is a conglomeration of all left-wing forces in the corporation. Before the introduction of municipal adult suffrage, it contended that the Congress hegemony over the corporation was largely a result of the restricted vote, based on property and educational qualifications. Its platform therefore included a demand for the introduction of a universal franchise. It also demanded the vesting of greater powers in the corporation, the curtailment of the commissioner's existing and still increasing authority, a reduction of the state government's interference in the corporation's affairs and an improvement in civic services. Its actual role in the corporation has been limited by its exclusion from membership of the standing committees; and, as an opposition group in the corporation-in-council, its principal strategy has remained one of destructive criticism and obstruction.

The Congress Party maintained control until the communist victory of

[1] Biswas Commission, *Interim Report*, p. 2.

1969. The defeat of the West Bengal Congress Party in the General Assembly and parliamentary elections of 1967, and its consequent loss of the state government, weakened its hold over the corporation. Moreover, the personal defeat of Mr. Atulya Ghosh in the parliamentary election undermined his political position nationally and provincially, and destroyed the influence which he previously enjoyed over the state government. Until his defeat, however, he wielded very great authority in the corporation's affairs, although he was neither a councillor nor a member of the state's legislative assembly. As President of the Congress Municipal Association in Calcutta, and buttressed by his strong position in the provincial and national committees of Congress, Mr. Ghosh appears to have exercised unchallenged power over the corporation, finally controlling all party nominations for municipal elections, determining the selection of persons to fill the corporation's higher positions, and issuing the municipal party whips from his office. If any single person could have given leadership to the corporation in the years between independence and 1967, it was he; and it is a significant commentary on his long stewardship that it was particularly characterized by a lack of leadership in civic affairs. This failure cannot be attributed solely to the 1951 municipal constitution, in spite of its serious defects.

The third major political event has been the introduction of universal suffrage. One reason often heard for continuing to restrict the municipal vote in Calcutta was that strong left-wing, and especially Communist, elements would take advantage of universal suffrage to capture the city's government. Increasing disaffection among the middle-class intelligentsia, and the fact that Congress registered great successes in Assembly and parliamentary elections in precisely those areas where the city's semi-skilled and unskilled workers were concentrated, seem to have induced the Congress leadership suddenly to change its stand and adopt full adult suffrage. As a result of the subsequent municipal elections held in March 1965 Congress lost its absolute majority in the corporation, and only forty-nine Congress councillors were returned as against a combined opposition of fifty-one. Since six of the opposition councillors had been jailed by the state government while it was still controlled by Congress, the party was able to elect five aldermen in its favour and thus ensure a working majority of three members. In 1969, however, the Communists won outright control.

It will be seen that widening the suffrage has certainly given greater opportunities for the mass of the people to interest themselves in municipal affairs, which are no longer closed to their participation. And it does entail that the parties must now overtly woo them, instead of virtually ignoring many of the poorer sections of the population. Undoubtedly, this political competition should eventually stimulate an increased involvement of other important groups of people in civic matters, and thus end permanently the long hegemony of Congress in local politics. It should force the party to clarify and announce its civic platform, and generally encourage the leadership which was so conspicuously absent as long as Mr. Ghosh and Congress were not seriously challenged. By the same token, opposition parties should be encouraged to prepare themselves for the possibility of city government, and offer more positive alternatives to the Congress platform than a vague promise to lower taxes and improve civic services (which may, in fact, be incompatible objectives). Hopefully, therefore, city politics in Calcutta should no longer be so boss-ridden, nor so parochial, as in past years; but it remains to be seen how far the immigrant population will be stimulated to take a proper interest in civic affairs.

MUNICIPAL POWERS AND FUNCTIONS

The corporation has responsibility for the following functions: water supply, conservancy, drainage and sewerage (which, however, are passing under metropolitan control), public health and sanitation, primary education, roads and public places (including gardens and parks), street lighting and the lighting of public places, markets and slaughterhouses (including their provision and maintenance), building schemes and the regulation of buildings, the improvement and clearance of *bustees* or slums, property rating and the licensing of carts and carriages, dogs, trades and professions, advertisements, hotels, food factories and places of entertainment.[1]

All of these functions (other than the financial) are *mandatory*, although, for instance, the state's slum-clearance agent is the Calcutta Improvement Trust, which also builds roads and dwellings.[2] The corporation's *optional* powers extend, among others, to the planting and preservation of trees, the construction and maintenance of public buildings, the construction and maintenance of hospitals and orphanages, the establishment and operation of industrial schools and the maintenance of free libraries.

It has already been pointed out that a large number of agencies are responsible for many other urban government services. These extend to quite vital functions, such as transport, housing, electricity, urban redevelopment and renewal, fire-fighting and physical planning. Indeed, the multiplicity of

---

[1] For a complete and detailed list of responsibilities, see M. M. Singh: *Municipal Government in the Calcutta Metropolitan District: A Preliminary Survey*, Calcutta Research Studies, No. 2, Asia Publishing House for Institute of Public Administration, New York, Bombay, 1965.

[2] See L. Green and A. Datta: *op. cit.*, Part I.

special agencies, each concerned with a specific service, has been partly responsible for lack of system and co-ordination in the city's development. This is clearly evident in such fields as transport, housing and slum clearance. The railways, the tramways, the bus service, traffic control and the design and maintenance of the road system, are all related one to the other, but the authorities involved have never been brought together for transportation planning purposes. Housing may be undertaken by the state, the union government, the West Bengal Development Corporation, the Improvement Trust, the railways, private companies and universities, as well as by the corporation.

Certainly, the corporation has not attempted to co-ordinate the activities of these many and varied agencies. It has done little enough to carry out its own limited functions, and the city's squalid living conditions are a testimony to the stagnation of its civic administration. It is no secret that Calcutta has dismally failed to match municipal performance and the multiplying needs of economic development, population growth and urban planning and improvement. There is not only a wide gap between the needs of the people and available civic amenities, but the gap is increasing at an alarming rate. Very recently, an international team of experts remarked: 'The [Basic Development] Plan deals with a city in a state of crisis. We have not seen human degradation on a comparable scale in any other city in the world.'[1] The Basic Development Plan itself sums up the dimensions of the failure in the following terms:

In spite of its awesome size, its wealth and bustling activity, its vital significance in the national and regional economy, Calcutta is a city in crisis. All who live in this metropolitan complex have daily experience of its characteristic problems: chronic deficits in basic utilities such as water supply, sewerage and drainage; and in community facilities such as schools, hospitals, parks and recreation spaces; severe unemployment and under-employment; congested and inadequate transportation; vast housing shortages and proliferating slum areas. . . .[2]

A brief description of the state of the city's services will illustrate their inadequacies. The World Health Organization team visiting Calcutta in 1959, pointed out: 'The provision of filtered or otherwise safe drinking water is inadequate to a serious degree and has been so for many years. Because of this inadequacy, hundreds of thousands of people are driven to a variety of unsafe sources of water for daily use.'[3] It is revealing that, between 1931 and 1965, the *per capita* supply of filtered water declined from 52 gallons a day to 28 gallons a day, and there must be a similar decline in the supply of unfiltered

---

[1] Concluding Statement, *International Planning Seminar on Calcutta Metropolitan Plan.*
[2] *Basic Development Plan*, p. 3.
[3] A. Wolman, H. F. Cronin, L. Gulick and R. Pollitzer: *op. cit.*

water. The latter is intended for washing and cleaning purposes, but it is widely used for drinking and cooking, and is thus a major source of cholera in Calcutta. Likewise, with regard to drainage and sewerage, the W.H.O. team pointed out that most of the areas outside the centre of the city are without underground drainage, and must rely on service privies emptied by Corporation sweepers.[1]

Housing conditions are in general deplorable. Two-thirds of Calcutta's inhabitants live in *kutcha* buildings,[2] and more than 57 per cent of its multi-member families live in no more than one room. Transportation in Calcutta is a nightmare. During the rush hours, it is a long and arduous struggle to get even a place on the rear platform of a tramcar or bus. During the monsoon, a few hours' heavy shower is enough to inundate the roads and streets and stop all traffic. As for primary education, the corporation's schools provide places for no more than 30 per cent of the children of school-going age. 'The dismal picture of overcrowded primary classes cramped into dilapidated and unsuitable buildings—usually rented or requisitioned—with inadequate toilet facilities, no playing areas, and with only makeshift equipment, is familiar to those who live in Calcutta.'[3]

The reasons for this abject failure to provide even the bare necessities of city life are economic and social, as well as administrative, political and financial. In the long run, the explanation lies in the extreme poverty of the mass of the people, and the apathy which their misery breeds. More immediately, there is no doubt that the responsibility must be shouldered by the central and state governments, and not only by local government. The former have been guilty of gross neglect of the problems of the whole of Greater Calcutta, let alone those of the city itself. In the worst instances, these problems far exceed the financial and administrative capacity of any local authority or combination of local authorities to solve. As regards problems of lesser dimensions, most need to be attacked on either a concerted or metropolitan scale, if there is to be any hope of success. It is only the residue which really falls within the province of existing local governments. Even so, there is little evidence of any serious intent on their part to find solutions. If the municipalities had done their best to improve urban life, they could no doubt be absolved of responsibility for failure. But, like the corporation, they have been too much controlled by parochial and sectional interests to concern themselves with the overall improvement of the towns they govern. Generally speaking, their negligence has been comparable to that of Calcutta, and their administration has been equally devoid of leadership.

[1] *Ibid.*   [2] These are insubstantial dwellings made of mud, bamboo or similar materials.
[3] *Basic Development Plan*, p. 30.

CITY DEPARTMENTS AND STAFF

The corporation's administrative organization is headed by the commissioner, and all officers and employees are subordinate to him.[1] There are now two deputy commissioners to assist him in his executive tasks, and numerous heads of departments. Prominent among the latter are the chief engineer, medical officer of health, law officer, education officer, and finance officer and chief accountant. The functions of these officers are indicated by their designations. There is, however, another important officer designated as secretary, whose main function in practice is apparently to maintain a liaison between the executive, on the one hand, and the corporation and the standing committees on the other.

The principal departments are established for the following purposes: assessments, buildings, licensing, engineering, valuing and surveying, waterworks, public health, education, records and public relations. There is in addition, a planning and development department headed by a development engineer under the control of the chief engineer, the main tasks of which are the planning and execution of development schemes for water supply, sanitation and drainage; and the corporation also employs a chief architect.

Apart from the commissioner himself, the corporation's staff may be divided into the following categories:

(a) statutory officers appointed by the state government on the recommendation of the State Public Service Commission, under which category falls the finance officer and chief accountant;

(b) statutory officers appointed by the corporation on the recommendation of the State Public Service Commission, and subject to the approval of the state government, such as the deputy commissioners, chief engineer, secretary and medical officer of health;

(c) officers appointed by the corporation on the recommendation of the Municipal Service Commission;

(d) officers appointed by the finance and establishment committee on the recommendation of the Municipal Service Commission; and

(e) clerical and lower staff appointed by the commissioner.

All appointments with a maximum salary of Rs. 250 a month are made by the commissioner; appointments between Rs. 250 and Rs. 750 a month are made by the finance and establishment committee; appointments between Rs. 750 and Rs. 1,500 a month are made by the corporation. The last two categories of appointments are made on the recommendation of the

---

[1] For detailed organization charts of the Calcutta Corporation in 1963, see M. M. Singh: *op. cit.*

Municipal Service Commission, which consists of a chairman and two other members, the former being a member of the State Public Service Commission and the latter being appointed one each by the state government and the corporation respectively. In the case of appointments with salaries above Rs. 1,500 a month, the corporation is required to act on the recommendation of the State Public Service Commission.

Since the commissioner is appointed by the state government, in these circumstances the corporation naturally has difficulty in exercising, for good or ill, significant control over its departmental machinery. Furthermore, the complicated provisions of appointment, involving the State Public Service Commission, the Municipal Service Commission, state departments, the corporation-in-council, the finance and establishment committee, and the commissioner himself, lead to much confusion about the locus of final authority and responsibility, and to divided loyalties. If the corporation does not have control, neither does the commissioner; as, for instance, a substantial number of municipal employees continue to owe their positions to the patronage of the councillors, whether acting in committee or as the corporation-in-council. The state's answer to these problems is to further weaken the corporation's hand, especially in response to the recommendations of a committee of inquiry of 1962, which advocated still greater independence of the commissioner from the corporation.[1] But it may be questioned if a complete divorce of the corporation's staff from the corporation-in-council (or in committee) is either feasible or warranted. Having no authority at all over its staff, the corporation would almost certainly be reduced to even greater impotence than it has displayed hitherto.

CITY FINANCE

Although the problems facing metropolitan Calcutta are immense, the sources of revenue available to its local governments are relatively inelastic and quite inadequate for the tasks that so urgently need to be performed. Generally speaking, 'The local authorities are caught in a vicious circle: low revenue from limited taxation fosters poor administration, poor administration puts a brake on the imposition of new taxes or the increase of existing taxes'.[2] About 72 per cent of the municipal authorities' ordinary income

[1] Government of West Bengal, Local Self-Government and Panchayats Department, *Report of the Corporation of Calcutta Enquiry Committee*, 1962, Vol. I.
[2] A. Datta and D. C. Ranney: *Municipal Finances in the Calcutta Metropolitan District: A Preliminary Survey*, Calcutta Research Studies No. 3, Asia Publishing House for Institute of Public Administration, New York, Bombay, 1965.

derives from taxation, for which a tax on property accounts for two-thirds. Apart from improving the collection of tax revenues, which is undoubtedly poor, there is thus little possibility of augmenting local income from existing sources, unless either property rates are increased or assessments raised. In practice, neither of these alternatives is possible, because the propertied interests controlling the urban local authorities are already subjected to heavy income tax and would find it difficult to bear a further financial burden from increased local taxes.[1] The most feasible answer thus seems to lie in the direction of increasing grants-in-aid from the state government. So far, however, the state has yet to evolve a system of grants to local authorities which is based on coherent principles.[2] It has given various development grants for specific projects in education and medical or public health services, but these have been erratic, sporadic and meagre. And by limiting capital grants to only the medical and public health services of urban local authorities, it has effectively relegated the latter to playing an insignificant role in the development programmes of a metropolitan complex which the state has neglected.

What is true for the metropolitan district is for the most part true of Calcutta City. There are long-standing problems of municipal poverty, of limited tax fields, or over-reliance on a property tax which is essentially regressive, and of unsystematic grants which, in this particular case, very largely represent state assistance for the payment of cost of living allowance to the corporation's employees and are totally unconnected with any programme for the improvement of city life. In his annual budget estimate for 1964–65, the commissioner remarked: 'Unless new resources can be tapped by which our revenue can be reinforced, the day is not far off when it may not be possible even to meet the normal cost of maintenance, not to speak of improvement and replacements.'

Income

The main sources of municipal revenue for 1966–67 were as follows:

	100,000 Rupees	*Percentage*
1. Consolidated rate	844·50	60·80
2. Licence fees and other taxes	81·34	5·84

[1] A. Datta and D. C. Ranney, *op. cit.*, p. 24. For the financial problems of the rural authorities in the Metropolitan District, see M. Bhattacharya: *op. cit.*

[2] For this, and the following reference to grants, see, A. Datta: *Inter-Governmental Grants in Metropolitan Calcutta*, Calcutta Research Studies No. 10, Asia Publishing House for the Institute of Public Administration, New York, Bombay, 1965.

3. Municipal markets and slaughterhouses	44·51	3·21
4. Building fees	40·55	2·92
5. Water supply receipts	37·56	2·11
6. Government contributions	213·19	15·35
7. Miscellaneous receipts	127·38	9·17
Total	1,389·03	100·00

It will be seen that receipts from the consolidated rate constitute more than 60 per cent of the corporation's income. This rate is a tax levied on the annual rental value of houses and land, and in the case of a building an allowance of 10 per cent is permitted for maintenance and repair. The rate combines a general property tax and service charges for water and conservancy. Its maximum permissible limit is 33 per cent of the annual rental value, and, in practice, it is levied on a graduated scale which rises from 15 to 23 per cent of such annual value.

This type of consolidated rate is open to serious objections where emphasis is to be placed on the development of a city. For example, Hicks has pointed out that a property tax discourages new buildings, slows down the improvement of existing ones and, if assessed on rental value, has more adverse consequences for growth than a property tax levied on capital value. Furthermore, in the case of Calcutta, where a Rent Control Act tends to freeze rents, the basis of the rate is artificially lowered;[1] and although the institution of *salami*, or the custom of paying key money at the time of taking lease, nullifies the benefits of this Act, the corporation still has to make assessments on the basis of the low rent that is actually paid by the tenant.

In addition to these shortcomings, there appear to have been serious defects in the administration of the property tax. There have been persistent complaints of widespread, gross under-assessment, and a falling rate of collection. The problem of under-assessment and under-collection in Calcutta is in fact very acute, and partly accounts for the very low *per capita* municipal tax receipts registered there as compared to some other metropolitan cities in India. A study of *per capita* municipal taxation in Calcutta, Bombay and Madras shows that, while in Calcutta it has remained at the level preceding the second world war, in Madras it has doubled, and in Bombay more than doubled, over the same period.

The next important source of income is represented by licence fees and taxes on trades and professions. The tax on trades and professions is levied at a flat rate, but there is a strong case for graduating the rate of tax according

[1] U. K. Hicks: *Development from Below*, Oxford, 1961, pp. 356–9.

to income. Such graduation would not, however, greatly augment the corporation's revenues; and neither would higher licence fees or the opening of new municipal markets and the municipalization of existing private markets, since receipts from this latter source constitute one of the smallest sectors of corporation revenue.

The miscellaneous items cover revenue from taxes on animals and carriages (including bicycles), receipts from the Tramways and Electric Supply Company, receipts from burial grounds, fines, the proceeds of sales of land and interest earned on surplus cash balances. Of these, the receipts from the Tramways and Electric Supply Company represent stereotyped levies fixed many years ago on undertakings which are scheduled for nationalization in five years' time. Water supplies are now being taken over by a metropolitan authority. Fines are controlled by various statutes. In short, while the total receipts are large, they are not expandable and are likely to be reduced in the near future.

It follows that, as in the case of the municipalities, the corporation is very much dependent on the property rate and government subventions for the augmentation of its income. As regards these subventions, the state's contributions to the corporation have already been stated to represent very largely a form of charity which can be defended only on grounds of expediency, i.e. 90 per cent of state assistance is given to defray the cost of living allowances paid to the corporation's own employees. The remaining state contribution consists very largely of a subvention made in lieu of receipts from motor vehicle licences, which the corporation itself issued before 1932. This subvention has recently been raised from Rs. 450,000 a year to Rs. 1 million, and is unlikely to be further increased in the foreseeable future. Nevertheless, it seems that the one item which could in fact be augmented is that of government grants, provided they are given regularly and systematically for development purposes, according to well-conceived development programmes.

Expenditure

The Calcutta Corporation is authorized to raise loans for specific purposes on the security of the consolidated rate, but prior sanction of the state government is necessary. The borrowing powers of the corporation are limited in that the sums payable for interest and for the maintenance of compulsory sinking funds may not exceed 10 per cent of the city's annual total property valuation.

Apart from a thorough overhaul of these financial arrangements, there is also a need to revise budgetary procedures. The budget has very limited scope for capital expenditures and the corporation's borrowing powers are seriously limited. The budget is also made annually without permitting flexibility for long-term investments spread over a number of years, and without reference to five-year development programmes, in spite of the long experience of economic and fiscal planning in India. This major defect is ventilated below in connection with planning, however, and need not be further discussed in this section.

The corporation's expenditure in 1966–67 was as follows:

	100,000 Rupees	Percentage
1. Conservancy	212·58	14·44
2. Water supply	166·09	11·28
3. Drainage	63·26	4·29
4. Roads	104·85	7·12
5. Lighting	40·32	2·73
6. Health measures	77·92	5·27
7. Primary education	61·73	4·28
8. Grants to hospitals, schools, etc.	12·12	0·82
9. Loan charges	179·58	12·19
10. Contribution to Calcutta Improvement Trust	57·24	3·88
11. Markets and slaughterhouses	21·49	1·46
12. General administration	150·60	10·22
13. Miscellaneous	324·12	22·02
Total	1,474·90	100·00

The most notable features of this breakdown are the very small proportions spent on primary education and health services, and the extremely high expenditure on the corporation's general administration and establishment. On a rule-of-thumb basis, these administrative charges appear to be at least twice as large as might reasonably be expected. Unless the corporation is to be regarded as a philanthropic employer of labour, they should certainly be reduced by an intensive economy drive. But, any such drive would no doubt meet with tenacious opposition from several powerful quarters, including the trade unions as well as vested political elements.

RELATIONS WITH HIGHER AUTHORITIES

In India, the central government has virtually no direct relationship with local bodies. Local governments derive their existence and authority from statutes made by the state governments. There are a number of statutory provisions under which the West Bengal Government exerts control over local authorities. Under the Calcutta Municipal Act, 1951, it is able to do so in the following ways:

(a) The corporation must submit to the state government a detailed annual report of its administration.

(b) The state may at any time require the corporation, the standing committees or the commissioner to produce any record or document, and to furnish any plan, estimate, statistics, account or report.

(c) The state may at any time depute an officer to examine and inspect any report on the city's administration.

(d) The state may, whenever it finds that any corporation activity is unlawful or irregular, or that a duty imposed on the corporation has not been performed, or that adequate financial provision has not been made for the performance of any duty, restrain the corporation from performing the act, or direct it to make arrangements for the proper performance of the duty, or direct it to make adequate financial provision, as the case may be.

(e) In the event of the corporation's failure to comply with the state government's directives, the latter may appoint a person to take the necessary action, and charge the cost to the corporation.

(f) The state prescribes the duties and powers of the commissioner and the standing committees, it appoints associate members to such committees, and by the amended Act names the standing committees which are to be appointed by the corporation.

(g) The corporation's by-laws must be sanctioned by the state government, which may modify any by-law before sanctioning it.

(h) The state has the power to make or authorize, as the case may be, certain senior appointments, including that of the commissioner and finance officer and chief accountant.

(i) The corporation may not raise loans without the previous sanction of the state government, which also approves the rate of interest on the loan and the period of repayment.

(j) In the last resort, the state government can supersede the corporation and place an administrator in charge of it.

These are very considerable powers of control, which deeply penetrate the corporation's organization and place it in a veritable strait-jacket. But they are negative powers which check and constrain. Instead of encouraging the corporation to act in certain desirable directions, they prevent it from acting in undesirable ones. Often, they can be exercised only by causing at least as much delay and obstruction as they are intended to remove; and whether or not the state exercises its powers may well depend upon the balance of political forces. In 1963, for instance, one observer remarked: 'Between supersession and the Corporation stands the massive figure of Atulya Ghosh. Twice in less than a year Chief Minister Prafulla Sen has made public statements on the changes he wants in the Corporation, twice he has been obliged to withdraw and retreat in face of Atulya Ghosh's unstated yet unmistakable resistance.'[1]

PLANNING AND DEVELOPMENT

It merits repetition that, until the establishment of the Calcutta Metropolitan Planning Organization in 1961, there was no planning organization for either the Hooghlyside conurbation as a whole, or for any urban area within its borders. Nowhere in West Bengal, in fact, was there any effective machinery for town and country planning. Thus, only six years have passed since the C.M.P.O. first began to plug the gap in physical planning, and the question of a suitable administrative structure for implementing the plans it formulates has still to be decided.

In December 1966 the C.M.P.O. published its first basic development plan for the Calcutta Metropolitan District between 1966 and 1986.[2] The purpose of the plan is to provide a rational and comprehensive framework of growth for metropolitan Calcutta over the next two decades, and its main objectives may be summarized as follows:

(*a*) to promote a more dynamic growth of the metropolitan economy in particular and of eastern India in general;

(*b*) to develop a proper urban environment for a population of 12·3 million people by 1986;

(*c*) to create machinery for the sustained planning of development and the effective implementation of all plans; and

(*d*) to strengthen local self-government and citizen participation.[3]

The plan recommends immediate action on a five-year development programme, including the development of three new towns, two urban renewal projects, the commencement of a long-run shelter programme involving slum improvements, the provision of basic utilities (including water, sewerage and drainage), the provision of over 200,000 primary and secondary school places, the development of urban community services and

[1] *Economic Weekly*, Vol. XV, No. 22, June 1, 1963.   [2] *Basic Development Plan.*
[3] *Ibid.*, p. 6.

facilities, the provision of open spaces, the initiation of a long-term programme for the renewal and development of a metropolitan transport system, and the institution of major administrative and fiscal changes. The latter include a strengthening of the local government system by consolidating all municipal authorities into nine only, with responsibilities extending to the maintenance of local roads, lighting, conservancy, building controls, local zoning, markets and slaughterhouses, and the registration of births and deaths. They also include: the establishment of a state planning agency; the transformation of the C.M.P.O. into a statutory body; the setting up of a state industrial development corporation; the creation of three area-wise urban development authorities for the metropolitan district; the creation of three metropolitan functional authorities for (i) traffic and transportation, (ii) the Hooghly bridge, and (iii) parks and recreation, in addition to the new Calcutta Metropolitan Water and Sanitation Authority; the establishment of a special administrative authority for *bustee* improvement; the creation of a state housing board; the probable creation of a metropolitan education commission; the enforcement of interim land-use control; the setting up of a Calcutta Metropolitan Development Fund; the introduction of central assessment for the metropolitan district; and the improvement of local government finance.

These proposals are intended to be incorporated in the next all-India Five-Year Plan, and beyond this first phase of immediate activities, the Basic Development Plan suggests a fifteen-year perspective plan that aims at an overall programme of action to arrest the deterioration of the metropolitan district, enhance its role as a major commercial, industrial and administrative centre, and revive its function as the cultural heart of the state.[1]

The plan calls for capital expenditures of approximately Rs. 1,070 million on specified activities during the first five-year phase, and naturally states that the long-term financial needs can be calculated with greater precision during the subsequent planning stages. It adds: 'The broad categories of expenditures contemplated in the plan may be listed as (*a*) those that may be expected to be self-balancing; (*b*) those that must be financed by local governments and may require increased taxation at the local level; and (*c*) those whose nature suggests that state and central government grant assistance may appropriately be sought.'[2]

This brief study cannot possibly do justice to the full scope, analysis and recommendations of the Basic Development Plan, which is a truly heroic

----

[1] *Basic Development Plan*, p. 170.
[2] *Ibid.*, p. 136.

document in view of the magnitude of the problems it sets out to solve. One can but contemplate the history of government in Calcutta for the last fifty years, take stock of the general economic and political situation of India today, review the more immediate reasons for the premature fall of the United Front Government of West Bengal towards the end of 1967, and wonder if the planners have not singularly failed to assess political realities. It is not a sufficient rebuttal to reply that planners are not concerned with these matters. Planning is a process beginning with survey and analysis, and ending with implementation. There could hardly be a political climate more adverse to the implementation of a plan of such breadth and depth than that prevailing in Calcutta, and especially since 1965.

At the same time, the poverty of eastern India sets its own narrow limits to planning possibilities in the city and its hinterland. Fiscal reliance on the local authorities of the metropolitan district and on the State of West Bengal is more easily recommended than achieved, and past experience of financial assistance from the central government offered little hope for the future. However, the colossal sum of Rs. 150 crores was allocated for two Calcutta Municipal Development Authority schemes during the Fourth Plan period.

While political, financial and national planning considerations thus lead to legitimate doubts about the feasibility of the plan as a whole, the least auspicious of its recommendations are certainly the administrative. Will urban local government really be strengthened by consolidating the existing fragments into nine large-scale authorities enjoying virtually no major municipal function at all? Is it wise to reorganize the improvement trusts as two out of three state-appointed area development authorities, established at the expense of the corporation and consolidated municipalities which, if reformed and adequately financed, might yet redeem themselves, provided they were made responsible for implementing quite important development projects planned and programmed by the C.M.P.O.? In such case, no more than a single state authority might need to be created to undertake major metropolitan development projects beyond the capacity of the consolidated municipalities. And, given Calcutta's political past and the explosive nature of its present problems, is it reasonable to transform the C.M.P.O. into a statutory body which, by definition, cannot form part of the state's departmental machinery and must for ever hover on the outskirts of the inner sanctum of the state government?

The truth is that, for many years to come, the C.M.P.O. will be deeply immersed in weighty and controversial issues of policy, which will be the stuff of state politics and resolvable only by the state government. It will

L*

thus be politically impossible for that government to abdicate to a statutory body the responsibility for any major stage in the process of decision-making in the field of metropolitan development. The C.M.P.O.'s plans necessarily set the frame within which final decisions are to be made, limit the alternatives placed before government, and define its field of choice. There is no doubt that the government itself must shoulder the responsibility for the social, economic and physical planning of metropolitan Calcutta. In that case, the planning organization should be placed as high as possible in the state's administrative hierarchy, and should have direct access to the Cabinet. Only this position would duly recognize the vital role Calcutta plays in the welfare of West Bengal, and the immense significance of decisions about its future.

Thus to raise the metropolitan problems of development to state significance would not, however, solve the crisis of local government in the metropolitan district. Even if the consolidated municipalities and the corporation were to be given something worth while to do, as suggested, there might still be no guarantee that they would in fact do it. The answer of the Basic Development Plan is to place no faith in local self-government, and to recommend the transfer of all major powers to state-appointed authorities, each concerned with a group of related functions, such as water, sewerage and drainage; traffic and transport; education; housing; industrial development; area development; and parks and recreation. Paradoxically, this counsel of despair is too optimistic. The state government has itself fallen apart more quickly than even the corporation. The corrosion of public life in West Bengal has many origins, moral, economic, social and political. The state appointment of metropolitan boards will not halt that corrosion. In the long run, only the people themselves can do so, and they must possess elective instruments for the purpose.

In short, there can be no guarantee that reformed municipal authorities would use the powers given to them; equally, there can be no guarantee that state-appointed boards would do so, either. But a possibility does remain of the people themselves yet rising to the challenge, given better tools of government and dynamic leadership. The problem thus resolves itself into one of designing locally representative and responsible governments to undertake important development tasks, with organizations tailored to this function and providing the greatest possible potential for effective and sustained leadership. The existing corporation is obviously not the prototype upon which to model these local (and possibly metropolitan) authorities; but the keys to success may very well lie in a study of its failings.

Chicago

MILTON RAKOVE

Born 1918. Roosevelt University, 1946–48, B.A. Political Science; University of Chicago, 1948–56, M.A. 1949, Ph.D. 1956 Political Science. Carnegie Teaching Fellow, 1955–56; U.S. Army, 1943–46; Professor of Political Science, University of Illinois, Chicago Circle, since 1958 and Lecturer in Political Science, Barat College; Lecturer, University of Chicago, Downtown Centre, 1957–60; Lecturer, Roosevelt University, 1957–60; Associate Professor, Loyola University Centre for Research in Urban Government, 1965–66; Field Research Associate and Director of the Chicago World Politics Programme, American Foundation for Political Education, Chicago, 1957–60; Research Consultant, Better Government Association, 1961–62; Research Consultant, American Foundation for Political Education, 1962–64; Research Consultant, Brookings Institution, 1967.

Author of: *Arms and Foreign Policy in the Nuclear Age* (ed.) Chicago, American Foundation for Continuing Education (1964); Monograph, *The Changing Patterns of Suburban Politics in Cook County, Illinois*, Chicago, Loyola University Press, 1965.

Articles in professional journals and magazines and the *Chicago Sun-Times*.

Chicago

NO ONE has ever described the city of Chicago better than the late poet and writer, Carl Sandburg, who once called it 'the city of the big shoulders'. Founded as a frontier post in 1803, and incorporated as a village in 1833, Chicago has never been a genteel town. It has always been, and still is today, a lusty, brawling, sprawling city.

Beginning with a population of 350 persons, Chicago grew rapidly. By 1860, the population had reached 100,000. After the great fire of 1871, which destroyed the central core of the city, the population literally exploded. By 1890 Chicago was the second largest city in the United States with a population of over 1,000,000, and by 1930 the city had 3,376,438 residents. Since 1930 the population has levelled off, rising slightly to 3,620,962 in 1950, and then declining to 3,550,404 in 1960. In area the city has grown from 10·186 square miles in 1840 to its present 224·2 square miles.

The population of the metropolitan area, including Chicago and its suburbs, some of which extend across the border of the State of Illinois' neighbouring State of Indiana, encompassed a population of 6,794,461 in 1960, more than tripling the 2,092,883 people who lived in that same area in 1900. In that same period of 60 years, however, the city of Chicago's percentage of the metropolitan area's total population decreased from 81·5 per cent in 1900 to 52·3 per cent in 1960. This trend will continue in the years ahead. It is estimated that in the Chicago Standard Metropolitan Statistical Area, which includes Chicago and its ring, the population will reach 8,619,000 by 1980. Of this total, the projection for Chicago is only 3,774,000 persons, while the metropolitan area outside of the city will contain 4,800,000 persons.

Within the Chicago metropolitan area, significant changes are taking place in the character of the population. Chicago and its suburbs are in the midst of the two great population movements which characterize contemporary American society—a massive migration of Negroes from the South into the cities of the North, and an exodus of whites from the city centres to the suburbs. The Negro population of Chicago has increased from 227,000 in 1940 to 509,000 in 1950, to 838,000 in 1960, and is expected to reach 1,540,000 by 1980 out of a projected population of 3,774,000. At the same time the Negro population of the suburban ring increased by only 37,000 persons between 1950 and 1960, and is expected to reach a total of about 347,000 out of 4,800,000 persons by 1980. Chicago, like many North American big

333

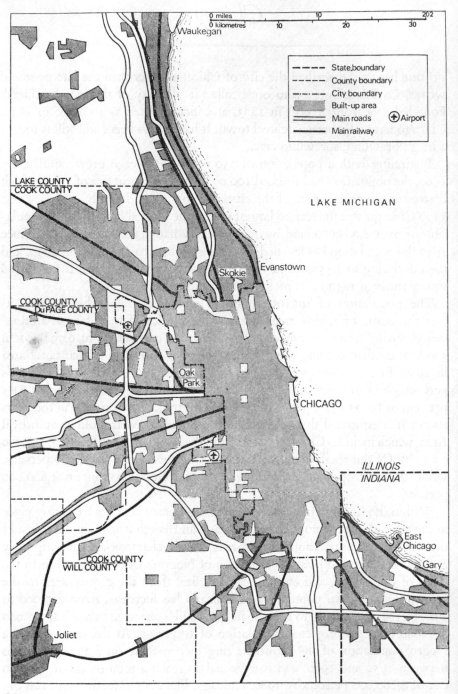

MAP 8 CHICAGO

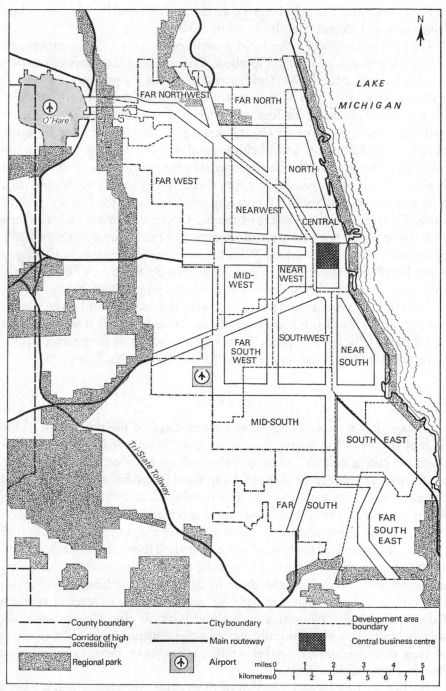

Map 9 chicago—comprehensive plan

The following labels appear on the map:

LAKE MICHIGAN

O'Hare

FAR NORTHWEST

FAR NORTH

NORTH

FAR WEST

NEARWEST

CENTRAL

MID-WEST

NEAR WEST

FAR SOUTH WEST

SOUTHWEST

NEAR SOUTH

MID-SOUTH

SOUTH EAST

FAR SOUTH

FAR SOUTH EAST

Tri-State Tollway

Legend:

- - - County boundary
——— City boundary
- - - Development area boundary
——— Corridor of high accessibility
——— Main routeway
▨ Central business centre
▨ Regional park
✈ Airport

miles 0 1 2 3 4 5
kilometres 0 1 2 3 4 5 6 7 8

cities, is becoming a largely Negro core city, surrounded by a heavily white fringe area and almost completely white suburban ring.

The primary reason for the rapid growth of the city and its surrounding area is a fortuitous geographic location. Chicago is in the heart of the rich farmlands of the Middle West with access to one of the great bodies of fresh water in the world, Lake Michigan, astride the main routes of almost all of the major railroad and main highway arteries of the United States, and close to the iron ore and coal of the Great Lakes region. Iron ore brought by barge cheaply from Minnesota and Michigan, and coal from the rich fields to the south and east have made the Chicago area the centre of a great iron and steel industry. On a normal day, approximately 35,000 railroad freight cars, with an average capacity of 50 short tons, are handled in the Chicago freight yards. Even before the opening of the St. Lawrence Seaway, which made Chicago an ocean port, the port of Chicago had the largest volume of traffic of any inland port in America. With the opening of the seaway, Chicago's water-borne commerce will be exceeded only by the port of New York. Iron, coal, steel, chemicals, petroleum products, wheat, corn, sulphur, limestone, sand, gravel, manufactured goods, machinery, and even sugar, molasses and coffee from Latin America are brought in and transhipped out of Chicago. Chicago's continued growth as a centre of commerce, manufacturing and transportation is assured for the foreseeable future.

THE PEOPLE

Chicago has 3,500,000 people, about one-third of the population of the State of Illinois. With many ethnic groups, and people of all religious affiliations, the city is a classic example of the melting pot that is America in the twentieth century, except that in Chicago and its environs, the melting pot has not melted very much. Chicago developed as a city of nationality, religious and racial neighbourhoods and has remained so until this very day. The ethnic, religious and racial divisions among the polyglot population of the city have remained fairly rigid and perpetuated themselves into the second and third generations of the children of the original immigrants. Chicagoans do not identify themselves with their city as an ancient Athenian would with his polis, an imperial Roman with his world capital, or even a modern Parisian, Londoner, Florentine or Berliner with his city. Chicagoans think socially, culturally, economically and, as a consequence, politically, in terms of their neighbourhoods or their ethnic, religious or racial groups, rather than in terms of their city.

The history of Chicago, like that of most great American cities, has been a chronicle of successive waves of immigrants pouring into the city seeking opportunities denied them in their homelands. Thus, the Germans, the Irish, the Poles, the Bohemians, the Lithuanians, the Italians and the Jews inundated the city in successive waves.

New immigrants almost always moved into old neighbourhoods, usually close to the terminus of whatever form of transportation they used to get to the city, the bus and train stations. Since those terminal points were usually located in or near the central core of the city, those were the areas in which the new immigrants settled.

The reasons for this tendency of new immigrants to settle near the terminals were quite simple. A new immigrant arriving in a strange environment was not likely to take a taxi or even public transportation with which he was unfamiliar into the distant reaches of the city. His natural inclination was to take his suitcase (if he had one) or his bag or box of belongings, walk around the corner from the terminal and find a room.

His next step was to find a job, preferably as close as possible to where he lived.

Once firmly rooted economically, he sent for his family (if he had one) and looked for a larger flat, possibly two or three rooms.

Then the brothers, sisters, cousins, aunts, uncles and grandparents began to arrive. They almost automatically went to the area where the enterprising pioneer immigrants were living and moved in with the relatives until they could afford a room or a couple of rooms of their own. Within a short period of time, shops stocking native foods appeared, restaurants serving native delicacies opened, taverns or wine houses dispensing native alcoholic spirits blossomed, recreational facilities endemic to the native culture were built and churches or temples serving the religious needs of the local population were established. Thus, islands of native culture were created in the heart of the city.

The process repeated itself with each ethnic group moving into the city. Chicago became a city of ethnic neighbourhoods with almost fixed boundary lines dividing the various nationality groups. Thus the Germans settled on the near North Side, the Irish on the near South Side, the Jews on the near West Side around Maxwell Street, the Italians on the near West Side north of the Jews, the Bohemians and Poles on the near South-west Side and the near North-west Side.

After the restrictive immigration law of 1924 was passed these communities began to gel as centres of ethnic culture. The people in them slowly assimilated somewhat to the life of the city as a whole, although still retaining strong feelings of identification with their own ethnic groups. As economic opportunities opened up they began to search for better living conditions in newer neighbourhoods.

However, the old ethnic clannishness and sense of identification with their cultural groups was still strong. As they moved from the older neighbour-hoods into newer communities farther out from the centre of the city, they literally moved *en masse*.

Thus the Jews moved from the near West Side to North Lawndale, the Italians moved steadily west up the centre of the city, the Poles and Bohe-mians moved west along the near southern streets of the city, the Irish and Lithuanians went south, and the Germans and Scandinavians went north-west.

Within each of these ethnic groups, fissures began to appear between the more successful *nouveau riche* and those immigrants who had not done so well in the new world. Wealthier merchant Jews moved out north to Albany Park and Rogers Park, and better-educated German Jews settled in Hyde Park and South Shore, close to the intellectual and cultural stimulation of the University of Chicago. Bohemian skilled workers went west to Berwyn. German machinists went to the far north-west reaches of the city. Polish middle-income workers moved to Cicero. Successful Irish politicians, civil servants, tavern owners and lawyers headed south-east and south-west. Italian and Greek doctors, accountants, restaurant owners and undertakers moved to Austin, Oak Park, River Forest, Elmwood Park and Westchester. Within each of the areas of the city and its suburbs new ethnic neighbour-hoods and enclaves were created. They were now middle class instead of working class, but they were still heavily Irish, Polish, Bohemian, Lithuanian, Greek, German, Italian and Jewish communities.

The approximately one million Negroes from the South who have emigrated to Chicago are the last of the great wave of immigrants, albeit being the only immigrant group made up of native American citizens. And they are following the traditional patterns of movement which characterize the behaviour of immigrant groups moving into a new environment.

Like the ethnic immigrants before them, southern Negroes moving into Chicago settled in the old neighbourhoods. As is traditional in such situations, the ethnic old settlers in these communities began to flee from the new immigrants. Most of the South Side, much of the West Side, and some of the near North Side have been denuded of their Irish, Jewish, Italian, Polish, Bohemian and German populations and have become Negro ghettoes. Only on the near South-west and North-west Sides are the Poles and Bohemians making a stand. The Poles, in particular, remain intransigent and resistant to the Negro pressure in the inner areas of the city. The older Polish settlers do not retreat easily from their hard-won homes and six-flat buildings. However, even in these neighbourhoods, the relentless pressure of the bursting Negro ghetto is slowly breaking down the barriers. The influx of a million Negroes into the city has fragmented the population even more deeply than the ethnic divisions. The division between two and a half million whites and one million Negroes has added another dimension to the ethnically separated city. In one sense, it has unified the ethnic whites on a single issue—blocking the movement of Negroes into white neighbourhoods. But, at another level, the rapid growth of the Negro population and the steady spread of the Negro ghetto has opened a wide chasm within the city's body politic between the non-white and white population of the city. Race has begun to replace nationality as the major factor in the life of the city. And the Negroes, even more than the ethnic whites, refuse to identify themselves socially, culturally or politically on a communal basis with a city which keeps them penned in a ghetto and forces them into a separate but not equal life within the city.

A third factor in Chicago's life is religion. In the largest Roman Catholic Archdiocese in North America no decision can be made without due consideration for the feelings and aspirations of the majority Catholic population of the city. It is with good reason that the State of Illinois annually awarded licence plate number one, not to the governor, but to the Roman Catholic Cardinal of Chicago. The influence of the hierarchy and the many parishioners of the Church of Rome is always present in decision-making in the politics, law, educational policy and cultural life of the city.

This is not to say that that influence is necessarily bad or necessarily good—merely that it exists. Roman Catholic power in Chicago has contributed mightily to the growth and development of the city and to the problems of the city. Some of the most liberal as well as some of the most conservative proposals and pressures in the life of Chicago have emanated from the many-splendoured, broad-based, variegated Roman Catholic clergy and laity of the city.

In contrast to the dominant Catholic religious community, the Protestant and Jewish communities, with the exception of powerful business leaders, are weak. This is not to say that they are ignored or are not consulted, but that their influence is nowhere near so great as that of the Roman Catholic community. Since most of the Protestants in the city are now the Negroes, they can be dealt with on the basis of race rather than religion. And since most of the Jews have fled the city for the suburbs, except for residence in a few fringe areas, they can be easily ignored, although recognized and tolerated in decision-making in the city.

To sum up, the city of Chicago is most affected by three major factors—the nationality make-up of its white population, the race issue stimulated by the exploding Negro population, and the religious dominance of the city's life by the Roman Catholic leadership and population.

THE GOVERNMENT OF THE CITY

Legally, all American cities are creatures of state government and have only those powers specifically delegated to them by their state legislatures. The city of Chicago is a legal creation of the State of Illinois governed under a body of state laws known as the Revised Cities and Villages Act[1] rather than under a specific muncipal charter.

The city government is divided into the traditional three branches of the American political system—executive, legislative and judicial. Chicago has a so-called 'strong council–weak mayor' form of government formally, although the realities of the relationship of the mayor and the city council have completely reversed the formal relationship. This can be attributed to two factors—the administrative and political skill of the incumbent four-term mayor, Richard J. Daley, and the dynamics of the political relationship of the Democratic Party in Chicago to the formal governmental structure of the city.

Elections for the three administrative offices of mayor, city clerk, and city treasurer are held every four years in April, and aldermanic elections for the city council are held in February and April[2] of the same year. Aldermen are elected on a theoretically non-partisan basis, with no party designation on the ballot, although most voters know the political affiliation of their local candidates. The elections are scheduled at a time when no other national, state or county office holders are being elected. This serves the laudable theoretical purpose of separating local elections from partisan national and state issues, and the practical political purpose of protecting the overwhelmingly dominant local Democratic Party from voter hostility based on possibly dangerous national political trends. It also insures a low voter turnout, since American voters are traditionally much more apathetic in local contests than in national elections. This tendency inevitably redounds to the advantage of the entrenched organization which can deliver the so-called 'machine vote' through an army of disciplined, hard-working precinct workers.

The mayor, city clerk and city treasurer are elected for four-year terms.

[1] Its proper legal title is the Illinois Municipal Code which was passed on May 29, 1961.
[2] If no aldermanic candidate receives a majority of the total votes cast in his ward the two candidates with the highest number of votes compete against each other in April.

The mayor's annual salary is $35,000, while the city clerk and city treasurer receive an annual salary of $15,000.

The mayor is the city's chief executive officer, directs city departments,

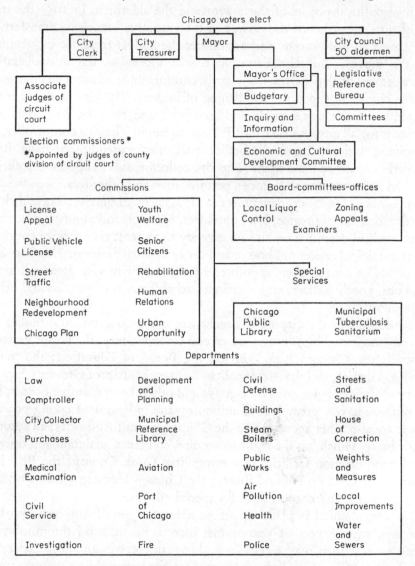

Chicago voters elect

| City Clerk | City Treasurer | Mayor | City Council 50 aldermen |

Associate judges of circuit court

Election commissioners *

*Appointed by judges of county division of circuit court

Mayor's Office
Budgetary
Inquiry and Information

Legislative Reference Bureau
Committees

Economic and Cultural Development Committee

Commissions

License Appeal	Youth Welfare
Public Vehicle License	Senior Citizens
Street Traffic	Rehabilitation
Neighbourhood Redevelopment	Human Relations
Chicago Plan	Urban Opportunity

Board-committees-offices

Local Liquor Control   Zoning Appeals
                Examiners

Special Services

Chicago Public Library   Municipal Tuberculosis Sanitarium

Departments

Law	Development and Planning	Civil Defense	Streets and Sanitation
Comptroller		Buildings	
City Collector	Municipal Reference Library	Steam Boilers	House of Correction
Purchases		Public Works	Weights and Measures
Medical Examination	Aviation	Air Pollution	Local Improvements
Civil Service	Port of Chicago	Health	
Investigation	Fire	Police	Water and Sewers

CHICAGO—Administrative Organization

and appoints the heads of city departments and other agencies with the approval of the council. He can remove his appointees (with certain exceptions stated by law). He presides over the city council and rules on procedure, although he can vote only in case of a tie. He has a veto power over ordinances and an item veto on appropriation bills. A two-thirds majority in the council is necessary to override a veto, a literal impossibility in view of the relative political power of the mayor and the aldermen. In 1955 the state legislature strengthened the power of the executive branch by transferring the power to plan, create, and administer the budget from the city council to the mayor. An administrative officer supervises the administrative management of all departments, boards, commissions and other city agencies.

The city clerk supervises the issuing of licences. The city treasurer is the custodian of the city's funds and securities, and receives, pays out, and accounts for all city and Board of Education funds. The city comptroller, an appointed official, decides whether particular expenditures have been properly authorized and spent. The city collector, also an appointed official, receives payments for all licences, permits, fines and other fees.

A number of staff departments serve the agencies of the city. These include the departments of finance; law; purchases, contracts and supplies; investigation; medical examination and emergency treatment; civil service commission; municipal reference library; and the budgetary division. There are also a number of commissions appointed by the mayor in such areas as human relations, youth welfare, senior citizens, rehabilitation of persons and urban opportunity.

In addition to the city government, six other governmental bodies are directly supported by Chicago taxpayers: Cook County; the Forest Preserve District; the Chicago Park District; the Board of Education; the Junior College District; and the Metropolitan Sanitary District of Greater Chicago. Some of these are governed by elective and others by appointive boards, but all of them have a great deal of autonomy and independent taxing powers. There are also other agencies like the Chicago Transit Authority, an autonomous body, which has the right to acquire, construct, maintain and operate local transportation facilities in metropolitan Cook County; the Board of Health; the Chicago Public Library; the Chicago Housing Authority; and various boards and corporations for special purposes.

The city council is made up of 50 aldermen, one from each ward in Chicago, who serve four-year terms; there is no limit on the number of terms an alderman may serve. Each alderman receives an annual salary of $8,000 plus $3,000 for office expenses, $660 for automobile expenses, and is provided with a secretary at a salary of $6,300. The council enacts ordinances; passes orders and resolutions; enacts the city budget; appropriates and borrows money; names streets and alleys; regulates garbage collection and disposal; issues and revokes certain licences and franchises; regulates traffic;

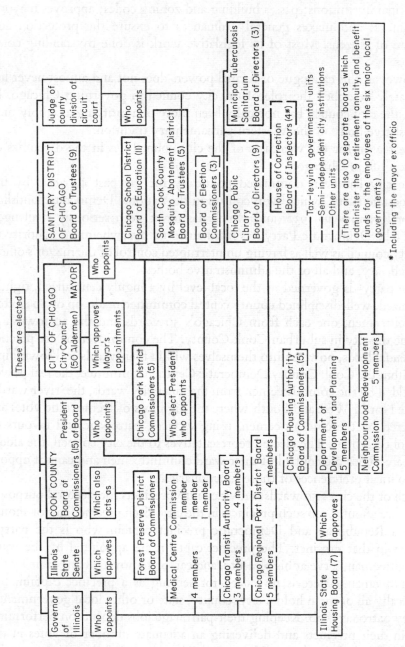

CHICAGO's Fragmented local government

* Including the mayor ex officio

provides fire, police and health protection; builds and operates various municipal institutions; passes building and zoning codes; approves mayoral appointees; and makes general ordinances to ensure the protection and welfare of citizens. Most of its legislative work is done by standing committees.

However, this catalogue of formal powers does not and almost never has accurately described the role of the city council in governing Chicago. In truth, the city council has normally been more of a ratifying assembly than a legislative body in the Western parliamentary tradition.

The reason for the weakness of the city council lies in the dynamics of political life in Chicago.

The city has been dominated politically for the past 40 years by the Democratic Party, which won control in the national Democratic landslide electoral victory in 1932, and which has never been seriously challenged since. The Democratic Party has maintained an overwhelming majority in the city council as well as having uninterrupted control of the mayor's office, the judiciary, and all of the administrative bodies.

The party[1] is governed at the local level by a highly centralized, tightly organized, well-disciplined county central committee made up of 80 elected committeemen, one each from Chicago's 50 wards and the 30 townships outside the city in suburban Cook County. The committeemen are practically feudal lords, powers unto themselves within their wards and townships.

Within the Cook County Democratic Central Committee, the real power is wielded by the committeemen from the inner city wards, the 'river wards' on the North, West and South where the big blocs of Democratic votes are delivered by the committeemen, using services, patronage and favours to control the voters. The elected representatives to the city council, the aldermen, are under the control of their ward committeemen and cannot oppose the political preferences of those functionaries.

Each of the city's 50 wards is divided into precincts for electoral purposes. There are about 3,500 such precincts in the city. Each precinct has (or should have) a Republican and Democratic precinct captain who is the party's worker in that precinct. The precinct captains are appointed by the ward committeeman, serve at his pleasure, and can be removed at any time by the committeeman. There is no salary for serving as a precinct captain, but practically all of them hold a city, county, state or other local governmental agency patronage job. Keeping their patronage jobs depend on performing well in their precincts and delivering an adequate number of votes in the precinct for the party's candidates at election time. Good precinct captains

[1] The Republican Party has an identical structure.

spend a great deal of time ministering to their constituents' needs—getting them jobs, providing welfare, making contacts with governmental agencies and providing a myriad of services. In Chicago, the precinct captains are the basic link and channel of communication between the citizens of the city, the political parties and the city government and its various agencies. This is particularly true of the Democratic precinct captains, since their party controls the city government. Many of the city's precincts do not have a Republican precinct captain because the Republican Party has not had enough patronage jobs to dispense, and very few people will serve as a precinct captain without being given a patronage job. However, personnel in city agencies will normally provide the same service to any citizen, regardless of his political affiliation. No one is asked his political affiliation by a municipal employee, but the Democratic precinct captains know how and where to go for help through the party organization and can often expedite a matter for a constituent.

The formal legal structure of the city government is weak, decentralized and lacking in any real power. The political organization of the Democratic Party is well organized, powerful and authoritarian. Inevitably the party controls the governmental apparatus and often uses that apparatus for its partisan political objectives. In many cases those objectives coincide with the interests of the city, but whether they do or not, the political preferences of the party take precedence over the administrative aims of the elected representatives and the administrative bureaucracy. In the city council itself, a mayor who is a powerful politician can dominate the council with some help from an inner circle of ward committeemen, some of whom may also hold aldermanic seats.

The present Mayor of Chicago, Richard J. Daley, is a classic example of what can happen when political and administrative power is fused in the same hands. Daley is the new American big city 'boss' *par excellence*.

No discussion of the city of Chicago today is relevant without recognizing Daley's role in the city's politics, government and life. Daley has proved to be one of the most capable administrators in the United States as well as the most effective political leader in Chicago's turbulent history.

Daley wears two hats—one as Mayor of Chicago, and the other as Chairman of the Cook County Democratic Central Committee. He operates from a broad-based power structure encompassing an army of disciplined, hard-working precinct captains in his political organization, and most of the important business, labour, religious, ethnic and racial leaders in the community. He juxtaposes his responsibilities as Mayor of Chicago with his duties as Chairman of the Cook County Democratic Central Committee. He gives service and loyalty to both masters impartially and sees no contradiction in his dual responsibilities. He uses his political power to get what he wants for his city, and his administrative power to strengthen the political organization in which he has spent his life. His favourite maxim that, 'Good government is good politics and good politics is good government', is, for him, not a cliché but a *modus operandi* and a guiding principle of both political and administrative behaviour. By conviction a Democratic liberal, at heart he is still a 'Back of the Yards' Irish Catholic. The marriage of the two personalities in the one man is the key to his political and administrative philosophy. He loves his Bridgeport neighbourhood and city, and his political organization and party.

Daley understands power and uses it effectively, both as mayor and political leader. City officials and politicians alike are held to a standard of excellence and are often unceremoniously dumped when they fail to meet their respective responsibilities. But Daley is also inordinately loyal to friends, neighbours, and fellow public servants and politicians. He finds them places on public payrolls, refuses to move them aside for younger men, puts their widows on public boards and other agencies, and finds other jobs for good Democrats who have been ousted by hard-hearted Republican office-holders.

Because of this effective fusion of political and administrative power Chicago is today probably the best run big city in the United States. The police department has been built into a first-class force after a scandal that rocked the city to its foundations a few years ago. The Chicago Fire Department is one of the finest in the country. A massive urban renewal, rodent control and street lighting programme has been launched. Public transportation facilities have improved tremendously under the Chicago Transit Authority and new extensions are under way. A network of expressways has been built to provide high speed access to the city for motorists. Chicago's central business district, the Loop, is in the midst of an unparalleled building boom encouraged by one of the most favourable tax rates of any major city in the country. The major crime rate has been decreasing while it is going up in most other American cities. In 1963 the National Safety Council rated Chicago the 'safest big city' in the United States for automobile traffic. There has been a cultural renaissance in the city with the successful launching of the Lyric Opera Company, the restoration of the world famous Auditorium Theatre, and the creation of a number of small theatre groups in the city and its environs. Job opportunities have increased steadily and unemployment and welfare rolls have been reduced. Race relations have been fairly stable between the city's 2½ million whites and 1 million Negroes, although a major riot in the summer of 1966 and occasional incidents have disturbed the peace of the city.

This is not to say that Chicago has no problems and that progress has been made in all areas. Many problems remain and some have grown worse, but the general direction of the city's momentum has been steadily forward in a period when the city had to absorb over 500,000 underprivileged Negroes from the South while losing a heavy percentage of its white, middle-class population to the suburbs.

FINANCE

Despite these population movements and their effect on the city's fiscal situation, Chicago is in excellent financial condition. Chicago ranks low among American cities in its bonded indebtedness which declined from $261 millions in 1960 to $216 millions at the end of 1965. The net bonded debt of the six major Chicago area governments totalled $612,678,755, a decrease of $51,264,184 during the year of 1965. On January 1, 1966, the *per capita* debt of the city government was the lowest of any large city in America—$61 for the city of Chicago only; $119 for the city, Board of Education and Park District combined; and $162 when the city taxpayer's share of the County of Cook, Forest Preserve District of Cook County, and Metropolitan Sanitary District of Greater Chicago was added to that of the governments within the city proper. A new bond issue of $195 millions was approved by the voters in 1966. The money will be used for street lighting, sewers, public transportation, urban renewal and other city services. The city also receives hundreds of millions of dollars in federal and state aid. The bulk of the federal grants are for urban renewal, education and other city services, while most of the state aid goes to the Board of Education for the city's school system.

Chicago has an executive budget, prepared by the mayor, which must be sent to the city council before November 15th each year, and enacted by December 31st by statute. The 1966 city of Chicago budget provided for expenditures appropriations of $572,332,251.

The major source of tax revenue is the real estate property tax, although other municipal taxes including a 1 per cent sales tax have been authorized by the state legislature for Chicago and other municipalities in Illinois. A personal property tax, which is collected by the county, is ignored by many of the taxpayers in the city. The law is so archaic and unenforceable that little effort is made to collect the tax from delinquent taxpayers because of the cost, the sheer number of delinquents, and possible political repercussions.

A summary of major sources of revenue and expenditures for the city of Chicago and the other major area governments is shown in Tables I, II and III.

STAFFING

The city employs about 48,000 people in its various departments, including employees of the municipal tuberculosis sanitarium, the public library and the non-teaching personnel of the Board of Education. The approximately 23,000 teachers are hired and promoted by the Board of Education.

TABLE I

1965 Current Account of the City

Revenue	Million dollars
Property taxes	109
Other municipal taxes	64·9
Licences, fees, service charges	25·5
Reimbursement of current expenses	13·9
Court fees, fines and forfeits	9·3
Surplus from prior years	7
City airports, port of Chicago, other rentals, reimbursements and miscellaneous income	2·3
Total income	231·9

Expenditure	
Protection to persons and property	134·5
Street maintenance and sanitation	34·8
Courts and correction	13·9
General government	13·9
General city purposes	11·6
Public highways, bridges and structures	9·3
Health and welfare	9·3
Public service enterprises	4·6
Total expenditure	231·9

Of the total number of city employees, about 80 per cent are under civil service. A Chicago Civil Service Commission of three members is appointed by the mayor for staggered three-year terms. The commission and its staff conducts examinations, maintains lists of eligible applicants, maintains personnel records, certifies payrolls, conducts investigations and holds hearings on complaints. It can dismiss employees for just cause, but the discharged persons may appeal to the courts. The commission classifies positions and proposes a pay plan, but the city council is responsible for wage and salary rates. The commission has jurisdiction over employees of the city of Chicago, the non-teaching personnel of the Board of Education, the public library, and the house of correction. Appointment, status and tenure of the majority of local governmental employees in Chicago are regulated by civil service laws passed by the state legislature.

TABLE II

Major Chicago Governments 1966 Resources and Appropriations

Resources	Million dollars
Property taxes	648·6
State and federal aid	439·4
Miscellaneous revenue	322·1
Bonds sold or authorized	55·5
Unexpended balances	106·1
Total	1,571·7

Appropriations	
Current expense	1,100·5
Capital improvements	189·9
Debt service	137·1
Pensions	56·7
Cost of property tax extension plus provision for loss	52·9
Total	1,537·1

The law permits appointment without civil service status of a few people in policy making and key administrative positions. But the law also permits the appointment, on a temporary basis for 120 days, of employees at all levels to departments where a shortage of personnel under civil service procedures exists. About 8,000 people, or about 20 per cent of the city's employees, are appointed on this basis. If the police and fire departments, which are practically all civil service, are exempted, the temporary, appointed employees make up about 35 per cent of the city's total work force. In fact, in city, county, state and local government agencies, there are about 35,000 patronage positions available to the political parties in the Chicago area. Table IV gives an approximate breakdown of these positions among the various governmental units.

Both the Democratic and Republican Parties attempt to maintain their party organizations by allocating these patronage positions at all levels of local government to party workers and the party faithful.

TABLE III

1966 Allocation of Chicago Property Tax

By government	Million dollars
City of Chicago	221·8
Board of Education	250·2
Chicago Park District	44·6
Cook County	42·0
Forest Preserve District	6·5
Sanitary District	33·6
South Cook County Mosquito Abatement District	·2
Total	598·9

By purpose	
Current expense	439·0
Debt service	62·3
Pensions	47·1
Miscellaneous	50·5
Total	598·9

Temporary appointments are made to positions at all levels from $295 per month clerks to highway inspectors at $12,000 per year and $25,000 per year departmental directors. Jobs are dispensed through the party organization to the ward and township committeemen on the basis of their political efficiency on the party's behalf in their wards and townships. Thus, an effective Democratic ward committeeman may be allocated 500 to 700 jobs for his ward, and a suburban Democratic committeeman, whose township is heavily Republican, might be given a half-dozen jobs. Conversely, a Republican township committeeman will be well rewarded with jobs by his party, whereas a Republican ward committeeman in one of Chicago's inner city river wards gets practically no patronage at all. One consequence of this system is that sometimes Republican ward committeemen in the city and Democratic township committeemen in the suburbs are given some patronage by the opposing majority party in return for maintaining a low level of political activity on behalf of their own party in the ward or township.

The 120 day temporary appointments can be renewed indefinitely, as long as qualified civil service personnel are not available. Since the Chicago Civil Service Commission does not schedule examinations in many categories for

TABLE IV

Patronage Positions in the Chicago area

Chicago departments and commissions	7,990
Chicago Park District	1,850
Metropolitan Sanitary District	200
Chicago Board of Education	2,245
County, under County Board	5,900
County Treasurer	368
County Sheriff	1,495
County Assessor	345
County Circuit Court and divisions	2,100
County Clerk	260
County Coroner	69
County Recorder of Deeds	320
State departments and commissions	8,995
Secretary of State	2,500
State Superintendent of Public Instruction	500
State Treasurer	90
State Auditor of Public Accounts	184
	35,411

years, or sets up qualifications so difficult that hardly anyone can pass the examination for a position, or does not post lists for long periods of time after an examination has been held, many of these positions are filled permanently by temporary employees.

Despite numerous attempts by Alderman Leon Despres, an independent Democrat from the University of Chicago's Fifth Ward, to bring about reform, there has been little significant change in the system. Neither political party is really interested in abolishing a system which enables it to take care of party workers and ensure their loyalty and responsiveness to the party leadership. Not every Chicago politician would be as blunt as Democratic Alderman Thomas Keane, chairman of the city council finance committee, who once declared, 'Civil service is for rum-dums' (alcoholics); or as forthright as former Cook County Board President Richard B. Ogilvie, who, when asked if he was going to put all of the 6,000 jobs under his control under civil service, replied, 'I don't believe in unilateral disarmament'; or as optimistic as 25th Ward Democratic Alderman Vito Marzullo, who believes 'that the qualities that make a man a good (precinct) captain make him a good job holder'. Perhaps the attitude of most politicians in Chicago, Republican and Democratic, is best expressed realistically by Democratic Ward Committeeman Bernard Neistein of Chicago's West Side 29th Ward, who, when asked his views on civil service, declared, 'If we're out, then I believe in it. If we're in, I'm against it.' Given the realities of politics in Chicago and Cook County, and the tacit acceptance of the system by the local citizenry, a major reform of personnel practices is unlikely in the near future.[1]

CITY POLITICS

Ten years ago political scientist Robert A. Walker, describing politics in the city of Chicago in the first edition of this book declared: 'The future of the political machine is uncertain. . . . Dangerous as it is to generalize, it may well be that as governmental policy in the United States itself has become more "democratic" in the sense of meeting an increasing share of the needs of the people (through relief, welfare, education, social security and related programmes), it has effectively undermined the political machine. To this extent, therefore, it has become increasingly difficult for any "boss" or small group of party leaders to deliver party and governmental support to the forces of special privilege or corruption without self-jeopardy. If this be true, we may look forward to an era in which the party will have to adhere to principle and be sensitive indeed to changing political opinion if it is to remain in power.'

A decade after these words were written, the political machine whose decline Professor Walker predicted was at the apex of its power, having just produced a smashing electoral victory and a fourth term for Mayor Richard J. Daley, who also doubles in brass as the undisputed 'boss' of the machine.

The resiliency of that Democratic machine, and its continued success, can be attributed to a number of factors—good organization, patronage, voter apathy, Republican ineptness and other reasons. But the root cause of the

[1] A court decision, which held that patronage employees cannot be required to do political work to retain their jobs, could significantly alter the personnel and party control systems, if it is upheld on appeal.

Democratic machine's dominance in the city of Chicago is its ability to understand, adapt to and serve the needs and interests of the nationality, racial and religious groups which make up the city's population. Chicago is both a kaleidoscope of nationality, racial and religious divisions, and a laboratory of nationality, racial and religious conciliation through the process of politics.

The traditional pattern of Chicago politics has for many years reflected the overriding influence of nationality on the political behaviour of the inhabitants of the city.

Guided by the Irish, the ethnic groups in the city have voted heavily Democratic for the past forty years. The great depression of 1929 and the New Deal made them Democrats. Franklin Roosevelt, assisted by the local professional politicians, locked them up in his broad-based coalition, the new Democratic Party. Big cities like Chicago became an essential ingredient in the formula for Democratic victories in national elections. Holding the South and delivering thumping majorities in the big cities of the North ensured national hegemony for the Democratic Party. Chicago, like most big northern cities, became a bulwark of the party of the Democracy in 1931 and has remained heavily Democratic.

With the exception of the Jews, however, the ethnic groups in Chicago became and remained Democrats, not out of any tradition of liberalism, but because of elemental, economic self-interest. The theoretical, liberal foundations of Franklin Roosevelt's New Deal had no appeal to them. The Irish, Polish, Bohemian, Lithuanian and Italian ethnic groups were, on the whole, orientated by instinct and background towards an innate conservatism. They embraced the Democratic Party and the New Deal because it offered them material rewards and opportunities they could not get, except through politics. The welfare state was and still is, for most of these nationality groups, not a condition of society, or a direction in which society should move because of its emphasis on middle-class liberal, democratic ideas. They were, and on the whole still are, unfamiliar with and unsympathetic and unresponsive to eighteenth-century Benthamite and Millsian Anglo-Saxon concepts of what the good society should be like. The Anglo-Saxon, white Protestant, Western European, middle-class ethos and concept of government has little or no meaning to the lower-class, peasant-descended, East and South European population of the city. Good government means services, favours, and concessions on a local basis rather than non-partisan, morally righteous, community-oriented, city-wide concern.

The major exception to this predominantly conservative outlook among the ethnic groups in the city are the Jews. Inevitably a minority in any

M

community, influenced by the traditional liberalism of Judaism, and emotionally committed to humanitarianism, the Jews have been a part of the ethnic coalition in the Democratic Party in Chicago, but have remained somewhat outside of the mainstream of the local party organizations.

It is this nationality conservative outlook which has given the Democratic Party in Chicago its peculiarly schizophrenic character.

The party has for forty years been riding the crest of a national Democratic liberal image, but has remained essentially conservative locally. Federal welfare programmes have been embraced and utilized, not out of any deep commitment to their intrinsically liberal ethos, but out of deference to their practical political results. Civil rights legislation has been supported, not primarily out of any inherent sympathy for the underprivileged Negroes, but mainly because it was good politics.

Liberal local Democratic movements are fended off, ostracized and kept beyond the pale, and national political issues and problems are subordinated to local interests of the organization.

The relationship of the essentially conservative local Democratic organization with the more liberal national leadership of the party has been a two-way street. Democratic presidents like Roosevelt, Truman, Kennedy and Johnson have collaborated with the local organization, funnelled federal funds through it, and bailed it out of trouble when necessary. The organization, for its part, has consistently delivered thumping majorities in the city for Democratic presidential candidates, except for Adlai Stevenson.

In essence, the Democratic organization in Chicago is non-ideological in its orientation. It is an organization dedicated primarily to gaining and retaining office and reaping the rewards of office. Its movers and shapers are relatively unconcerned with philosophical terms like liberalism and conservatism. Its primary demands on its members are loyalty and political efficiency. In return for that loyalty and efficiency it carries out its obligation to its members by providing them with jobs, contracts, contacts and its own social security system of protection against adversity and old age.

A member of the organization remains in good standing as long as he delivers his precinct or ward. Service to the people is considered to be the prime requisite of good politics. To give that service, a politician should live in his neighbourhood, be of the same ethnic, racial and religious background as his constituents, have the same outlook and aspirations as his people, and reflect and represent that outlook and those aspirations. There is an inherent, implicit recognition of the principle of democratic representation, not just on the basis of numbers or territory, but on the basis of ethnic, religious, racial, social and cultural aspirations and needs.

Thus, at the local grass roots level of Chicago politics, the practical political needs of the organization are fused with the basic aspirations of the population of the city. This marriage of convenience rather than love is the foundation of the relationship of the great majority of the people and the Democratic organization, and is the major reason why the organization has maintained its power for thirty-five years.

If the primary purpose of a democratic political system is to ascertain and carry out the will of a majority of the people, the Democratic Party in Chicago fulfils its obligations exceptionally well.

Since the great majority of the ethnic citizenry espouse a moderate conservatism in issues like civil rights and welfare, the great majority of the political leaders manifest the same attitudes on those issues. And, since the political leaders are drawn from those ethnic groups and have the same backgrounds and attitudes as their constituents, there is little conflict between the private political beliefs of those politicians and their public attitudes.

The great influx of Negroes from the South into Chicago has not significantly altered either the political techniques of the machine or its basic conservatism. The Democratic organization deals with the Negro population of the city and its political leaders in exactly the same way that it has always dealt with the nationality groups—by apportioning recognition and prerogatives in direct proportion to demonstrated political power, except that recognition is granted on the basis of race rather than nationality.

Political scientist James Q. Wilson has argued in his study of Negro political leadership, *Negro Politics*, that Negro politics in an American city reflects the politics of the city. Negro politics in Los Angeles reflects the non-partisan, non-machine politics of that city; Negro politics in New York City reflects the rather localized borough politics of that city; and Negro politics in Chicago reflects the materialistic, non-ideological machine politics of the city. Like their white ethnic counterparts, Negro voters and Negro politicians in Chicago are more interested in bread and butter material rewards like welfare, jobs and contacts rather than in the more esoteric, spiritual and ideological goals espoused by civil rights leaders like the late Martin Luther King, Jr., Albert Raby and Edwin C. Berry.

Given the realities of political life in Chicago, it is unlikely that the character of Chicago politics will change much in the foreseeable future or that the Democratic organization will loosen its hold on the city government. The most important change, one which is already taking place, is that the Negro population and political leaders will get a larger piece of the pie that is cut up quadrennially, and the share of the ethnic whites will be reduced proportionately. Ten years from now, Professor Walker's prediction of things to come in Chicago politics will probably be no more valid than it is today. To paraphrase former 43rd Ward Democratic Committeeman and alderman, Mathias (Paddy) Bauler, 'Chicago still ain't ready for that kind of reform'.

PLANNING THE CITY

Chicago has for many years been a city with a magnificent front yard, and a generally depressing, unimaginative and deteriorating back yard.

Chicago's front yard is its lake front area stretching from the northern boundary of the city to the far South Side. A scenic eight-lane high-speed expressway, the Outer Drive, spans the length of the city from north to south, bordered on one side by Lake Michigan, and on the other side by miles of parks and modern high-rise apartment buildings. But inward from the lake front is mile upon mile of older, rundown neighbourhoods, interspersed with industrial development, before one reaches the newer, cleaner, middle-class residential areas of the city on the far South, South-west, North and North-west Sides.

The rapid industrial expansion and population explosion of the last quarter of the nineteenth century and early years of the twentieth century resulted in a city which grew with little or no planning. Two exceptions to this general lack of interest in planning were the rectangular street system of square-mile land sections, bounded by section-line streets one mile apart, which became major traffic and commercial arteries; and a magnificent park system which provided recreational open space for the citizenry.

In 1909 Chicago pioneered in planning among American cities with its famous Burnham Plan, sponsored by the influential Commercial Club made up of civic and business leaders, and drawn up by the director of works for the 1893 World's Fair Exposition, Daniel Hudson Burnham, and architect Edward Bennett. The plan was influenced heavily by the boulevard system of Paris devised by Baron Haussmann.

The Burnham Plan, while comprehensive for its time, and metropolitan in scope, was primarily concerned with physical planning. It was designed to save Chicago's lake front as an aesthetic and recreational area, to provide a city-wide park system, and to lay out a network of streets and future expressways to ensure adequate transportation in and from the city. The plan was broad in scope, was pushed actively by the business and political leadership of the city, and was supported generally by the citizenry. But it was not designed to deal with the social and economic life and problems of the city and its people. The plan has been exceedingly successful within its scope.

Formal planning by governmental agencies began with the creation of the

Chicago Plan Commission as an advisory body to study and carry out the Burnham Plan. The commission functioned as a promotional agency until 1939, when it was made an official agency, the planning arm of the city of Chicago.

Although it is an advisory body its recommendations are almost always accepted by the city council, especially since Mayor Daley and Alderman Thomas Keane, who is chairman of the city council finance committee and the most powerful Democratic politician in Chicago next to the mayor, are both members of the Plan Commission. In addition, Illinois State Law requires all public improvement proposals to be submitted to the Plan Commission for review and recommendation. The Plan Commission consists of 17 members, 9 private citizens appointed by the mayor with the approval of the city council, and 8 members who serve *ex officio* during their terms in public office. Of course, practically all of the planning and work done in this area is done by the staff of the department of development and planning.

In 1957 the department of city planning was formed and the commission was reconstituted as a policy-making body. The department of city planning was replaced in 1965 by the department of development and planning which supervises and co-ordinates the formulation and execution of physical improvement projects and programmes for industrial growth, development of the city's central and outlying areas, development of culture and art, urban renewal, housing, public works, recreation, transportation and community improvements. The department is responsible for revising, maintaining and expanding the new Comprehensive Plan of Chicago issued in 1966; reviews all improvement projects undertaken by other local governmental agencies like the Board of Education, Chicago Park District, Sanitary District, Port Authority, hospitals, highways, anti-poverty, youth welfare agencies, and other public and semi-public agencies; and makes recommendations to the city council and zoning board of appeals on zoning matters. Other agencies involved in the planning field are the department of urban renewal, the mayor's urban renewal committee, the Chicago housing authority, the neighbourhood redevelopment commission, the medical centre commission, the Chicago dwellings association, and the department of buildings. The city council still retains authority over zoning matters, except for some applications for variation, which are made to the zoning board of appeals.

Twenty years ago the city, in collaboration with state and federal agencies and private developers, began a programme of urban renewal designed to halt and reverse the spread of blight. Over 7,000 new homes and apartments have been completed in renewal sites and another 10,000 are committed.

The city has spent $85,000,000, which has brought in $196,000,000 in federal funds for a total public expenditure of $281,000,000, which in turn has generated private redevelopment expenditures of approximately $1 billion. Chicago's Loop is in the midst of a building boom. Carl Sandburg Village on the Near North Side, Lake Meadows and Prairie Shores on the Near South Side, and the rebuilding of the Hyde Park area around the University of Chicago are examples of private-public co-operation in middle-income housing redevelopment. A great deal of low-income public housing has been built on the South and West Sides.

Recognizing, however, that housing is only one aspect of the total problem, the city has launched a programme of attracting industry to provide jobs and income for the citizenry. Much of the new industrial development in the Chicago area is taking place in the north-west suburban area of Chicago's hinterland, far from the people of the inner city who need jobs the most.

In December 1966 the department of development and planning issued a new comprehensive plan of Chicago, the first major plan since the Burnham Plan of 1909.

The new plan has three fundamental goals for the future of Chicago: 'To enlarge human opportunities, to improve the environment, and to strengthen and diversify the economy', by spending about $400 million a year for the next 15 years to improve the physical and social environment of the city. The money will come from expanded state and federal aid and a continued growth of the city's tax base and resources.

The plan envisions the creation of 16 development areas or urban towns within the city of 150,000 to 250,000 people. Each of these would be a cohesive, identifiable neighbourhood, bounded by expressways or major streets, with shopping centres, schools, parks, recreational facilities and green malls. About 235,000 units of new housing will be built, and all substandard housing will be razed or salvaged. Transportation corridors of expressways and rapid transit lines will carry the major traffic around the urban towns. New industry, and 3 senior colleges, 8 junior colleges, 40 to 50 high schools, and 200 elementary schools will be built along these corridors. Additional police will be hired and 38 new fire stations built. Rapid transit lines will be laid in all of the existing expressways and a new north–south expressway built on the Far West Side. The traffic capacity of 21 major streets will be improved, the elevated lines encircling the Loop torn down and replaced by a subway, and greater use of parking facilities on the fringes of the Loop provided. Eighteen hundred acres of park space and recreational facilities will be added. Land fill in Lake Michigan will add an additional 1,200 acres of recreation land. Community and neighbourhood health centres and additional mental health facilities will be provided. Air and water pollution programmes, and refuse disposal and sewage treatment facilities will be expanded. Regional business centres will be established, existing industrial areas will be renovated, and new industrial parks will be built. Every attempt will be made to co-ordinate the plan with the metropolitan area planning of the North-eastern Illinois Planning Commission.

In essence the plan is an attempt to provide for the health, safety, economic security, and social well being of the 3,700,000 citizens the city will have by 1980.

Will the plan work?

'This is a constructive plan,' says Professor Harold M. Mayer, of the University of Chicago's Centre for Urban Studies. 'It does not do the whole job and it has minor shortcomings, but it is a milestone in planning both nationally and locally.'

THE GOVERNMENT AND POLITICS OF THE METROPOLITAN AREA

The city of Chicago is a part of the county of Cook, which encompasses the city and 30 townships outside the city limits. Cook County is the largest county in the State of Illinois with a population of approximately 5,400,000 people, more than the total population of all of the other 101 counties in the state.

Cook County is governed by a board of commissioners, composed of 15 members elected at large, 10 from the city of Chicago, and 5 from the suburban area outside of the city. The members serve for 4 years, and have administrative and regulatory rather than legislative powers. The board supervises, and controls all county activities, levies and collects taxes, issues bonds, formulates and adopts an annual budget, constructs and maintains roads and highways, maintains charitable institutions and welfare services, and administers election procedures.

The president of the board is elected on a county-wide basis and also runs for office as a commissioner. He dominates the board because of his powers of appointment (he controls thousands of patronage jobs), and through his veto power. He can veto any appropriation, item, ordinance, resolution or motion, and a four-fifths majority of the board is needed to override a veto.

The board has been traditionally dominated by the Democratic Party which always elects the 10 commissioners from Chicago while the Republican Party elects the 5 minority commissioners from the suburban areas. The

President is usually a city Democrat because the Democratic majority vote in Chicago is normally heavy enough to overcome the Republican suburban vote in a county-wide election.

Other elected officials are the county clerk, recorder of deeds, assessor, treasurer, board of tax appeals, sheriff, state's attorney, coroner, and superintendent of schools, all of whom serve terms of 4 years.

There is still a degree of township government in the 30 functioning townships outside of Chicago. Township voters elect a supervisor, clerk, assessor, collector, highway commissioner and 3 auditors. Townships administer public welfare assistance, build and maintain roads in unincorporated areas, assess personal property, prevent the spread of communicable disease, collect agricultural statistics and can provide such services as mental health facilities, libraries, cemeteries, hospitals and youth commissions. An annual town meeting is held at which interested township electors adopt the annual budget and determine the tax levy.

The other units of local government in Cook County include cities, villages, school districts and special administrative districts, all with taxing powers. In 1966, there were 486 governmental units with power to levy taxes in Cook County.

However, despite this hodge-podge of political, administrative and fiscal responsibility, and a population explosion in the suburbs, there is little chance of any serious consideration of or move toward a metropolitan government with real political and administrative power. In the face of the political reality of the contemporary situation former County Board President Richard B. Ogilvie[1] proposed the creation of a voluntary council of local governments to try to work out co-operative efforts to deal with problems of flood control, air and water pollution, transportation and other administrative problems common to the burgeoning metropolitan area. Whether such voluntary effort, without adequate political and administrative power to back it up, will be adequate for the needs of the metropolitan area is a moot question.

Chicago's suburbs, like the city, are also undergoing radical change. The Negro migration into Chicago has stimulated a massive exodus of white middle-class and working-class citizens to the suburbs. While the Negro population of the city doubled between 1950 and 1960, going from 400,000 to 800,000, the total population dropped 2 per cent. In the same period, the population of the suburban area of Cook County increased by 71 per cent.

The face of the suburban area of Cook County is being altered in two

[1] A Republican who served from 1962 to 1970.

major ways. First, many new development suburbs have sprung up where farmers' fields once graced the landscape. Second, the old, established, close-in suburban cities and villages are undergoing a transformation.

Chicago's working-class and lower middle-class ethnic, heavily Catholic, white population is leaving the city for new tract development suburbs. New, fairly homogeneous population centres of cheap and moderately priced housing are being established by the fleeing working-class and lower middle-class white Democrats from the city.

Contrary to popular mythology, these fleeing Democrats are not becoming Republicans in their new communities. Isolated from surrounding established towns, in close proximity physically to other emigrant Democrats like themselves, and relatively untouched by established Republican-dominated suburban organizations, most of the former city Democrats are retaining their traditional affiliation with the Democratic Party nationally.

However, on local issues, they have tended to become relatively non-partisan, as homeowners and taxpayers without regard to any formal party affiliation or doctrine. Traditional Democratic New Deal liberalism, or Republican hostility to welfare state measures and governmental activity in a broad range of programmes, are both relatively meaningless to these new suburbanites. Their primary concerns are with administrative, not political matters, at the local level. Taxes, sanitation, flood control, schools, zoning and property values occupy whatever time they have to devote to public affairs. Appeals to their civic mindedness on an ideological basis fall on deaf ears. They are practical, pragmatic, self-centred, narrowly oriented and concerned, and non-ideological politically in so far as local problems and issues are concerned. As for the city which they left, the county of which they are a part, the state which spawned them legally and the nation which guides their ultimate destinies—those are matters of relatively little concern in comparison to their immediate local problems. Their major interests are to make sure the Negroes do not follow them into their new communities and to keep their taxes down even if it means unsatisfactory and inadequate local services and facilities.

These are not Jeffersonian New England town-meeting communities governed by Anglo-Saxon ideas of what the good society should be like. They are rather first and second generation Eastern and Southern Europeans, influenced by their peasant and proletarian backgrounds, and dominated by still-retained prejudices and fears of the strangers beyond the fence.

In contrast, the old, established cities and villages of Chicago's suburban hinterland are undergoing a significant political transformation.

M*

These communities are attracting upper middle-class city Democrats moving in search of good schools, safe streets, clean government and all the other trappings of the middle-class American dream.

Most of these new suburbanites are the newly arrived middle class in America. Their fathers were labourers, small businessmen and skilled tradesmen. They are doctors, lawyers, teachers, corporation junior executives and successful businessmen. Their wives are college graduates and their children are born to the upper middle class. The Catholics and Jews among them have assimilated as much as possible the dominant Protestant middle-class values of white America, in the pattern described by Will Herberg in *Protestant, Catholic, Jew*. They have not left their faiths, but they have adapted socially, culturally and often politically to what they believe are American traditions.

Unlike the city emigrants to the development suburbs, they have retained their Democratic liberalism, applied it to local community problems, and combined it with their new-found Anglo-Saxon Protestant concepts of conservative, anti-machine, non-partisan, well-run local government. They are hybrids, fusing the old with the new, the untried with the true, that which they are with that which they would like to be. They are Ortega y Gassett's revolting twentieth-century masses who pursue culture, politics, recreation and community life with a passion not seen in their newly discovered conservative communities for many years.

They have left the city behind, but most of them work there, have attachments there, and are concerned with its problems, unlike the old settlers in their new communities. They will probably never go back, but they think they will. In the meantime, they are in the process of urbanizing their new communities, even while they are adapting to them. They are a disturbing force in these old communities, partially adaptive, partially disruptive, accepting the values but challenging them at the same time. They are in the process of creating a new, more partisan politics in the once tranquil, administratively oriented, non-partisan Republican established suburbia of Chicago. They are Democrats who have half-adopted some of the better tenets of Republicanism and are forcing their neighbour Republicans to rethink and re-evaluate their own party principles and their communal values.

These suburban communities are the opposite of the development suburbs, where politics is negligible and administration is all important. In the old suburban communities, non-partisan administrative matters are becoming increasingly political and intertwined with county, state and national political directions and ideologies.

However, any attempt to unify the city of Chicago and the suburbs politically would be met by opposition from both the people of the city and the suburbs.

Suburbanites who have left the city because of its machine politics, Negro population growth, greater crime and delinquency rates, fiscal problems, school problems, urban deterioration, and all the other ills of contemporary big city life in America, are violently opposed to being tied in politically to the city. The older suburban natives have never had any understanding of or concern for the city's problems. And, within the city, the Negro population and political leaders, whose power is growing and who will probably dominate the city's politics in the future, will be unwilling to subordinate their power as a minority bloc in a county-wide electorate to the dominance of a majority white, suburban-centred population. In the light of these political realities, the prospects for metropolitan government in the Chicago area are dim indeed.

BOUNDARY PROBLEMS

The city of Chicago's boundary problems are quite minimal. The only annexation of any significance has been a strip of territory incorporating a corridor to O'Hare Airport, the new municipal airport north-west of the city. The airport itself has also been annexed to the city. The city authorities have no interest in annexing any of the incorporated municipalities adjacent to the city, and the people in those cities and villages would strongly oppose annexation to Chicago. Chicago, like all municipalities in Illinois, is empowered by the state legislature to annex adjacent unincorporated areas up to 60 acres by action of the corporate authority, in this case the Chicago city council. Annexation of an incorporated city or village would require approval of the corporate authorities of both municipalities. Those corporate authorities can also order a referendum in the municipality, and the people in the municipality have the right to petition for a referendum on the issue. The state legislature has the power to provide for the annexation of a part of a municipality to another city or village. The legal appeal for adjudication of boundary problems would be to the circuit court of Cook County.

RELATIONSHIPS WITH OTHER AUTHORITIES

In addition to the problem of Chicago—suburban relationships, and metropolitan area co-operation and conflict, Chicago, and more recently, Cook County, have traditionally been exploited by the rural, small-town area of the State of Illinois, which has always controlled the state government in Springfield.

Illinois, like many other American states, has traditionally been divided between a major industrial city and a rural hinterland. Like most other such American states, the marriage of the two parts has not been a union of compatible partners, but rather a shotgun wedding of contending parties.

In contrast to Catholic, ethnic, Negro Chicago, downstate Illinois has traditionally been Protestant, white, Republican, small town and conservative. This is the land of the Lions, the home of the Kiwanis and the territory of the Elks. The sanctity and validity of traditional white, Protestant, conservative rural America guides the outlook and the aspirations of the majority of its population, except for a few industrialized small cities.

The state government at Springfield has been the private province of this part of Illinois. Chicago, the colossus of the North, with its Negroes, Catholics, Jews, crime, delinquency and corruption, has always been regarded as the Babylon of Illinois, a place to visit but not to live in. In truth, there has usually been as much crime, delinquency and corruption proportionately in the towns of downstate Illinois as in Chicago, but this fact has been conveniently overlooked by the local citizenry.

Castigating the Northern colossus has been a way of life for generations in rural Illinois. Protecting the state government from undue influence by the big city slickers has been a self-appointed holy mission. Exploiting the urban masses financially and politically in the interests of the rural section of the state has been regarded as proper. If this violated the state constitution, if it deprived Chicago's citizens of a fair share of the state's revenues, if it discriminated against Chicago's children in providing equal educational opportunity, and if it denied equal representation or consideration of their interests to Chicago's population, it was all being done in the name of the sanctity of the real American values which happened to coincide with the interests of the economic and political leadership of the downstate areas.

The major problem has been a steady growth of population and political and economic power in Cook County, in Chicago and its surburban ring. Cook County, with over five million people, has a population equal to all the other 101 counties and a disproportionate share of the industry and wealth. Keeping some balance in the state's politics and economics against the growing power of the giant northern county is, of necessity, a major political consideration. The success with which downstate Illinois has accomplished this task is a testament to the tenacity, ingenuity and dedication of downstate Illinois' political leadership.

Downstate Illinois has many problems of its own, some similar to those in

Cook County and many different. Saving the towns from deterioration, keeping industry from leaving, bringing in new industry, offering young people adequate opportunity at home, trying to compete culturally with the big urban area and maintaining and protecting a way of life and traditional values are of major concern to the residents of downstate Illinois. Like their northern counterparts in Chicago, downstate politicians not only represent but also reflect the aspirations, needs and values of their constituents. Like their big city counterparts, their behaviour and policies are based on a mixture of self-interest and honest belief in the value of what they defend. And who is to say that they are not partially correct in what they do, that what they strive to maintain is not in the best interests of their constituents and of the state?

Rural downstate power has been maintained for decades because of a consistent refusal on the part of the downstate-controlled legislature to redistrict the legislative seats and reapportion the legislature to conform to the growing population of Chicago and Cook County. Despite a state constitutional requirement that the legislature be redistricted every ten years on the basis of the national census, the legislators refused to redistrict the state between 1901 and 1954. An agreement reached that year gave Chicago and Cook County fair representation in the House of Representatives of the state legislature in return for giving the downstate area of Illinois a permanent majority in the state senate. However, the recent decisions of the United States Supreme Court requiring districting of both Houses of all state legislatures in the United States on a one-man-one-vote basis ensures fair representation of both Chicago and Cook County in the state legislature. Such representation should, in time, lead to more consideration and assistance by the state for the needs and problems of Chicago and Cook County.

CHICAGO'S FUTURE

Chicago has made significant progress during the past decade. But a number of unresolved problems remain which must be dealt with if the city is to continue to grow and prosper.

At the heart of the city's future development is the issue of race relations. The rapid growth of the Negro population and the white exodus to the suburbs are affecting the life, the character, the politics, the planning and the economic and financial status of the city. Despite a great deal of effort on the part of the leadership of the Negro and white populations, and a fair amount of success in conciliating the interests of both groups, Chicago is still very much made up of two communities, an expanding Negro community and a contracting white community. Unless the white exodus is stemmed and the Negro standard of living is raised significantly, continued progress will be difficult, if not impossible.

Almost all of Chicago's problems are subordinate to this overriding consideration. Adequate tax revenues, safe streets, good schools, improved housing, urban renewal, decent recreational facilities and better economic opportunities all hinge on creating and maintaining co-operation between Chicago's white and non-white citizens.

There are, of course, many administrative problems that must be dealt with—air and water pollution; relationships with the suburban area, the county and the state; improvement of the administrative apparatus of the city government; and maintaining a high level of performance for the manifold services the city must provide. But Chicago's most pressing and critical problem is political and sociological. Can Negro and white citizens live together in peace and harmony, with mutual respect for each other's needs and interests, and adjust and conciliate those interests?

If that question is answered affirmatively, Chicago's future progress is assured. But if the response is negative, Chicago, like many other American cities, could well become a Negro city, surrounded by a Chinese wall of white suburban communities, and left to simmer in the bitter juices of racial tension and conflict.

Resolution of the racial problem will be primarily the task of the people who live in the city today. Very few of Chicago's emigrant citizens who have moved to the suburbs will ever return to the city to live, regardless of what plans are made for rebuilding the city. They will have been gone too long, will have adjusted to a new way of life, and will have formed too many new associations and abandoned too many old ones to ever come back. The more civic-minded among them may assist in promoting the quality of life in the city they left, but most of them will not live there again. The necessary compromises and adjustments between Negroes and whites will have to be made by responsible leadership of the two groups within the city, and accepted by the people of the Negro and white communities.

Those compromises and adjustments will have to be worked out primarily through the process of politics much more than by administrative fiat or regulation. Great national programmes in countries like the United States can be instituted and carried out by the administrative bureaucracy in Washington, but the local, day-to-day 'gut issues' of individual and group relationships can still best be ameliorated and resolved by political compromise, bargaining and adjustment. The great cities are the last stronghold of politics in the United States today, since the administrative bureaucracy has gained control of the national government and most of the state governments. That administrative control was made possible by the achievement of a basic national political consensus. No such political consensus at the local level exists yet in cities like Chicago, and the first order of business is the task of building and maintaining such a consensus. This can only be done through the process of politics. 'For politics', in the words of T. E. Utley, 'does not consist of deciding in the void what is good for man and proceeding to do it. It has its own methods and conventions which are directed to maintaining divided societies in existence by reconciling conflicts within them or by keeping those conflicts within bounds.'

If it is true that conflicts within divided societies can best be reconciled by politics, the prospects for a successful amelioration of Chicago's central problem are good, for no city in the world has had more dynamic and successful politics than the city of Chicago.

The city has experienced great fires, financial crises, economic depressions, nationality differences, racial tensions, spreading blight, gang wars, political corruption and all the other problems common to urban life in America. But it has survived them all, eliminated some, reduced others, learned to live with still others, and progressed steadily far beyond the hopes of the city's founders.

The key to that progress has been the optimism, determination, and political realism of the civic, business, political, ethnic, religious and racial leaders of the city, and the willingness of the citizenry to live together in some degree of harmony and help build one of the great cities of the world, in spite of their ethnic, religious and racial differences.

If past history is any criterion Chicago will surmount the most recent of its many crises and move forward into the future.

Copenhagen

AXEL HOLM

AXEL HOLM

Born 1897. Higher School Certificate, 1916; *candidatus politices*, University of Copenhagen, 1922.

Deputy Director of the Statistical Office of Copenhagen; Visiting examiner in National Science at Denmark's Technical High School; President, Danish Statistical Society, 1959–64; Member of the Supervising Committee relating to the education of the clerical staff of the Municipality of Copenhagen.

Author of: *A Textbook on Local Government of Copenhagen* (1938, 1954 and 1964); *Economy of the Municipality of Copenhagen, 1840–1940* (1941); *Parliamentary Elections through 100 years* (1949); also several publications of the Statistical Office, and periodical and newspaper articles.

Copenhagen

IN the summer of 1967 the city of Copenhagen celebrated, with many festivities, the fact that 800 years had passed since Bishop Absalon in 1167 had built a castle on a little island on the coast of the Sound, for protection against attacks from the Wends (a North German slavic tribe) who ravaged the Danish coasts. However, archaeological studies have shown that for many centuries before Absalon, the area where Copenhagen lies had been inhabited by fishermen and farmers.

The construction of the castle and the foundation of the city's first fortress meant that there was now a much greater potential for commercial development, such that the city which had originally been called Havn (Haven), now became a real *portus mercatorum*, hence the name: *købmannae hafn* (Merchants' haven), and this came later to be København—Copenhagen.

HISTORY AND GROWTH

Beyond the area of the fortress boundaries, Bishop Absalon, who as well as his priestly mission was a leading statesman and military leader, received from King Valdemar the Great in gratitude for his services large tracts of land around Copenhagen. For about the next 250 years, the city and the surrounding country was in the possession of the Bishops of Roskilde. It was also a bishop who in 1254 gave the city its first charter. The area encompassing the first city ramparts was in total only about 70 hectares and this now forms the core of the city's 'old town'.

The city had often in the course of these years to fight hard for its existence; several times it was attacked by the Hanse towns, especially Lubeck, but it survived and in 1417 after a rather problematic lawsuit between King Eric of Pomerania and the Roskilde Bishopric, the city came to the Crown.

Copenhagen, at that time when the southern Swedish provinces belonged to Denmark, had an advantageous position in the very centre of the kingdom, and in the following years it naturally developed into the capital city. The King took up residence in the old castle which after rebuilding became the palace of Copenhagen and was later still supplanted by the Christianborg palace which is now the seat of government, Parliament (*Folketing*) and Supreme Court.

The year 1479 saw the foundation of the University of Copenhagen which strengthened the tendency for the city to become the centre of the nation's

371

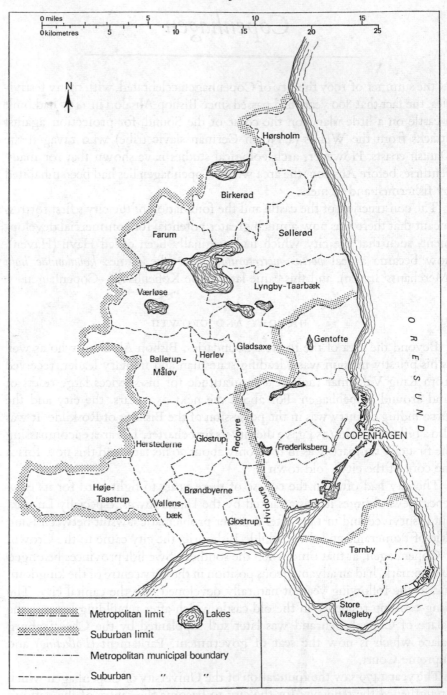

MAP 10   COPENHAGEN—municipal boundaries

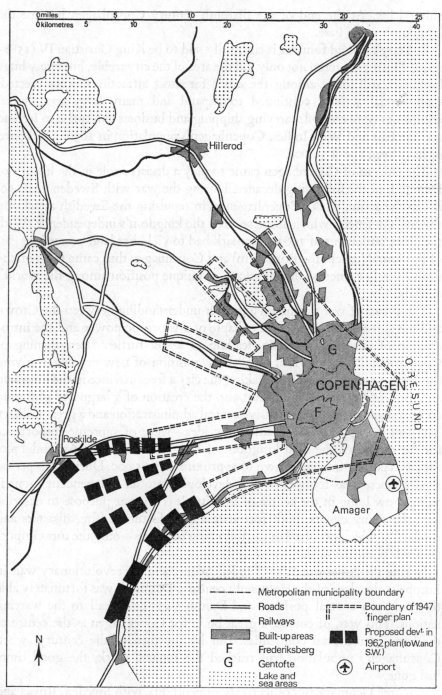

	Metropolitan municipality boundary
Roads	
Railways	
Built-up areas	Boundary of 1947 'finger plan'
F Frederiksberg	Proposed devt in 1962 plan (to W. and S.W.)
G Gentofte	
Lake and sea areas	Airport

MAP 11   COPENHAGEN

cultural life. At the end of the fifteenth century Copenhagen became the kingdom's naval base.

The city's second founder is rightfully said to be King Christian IV (1588–1648). During his reign not only did the area of the city treble, but many huge buildings, still today among the city's foremost attractions, were erected. Commercial activity continued to expand and many large commercial companies were created, carrying shipping and business enterprise to Iceland and the East and West Indies. Copenhagen's population in 1650 is reckoned to have been about 30,000.

The citizens of Copenhagen came to play a decisive role in the history of Denmark in the following decades. During the war with Sweden 1658–60, it was the action of the Copenhageners in repulsing the Swedish attacks on the city's defences, which alone secured the kingdom's independence. With the peace settlement of 1660, Denmark had to yield her land possessions east of the Sound (except for Bornholm) and Copenhagen thus came to lie on the most easterly corner of the kingdom—a unique position among the world's capitals.

The events of war promoted a greater understanding between the Crown and the citizens; this led to the collapse of aristocratic power and the introduction of autocracy in 1660, leading to a still further strengthening of Copenhagen's position. Not only the acquisition of new privileges, giving the citizens certain rights and making the city a free province in the kingdom and the seat of the monarchy but also the creation of a large and glittering court, a strong and comprehensive central administration and a great military base—all in support of the autocratic idea—were of supreme importance for the capital of the dual kingdom of Denmark–Norway. Around 1700, the city's population had grown to approximately 65,000. During this period Frederiksberg was founded and it developed into an independent municipality, now lying in the centre of the city. It is not our purpose to describe here the many events, both fortunate and unfortunate (fire, disasters and epidemics) which occurred in the following centuries—only the most important will be mentioned.

During the American War of Independence and the revolutionary wars in Europe at the close of the eighteenth century, Denmark was fortunately able to maintain a neutral position and Danish ships could sail to the warring nations. This was, of course, a great boon for Copenhagen as the centre of the large commercial companies. But by the turn of the century, when Copenhagen's population had reached the 100,000 mark, the good times had gone.

To force Denmark out of its treaty of neutrality with Sweden, Russia and

Prussia, England attacked Denmark for the first time in 1801 (the naval battle off Copenhagen on April 2, 1801) and the second time in 1807 when Copenhagen was bombarded and the English sailed off with the Danish fleet.

Denmark and its capital were, as a matter of course, politically and materially weakened in the following decades; in 1814 Denmark had to cede Norway to Sweden. By about 1840, the nation and capital had thrown off the results of the disasters of the beginning of the century. Autocracy was abandoned and democracy was introduced with the Constitution of 1849. In 1857 the city received a new constitution which gave the citizens greater self-government and in the same year guild privileges were abolished and free trade established. In 1867 the city's fortress was finally demolished and large areas opened up for building development.

Even without the special privileges attaching to autocracy, Copenhagen was able to maintain its position as the political, cultural and business capital. In 1880 the population numbered 235,000 and after the incorporation of several neighbouring municipalities in 1901 and 1902, the city at the beginning of the twentieth century covered an area of 7,000 hectares and had 400,000 inhabitants. With the incorporation of the other municipalities the previously mentioned Frederiksberg municipality became completely surrounded by Copenhagen.

The two municipalities, together with the adjacent municipality of Gentofte, have during the last fifty years been treated in all official, administrative, and statistical publications as a corporate body known as the capital of Denmark.[1]

The total population of the capital reached the proportion of 974,900 inhabitants in 1950, whereof 768,100 were in Copenhagen, 119,000 in Frederiksberg, and 87,800 in Gentofte. But since then the population has considerably declined—with removal to the suburbs, and with the thinning out of older dwellings in the old town areas—and on October 1, 1969, Copenhagen had 640,500 inhabitants, Frederiksberg 103,700, and Gentofte 80,000—or a total of 824,200 in the municipalities of the capital. Since 1950 this has meant a decline of total population in the capital of 150,700 persons or 15 per cent.

The three metropolitan municipalities together cover an area of 11,808 hectares of which Copenhagen has 8,400, Frederiksburg 870 and Gentofte 2,538 hectares. Concurrently with the development of the population in the

[1] The capital of Denmark is in the strictest legal sense only the municipality of Copenhagen, but for practical administration and in all statistical publications 'the capital' means the three municipalities of Copenhagen, Frederiksberg and Gentofte, which are also called the metropolitan municipalities (*Hovedstadskommunerne*). These three municipalities co-operate in several ways, but have no common administrative organ.

capital there has been a tremendous development and expansion in the suburbs of the capital. These suburbs together with the 3 municipalities of the
capital form the concept called the Metropolitan Area.

The fact that the administration of the capital is split up into three independent municipalities has naturally produced several complex problems,
especially with regard to taxation. These problems have recently been
referred for consideration in conjunction with the whole question of a
rational solution of the administrative, economic, traffic and town-planning
problems of the whole metropolitan area. This area comprises, in addition
to the metropolitan municipalities already mentioned, a considerable
number of suburban municipalities.

SUBURBAN DEVELOPMENT

Up to the beginning of this century the greater part of the suburban
municipalities were more or less rural districts, whose inhabitants were
chiefly engaged in farming and gardening, but the development of modern
traffic and increasing industrialization have gradually made the structure of
these suburbs purely, or at any rate chiefly, urban. At the same time those
very factors have induced an ever increasing number of people engaged in
industrial and business pursuits in Copenhagen, or attached to the central
administration or the cultural institutions of the capital, to take up their
abodes in these suburbs. Added to this is the fact that the commercial undertakings found in suburban municipalities are often branches of those in the
capital.

On these criteria the Statistical Office of Copenhagen in 1930 defined
the metropolitan area as including, besides the three municipalities of
Copenhagen, Frederiksberg and Gentofte, those of Taarnby, Hvidovre,
Rødovre, Glostrup, Brøndbyøster-vester, Herlev, Gladsaxe, Lyngby-Taarbaek, Søllerød, Hørsholm and Birkerød.

Since 1930 the metropolitan area has, however, been further extended.
This is chiefly due to the fact that the municipalities of Copenhagen and
Frederiksberg have by a gradual process been almost completely developed,
to the point where the new buildings necessary to absorb the excess of births
over deaths, to provide for the influx of new citizens, to meet the housing
requirements caused by the conversion of old residential houses into business
premises or the pulling down of old, unhealthy residential blocks, and finally
to cater for the changed age distribution and habits of the population, have
had to be placed in the suburban municipalities. In addition the electrification
of the railways connecting the capital and the suburbs, and the extension of

the motor coach service, have rendered possible a considerable distance between residence and working place.

After a renewed investigation by the Statistical Office of Copenhagen in 1950, eight more suburban municipalities were included in the metropolitan area, so that the entire area comprises twenty-two municipalities in all, namely, the three metropolitan municipalities, the eleven suburban municipalities mentioned before, and also those of Farum, Vaerløse, Ballerup-Maaløv, Herstederne, Høje-Taastrup, Vallensbaek, and St. Magleby and Dragør in the Island of Amager.

In the course of the last ten years, urban development has continued beyond the boundaries of the metropolitan area as defined in 1950 and this development is expected to continue even more strongly in the coming years. The Statistical Office has, therefore, had plans for a new statistical-economic survey to determine new boundaries for Greater Copenhagen. But for the reasons elaborated in the section below entitled 'The Planning of Greater Copenhagen', this survey has not yet been set in motion.

THE METROPOLITAN AREA

The concept of the metropolitan area, after its gradual acceptance in statistical terminology has come also to be accepted in the legislative field for certain activities such as taxation, building and housing, etc., but without creating any joint administrative organ for this area which still embraces the three metropolitan municipalities and the 19 above-mentioned suburban municipalities.

The total metropolitan area is thus 57,700 hectares, of which 11,800 are covered by the three metropolitan municipalities and 45,900 by the nineteen suburban municipalities. Only 17 per cent of the area of the latter municipalities is now farm land, compared with 75 per cent in 1907.

The total population of the twenty-two municipalities on October 1, 1969, numbered 1,383,400 inhabitants, viz. 824,200 in the capital and 559,200 in the suburban municipalities. To illustrate the development of these suburban areas we may note that the population in 1901 numbered only about 40,000; in 1930 it had risen to about 105,000, in 1950 to 241,700 and during the last nineteen years it had further increased by 317,500 people.

This great increase in population has resulted in the populations of several of the suburban municipalities exceeding those of most Danish provincial towns in terms of population size. Thus, Gladsaxe had on October 1, 1969, 74,500 inhabitants, Lyngby-Taarbaek 61,000, Hvidovre 45,800, Taarnby 46,100, Rødovre 45,100 and Ballerup-Maaløv 47,100 inhabitants.

The fact that the inhabitants of these suburban municipalities draw their incomes largely from Copenhagen is revealed by the information that of the total income earned by the suburban population about 50 per cent originated from independent trading and employment in the municipality of Copenhagen proper.

COPENHAGEN'S DOMINANT POSITION

In spite of Copenhagen's situation on the most easterly part of the country, it can be said, in comparison with other capitals in the world, to have a relatively dominating position. As the capital it is the seat of the royal court and the government, the legislature and the Supreme Court. Consequently the whole of the central administration is gathered here. Further it is the largest national port and contains the country's only free port. After the breakthrough of industrialization in the last century, commerce and industry were concentrated in the capital and the larger financial institutions—banks, savings banks, insurance companies, etc., made it their main seat. The only stock exchange in Denmark is also situated in the capital.

Copenhagen is the cultural centre of the nation. The oldest and largest university, the technical high school, the veterinary and agricultural college and many other scientific institutions as well as museums and art collections are all found in the capital.

At the same time it must be recognized that in the last ten years Copenhagen has had to cede some of its former domination. Some figures will serve to illustrate the position of the city today. As was mentioned above the capital had in 1969, 824,200 inhabitants or 17 per cent of the total population.

To illustrate the concentration of business activity—in 1958, 35 per cent of all personnel employed in crafts, industry, commerce and transport were located here. It must, however, be stressed that the capital's percentage of total *industrial* personnel in the last ten years has decreased. A survey covering all industrial activities which regularly employ at least six workers, reveals that the city's percentage of total industrial personnel in 1964 was only 29·2 as against 39·1 in 1958. In contrast the percentage in the suburban municipalities has risen from 8·8 in 1958 to 11·8 in 1964.

Another sign of this concentration is that about 60 per cent of the share capital of the total number of joint stock companies belongs to companies situated in the capital; 75 per cent of the total mercantile shipping is registered in Copenhagen. Its importance as a port is shown by the fact that in 1965 it was a port of call for no less than 13,100 ships aggregating a tonnage of 8·8 million and of these 8,300 (7·9 million tonnage) were ships from foreign ports.

In aviation too, Copenhagen has a dominating position. At Copenhagen's airport (Kastrup) in 1969 there were 145,000 take-offs and landings and the passenger total was 5·8 million. Copenhagen airport is now the fifth largest in Europe.

THE CITY'S CONSTITUTION

The government of the city of Copenhagen is founded on an act of March 4, 1857, with amendments of March 18, 1938, together with various other Acts, the most important of which is the electoral law of 1924, with subsequent amendments the latest being in 1965, and the city statutes of 1920, with amendments of 1938 and later. The fundamental constitution of Copenhagen is embodied in the Danish Constitutional Law of June 5, 1953, which says that the right of municipalities to manage their own local affairs under supervision of the state shall be established by law. In our time, this fundamental principle of local self-government, which was originally adopted in Danish administration by the first democratic Constitution of 1849, has in reality been considerably curtailed through the many encroachments on local administration and finance effected by the central government.

According to the constitution now in force, the municipal corporation of Copenhagen consists of an executive council (*magistrat*) and a town council (*borgerrepraesentation*). The town council, whose members are elected directly by the electors, constitutes the approving authority in municipal affairs, whereas the executive council, i.e. the mayors and aldermen, who are elected by the town council, constitute the executive or administrative power. Compared with central government institutions, the town council corresponds to Parliament, and the mayors and the aldermen to the ministry.

THE TOWN COUNCIL

The town council consists of fifty-five members, all of whom are elected for four years.

Every citizen, man or woman, who meets the electoral requirements for the *Folketing* (Danish Parliament), i.e. who is aged 21 years or over, has Danish citizenship, is domiciled in the town and is not a person declared to be incapable of managing his own affairs, is entitled to vote.

Every citizen who is entitled to vote, except persons who have been punished for a criminal offence which according to public opinion makes him unworthy to be member of the municipal council is eligible for election.[1] The candidates who may be sponsored must be nominated by from five to fifteen electors. Members of the executive council of Copenhagen and the lord lieutenant cannot be elected to the town council.

Elections take place every fourth year in the first half of March. After their names have been checked on the electoral register, the electors at some fifty polling-stations enter an electoral booth where in complete secrecy they can place a cross on a slip of paper against the list they prefer. Elections are conducted on party lines, each list representing a political party, e.g. List A = Social Democrats (Labour), List B = Radicals (Social Liberals), List C = Conservatives, and so on. It is also possible for an elector to write the name of the candidate for whom he wishes to give a personal vote. Few electors, however, avail themselves of this right. The number of candidates to be allotted to each list is calculated according to the d'Hondt system of proportional representation.[2] The parties which in Copenhagen and, increasingly in most towns participate in municipal elections are the same as those which contest Parliamentary elections at the national level. In local government the most important party differences concern the level of taxes and duties, the size of establishments and the extent of reliance upon loan finance. The socialist parties (lists A, F, K and Y) are identified with greater

---

[1] Conviction of a criminal offence does not automatically deprive a candidate of eligibility to serve on a local council. Previously it was left to local councils themselves to decide whether a nominated candidate who had been punished for an offence should be regarded as ineligible. Since 1965, however, such issues have been determined by an 'eligibility board' consisting of a chairman (who must be a judge), deputy chairman and civil servant appointed by the Minister of the Interior and four other members appointed by the four local authority associations.

[2] d'Hondt's system of proportional representation may be explained as follows: Suppose that the following number of votes have been registered in a municipality where 9 councillors are to be elected from three lists:

List A	List B	List C
5,050	3,460	1,490

These figures are then divided by 1, 2, 3, and so on until the 9 greatest quotients have been calculated:

Division by	List A	List B	List C
1	5,050 (1)	3,460 (2)	1,490 (6)
2	2,525 (3)	1,730 (4)	745
3	$1,683\frac{1}{3}$ (5)	$1,153\frac{1}{3}$ (8)	$496\frac{2}{3}$
4	$1,262\frac{3}{4}$ (7)	865	$372\frac{2}{4}$
5	1,010 (9)	692	298
6	$841\frac{4}{6}$	$576\frac{4}{6}$	$248\frac{2}{6}$

The figures in parentheses after the quotients indicate the succession of candidates elected from the three parties. It will be seen that party A returns 5 councillors, party B 3, and party C only 1. If the quotients are equal, there will be a drawing of lots.

municipal enterprise and therefore higher taxes than the liberal parties (lists C, D and, partly, B).

During the last fifty years municipal elections have reflected fairly accurately elections to Parliament—the same political parties have gained a majority in both national and municipal elections.

At the election to the town council in March 1970, 474,600 persons had the right to vote. 61·4 per cent of these voted, namely 62·3 per cent of the men and 60·6 per cent of the women.

The number of votes received by the various lists and the number of members returned was as follows:

List	Number of votes	Per cent	Candidates elected
A Social Democrats	154,861	53·9	31
B Radicals (Social Liberals)	23,580	8·2	5
C Conservatives	57,790	19·1	11
D Liberals	6,335	2·2	1
F Socialist People's Party	28,761	10·0	5
K Communists	9,193	3·2	1
Y Left Socialist	7,898	2·8	1
Other Lists	1,992	0·6	0
Total	287,360	100·0	55

Fourteen of the fifty-five town councillors are women. The persons elected are largely recruited from the trade unions and political organizations. In many cases participation in local politics serves as a training ground for parliament.

Theoretically, every citizen is bound to accept membership of the town council, which is unpaid. Members receive an annual remuneration of 3,200 kroner, but this is merely an allowance for the extra meals and travelling involved.

As to the jurisdiction of the town council, the Act of 1938 provides that the town council has the power of ratification in municipal affairs, and is entitled to debate and decide upon any municipal matter. In consequence of this power, the town council alone can grant money, which in turn means that no municipal expenditure can be defrayed without the consent of the town council, nor can the real property and revenues constituting the capital of the town be touched or any loan negotiated without the approval of the town council.

As this body elects every eighth year the mayors and aldermen (see below), the centre of gravity in the administration of Copenhagen lies not only nominally but actually in the town council.

The standing orders of the town council are embodied in the rules of procedure passed by the council itself, according to which the members every year elect a chairman from among themselves and a first and a second deputy chairman. The principal task of the chairman is to preside at the meetings of the town council, which are held at the town hall (*r°dhus*) of Copenhagen, generally on every second or third Thursday at 6.30 p.m., except in July and August.

The matters considered by the town council may be either motions from the mayors and aldermen or motions, questions and petitions from the members of the council or from persons and institutions outside the council. Motions from outside the council have to be introduced through a member; he passes them on to the chairman, who is bound to include them in the agenda as soon as practicable. By far the greater number of the matters dealt with by the town council are, however, motions by the mayors and aldermen.

If a question discussed by the town council is not initiated by the mayors and aldermen, it must, before any final decision is taken, be submitted to the mayors and aldermen, who are allowed a certain time to express their views.

Motions from the mayors and aldermen are introduced by the mayor to whose department the matter relates. All motions involving expenditure must be read twice, at intervals of at least three days; other matters require only one reading, but often motions of supply as well as other motions are referred to one of the committees appointed by the council. These include the ten permanent or standing committees, which are appointed every year for the chief municipal services, such as lighting, hospitals, education, tramways, etc., the important budget committee, or select committees appointed for special purposes. The members are elected by proportional representation. The object of the committees may be partly to work out the details and implications of a motion, and partly to make suggestions on certain matters.

A fundamental difference between the government of Copenhagen and that of other Danish municipalities, as well as many foreign ones, is that the committees appointed by the elected council do not directly participate in the administration, which is entrusted to the mayors and aldermen alone. The committees deal only with matters of fact, which are referred to them for examination and report to the town council although their reports contain recommendations. On the basis of the committee's report the motion is read a second time. The question is then opened by the spokesman of the committee, and the spokesmen of possible minorities propound their views.

When the matter has been debated, it is put to the vote. The issue is decided by a simple majority of those present and voting. The presence of at least 50 per cent of the members constitutes a quorum. An absolute majority of the whole assembly (which means at least twenty-eight members in favour) is required for the election of the chairman and other individual elections.

The mayors and aldermen are entitled to attend the meetings of the town council and address the assembly; and as the law requires the presence of the respective mayor or alderman at the readings of all motions of supply in order to offer information, the meetings are practically always attended by them. The first meeting in each month is specially reserved for the answering of questions, the time for the asking and answering of each question being limited to ten minutes. The importance of these 'question-times', which were introduced in 1948, has not, however, proved to be very great.

The meetings of the town council are held in public. Certain matters of a confidential nature, such as appointments to office and transactions in real property are, however, dealt with at meetings from which the public is excluded. On the proposal of the chairman or six members it can be moved that other matters also shall not be discussed in public.

The deliberations are taken down in shorthand and published in print. The publication named 'Proceedings of the Town Council of Copenhagen' (*Københavns Borgerrepraesentanters Forhandlinger*) dates back to 1840.

THE BUDGET

The most important matter dealt with by the town council in the course of the year is the municipal budget, and the additional grants made in connection with it. The budget is divided into two main parts: the current budget and the capital budget.

The current budget is an estimate of the operating revenue and working expenses of all the municipal organs during the coming financial year, which runs from April 1st to March 31st, and of the rates that will have to be collected to balance the budget. The various institutions begin working on the budget in the month of April. Estimates are sent by the heads of the various institutions to the mayor of the respective department. When the respective mayors have drawn up the estimates submitted by their departments, the proposals are sent to the chief mayor before the end of May. Any amendments desired by him are discussed with the respective mayors. On the basis of the figures representing expenditure and revenue the chief mayor draws up his motion concerning the rates to be collected during the coming financial year, and after that the whole budget is presented to all the mayors and aldermen. After it has been considered by the latter, and possibly criticized by minorities, the budget is presented by the chief mayor to the town council for approval. This has to be done before the end of June. After the opening speech by the chief mayor, which take the form of a general survey of the whole economic situation, the budget debate begins, when not only the financial status of the municipality is discussed by the members, but all sorts of local political problems, and the mayors have to answer numerous questions.

When the budget has been through the first reading, it is sent to the budget committee, which at present consists of fifteen members, to be examined in detail.

Here it is gone through very carefully and finally reported upon, after which the second reading takes place. The budget must be completed by 1st October.

Nominally the passing of the budget does not require the confirmation of a superior authority. But this does not really mean that the town council has a free hand concerning the nature or the extent of the expenditure and revenue contained in the budget. This aspect will be considered later.

The budget determines the scope within which the activities of the administration (i.e. the mayors and aldermen) are confined during the financial year. Should questions arise in the course of the year involving additional expenditure not included in the budget, a further grant will be necessary. This, as mentioned before, has to be read twice by the town council, possibly with an intervening committee stage. Small amounts of less than 3,000 kr. may, however, be granted by a standing committee appointed by the town council. At the end of each financial year a report and accounts are published.

The audit of the municipal accounts is carried out partly by a special directorate of professional auditors, which is responsible for the correctness of the municipal accounts, and partly by the municipal auditors, who number five persons elected for a period of four years by the town council, one of whom is elected chairman. These auditors must see that no expenditure is incurred which has not been granted, and that the dispositions of the administration conform with the decision taken by the corporation, and the existing laws and regulations. When the municipal auditors have completed their report it is sent to a decision committee, which in its turn reports to the town council, by which the municipal accounts must be finally approved.

Unlike the current budget, the municipal capital budget cannot be made for a certain period, but results from the special allocations made for new plant and extensions of existing plant and activities according as they are required. But every year a working plan is made showing the amounts available for capital expenditure during the coming year and supplemented with a more long-term investment plan, a so called flexible five-year plan.

Whereas the current budget, as already mentioned, does not require the approval of higher authorities, all purchases, sales and mortgages of municipal property must be sanctioned by the Ministry of the Interior (*Indenrigsministeriet*). Likewise the negotiations of loans to a larger amount than can be repaid out of the annual revenue. This last provision is, of course, of great importance to all municipal investment which is largely financed through loans (such as the building and extension of gas and electricity works, streets and schools).

THE EXECUTIVE COUNCIL

The executive council (*magistraten*) is composed of one chief mayor (*overborgmester*), five mayors (*borgmestre*) and five aldermen (*raadmaend*), who are all elected by proportional representation every eight years by the town council. Everyone who has a right to vote for the lower house of Parliament is eligible for these offices. As no one can be at the same time a mayor or an alderman *and* a member of the town council, a town councillor has to retire from the council if he is elected a mayor or an alderman. Whereas a mayor was formerly chiefly an official he is now more of a politician, and mayors as well as aldermen are mostly recruited from among the town councillors, who are elected on political lines. Of the present mayors, who were elected in 1970, four (among them the chief mayor) were elected by the Social Democratic Party, one by the Conservatives, and one by the Social Liberals. Of the five aldermen, three were elected by the Social Democrats, one by the Conservatives, and one by the Socialist People's Party.

The mayors receive salaries and are entitled to pensions on retirement. The chief mayor receives a basic salary which, together with certain additional payments dependent on the price-index, brings his present total salary up to 136,000 kr. The salaries of the mayors with similar additions amount to 125,000 kr.

The aldermen are not entitled to pensions, but receive a basic fee with additional payments, so that each alderman at present receives 45,000 kr.

As mentioned before, the mayors and aldermen constitute the executive power in municipal affairs. They act partly as a body through collective

N

decisions made by all of them, and partly through departments, each headed by the chief mayor or a mayor.

Matters concerning the municipality in general, such as the statutes and the annual budget, or which affect several branches of the administration, or are of vital importance to the administration and economy of the town, are dealt with by the executive council. As chairman the chief mayor may cause any matter to be brought before it, just as each of the mayors can submit matters belonging to his department.

In pursuance of the city ordinances matters concerning the appointment and dismissal of officials and employees are decided by the executive council, with a few exceptions. The highest municipal officials, such as directors of the departments, are nominated by the executive council but appointed by the town council; moreover, the town council or a committee appointed by it, is in certain cases called upon to decide questions relating to the pensioning of an official.

The executive council normally meets every Monday at 10 a.m. at the town hall, except in July and August. The meetings are not public, like those of the town council, and even officials cannot attend except the lord lieutenant, who attends in his capacity of state superintendent. Matters are decided by a majority. Resolutions are drawn up in the name of the executive council and signed by those present, unless the matter belongs to a single department.

As chairman of the executive council, the chief mayor is invested with certain special powers. If, for instance, he finds that a decision taken by a mayor, or by an alderman acting on his own initiative, exceeds his authority, or is in conflict with the law, or is detrimental to the municipality, or neglects a duty incumbent on the municipality, it is his duty to protest, and the decision is suspended. If the matter is not settled by arrangement between the chief mayor and the mayor or alderman in question, the former may cause it to be submitted to the executive council. If he considers it necessary, he can insist upon the matter being finally settled by the town council.

To make sure that the chief mayor (and consequently all the mayors and aldermen) keeps in touch with the work of the town council, he has a statutory right to be informed, not later than the night before each meeting of the town council, as to the business to be debated.

Finally, the chief mayor is entitled temporarily to transfer the business of a mayor or alderman to one of his colleagues. Similarly, pending the decision of the town council, he can appoint one of the mayors or aldermen to be acting chief mayor during his absence.

The most important thing about the chief mayor is that he is the head of the municipal treasury. In consequence, every motion of supply has to be submitted to him to receive his comments before it is sent to the executive council, as well as before it is brought before the town council. In this way he is enabled at his leisure to decide whether he considers the contemplated financial measure justified or desirable, having regard to the financial position of the municipality as a whole.

As previously explained, the chief mayor or a mayor is at the head of each department. The election itself determines who is to be chief mayor and the city ordinances contain special rules for the distribution of departments among the mayors. Thus the elected mayors and aldermen, at the first meeting of the executive council, choose in accordance with their seniority on the executive council the departments they would like to direct, so that one mayor and one alderman are allotted to each department. If any of the elected mayors or aldermen has at any time served in the same capacity, a request to remain in the same department will, however, be complied with, if the chief mayor has been notified before the meeting takes place.

Each mayor has charge of all matters referred to his department, and acts independently and on his own responsibility. No appeal from his decision can be made to the executive council, but if anyone has cause for complaint an appeal lies to the central government provided that the matter does not belong to the law courts. In theory the mayors in Copenhagen thus have great administrative powers, and unlike the mayors of other towns, they are not tied by committees appointed by the elected council. Nevertheless, as the town council fixes the regulations and has to vote all appropriations for the administration and as the chief mayor has the important powers mentioned above, the occasions on which a mayor is entirely independent are in practice rare.

The city ordinances define how the municipal tasks and business are assigned to the six departments.

To the chief mayor's department belong in the first place the institutions dealing with municipal accounts, audits, wages, pensions and rates.

To the first department are assigned (among other things) certain legal functions, education, libraries, statistics, population registration and the funeral service.

To the second department are assigned (among other things) hospitals, mental hospitals and housing.

To the third department are assigned public assistance, social insurance, and the child guidance service.

To the fourth department are assigned the technical institutions such as the town engineer's office, the town architect's office, the surveyor's office and the fire brigade.

Finally the fifth department is in charge of the municipal trading services, such as the supplies of gas, electricity and water, tramways, etc.

As previously mentioned, the executive council includes five paid but unpensioned aldermen, who are supposed to act as intermediaries between the mayors' naturally more official outlook and the councillors' more political point of view. In the executive council, the aldermen are on equal terms with the mayors, and their votes are of equal weight. Within their respective departments the aldermen may be entrusted with certain administrative tasks, but in reality this does not amount to much. On the other hand, the aldermen are largely employed in various committees as representatives of the executive council.

Certain services are directed by special authorities, committees or boards. Local education is thus administratively and educationally under the supervision of an education committee consisting of the mayor of the first department as chairman, the alderman of the same department, four members elected by the town council and four members elected by and from among members of the boards of managers who were elected by parents, attached to each school. These school boards of managers in their turn consist of two members elected by the town council and three elected by the parents who have children attending the school in question. The idea of the boards is to obtain information about the working of the school, and they are entitled to deal with all questions concerning the school and to make recommendations to the education committee.

The education committee appoints the teachers, draws up the syllabus and curriculum in accordance with the legislative prescriptions, whereas the corporation decides all questions concerning the economy or finance of education.

Health services are in the hands of a public health committee consisting of the police director (a government official) as chairman, the mayor of the second department, the medical officer, and two members elected by the town council.

The municipal libraries also have an administration of their own, presided over by the mayor of the first department. This committee, which plans and superintends the working of the libraries, is invested with rather limited powers concerning the appointment and dismissal of the staff.

The port of Copenhagen is the only institution which is not administered by the corporation, in contradistinction to the situation in certain other towns. This is a self-supporting institution administered by a board consisting of the Lord Lieutenant of Copenhagen (see following section) and sixteen members, of whom only four are elected by the corporation of Copenhagen, while the others are elected by the central government, Parliament, and the trade organizations.

RELATIONS WITH CENTRAL GOVERNMENT

An account of the constitution of Copenhagen would be incomplete without some mention of the relations between the state and the municipality. The influence of the central government on municipal administration is steadily increasing.

The formal relations between the state and the municipality are apparent from the words of our constitutional law, which declares that the right of municipalities *under the supervision of the state* to govern their own affairs shall be established *by law*. This implies that the very rules according to which the municipalities are governed are embodied in Acts of Parliament, and consequently municipal statutes are to be approved by the Internal Affairs Ministry. As the statutes contain a list showing the number of public servants and their wages, the latter provision involves among other things that the creation, amendment and abolition of posts within the local government service have to be approved by the Internal Affairs Ministry. In Copenhagen, however, this provision has been limited to the higher officials only.

The right of the Internal Affairs Ministry to sanction the raising of loans in connection with capital expenditure, and the purchase, sale or mortgaging of municipal property has already been mentioned.

The state has also to supervise the municipalities. In Copenhagen this supervision is performed by a lord lieutenant (*overpraesident*), whose office dates back to the charter of 1661, when all the mayors of the town were chosen by the King, and the first mayor got the title of '*praesident*', and later on '*overpraesident*'. Although the constitution of the town had been made more democratic in 1840 and 1857 the lord lieutenant survived as president of the executive council, whose members were by now all elected by the town council. In 1938 the lord lieutenant left the corporation, and is now only the superintendent representative of the state. In this capacity he has a right to demand information from and to negotiate with the corporation and to attend the meetings of both the executive council and the town council. If the lord lieutenant finds that a decision taken by the corporation exceeds the authority conferred upon it or is otherwise contrary to law, or tends to prevent the performance of a duty incumbent on the municipality, he should without delay report to the Ministry of Internal Affairs, who after hearing the corporation decides whether the decision shall be cancelled. It goes without saying that the Ministry of Internal Affairs may also take action without the intervention of the lord lieutenant.

The local administration is in practice largely dependent on the central administration. To show this in detail would be beyond the scope of this work so we must confine ourselves to the main points. In the first place it should be emphasized that the corporation has no real authority as regards taxation. The provisions according to which municipal rates and taxes are levied have all been made by central legislation—The King and Parliament—and the administrative rules for their execution have been largely fixed by the central government.

In the second place the state contributes towards the costs of municipal purposes, primarily towards social insurance and social welfare, hospital services and schools. This means that the state has a great deal of influence on the administration of these municipal activities.

A further estimate of these conditions will appear in the following section illustrating the balance sheet of the municipality of Copenhagen.

Of municipal institutions principally rooted in central legislation and central administration, education should be mentioned (together with public assistance and social insurance) for the whole educational system and structure has been largely determined by the state. The corporation is supreme, however, as regards the construction and equipment of school buildings.

The regulations of the funeral service and the local libraries must be approved by the Ministries of Church and Education respectively. The register of population was established under an Act of Parliament and is administered according to regulations made by the Internal Affairs Ministry. Likewise the health service is administered largely in accordance with regulations made or approved by the central government. Also the technical departments, which are in charge of sites, streets, roads, sewers, etc., must be administered on the basis of special acts concerning streets and roads, building laws, town planning, etc.

These central controls do not amount to an abolition, but only a limitation of local self-government. In a municipality the size of Copenhagen the elected corporation will naturally find ample scope for self-government and consequently for the realization of the local political views of the majority in the corporation.

MUNICIPAL FINANCE

To illustrate the extent of municipal administration, a broad survey of the net revenue and net expenditure of Copenhagen for the year 1969–70 is as follows:

Net revenue			Net expenditure	
		1,000 kr.		1,000 kr.
1. Taxes and rates:			I. Central administration	175,187
Income tax	774,161		II. Social insurance, assist-	
Property Tax	344,838		ance, and relief	417,625
Other rates and duties	26,126		III. Hospitals	270,229
			IV. Public Health	8,156
Total	1,145,125		V. Education	177,069
2. Contributions from Frederiks-			VI. Libraries	17,550
berg and Gentofte as per			VII. Roads and sewer service,	
intermunicipal clearing	24,551		public cleaning and	
3. Surplus on municipal services,			lighting	110,299
and real property:			VIII. Fire brigade	39,035
Gasworks	1,546		IX. Lavatories and baths	8,009
Electricity works	32,553		X. Appropriation for	
Heating works	18,940		financial investment	172,583
Water supply	13,468		XI. Other expenditure	63,974
Tramways	−71,938			
Land and real property	3,990			
Other activities	−12,920			
Total	−14,361			
4. Interest	35,929			
Total	1,191,244			
Deficit	268,472			
Total	1,459,716		Total	1,459,716

The total expenditure of Copenhagen in the period 1969–70 thus amounted to nearly 1,500 million kr. of which 29 per cent went to social insurance, assistance and relief, 20 per cent to hospitals and 12 per cent to education. Expenditure is mainly covered by taxes and revenues (see below) while the large surplus coming from electrical and heating works and water supply is swallowed up by the large deficit from tramways and other activities.

It must be emphasized the municipality of Copenhagen's budget is based on the *net* principle so that, for example, figures showing a surplus on municipal utilities arise after expenses for salaries, equipment, raw materials, etc., have been deducted from gross revenue and on the expenditure side first and foremost the large state subsidy (see below) which the municipality receives is deducted from gross expenditure. Thus in 1969–70 the municipality's total gross expenditure was 4,178 million kr.

In connection with the most important section of revenue income '*Taxes and Rates*', it should be noted that these are raised according to procedures established by statute. The financially most important item, as the table indicates is that of income tax. The income of companies, associations institutions and foundations is assessed on a joint tax, to state and municipality. 15 per cent of the tax goes to the local authority where the establishment is situated.

Municipal property taxes are collected partly on a land tax rate and partly on a building tax rate. For the land tax a minimum thousandth rate has been established which is, so far as Copenhagen is concerned, 25 per thousandth and in 1969–70 the rate was 42 per thousandth, the building tax rate is fixed by statute and in 1969–70 was 19·07 per thousandth (assessed on the basis of quite detailed procedures).

Regarding the item of contributions from Frederiksberg and Gentofte towards intermunicipal clearing the point should be made that the object of the equalization between Copenhagen and these two municipalities is to make the total net proceeds from the number of rates and taxes per inhabitant in each of the municipalities equal to the corresponding proceeds per inhabitant in Copenhagen plus Frederiksberg and Copenhagen plus Gentofte respectively. This rule which has existed since 1938 and is now in process of being wound up, has since 1958–59 meant in effect a fixed amount. As it is expected to be shortly supplanted by another form of equalization procedure among all the metropolitan municipalities, there is no point on dwelling further on the special arrangement.

To illustrate the great importance of state subsidies within the various areas of expenditure the following figures for 1969–70 are given:

State subsidy to:	million kr.
Social insurance and welfare	1,195·6
Hospitals	402·4
Public Health	3·2
Education	183·4
Roads	67·6
Libraries	7·3
Others	12·5
Total	1,872·0

As a supplement to this brief survey of the expenditure involved in the administration of Copenhagen the following table illustrates the personnel employed in the most important municipal institutions.

Number of Persons Employed, 1969–70

	Permanent officers	Wage earners	Other employees	Total
Taxation department	735	—	717	1,452
Statistical office and register of population	156	—	237	393
Libraries	171	16	132	319
Funeral service	107	271	42	420
Education	3,089	755	1,324	5,168
Public markets	69	90	10	169
Hospitals	2,886	2,461	6,073	11,420
Public health	44	13	70	127
Municipal residential properties	60	13	199	252
Administration of the town hall	284	334	110	728
Social insurance and public assistance	1,618	851	2,717	5,186
Fire brigade	613	69	58	740
Administration of streets, roads and sewers	379	942	222	1,573
Town architect's and engineer's offices, etc.	222	—	230	452
Gas, electricity and heating works	948	826	293	2,067
Water supply	206	240	58	504
Tramways	2,475	606	87	3,168
Department for Handicraft	38	450	37	525
Other institutions	269	282	222	773
Total	14,369	8,219	12,818	35,406
Of these women	5,422	4,522	9,725	19,469

To give some idea of the magnitude of the various activities carried out by the municipality of Copenhagen, capital expenditure figures for 1969–70 show that these totalled 443 million kr. of which the largest part went to gas and electricity works (174 million kr.), tramways (26 million kr.) this involved modernization and rationalization including the replacement of tramways by buses, hospital works (67 million kr.) and schools (31 million kr.). It is expected in 1971–72 that there will be a total investment figure of 608 million kr.

N*

A COMPARISON WITH OTHER DANISH LOCAL AUTHORITIES

A comparison between the constitution of the local authorities in the Copenhagen area and the rest of Denmark would be pointless at present, because the legislation reforming local government, passed on April 1, 1970, did not apply to the municipalities of Copenhagen and Fredericksborg and the county of Copenhagen, in other words Greater Copenhagen. No scheme of local government reform has yet been prepared for the capital.[1]

The main points in the above-mentioned reform of local government should be briefly surveyed. Before April 1, 1970, Denmark outside Greater Copenhagen was divided into two groups of local authorities: *købstad-kommuner* (urban municipalities) which correspond roughly to English county boroughs, and *landkommuner* (rural municipalities). The latter form a two tier system, the top tier being *amtskommuner* (counties) and the lower tier *sognekommuner*, broadly equivalent to English rural districts, or parishes. There were 85 boroughs, 25 counties and 1,250 rural districts. The boroughs were governed by a town council (*byrådet*) of 7 to 25 members, who were elected according to the provisions of municipal election law for a four year term of office. The town council elected a chairman called the mayor (*borgmester*) who directed the administration in conjunction with various committees set up by the council. The boroughs were subject to the supervision of the Minister of the Interior especially with regard to their capital programmes. Counties were governed by a county council (*amtsråd*) of 9 to 15 elected members and they had a state appointed chairman. The responsibilities of the county councils were primarily the provision of hospital services and roads and the supervision of the rural districts; the counties themselves were subject to the Minister of the Interior. The rural districts undertook primarily local tasks such as schools, social welfare, local roads, etc. They were governed by a district council (*sogneråd*) of 5 to 19 members elected according to the provisions of municipal election law. The chairman of the district council directed the administration in conjunction with the relevant committees.

This centuries old system was radically changed by the reforms mentioned above. The first step was an Act of June 1, 1967 which gave the Minister of the Interior power to institute a structural reform on the following basis:

(1) The establishment of new counties to embrace boroughs as well as rural districts.

(2) The reorganization of local government around towns so that urban areas which had previously extended over several local government boundaries, but which should be regarded as entities, would now be contained

1 For further reference see the following section.

in one local authority area. In this connection reference would have to be made to expected population changes and economic developments.

(3) To bring into being larger and more viable units in terms of population, resources and area so as to carry out their tasks more effectively.

The result of this Act is that since April 1, 1970, Denmark has been divided into 276 primary or lower tier local authorities (as against the former 1,335) and 14 secondary or top tier units, called counties. It seems likely that the number of units will be further reduced in the course of the next few years. Greater Copenhagen as was mentioned remains outside the provisions of the Act.

Regulations for the government of these new local authorities are set out in an Act of May 31, 1968. It lies outside the scope of this article to examine these regulations in detail. Perhaps, however, it should be mentioned that the 276 primary local authorities are governed by a *kommunalbestyrelse* (communal council) of 5 to 31 members elected according to the existing law. The chairman with the title of mayor (*borgmester*) undertakes the provision of daily administration in conjunction with the various committees.

The counties are governed by a county council (*amstråd*) of 13 to 31 members with a chairman elected by the council called the county mayor (*amtsborgmester*). The former state-appointed chairmen of the county councils now exercise other state responsibilities; they also act as the chairmen of the county supervising committees (*tilsynsrådene*) whose other members are appointed by the county councils. Their supervision includes the confirmation of the primary units capital programmes especially loan authorization. Counties still remain subject to the jurisdiction of the Minister of the Interior. It must be mentioned that the allocation of responsibilities between the state, the primary units and the secondary units has not yet been finalized. Likewise no rules have been drawn up for the division of their resources, for example, the exact allocation of taxes.

Such questions will be of great significance for the devising of a scheme for the capital which has now been set in hand. So far as the difference between the existing unaltered local government system in Copenhagen and the rest of Denmark is concerned only the following important differences will be mentioned: that whereas the approving authority in the former is separated from the executive, the councils of the latter, though elected on the same lines as the town council of Copenhagen, are in control of the executive as well as the approving power. This will at once appear from the fact that, whereas the mayors and aldermen in Copenhagen cannot at the same time be members of the town council, the opposite is the case in other towns. Secondly, the administration in other towns is largely carried out by committees appointed by the town council, whereas the committees appointed by the town council of Copenhagen do not participate in the administration of the capital. This difference means that in Copenhagen the adminstration is entrusted to the 'efficient' element (i.e. the chief officials) in a higher degree than elsewhere, though the mayors are responsible to the town council, whereas in the smaller towns, at least, the town council—the 'democratic' element—is in closer touch with the daily administration.

RELATIONS WITH NEIGHBOURING MUNICIPALITIES

In the foregoing we have dealt with the municipality of Copenhagen as a constitutional and administrative unit alone, but, as already mentioned, the formal boundaries of the municipality were burst long ago by the economic and political development of the city.

The fact that even by 1950 the twenty-two municipalities, and even more so now, constitute one economic community, naturally involves a considerable interest in the administration of public affairs on the part of the inhabitants, not merely in the municipality where they live, but also in the one where they work. They are interested in reliable and fast means of communication, roads, bus-lines, railways and tramways; and the establishment and efficiency of gas, water, electricity and heating facilities become matters of importance to a circle of consumers extending beyond the formal boundaries of the individual municipalities. The same thing applies to hospitals, schools, etc. A real co-ordination of all these matters of mutual interest is beset with considerable difficulties, not only because the metropolitan area is split up into different independent municipal units, but also because the municipalities outside the capital are parish councils, which are under the supervision partly of the county council of Copenhagen, and partly of the county councils of Frederiksborg and Roskilde, which also administer the hospital service of these municipalities, along with the most important main roads.

Besides the mutual interests mentioned, which are bound to result in the demand for a rational administration of the metropolitan area, attention should be turned to another important problem, which is not a question of mutual interest to all the inhabitants of the metropolitan area, but rather a question of guarding the legitimate economic interests of some municipalities against others within the area. The distribution of vocational and income classes, and consequently the social structure of the population, vary considerably in the different municipalities. Some municipalities are inhabited chiefly by the more well-to-do business people and superior civil or public servants and employees, others by members of the working classes. The public expenditure per head being about the same in the municipalities—somewhat higher in the 'poor' municipalities than in the 'rich' ones—a rather considerable discrepancy arises as regards municipal taxation. Endeavours have been made to remedy this discrepancy by the imposition of a so-called trade tax on persons receiving an income exceeding a certain amount from a municipality outside the one where they are domiciled. This tax is added to the revenue of the municipality in which the income is earned, but is refunded to the ratepayer partly or entirely by the municipality in which he resides. Between Copenhagen on the one hand, and Frederiksberg and Gentofte on the other the trade taxation has, however, been replaced by a clearing system, as mentioned above.

As, however, the trade tax regulations and the equalization agreements among the three municipalities of Copenhagen no longer corresponded to the overall economic development among the municipalities and led to great economic difficulties, an Act of 1959 provided that those amounts which the suburban municipalities paid to Copenhagen should be fixed at an annual sum, calculated on the basis of the 1957–58 trade taxes. The equalization agreement among the three Copenhagen municipalities was likewise fixed to the amount which Copenhagen received in 1957–58. This provision which was only intended to apply for a few years, is still in existence whilst the great municipal and tax reforms mentioned above, are put into effect.

To inquire into these problems the Ministry of Internal Affairs even as early as 1939 appointed a committee, called the Metropolitan Committee, to consider what alterations to the existing municipal administrative structure, changes in population and economic and technical development in the metropolitan area might make necessary.

In January 1948 the committee made a report. This report began by pointing out that the municipal boundaries fixed centuries ago under widely different administrative and economic conditions, do not at all suit modern developments as regards the built-up area, trade, commerce and traffic, which often utterly disregard these boundaries. In the metropolitan area the problem is exceptionally acute owing to an almost explosive development.

The report then considers the various possibilities of reform, specially dwelling upon the arguments pro and con three separate solutions: (1) an arrangement for the purpose of adjusting the economic discrepancy between the municipalities already mentioned; (2) the establishment of a sort of municipal league so that certain business of an intermunicipal nature could be assigned to a major municipality, whereas the more local business would be left to the primary municipalities of the league, i.e. a system somewhat corresponding to the relations between the Greater London Council and the

London borough councils, and (3) the incorporation in Copenhagen of a number of municipalities and the amalgamation of others.

It would require too much space to deal with the various arguments for and against the several possibilities and combinations. We shall therefore only say that the committee did not succeed in making a unanimous recommendation, and the majority obtained in favour of a certain solution could only be secured by the sacrifice of principles all round.

There was no majority decision on the government's part and the proposals have been definitely abandoned, including those for a comprehensive incorporation within Copenhagen and the setting up of a Copenhagen Council.

A METROPOLITAN ADVISORY COMMITTEE

After the abortive attempt to provide an administrative organ to consider the joint interests of the city's municipalities, discussions followed to create on a voluntary basis (i.e. having no legal base), an organ for collaboration. This resulted in 1956 in the creation of a Metropolitan Municipalities Joint Committee. It has 34 representatives, 7 from the municipality of Copenhagen, 2 from Frederiksborg, 3 from Copenhagen county council and 1 from each of the 22 attached municipalities outside Copenhagen and Frederiksborg. The Joint Committee's task is to discuss questions of mutual interest, to consider probable joint municipal agreements as well as, of course, initiating research into problems which would naturally fall to its consideration; to reach the eventual position of sending recommendations to the relevant municipalities or others, or if the situation so requires, to the Ministry or other authorities. Such recommendations require at least a two-thirds majority of all representatives regardless of the number present at the meeting. This procedure underlines the fact that the council can only be considered as a forum for debate and that it has no decision-making authority.

The council has also taken up the question of the creation of a legally based union of local authorities and has made several attempts at formulating proposals for a rational arrangement of the metropolitan local authorities, but this work has been rendered difficult because of the classical conflict between the 'rich' and 'poor' municipalities and between the old well-consolidated municipalities and the new developing ones. The executive councils of the suburban municipalities all agree that their primary aim must be to take care of the economic interests of their own communities, and they can with some justification declare that it is for this purpose they have been elected.

To summarize the position and illustrate how economic displacements have changed—the municipality of Copenhagen had, twenty years ago, an average income only a little below the average for the whole metropolitan area but developments have been such that Copenhagen now has the lowest average income per taxpayer among the 22 municipalities. In 1968 this was 26,143 kr. for Copenhagen whereas the overall average was 30,555 kr. and in Gentofte it was 45,862 kr., Søllerud 45,003 kr. and in Lyngby-Taarbaek 38,109 kr. It is easy to understand that these disparities of economic status to a great extent impedes agreement towards new arrangements for the metropolitan area.

In 1965 the metropolitan committee put forward a proposal for a re-organization of the capital area but it was territorially too limited, too narrow and took no account of the financial and taxation problems. It suffered from various other deficiencies and accordingly has received no backing from the Ministry of Internal Affairs. Nothing would be achieved by elaborating on it here.

After another abortive attempt between 1967 and 1969 by the local authorities concerned to reach agreement on a scheme for reforming local government in Greater Copenhagen, the state finally decided to set up in May 1970 a Capital Reform Commission (*Hovedstadsreformudvalg*). The Commission's terms of reference are to recommend what changes in the existing structure of local government in the capital area it considers desirable to bring about a more rational administrative and economic basis for the future provision of services.

The Commission consists of a *departementschef* (divisional head) from the Ministry of the Interior together with two other officials from the same Ministry, five members chosen by the political parties in the *Folketing*, four by local authority associations and five by local authorities in the capital area. Thus the latter authorities' representatives in contrast to previous inquiries do not predominate. The Commission is to report by April 1, 1971 and it can be expected that there will be both a majority report and one or more minority areas. The main points upon which discussion will focus will certainly be:

(1) Which local authorities will be included in the capital area.

(2) Which functions will be allocated to a Greater Copenhagen authority.

(3) How the government of such an authority will be chosen—by direct or indirect election.

(4) How comprehensive will be the division of resources among the new local authorities.

After the Commission has reported the government will consider its proposals and present its conclusions for discussion and decision to the *Folketing*. The reorganization of local government in Greater Copenhagen (which includes not only the municipalities of Copenhagen and Fredericksberg but the counties of Copenhagen, Fredericksborg and Roskilde) will at the earliest be implemented by April 1, 1974. So the problem will have been on the agenda for 40 years!

At the same time as there has been work in progress to create new metropolitan arrangements, several commissions have been set up in the rather important transport sector with the object of co-ordinating the public transport services in the metropolitan area. These are administered at present partly by the state (railways), partly by the local authorities (tramways and buses) and partly by private companies (buses).

The last commission in 1955 urged the setting-up of an independent Traffic Council to co-ordinate all of the surface traffic in Greater Copenhagen, but even this proposal has not been activated.

If the above picture gives the reader a somewhat pessimistic impression of collaboration among the metropolitan municipalities, the position must be rectified by stressing that in a whole range of decisive areas there has been impressive administrative and technical co-operation. This applies to such activities as the tramways, the provision of gas and electricity, water supply, hospitals and the fire service.

The main deficiency is that of a joint supreme executive council which would have decision-making authority, not just consultative authority, in both the administrative and economic spheres—so wide are the vital interests of joint concern.

Simultaneously with the many, but unfortunately up to now abortive, attempts to instititue a rational metropolitan organization by the creation of a regional county or a union of municipalities, there has been in both the spheres of population and commerce in the Greater Copenhagen area, a development which steadily expands the boundaries of the metropolitan conurbation. The following section will look at this development.

THE PLANNING OF GREATER COPENHAGEN

One of the most serious consequences of the lack of co-ordination in a policy for the metropolitan area has been the inability to develop an overall planning structure for the entire Copenhagen region. The planning of residential districts, commercial areas (industrial quarters and business centres) and traffic lines (railways and buses) which has had to take place, has happened in various stages and through a variety of municipal and state organs. State authorities have, in particular, taken charge of major transport facilities without any comprehensive consultation with the municipal authorities and with no satisfactory regard to other planning features in the region.

The great uncertainty surrounding any overall policy direction for the metropolitan region, has also prevented Copenhagen's Statistical Office from carrying out, as it did in 1930 and 1950, a new statistical-economic delineation of the region. There has been no lack of plans but most of them have been formulated on a private or semi-official basis.

The first significant planning work was carried out by a regional planning committee appointed on private initiative. This committee was originally appointed in January 1928 at the request of the Danish Town Planning Committee. But after the committee in 1936 had finished a task which at that time was rather urgent and important, concerning the green areas of Copenhagen, i.e. woodland and parks for open-air recreation, etc., the committee came to a standstill. As the work of the metropolitan committee dragged on, however, the demand for a general plan for the Copenhagen region grew more and more urgent, especially after the Town Planning Act of 1938 had required the municipalities of the area to draw up separate town plans. In March 1945 the regional planning committee then resumed its work. The membership of the committee consisted of representatives of the municipalities of the Copenhagen area and representatives of a great number of authorities and institutions interested in planning. It was, however, an unofficial body without executive power.

In 1947 the regional planning committee issued a plan for Greater Copenhagen. This is a rather comprehensive work treating all the problems connected with the planning of a future Greater Copenhagen. One of the points of departure is, of course, the number of inhabitants, and here the figures are based on a population prognosis, made by the Statistical Office of Copenhagen, which on certain assumptions estimated that in 1965 the metropolitan area would contain 1·4 million inhabitants (a prediction virtually fulfilled) and in the somewhat longer term the population would reach 1·6 to 1·7 million. The plan proceeds to show which areas are most suitable for residential building, specified according to housing, and indicates the localities for the different kinds of industrial and commercial development. It deals with traffic routes, recreation grounds, etc.

The plan proposes that the future development of the metropolitan area should be connected with the radial railway lines. These lines are the electrified north and north-west railways, and partly constructed and partly projected electric railways to the west. The structure of the future metropolitan community could therefore, as shown in Map 11, be illustrated by a hand, the palm forming the municipality of Copenhagen while the five spreading fingers indicate building development along the five radial railways. The spaces between the fingers were intended to be largely laid out as green areas.

An Act of 1949 on the regulation of built-up areas became of great importance for town planning in the metropolitan area, and in other town areas in Denmark.

According to this Act town development plans may be drawn up for periods of not less than fifteen years for areas further defined, and of course also for the metropolitan area, prescribing those areas which may be used for urban building (inner zones), those which may be laid out as garden links for later development (intermediary zones), and those which are to be kept free of urban building (outer zones). In the autumn of 1949 a town development committee was appointed for the Copenhagen region to draw up these plans. This committee finished its work in 1951.

In the following years, many detailed plans appeared but whilst the whole collection of planning proposals had achieved practically nothing, population was growing, housing and commercial building expanding and the volume of traffic—especially motor cars—greatly increasing.

In 1958 planning work was renewed with the support of the Metropolitan Municipalities Joint Committee and with the influence of the State Town Planning Committee behind it. In 1962 it produced a new outline of principles for a regional plan for the metropolitan area.

Taking into account developments which had taken place since the 'finger plan' of 1947, the outline suggested a slowing-down of residential growth in the north and the greater concentration of residential and commercial building in the urban regions of the west and south-west (see Map 11). This outline was laid before a technical committee by the town planning committee. This committee had difficulty in reaching agreement and finally two alternatives were produced; one suggesting an expansion of development towards the south-west with an extension of the suburban electrical railway to Roskilde and Køge as well as a limited expansion of the railway between them, and the other alternative suggested a continuation along the existing lines of expansion including the north and north-west.

The committee was unanimous in recommending the initiation of those proposals common to both alternatives, namely the railway extension to Roskilde and Køge. They also recommended that in the interests of a more intensive regional policy, much more background work was necessary to create a situation whereby a real choice among the various possibilities open to planners could be made. But instead of setting into motion this necessary work, there is again to all intents and purposes a standstill in producing an overall planning policy for the metropolitan area, presumably because, among other things, there is still this lack of a politically responsible co-ordinating body.

A REGIONAL PLANNING COUNCIL

Since April 1967, the situation has looked brighter with the establishment, after initial difficulties, of a joint regional council for Copenhagen, Frederiksberg and the three so-called metropolitan counties: Copenhagen, Roskilde and Frederiksborg. This joint municipal body which has 17 members will look at future regional planning work in the area and will attempt to co-ordinate the work of municipal, county and state planning authorities. How much weight the new council, which has no legal basis and no decision-making powers over the local authorities, will come to have, only the future can show. It is interesting to note, however, that the council now covers the whole of north-eastern Zealand i.e. almost a total of 100 local authority areas comprising 260,000 hectares and it is reckoned that the total area in 1980 will have a population of around 2 million people.

In the meantime metropolitan planning policy has been greatly complicated by the fact that during the period when planning on a regional basis was inoperative, major planning dispositions have taken place within the individual municipalities.

In the more scenically attractive areas of North Zealand, a great deal of urban building has taken place, in spite of the intentions of the outline principles of 1962. A confirmation of past experience, is that it is in practice impossible for a local authority to limit its growth by its own efforts; the expansion of local communities is seen as a 'law of nature'. Simultaneously many of the western municipalities, such as Taastrup, have planned commercial centres of fairly large dimensions. But of by far greatest importance for collective metropolitan planning has been the major plan for the development of West-Amager, which the municipality of Copenhagen has been working with since 1964.

For the benefit of those readers who are unacquainted with the local geographical position, and to help them understand the Amager problems better, the whole of the western part of the island of Amager, of which the northern half belongs to Copenhagen and the southern half to the Tårnby municipality, has a very flat and low-lying terrain. It has been regarded until now as unfit for development and large parts of the area which are owned by the state have been used for military purposes (firing ranges). In the 1930s large damming operations were carried out on the Amager bank of the Kalvebod Strand. These operations did not originate in connection with any regional policy but were employment measures in a period of unemployment. Even in the above-mentioned 'finger plan' of 1947 consideration was brushed aside for any future extensive developments on Amager. The reasons for this were firstly, the very complicated water and sewage problems (because of its low-lying position), secondly, the transport problem because at this time Amager was only joined to Copenhagen proper by two bridges (another has been added) which have to be opened frequently because of sailing to and from Copenhagen's southern harbour, and thirdly, was the factor of Copenhagen's airport which is positioned at Kastrup (in the Tårnby municipality).

In 1964 an agreement was reached between the municipality of Copenhagen and the state, whereby as the military gave up the area, in conjunction with the state Copenhagen would have large sections at its disposal. The West-Amager areas comprises about 1,200 hectares. The municipality of Copenhagen as was shown previously had for several years been suffering a drop in population and its economy had been further weakened by the removal of many of the wealthier taxpayers to the suburbs. Copenhagen's lord mayor, Urban Hansen, saw a chance, with great residential development on West-Amager, to rectify from Copenhagen's point of view this unfortunate tendency.

In conjunction with the so-called 'Urban plan', a Nordic architectural competition was held in 1964 to consider development of the West-Amager area. The results, which are outside the scope of this article, were published in 1965. It should be mentioned, however, to indicate the vastness of the Amager project that provisional plans estimate the construction of 50,000 flats i.e. an urban quarter of up to 150,000 inhabitants. Discussion of this Amager project has been so detailed because of the implications which a project of this size must have on the whole planning concept of the Greater Copenhagen area. Great objections have been raised against the project by the other municipalities and from a regional policy aspect. Firstly it runs counter to previous proposals involving development mainly in the west and south-west, and secondly it will create traffic problems of great magnitude because traffic connections between Amager and Copenhagen as mentioned before must either go over or under the harbour course i.e. more bridges and roadworks and eventually tunnels will be required. This will involve large capital investment programmes which can only make it more difficult for the other smaller municipalities in the region to get their capital costs covered.

To complete the discussion of planning problems of the Greater Copenhagen area, it should be mentioned that besides the really great problem of an organized policy for the metropolitan area and the consequent rational, physical and economic regional plans, there are four important planning projects on the agenda for Greater Copenhagen.

First, after many years' discussion 1967 has seen the enactment of proposals for an underground railway in Copenhagen, though only as the first stage of a wider project. Such an underground system will naturally lead to alterations in the street network and at the same time will mean an expansion of the motorway network in conjunction with the road network outside the municipal boundaries.

Secondly, Copenhagen's airport at Kastrup must in the course of a few years be considerably expanded. If this expansion takes place in its present position it will carry great implications for developments on Amager. As an alternative, it has been proposed to remove the airport to the island of Saltholm which lies 5 kilometres east of Amager.

Thirdly, this last plan is linked to the vast project of a bridge across the Sound Øresundsbro (or an eventual combination of bridge and tunnel) connecting Copenhagen to Malmø on the Swedish Coast of the Sound.

Fourthly, this bridge creates another important element in the plans which are afoot, with the idea of Greater Copenhagen and Greater Malmø as a centre, involving a traffic and commercially linked Sound Region (*Oresundsregion*). A Sound Committee has been set up by Danish and Swedish local authorities in the region to consider this question. There are also alternative plans that the contemplated bridge connection should be between Helsingør and Helsingborg, i.e. across the narrowest stretch of the Sound. There are also those who think that both these bridges should be built!

Finally, it must be stated that the many plans for the Copenhagen region will, in the end, have to collaborate with national planning policy simultaneously being considered and whose primary aim is a co-ordination of regional planning for the country as a whole.

Delhi

ABHIJIT DATTA
J. N. KHOSLA

ABHIJIT DATTA

Born 1934. Educated in Calcutta and London Universities. M.A.,
1955, M.Sc.(Econ.) in Public Finance, 1961 (at the London School
of Economics and Political Science). Research Fellow in Urban
Studies, Institute of Public Administration, New York (Calcutta
Project), 1962–64; part-time Lecturer, Calcutta University,
1962–64; Senior Research Fellow, Indian Institute of Public
Administration, 1964–66; Reader in Municipal Administration,
Indian Institute of Public Administration, since 1966.

Author of: *Inter-governmental Grants in Metropolitan Calcutta*,
1966; with David C. Ranney, *Municipal Finances in the Calcutta
Metropolitan District: A Preliminary Survey*, 1965; with Leslie
Green, *Special Agencies in Metropolitan Calcutta: A Comparative
Study*, 1967; and with Mohit Bhattacharya, *Centre-State Relations
in Urban Development*, 1966 (mimeographed).

Articles in the *Indian Journal of Public Administration* and the
Journal of the Institute of Town Planners, India.

JAGAN NATH KHOSLA

Born 1906. Director, The Indian Institute of Public Administration, New Delhi, since January 1964; and President, The Indian
Council for Cultural Relations, New Delhi, 1968; *educ.* Govern-
ment College, Lahore (B.A.), University of the Punjab; London
School of Economics, London University (B.Sc., Ph.D.). Called
to the Bar, Middle Temple 1931; Lecturer, Law and Political
Science, Punjab University, 1933–40; Reader in Political Science,
1940–44; Head of Department of Political Science, 1944–48;
Principal, East Punjab University College, 1947–48; President,
Indian Political Science Association, 1947.

Entered Government Service with Indian High Commission
in London, 1948; Secretary, Consular Department, 1949–51;
Charge d'Affaires, Rome (also Belgrade), 1951–52; Prague,
1952–53; Director, Historical Division, Ministry of External
Affairs, 1953; Chairman, International Commission for Supervision and Control of Laos, Vientiane, 1954–55; Minister and
later Ambassador to Czechoslovakia (concurrently accredited to
Rumania, 1958), 1955–58; Ambassador of India to Indonesia,
1958–61; Ambassador of India to Yugoslavia, and concurrently
accredited to Greece and Bulgaria, 1961–64. Member, India
Delegation to XVIth and XVIIth Sessions, U.N. General
Assembly. Member of several political and scientific associations.

Publications: Editor, *Indian Journal of Political Science*, 1945–48;
has contributed numerous papers in Indian and foreign journals
devoted to political, constitutional and administrative subjects.

Delhi

DELHI has a hoary past. It has seen the rise and fall of mighty empires through-out the annals of history. Historians write about the seven cities of Delhi, and the present city is supposed to be the eighth capital in independent India. However, the only surviving link with the medieval age in the city is the walled city of Shahjahanabad built by Mogul Emperor Shah Jahan in the seventeenth century. Modern Delhi was born with the transfer of the capital by the British from Calcutta to Delhi in 1912. Before the transfer took place, a small British community had already settled in an area to the north of the walled city, known as the Civil Lines, characterized by open spaces and interspersed with Victorian and Edwardian bungalows. Imperial Delhi was created to the south of the walled city at the site of Raisina Village during the 'twenties, which came to be known as New Delhi. Both Civil Lines and New Delhi were separated from the congested old city by wide parks and open spaces. With the growth of urbanization to the east and west of Old Delhi, as also to the south of New Delhi, new urban colonies and settlements developed so that during the 1951 census Delhi was characterized as a 'town group' (continuous urban area) consisting of two cities, three major towns and one minor town. This picture was completely changed with the amalgamation of all the urban areas in a single municipal corporation in 1958, except New Delhi and the cantonment which still retain their indivi-dual entities. Thus, although different areas of urban Delhi grew at different times as functionally self-sufficient units, these were merged into a single metropolitan complex only recently and, as a result, the city presents the picture of an amazing variety of urban growth.

The total area of Delhi, according to the Surveyor-General of India, stands at 573 square miles, of which 78 per cent is rural and the remaining 22 per cent urban. The corresponding population distribution in rural and urban areas works out at about 11 per cent rural and 89 per cent urban, according to the 1961 census. This clearly indicates the rural character of the metropolis in terms of land use and the urban composition of the population from the point of view of occupational classification. This dichotomy has resulted in a heavy density of population in the urban area, more than 7,000 per square kilometre and a few urban pockets can claim to contain some of the world's most densely populated areas.

From the point of view of topography, the two important features are the rivers Jamuna and Hindon in the east, and the extension of the Aravalli hills

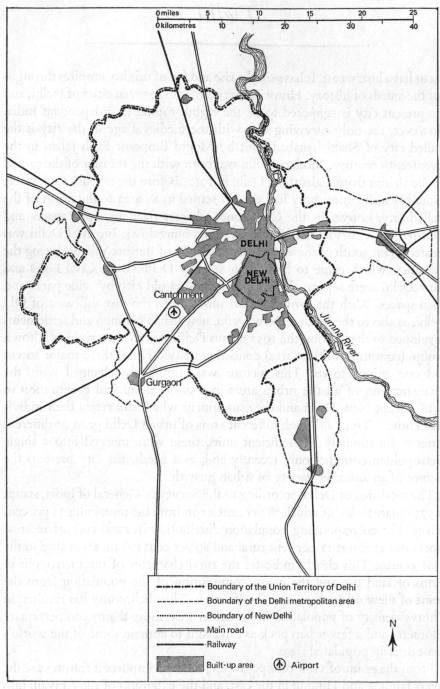

Boundary of the Union Territory of Delhi
- - - - - Boundary of the Delhi metropolitan area
. . . . Boundary of New Delhi
═══════ Main road
─────── Railway
▨ Built-up area   ⊕ Airport

N ↑

MAP 12 DELHI

terminating at an angle on the western bank of the Jamuna to the north of the city, with another range of the Aravalli to the south of the city acting as a base. It is this triangle which contains about 70 per cent of the total population of Delhi and includes such areas as Shahjahanabad, Civil Lines, New Delhi and the newly developed colonies to the west and south of the city centre. The future urbanizable limits of Delhi are also conditioned by geographical constraints, such as the low-lying areas in the east, north and south-west, the rocky land in the south, and the presence of saltpetre in the soil in the south-west. The directions for future urban growth would, therefore, lie in the west and north-west of the present urban area.

The total urban area of Delhi comes to about 170 square miles, while the rural areas occupy about 400 square miles. The Delhi metropolitan area, a concept developed in the master plan, has an area of about 800 square miles and goes beyond the territorial limits of Delhi to embrace the adjoining urban areas in the neighbouring States of Haryana (Bahadurgarh, Sonepat and Faridabad) and Uttar Pradesh (Ghaziabad) besides including semi-urbanized Narela within the territory. Delhi's area of influence, termed the national capital region in the master plan, comprises about 4,500 square miles.

Delhi's population stood at about 2·7 millions for the entire union territory, of which about 2·4 millions were urban and only about 0·3 millions rural, during the last census in 1961. Up to 1911, the growth in Delhi's population was almost insignificant. Since then three important factors have been responsible for a rapid increase in population—the establishment of imperial Delhi in 1912, the partition of the country in 1947 which brought in its trail an enormous refugee influx into Delhi, and the city becoming the capital of the new republic of India. The highest rate of population growth was registered during 1941–51, an annual rate of 9 per cent for the entire population and about 11 per cent for the urban population. The annual rate of growth dropped to about 5 per cent for the total and about 6 per cent for its urban component during the next decade, 1951–61. An interesting development in the present decade is the net depopulation of the rural areas at an annual rate of −0·25 per cent which shows the growth of urbanization and immigration into the urban area within the territory. Migration of population from the neighbouring States of Uttar Pradesh, Punjab, Haryana and Rajasthan account for more than half of the immigrants most of them coming from rural areas. The share of immigration to the growth of total population in Delhi comes to about 62 per cent, the remaining 38 per cent representing natural increase. Among all the states and union territories, Delhi had the highest percentage of urban to rural population in the last two decades. Among the major cities in India, Delhi shows the highest rate of growth of population since 1921, and occupies the third place in terms of total population, after Bombay and Calcutta, since 1951. The total annual increase in Delhi's population works out at the rate of about 100,000 during the last decade.

In 1951, almost 20 per cent of Delhi's labour force was engaged in commerce and finance, and only a slightly lesser percentage in industry and public service. These three sectors together provided gainful employment to more than 55 per cent of the labour force. In 1961, the share of industry in the labour force increased slighly in relation to commerce and finance, and among all the states and union territories, Delhi occupied the highest position in regard to both, and second highest with respect to public employment. The share of agriculture in the labour force, on the other hand, has now fallen below 10 per cent. In terms of income also in 1955 about 25 per cent was earned in commerce and finance, 20 per cent in public service and 18 per cent in industry and mining—together accounting for about 63 per cent of the total. Thus, contrary to popular belief, Delhi is not a predominantly administrative capital, but also an important centre of commerce and finance. In this respect, Delhi resembles more the older capital cities like London and Paris, than the newer capital cities like Washington and Canberra.

Because of the small size of the territory compared to the other states and territories in India and its overwhelming urban characteristics, it is not surprising to find that Delhi has the highest *per capita* income in India. It is more than twice the average all-India figure. In 1955, the all-India estimate of *per capita* income stood at Rs. 261, while the corresponding figure for Delhi was computed at Rs. 690 at current prices. The rate of growth of *per capita* income in Delhi is also among the highest.

THE ORGANS OF METROPOLITAN GOVERNMENT

Although the town planning concept of the metropolitan area of Delhi includes a few urbanized tracts of the adjoining states of Haryana and Uttar Pradesh, for the purpose of examining the local government set-up within the union territory of Delhi, issues which are essentially inter-state in nature are irrelevant. However, this aspect will be touched upon in a later section on boundary problems. Similarly, Delhi being the seat of the union government of a federal country, its government has assumed certain characteristics which tend to avoid any constitutional division of power. The peculiarities of governmental arrangements in Delhi will also be explained later. Here our primary concern is to discuss the system of local government in the territory.

Prior to 1958, Delhi had a number of local government units and *ad hoc* authorities. There were, for instance, five municipal committees, one of which was nominated (New Delhi); five nominated urban authorities (the notified area committees), one district board for the rural areas; four *ad hoc* authorities for water supply and sewerage, city transport, electricity, and land improvement and development; and one partially elected cantonment board—the municipal authority for the permanent military station. In 1958, excepting for the New Delhi Municipal Committee, the Delhi Cantonment Board and the *ad hoc* authority for land improvement and development, all the other bodies were merged into a single municipal corporation of Delhi. At the moment, therefore, there are three multi-purpose urban local authorities: (*a*) Municipal Corporation of Delhi, (*b*) New Delhi Municipal Committee, and (*c*) Cantonment Board, Delhi. Among the three, only the municipal corporation is an elected body, while the New Delhi Municipal Committee is nominated by the central government, and the Cantonment Board consists of partially elected and partially nominated and *ex-officio* members.

The reasons for the reorganization of local government in Delhi are not wholly local in origin, although an inquiry committee which examined the question of municipal reorganization after independence recommended in favour of a single municipal corporation.[1] The need for such reorganization became imperative as a result of the abolition of statehood in Delhi in 1956, consequent on the recommendations of the States Reorganization Commission.[2] The commission came to the conclusion that being the union capital, Delhi 'cannot be made part of a full-fledged constituent unit of the Indian Union'.[3] Delhi's problems being essentially urban, and since the same territory could not sustain both a state government and an elective civic body at the same time, the decision was to dismantle the state and create the municipal corporation, with a total area of about 540 square miles.

The municipal reorganization in Delhi has created a few anomalies and contradictions in the existing set-up. Owing to the abolition of the state, certain functions which are not strictly municipal have been thrust on to the corporation, such as the large undeveloped rural areas which constitute about 83 per cent of the total corporation area, or the management of secondary schools and hospitals transferred to the corporation. It is true that the corporation did receive some ear-marked grants for the transferred institutions and also liberal doses of general purpose grant, but on the whole its finances were strained from the beginning to sustain its non-statutory

[1] *Report of the Delhi Municipal Organization Enquiry Committee*, Government of India, 1948.
[2] *Report of the States Reorganization Commission*, Government of India, 1955.
[3] *Ibid.*, p. 158.

responsibilities. Again, the artificial distinction between Delhi and New Delhi has been perpetuated even when the central government assumed direct responsibility for administering the territory.

The total area and population of the three local governments in Delhi is indicated in Table I.

It is apparent that the municipal corporation is the principal city government as well as metropolitan government of Delhi. At the time of municipal reorganization, nearly half of the area of New Delhi was ceded to the corporation so that the remaining area of New Delhi consists of mainly government

TABLE I

Area and Population of Local Governments in Delhi Territory

Local governments	Area in sq. miles	% age to total	Population 1961	% age to total
Municipal Corporation of Delhi	539·91	94·23	2,360,962	88·9
New Delhi Municipal Committee	16·50	2·88	261,545	9·8
Cantonment Board, Delhi	16·59	2·89	36,105	1·3
Total (Delhi territory)	573·00	100·00	2,658,612	100·00

Source: *Census of India,* 1961.

properties. The present size of New Delhi is considered to be the minimum viable area for a separate entity to function effectively. The cantonment, on the other hand, is located on the outskirts of the built-up area and its contacts with the city's urban life are few.

The municipal corporation is governed by the Delhi Municipal Corporation Act, 1957. It is the only self-governing body in Delhi either at the local level or at the territory level. The corporation is a body of elected councillors and a few co-opted aldermen. Its functions include all local services and amenities for the entire union territory, except those performed by the Delhi Administration or the other local authorities namely, the New Delhi Municipal Committee, the Cantonment Board, and the Delhi Development Authority. Apart from civic functions normal for urban local bodies in India, the corporation is responsible for water-supply and sewage disposal, operating city transport and generating electricity for the entire territory. The cantonment Board and the New Delhi Municipal Committee are bulk consumers of water and electricity from the corporation, and local distribution is the responsibility of the individual local bodies. The corporation has three undertakings, which used to be statutory *ad hoc* bodies before the municipal reorganization, to operate these metropolitan facilities. The essential features of the Corporation Act follows the Bombay pattern, with an important exception. In Bombay, city improvement and development is the responsibility of the municipal corporation; in Delhi, this is entrusted to a statutory *ad hoc* body called the Delhi Development Authority. The Delhi Development Authority came into being as a successor to the erstwhile Delhi Improvement Trust in the same year that municipal reorganization took place in Delhi.

The New Delhi Municipal Committee was created in 1933 and it is governed under the provisions of the Punjab Municipal Act, 1911. The committee consists of 11 nominated members, 5 officials and 6 non-officials, headed by an official President. The functions of the committee include all local services and civic amenities within its jurisdiction. New Delhi is located in the heart of the Delhi urban area, and houses the central secretariat complex, Rashtrapati Bhavan (formerly Viceregal Lodge), the Parliament, other important government offices, foreign embassies and missions, official quarters for the ministers and civil servants, etc.

The Delhi Cantonment came into being in 1912 and is situated in the south-west of Delhi, at a distance of about 11 miles. The cantonment is administered under the provisions of the Cantonments Act, 1924. The total membership of the board is 14, of whom 7 are elected. The board is headed by the officer commanding the station and functions under the supervision of the Ministry of Defence. The board is charged with the responsibility of maintaining civic administration within its jurisdiction.

THE CITY CONSTITUTION

The Indian Constitution lists Delhi as a union territory and provides for its administration by the President acting through an administrator. Among the ten union territories, five are governed under the provisions of a special act of Parliament—the Government of Union Territories Act, 1963—which provides for elected legislative assemblies with jurisdiction over concurrent and state list subjects, a council of ministers headed by a chief minister, and so on. This Act, however, does not apply to Delhi so that the union Cabinet and the Parliament are directly involved in its administration. In practice,

Delhi is administered through a lieutenant-governor, on behalf of the President, who is assisted by a deputy commissioner or district magistrate and a few secretaries and heads of departments. This is the Delhi Administration.

An experiment with statehood in Delhi was tried for a brief period of about four years (1952–56), but was abandoned following the recommendations of the States Reorganization Commission. Recently, another attempt is being made to associate political leadership with the territory administration through the creation of an elected metropolitan council, under the Delhi Administration Act, 1966. The council, which is concerned with the whole Union territory, is a deliberative body, but does not enjoy the power to legislate. There is a standing committee of the council appointed by the President, called the executive councillors, consisting of four members headed by a chief executive councillor, to advise the lieutenant-governor with respect to concurrent or state list functions excluding certain matters called 'reserved' powers of the lieutenant-governor which include law and order, services, revenue administration, and land acquisition and housing. All other state-level functions are 'transferred' and can be discussed by the council. However, responsibility of legislation for Delhi is vested solely in Parliament. As the Delhi Administration is not a sovereign body, it has no power of taxation, no separate budget, nor can it claim a share of central taxes in the divisible pool as a matter of right.

The anomaly of the situation becomes clear with respect to local government in the territory. The metropolitan council can discuss matters pertaining to the Delhi Municipal Corporation, since local self-government is a transferred subject. But the council's views on any matter relating to the New Delhi Municipal Committee require the concurrence of the lieutenant-governor. In other words, not only is there total denial of responsible government at the intermediate level performing state-level functions, but also there is total disfranchisement at the local level in New Delhi and the cantonment area. With what seems to be more than adequate safeguards at the intermediate level, this position is rather anomalous.

Till recently, Delhi was the only city with such an authoritarian system of government. But of late another city Chandigarh, the capital of Punjab and Haryana, has been treated in a similar manner. All other cities in India are subject to state legislatures and enjoy representative and responsible government. The system of government in Delhi operates without the guidelines of a comprehensive legislation and relies too heavily on a process of delegation of authority to the lieutenant-governor by the various ministries of the central government. The result, inevitably, is a very great reliance on *ad hoc* arrangements and the personal relation of the key administrator in the capital territory to the central government. Instead of taking directions and deriving his authority from law, the lieutenant-governor is forced to look up to the central government for support.

At the local level, the municipal corporation is a fully representative body of 100 elected members and 6 co-opted aldermen. The city is divided into 100 single-member constituencies or wards. A few electoral wards, at present 13, are reserved for the representation of scheduled castes or the backward communities in the proportion that their population bears to the total population. Elections take place on the basis of adult suffrage and any adult resident can stand for election subject to disqualifications for being of unsound mind, an undischarged bankrupt, an alien, a criminal, holding an office of profit under the corporation or the government, in arrear of municipal taxes, and so on. The aldermen are chosen by the elected councillors from among the citizens who are qualified to stand in municipal elections. The number of aldermen is fixed at 6, while the number of councillors can vary between 80 and 100. The term of office of a councillor or an alderman is 4 years. The periods of casual vacancies terminate with the period of the council as a whole. A councillor or an alderman is entitled to an allowance of Rs. 25 for each day he attends a meeting, up to a maximum annual limit of Rs. 300.

The general council meetings are presided over by the mayor, or in his absence the deputy mayor, and in the absence of both, by a senior councillor. The mayor and the deputy mayor are elected every year—in recent years they have been re-elected till a fresh election of the corporation takes place after 4 years. The mayor is entitled to have a furnished residence, the use of a car, official entertainment up to Rs. 6,000 a year, and the use of a special flag.

Under the general council of the corporation there are seven statutory authorities with clearly defined powers, viz.: (i) the standing committee; (ii) the Delhi electric supply committee; (iii) the Delhi transport committee; (iv) the Delhi water supply and sewage disposal committee; (v) the commissioner; (vi) the general manager (electricity) and (vii) the general manager (transport). The commissioner himself acts in the capacity of a general manager for the water supply and sewage disposal undertaking. Each of these authorities has co-ordinate powers of decision-making and execution. Thus, the general council is concerned with the general and over-all policy of the civic body, but the real decision-making authorities are the statutory committees. The statutory committees are not subordinate but co-ordinate to the general council of the corporation, deriving their status and authority from statute. Once a policy decision is made, these are left to be executed by the statutory executives—the commissioner and the general managers. Apart

o

from the statutory committees, there are a number of functional committees like the education committee, rural areas committee, works committee, law and general purposes committee, assurances committee, medical and public health committee. In addition, there are a few *ad hoc* committees for particular problems and the territorial or zonal committees for each of the 8 zones into which the whole municipal area is divided. These non-statutory committees are creatures of the general council of the corporation and thus subordinate to it.

The division of deliberative and executive functions in the corporation is sought to be maintained by defining precisely the role of each organ with the idea that once a decision is taken by the elected representatives, the appointed executives should be free to implement these decisions. The theory of separation of powers in municipal corporations is, by and large, accepted in India, although one can entertain reasonable doubts if it is really practicable to maintain the distinction between policy and administration. Without either a cabinet or a presidential system, it is very difficult to involve the elected representatives in the business of government in an effective manner. Experience of municipal administration, as it has worked in Delhi, shows that its working has not been smooth and the team work between the political leaders and the appointed officials is not easy. The councillors blame the officials as high handed, and the officials regard the councillors as irresponsible. There is no unity of command and leadership in such a situation.

In order to remove these difficulties, there is a recent proposal to introduce the mayor-in-council or a cabinet type of government in the municipal corporation, where the mayor would act like a chief minister and his colleagues in the team would be in charge of various functions of the corporation. With the emergence of a two-party system in the corporation, and the municipal elections being run on party lines, the proposed system seems workable.

LOWER-TIER AUTHORITIES

Within the municipal corporation, there is an attempt to decentralize its activities through delegation to 8 special zonal committees. Under the Municipal Corporation Act, section 40 empowers the corporation to establish ward committees, for a single ward or a group of wards, by a special resolution. Initially, there were 10 such zonal committees, 8 urban and 2 rural. But, recently, the rural and the city zones have been merged into one each. These zones are: (i) Shahdara, (ii) City, (iii) Civil Line-Subzimandi, (iv) Sadar Pahar Ganj, (v) Karol Bagh, (vi) Delhi West, (vii) New Delhi–South Delhi, and (viii) Rural. These zones are under the charge of zonal committees consisting of the local councillors and one or more aldermen. The zonal committees have power to sanction local improvement in a particular zone up to Rs. 50,000, provided there is a budgetary provision for it. The executive functions of a zonal office are placed under an assistant commissioner. All minor civic functions, as far as possible, are carried out by the zonal offices, in addition to assessing local needs of the area. Most of these zones correspond to the areas of the former urban local bodies merged into the corporation in 1958, and thus have some tradition of articulation of local interests. However, it is generally felt that the limited delegation to the zonal committees has not brought the municipal corporation sufficiently near to the citizens and a governmental decentralization within the metropolis is well worth trying. Such a decentralization will have to await another reorganization of metropolitan government in Delhi.

OTHER AUTHORITIES

Before 1958, there were four single-purpose *ad hoc* authorities in Delhi, viz. (i) Delhi State Electricity Board, (ii) Delhi Road Transport Authority (iii) Delhi Water and Sewage Board, and (iv) Delhi Improvement Trust. At the time of municipal reorganization, the first three statutory bodies were merged into the new municipal corporation and the improvement trust was transformed into a development authority under the Delhi Development Act, 1957.

The Delhi Development Authority was created as a high-powered body and kept separate from the municipal corporation on the ground that the central government would have to find large funds for Delhi's development in accordance with a comprehensive master plan. The authority is composed of 13 members, 7 officials and 6 non-officials, with the lieutenant-governor as the chairman, including two councillors and the commissioner of the municipal corporation and the executive councillor of the metropolitan council.

During the initial years, the authority was busy preparing the draft master plan for Delhi in collaboration with the Town Planning Organization of the Ministry of Health. A draft plan was prepared in 1960, which was approved by the central government and came into effect from September 1962. Since its inception, the authority has received about Rs. 50 millions from the central government to be operated as a revolving fund. Also, the authority is responsible for the management and control of *nazul* (viz. government) lands in the territory which were vested in the central government for establishing the imperial capital in Delhi.

The major function of the authority is to acquire undeveloped land and, after proper development, hand it over to the municipal corporation for servicing. Experience, however, shows that this has not been a smooth process and occasions have arisen when the municipal corporation has been rather reluctant to take over the developed land or to extend primary civic facilities, like water supply and sewerage, electricity and so on.

Recently, there has been a move to create *ad hoc* bodies in Delhi for the three undertakings of the municipal corporation. This, if implemented, would be a major departure from the Bombay system on which the municipal corporation was modelled. This would also create problems of co-ordination at the territory administration level. So long as the territory administration is divorced from the political forces, co-ordination between the municipal body and the *ad hoc* authorities may indeed prove to be a difficult proposition.

PARTY POLITICAL CONSIDERATIONS

In Delhi, municipal elections take place on party lines. The municipal

TABLE II

*Number of Seats secured by Major Political Parties in the Municipal
Corporation of Delhi*

Political Party	1958	1962	1967
Congress	31	64	40
Jana Sangh	25	9	53
Communists	7	2	1
Left Communists	—	—	1
Independents and others	17	5	5
Total	80	80	100

corporation was introduced in a period when universal adult suffrage was already introduced, in the early 'fifties, and the official president of the Delhi municipal committee (old city council) was abolished in 1946. The relative party position in terms of the number of seats secured in the municipal corporation during the last three elections is given in Table II.

The first election did not give an absolute majority to any major political party and although the Congress Party wooed the independents to hold power, it was an uncomfortable existence. The first few years of the municipal corporation, in spite of the goodwill and blessings of no less a person than the Union Home Minister, Pandit Govind Ballabh Pant, was full of instances of bitter political struggle. This tussle manifested itself in the mayoral elections, the working of the statutory committees, staff appointments, relations with the municipal commissioner, unruly conduct in the meetings including frequent walk-outs, and so on. It is on record that in a corporation meeting (April 4, 1961) one councillor challenged another to a wrestling bout outside the corporation buildings to settle an issue.

This instability was corrected in the next election when the Congress Party was returned with an overwhelming majority in the municipal corporation. This time the ruling party had no difficulty in keeping the opposition in its place and this was done with little regard for healthy democratic traditions. As a result, the opposition parties were in a political wilderness and developed cynicism about constitutional means.

The 1967 municipal election, which was delayed by a year to coincide with the general elections in the country, ended the Congress rule and brought Jana Sangh into power. Although Jana Sangh enjoys an absolute majority in the corporation, the combined strength of the opposition parties is not inconsiderable. One healthy aspect of the present situation is the emergence of a two-party system of government without, however, the benefit of an effective machinery to take advantage of it. The Congress Party enjoys the status of the official opposition party and the other parties and independents have formed into a 'progressive' group which act as a third force. Two of the statutory committees are headed by Congress members, and the party composition of the most important statutory standing committee is: Jana Sangh 8, Congress 5 and Independent 1.

Till the last general election in February, 1967, the Congress Party was in virtual control of the Delhi situation—the central government, the Delhi legislative assembly and the interim metropolitan council during the brief period of their existence, and the municipal corporation. All the parliamentary seats from Delhi returned Congress members in the three successive general elections in 1952, 1957 and 1962 after independence. The recent general election has radically changed the situation. Jana Sangh has come out as the ruling political party in Delhi with absolute majorities in the municipal corporation as well as in the metropolitan council. Out of 7 parliamentary seats for Delhi, 6 have gone to Jana Sangh. This has added piquancy to the situation where the central government is run by Congress, but it is not the ruling party in Delhi. The reason why this has not created complications is not far to seek—essentially the two parties are not radically opposed to each other on ideological grounds, excepting on a few issues which have either religious overtones (cow slaughter), or regional bearing (introduction of Hindi as the official language). On purely civic matters, like the status of New Delhi, experiment with the mayor-in-council form of municipal government, central–local relations, etc., there is surprising unanimity of views among all the political parties. The inference from this is obvious—the dialogue between the Congress high command and the Delhi Pradesh Congress Committee seems curiously one-sided. This has happened for two reasons. After independence, Delhi did not have the benefit of political leadership which enjoyed wide popularity and public esteem. Leaders like Asaf Ali, Deshbandhu Gupta were dead, and the Congress organization fell into the hands of powerful party bosses who could not rise above party factions. On the other hand, Delhi being the country's capital, national leaders like Prime Minister Nehru and Home Minister Pant took a good deal of interest and influenced decisions about the governmental set-up in Delhi. With the changed situation after the recent elections and the passing away of great national leaders like Nehru and Pant, the future of Delhi once again assumes considerable importance.

The civic leadership in Delhi springs from the urban middle classes. This is true of all political parties of any consequence in Delhi—the Congress, Jana Sangh and the Communists. It is for this reason—more than anything else— that there is a strong opposition against any rise in property taxes, a major source of municipal revenue. With the introduction of universal franchise even before the municipal corporation came into being, this situation was expected to change. That the rate of property taxation is about half of the prevailing rates in Bombay and Calcutta testifies to the degree of influence of a minority of the electorate in the city government. So long as the majority of the city population remains apathetic and indifferent to the functioning of local government in Delhi, it is idle to expect that the municipal corporation would be able to rise from its present slumber unless, of course, large-scale aid is forthcoming from the union government.

MUNICIPAL POWERS AND FUNCTIONS

The functions of the municipal corporation are enumerated in detail in the Act itself (sections 42 and 43), which resemble the Bombay Act, and are divided into two broad categories: obligatory and discretionary. Among the obligatory functions, mention may be made of the following:
(1) water supply, drainage, sewerage, conservancy, scavenging;
(2) abatement of nuisances;

(3) disposal of dead;

(4) registration of births and deaths;

(5) measures for preventing and checking dangerous diseases;

(6) construction and maintenance of hospitals and other places of medical relief;

(7) construction and maintenance of municipal markets, slaughterhouses and their regulation;

(8) regulation and abatement of dangerous trades;

(9) demolition of dangerous buildings;

(10) construction and maintenance of public streets, bridges, culverts, etc.;

(11) lighting and cleansing of public streets, including their naming and numbering;

(12) removal of obstructions on streets and other public places;

(13) establishment and maintenance of primary schools;

(14) laying out and maintenance of public parks, gardens, etc;

(15) maintenance of a fire-brigade.

The discretionary functions of the municipal corporation include items like the construction and maintenance of houses for the poor, infirm, deaf and dumb, orphans and handicapped children, destitute and disabled persons, lunatics, etc.; the establishment and maintenance of cultural and sports centres; provision for relief of the destitute and the disabled; establishment and maintenance of veterinary hospitals; construction and maintenance of public washeries, bathing places and the like; management of farms and dairies for distribution of milk and milk products; provision for unfiltered water supply; city improvement according to approved schemes; housing for the inhabitants of any area or for any class of inhabitants; any measure likely to promote public safety, health, convenience or general welfare.

Although the list appears to be quite comprehensive, the range of functions that the municipal corporation is expected to perform does not include, by and large, social welfare services and public assistance programmes. Functions like city transportation, and the generation and distribution of electricity are performed by the corporation, although these are neither obligatory nor optional, except in a vague way to promote general welfare. Milk supply is the responsibility of the central government in Delhi through a departmental agency and, in recent times, there has been some talk of transferring this activity to the civic body. Similarly, supply of unfiltered water in certain parts of the city, like the Civil Lines area, New Delhi, newly developed colonies in the south, etc., is the responsibility of the public works department of the union government. Renewal and improvement of the old city is the responsibility of the municipal corporation, while the development authority develops new areas called the 'development areas'. Regulation of city traffic, maintenance of law and order including the control of police force vest in the territory administration under the lieutenant-governor. Although housing is an optional municipal function, the municipal corporation has not entered into this field in a big way owing to lack of financial resources, and the territory administration operates the public housing schemes launched by the central government under the five-year plans.

Generally speaking, the level and quality of municipal services leave much to be desired. Essential services like water supply, sewerage, city transport, are inadequate to the needs of the citizens. About 70 per cent of the residents get continuous water supply and the rest, in the new colonies, have only intermittent supply. The average daily supply of water comes to about 35 gallons *per capita*. Only about 20 per cent of the population is covered by the sewerage system. During peak hours, the city transport is packed to capacity with office workers even though only 21 per cent of the passengers use public buses on the intra-urban routes. The serious power shortage which Delhi experienced from 1957 has been removed recently with the commissioning of a new thermal station. It is to the credit of the municipal corporation that the villages in Delhi have been electrified. The communications system has improved and educational and medical facilities are available throughout the length and breadth of the territory. Delhi's literacy rate is the highest in India; so also is the ratio of beds in the hospitals per 1,000 population.

The quality of the various municipal services is not up to the mark and certainly not befitting the capital city. The public transport service is notorious in this respect as regards punctuality, the maintenance of the fleet, the behaviour of the conductors and so on. As regards electricity supply, the voltage fluctuations are such as to cause damage to household electrical appliances. During the monsoon, water supply is prone to be contaminated from the overflow of open drains and flood waters of the Jamuna causing public health hazards like the outbreak of epidemic jaundice in 1956 and contamination of drinking water in 1964. Ever since the partition of the country, Delhi saw the growth of tent schools with inadequate facilities for sports, recreation and ventilation in the class rooms. Recently, the number of such tent schools has considerably declined and the municipal officials claim that not more than about 20 per cent of the corporation's schools are housed in tents. Maintenance of roads is frankly admitted to be below standard and the city streets are full of pot-holes and uncovered pits. The responsibility on this score does not fall entirely on the corporation, as several national and territorial highways are in no way better maintained. Also, lack of co-ordination among various public authorities in Delhi (including different wings of the corporation) contribute to the present state of affairs.

ADMINISTRATIVE ORGANIZATION AND STAFFING

The administration of the municipal corporation may be divided into four broad wings: (a) general, (b) water supply and sewage disposal, (c) electricity and (d) transport. The municipal commissioner is the administrative head of the corporation and he is specifically responsible for the working of the general wing and the water supply and sewage undertaking. The other two undertakings on electricity and transport are each headed by a general manager.

Various activities in the general wing are organized in terms of departments, of which the most important are general administration, finance, audit, taxation, licensing, lands and estates, engineering, building, town planning, garden, fire, health and medical, education, vigilance, slum clearance, labour welfare, stores and purchases, public relations, information, and community services. Each department is headed by an officer, while the over-all supervision is vested in the commissioner who is assisted by five deputy commissioners, one assistant commissioner for the headquarters, and nine assistant commissioners for the nine zones into which the city is divided. The water supply and sewage undertaking is headed by the commissioner in his capacity as the general manager and he is assisted by a deputy commissioner, one chief engineer (water) and one superintending engineer (drainage). In the other two undertakings, the respective general managers are assisted by a team of deputy manager and chief engineer. The secretary and the municipal auditor function directly under the standing committee, although for establishment purposes they come under the commissioner. The secretary's department is the liaison between the deliberative and administrative parts of the corporation and acts as the secretariat of the deliberative bodies. The municipal auditor is an officer of the corporation with statutory powers under the Act. Apart from the various departments, there are a number of institutions run by the corporation like hospitals, clinics, laboratories, crematorium, press and so on.

The total staff strength of the municipal corporation, including its three undertakings, would be around 40,000 of whom about 27,000 would come under the category of labourers and unskilled staff, about 12,000 clerical and subordinate staff including skilled technicians, and the remaining 1,400 supervisors and officers. The total staff strength of the general wing is about 24,000: water and sewage undertaking has about 2,000, electricity

o*

undertaking about 7,700, and the transport undertaking about 8,300. The combined staff strength of the general wing and the water and sewage undertakings comes to about 26,000—the corresponding figures stood at a little over 26,000 for Calcutta and around 28,000 for Bombay in the early 'fifties.

The officers and employees of the municipal corporation may be categorized under the following broad heads: (a) statutory officers with defined powers and functions, like the commissioner and the general managers; (b) statutory officers prescribed under the Act, such as the chief engineer (water supply), the municipal engineer, health officer, education officer, chief accountant, secretary, chief auditor and the deputy commissioners; (c) officers carrying a monthly salary of Rs. 350 and over; and (d) other officers and staff having a monthly salary of less then Rs. 350.

The municipal commissioner is appointed by the central government by a gazette notification for a period of five years in the first instance, and thereafter the term is renewable annually. The salary and allowances of the commissioner are fixed by the central government which also reserves the right to appoint an officiating commissioner, for a term not exceeding two months, till the permanent incumbent is chosen. The Act enjoins that the commissioner is removable if at a special meeting of the corporation there is a three-fifths majority demanding such a removal. The central government may also remove the commissioner if he is incapable of performing his duties or has been guilty of negligence or misconduct. So far all the commissioners except one have been seconded from all-India service and, on an average, each incumbent served for a period of 2½ years. Appointment of the general managers is, however, made by the corporation with the approval of the central government, and their removal also requires a majority of three-fifths of the total councillors in a special meeting. The appointment of the chief auditor requires the prior approval of the central government, while in the case of any other officer required under the Act, except the chief accountant and the secretary, the confirmation of the central government is necessary. The municipal auditor is debarred from holding any office under the corporation after his retirement.

Other officers of the corporation, drawing monthly salaries more than Rs. 350, are appointed by the corporation on the recommendation of the statutory committees and after consultation with the Union Public Service Commission. Such consultation is not necessary if a post is temporary or if the person is already in a class I post of the central or a state government. All other appointments in posts carrying monthly salaries below Rs. 350 are made by the commissioner and the general managers, subject to approval by the statutory committees. Posts subordinate to the secretary and the chief auditor, carrying monthly salaries less than Rs. 350 are filled by the standing committee. The standing committee may, however, delegate the power of such appointments to the secretary and the chief auditor.

Municipal officers at the higher level, those carrying monthly salaries above Rs. 350, are fully competitive in the employment market as their qualifications are examined by the Union Public Service Commission. However, in the case of lower categories of staff this is not so—although efforts are made to recruit persons registered at the employment exchange. Often seniority is more respected than merit. A few posts are reserved for the scheduled caste candidates. By and large, in the technical posts, it is difficult to make the selection as not many qualified and suitable candidates apply, partly because of unattractive pay-scales and also because of the general image of inefficiency of local government in the country.

There is no well-organized method of in-service training of local government officers and staff in the country excepting limited attempts by the All-India Institute of Local Self-Government, Bombay, the Indian Institute of Public Administration, New Delhi and three regional training centres at Calcutta, Lucknow and Hyderabad. The municipal corporation officials have been seconded to training courses and study tours in India and abroad, but so far this has not covered a large segment of the staff. There is no systematic effort for staff development within the corporation and incentive plans do not exist to encourage those who undergo such training.

There is no doubt that by making the commissioner and the general managers more or less independent of the corporation and seconding serving government officers to the top posts—the commissioner, the general managers, the deputy commissioners and a few others—the effective control of the corporation over civic administration is a matter of conjecture. On the other hand, there is no denying that the commissioner and the general managers have great powers of patronage through the appointment of subordinate and menial staff. One of the reasons why none of the previous commissioners could function for the full period of their tenure is precisely this—the duality of authority in the municipal corporation and the consequent tension and acrimony between the deliberative and the executive wings. In order to resolve this *impasse*, the mayor-in-council proposal intends to abolish the post of commissioner and substitute for it a chief executive officer who will be appointed by and directly responsible to the corporation.

FINANCE

The circumstances under which the municipal corporation came into being have greatly conditioned the pattern of its finance, the chief characteristic being heavy reliance on subventions from the central government. From this point of view, the revenue structure of the corporation resembles more the states in India, with total reliance on plan grants and major reliance on shared taxes, than the city corporations where the quantum of state grants constitutes an insignificant proportion of total revenue receipts. Since its inception, the receipts from the central government have exceeded the domestic income of the corporation. During the initial years, the corporation received a budget balancing grant to tide over its teething troubles, but since the grant was withdrawn in 1962–63, the successive budgets show increasing deficits and in the estimates for 1968–69 the gap comes to about Rs. 40 millions.

Excessive reliance on the central government for financial assistance has resulted in low rates of municipal taxes in Delhi, and also laxity in expenditure control. That the rate of property taxes in Delhi stuck to the minimum 10 per cent of annual rateable value for the first five years and with a great deal of pressure from the government, increased to 11 per cent, is common knowledge. The corresponding rates in Calcutta and Bombay exceed 20 per cent. There has been a recent attempt to link a general purpose grant to the corporation with the increase in its tax receipts by providing for Rs. 7 as grant for every Rs. 3 of new taxes. But the experiment has not been successful. On the other hand, there is no doubt that the large rural tracts within the corporation's area are being provided with municipal amenities at the cost of urban tax payers and the grants are not specifically related to rural development as such. The only tax that the rural population pays is the land revenue which accrues to the central government. Similarly, the grant for the transferred institutions stands more or less frozen at 1958–59 level of expenditure, although the actual expenses for running these institutions have gone up threefold during the last ten years of the corporation's existence.

The unbusinesslike manner in which the municipal corporation functions may be illustrated by the financing of the water supply and sewage undertaking. The annual deficit of the undertaking comes to about Rs. 4 millions and is met from the general revenues of the corporation. The main reason for a continuing deficit in the undertaking is the extremely low rate of water charge—at Rs. 0·50 for the first 6,000 gallons and Rs. 0·75 for subsequent one thousand gallons—while the cost of supplying filtered water is much higher than the prevailing rate, about Rs. 0·83 per thousand gallons. Where the metering system is not introduced, the rate of water tax is only 3 per cent of the rateable value of properties, while the corresponding rate in Bombay is 4½ per cent.

TABLE III

Revenue Income and Expenditure of the Municipal Corporation of Delhi

[*General Wing*]

Rupees millions

Expenditure	1964–65 (Accounts)	1965–66 (Budget)	Income (a) Domestic	1964–65 (Accounts)	1965–66 (Budget)
(i) General admn.	6·5	6·5	(i) Property taxes	25·7	30·0
(ii) Education	23·2	25·4	(ii) Duty on transfer of property	4·7	5·0
(iii) Medical and public health	34·4	58·3	(iii) Fire tax	1·0	0·9
(iv) Roads, public lighting and new works	17·8	16·6	(iv) Reimbursements	2·5	2·5
			(v) Tax on electricity	2·8	6·0
(v) Miscellaneous	26·3	39·8	(vi) Income from lands and buildings	4·2	7·3
			(vii) Miscellaneous	8·8	15·5
			(viii) Transfer from electric and transport a/cs	1·0	2·5
			Total domestic	50·7	69·7
			(b) Receipts from Govt. of India		
			(i) Assigned taxes (terminal tax)	33·4 (21·5)	50·9 (37·4)
			(ii) Transferred institutions[1]	10·1	9·7
			(iii) Education	9·0	10·6
			(iv) Slum clearance	—	1·0
			(v) Miscellaneous	1·3	3·9
			Total from government	53·8	76·1
			Total income (a)+(b)	104·5	145·8
			deficit	3·7	0·8
Grand Total	108·2	146·6	Grand Total	108·2	146·6

[1] These are the secondary schools and hospitals transferred from the Delhi Administration to the Municipal Corporation of Delhi. See *ante*, p. 413.

Among the shared taxes, the most important is the terminal tax which is collected by the municipal commissioner, as the appropriate authority on behalf of the central government, and the proceeds are distributed among the three local authorities within the territory, the share of the corporation being 80 per cent. The rates of terminal tax, which are levied on commodities brought in from the rest of the country for consumption within the territory, have been raised in 1965. The relative share of property taxes and the terminal tax to total revenue receipts of the corporation is an index of some significance; it shows whether the balance is tilted towards self-reliance or dependence on external assistance.

In presenting the budget estimates for 1968–69, the municipal commissioner suggested several tax increases. To what extent the suggestions will be accepted by the councillors is yet to be seen, but the leader of the ruling Jana Sangh party has already attributed the current deficit in the corporation's budget to Congress misrule in the previous decade, while the leader of the Congress group in the corporation remarked that the proposals have been made without any promise for improving the civic amenities.

The loan liability of the municipal corporation at the beginning of 1965–66 stood at about Rs. 150 millions. The corporation is empowered to raise loans from the public by way of debentures on the security of its tax revenue for undertaking any permanent work or repayment of its previous loans with the sanction of the central government. The central government also determines the amount of money to be raised, the interest rate and other terms including the date of flotation, the time and method of repayment and the like. Generally speaking, the maximum duration of a loan is 60 years, unless extended by the government. With the exception of one debenture loan (1959–71), all the other loans taken so far have come from the central government. It is enjoined in the municipal Act, that if the conditions of a government loan are not honoured the central government may attach the municipal fund of the corporation.

The municipal budget is divided into four sub-budgets prepared by the four statutory committees, and these are finally reviewed and approved by the corporation itself. Initially, these budgets are prepared by the chief executives for adoption by the statutory committees, and contain estimates of income and expenditure for the coming fiscal year, the revised estimates for the current year and the actual figures of the previous year as in the case of government budgets in the country. However, unlike the state or central governments, the corporation is statutorily required to keep a minimum cash balance of Rs. 100,000 at the close of the fiscal year.

RELATIONS WITH HIGHER AUTHORITIES

The relationship of the municipal corporation with higher authorities, viz., the lieutenant-governor and the central government may be described as one of uneasy intimacy. The central government has considerable powers of control and supervision over the civic body through normal and emergency powers under the Act—although these are in most cases negative and obstructionist. In fact, most of the powers of control and supervision have been delegated to the lieutenant-governor, keeping only the reserve powers with the central government, in the hope that this would co-ordinate overall supervision and control of the civic body. In fact, the lieutenant-governor himself has to run the territory administration with the goodwill of the municipal corporation and, therefore, cannot perform the role of an impartial observer. On the other hand, several central ministries in charge of works, housing, health, family planning, town planning, power, transport, education, finance and so on, are directly involved in the working of the municipal corporation, especially its development projects. In the circumstances, the territory administration cannot effectively co-ordinate all central plan assistance to the corporation.

Among the normal powers of the central government mention may be made of the power of rule-making under the Act with the concurrence of the Parliament, the power of appointing or approving the appointments of the statutory officers of the corporation like the commissioner and the general managers, power to sanction by-laws prepared by the corporation under the Act, power to sanction the terms and conditions of municipal borrowing from the market, and so on. The emergency powers of the central government include the power to require the production of any record, document, statement, etc., from the commissioner; the power of inspection of any municipal department, office or any service or work undertaken by the corporation; the power to give directions to the corporation to make necessary arrangements for the proper performance of municipal functions including the management of the undertakings; the power to make necessary arrangements by the government, in the case of the corporation's failure to comply with the government's directions, and charge the costs to the municipal fund; the power to give directions in relation to primary education; and finally, the power to supersede the corporation if it is not competent to perform, or persistently defaults, in its duties.

These are considerable powers indeed, and one may legitimately question the propriety of supersession of an elected body like the municipal corporation by the executive arm of the central government and not through a resolution in the Parliament. Even apart from this, the overlordship of the central government *vis-à-vis* the municipal corporation shows the limited degree of local self-government in the capital.

Instances where the corporation and the lieutenant-governor have come into conflict are numerous and most of these arise because of the possibility of overlap of functions and responsibilities. For instance, when the lieutenant-governor takes action for traffic control in Delhi, certain roads may have to be closed which means ratification of the action by the municipal corporation, or signboards which prove to be traffic hazards may have to be removed even though the municipal corporation approved the sites and levied taxes on advertisements. On the other hand, the municipal corporation has to depend on the territory administration for police assistance during any eviction or demolition operation. It is clear that without a rapport between the corporation and the lieutenant-governor, the civic administration in the capital may come to a standstill.

Under the powers conferred on the lieutenant-governor, special audits have been carried out in respect of the activities of the slum clearance department, the general wing, and the water and sewage undertaking of the corporation. Again, following the financial crisis under which the municipal commissioner has recommended increases in existing taxes and the levy of a few new taxes, the lieutenant-governor is reported to have recommended (December 1967) to the central government that the corporation be superseded or stripped of its powers to levy taxes.

Whether the municipal corporation is ultimately superseded or not depends on the balance of political forces, but it is clear that a tutelary system of local government having conflicting powers and jurisdictions with the higher authority, and different political parties governing the civic body and the central government contributes to tension and misunderstanding in central–local relations and perpetuates inefficiency and irresponsibility in the civic body.

PLANNING AND DEVELOPMENT

In order to tackle the problems created by large-scale migration to Delhi after the partition and the haphazard and unplanned growth of the urban area, the central government created a development authority which came into being at the same time as municipal reorganization took place in 1958. It was enjoined on the development authority to prepare a comprehensive master plan for Delhi for the orderly development of the territory. Accordingly, a master plan was prepared which came into force from 1962. The plan gave a perspective of development for a period of 20 years (1961–81), and was conceived in the regional context. The total capital cost under various heads of development was estimated at Rs. 7,320 millions and it was hoped that about 70 per cent of the capital cost would be realized. The recommended capital outlay for the first five years was in the neighbourhood of Rs. 1,250 millions.

The plan envisaged, in the main, the following features:

(a) optimal distribution of work centres;
(b) elimination of slums and squatting on public lands, and provision of adequate housing and community facilities;
(c) provision of adequate transport for people and goods;
(d) rebuilding of derelict areas according to a balanced plan;
(e) balanced distribution of population densities including lessening of congestion in the old city and raising densities in the thinly populated areas; and
(f) provision of an inviolable green belt around the city.

TABLE IV

Suggested Land use in Delhi Urban Area

Land use	Area in acres	Percentage to total
Residential	48,638	40·2
Commercial	1,615	1·3
Industrial	8,109	6·7
Governmental	1,149	0·9
Recreational	27,342	22·6
Public and semi-public	9,982	7·7
Railways	2,251	1·9
Airports and transportation	5,175	4·3
Defence	8,638	7·1
Agricultural	8,805	7·3
Total	121,004	100·0

The master plan also recommended a balanced land-use policy, after taking into consideration such factors as the future growth of population and the directions of urban expansion. The proposed land use suggested in the master plan for the urban area of Delhi is shown in Table IV.

Simultaneously with the development of Delhi, the master plan proposed the creation of a ring of towns around the present urban area of which two are in Uttar Pradesh, five in Haryana, and one in the territory itself. These may act as counter-magnets, and prevent a lop-sided growth of Delhi. Community facilities like schools, hospitals, playgrounds and open spaces, shopping and cultural centres have been envisaged. Detailed proposals have been made regarding water supply, sewerage, electricity, transportation, housing, etc. The main strategy for urban development suggested in the master plan and accepted by the development authority and the central government, is large-scale acquisition of undeveloped land and its public ownership.

The master plan is subject to quinquennial revision by the central government to adjust the planning exercise to the needs of the future. Accordingly both the development authority and the central government have recently been seized with the question of reviewing the plan in the light of its implementation during the last five years, especially so because the population projections have proved to be too modest, legal difficulties have arisen in large-scale acquisition of land, funds have not been found to the extent contemplated, and the implementation agencies could not be made to work together.

The problem of implementation of the master plan in Delhi has baffled the administrators, political leaders and the lay public. It must be said to the credit of the development authority that in the initial years considerable progress has been achieved in developing new areas in Delhi, but the process has not been entirely smooth. The programmes of the development authority and those of the municipal corporation have not gone hand in hand, with the result that many new colonies could not attract settlers owing to lack of civic facilities. Even the central government faced the same difficulty when the central public works department built a number of multi-storeyed buildings to the south of the city for accommodating government offices and their staff. Again, no improvement could be made with regard to the old city, partly because of the lack of a detailed zonal plan, higher costs of land acquisition in the congested areas and the problem of rehousing the displaced population. Similarly, there has been resistance to any attempt to violate the character of Lutyen's garden city. In spite of the prohibition against the location of new government offices in the capital city, more than 500 new government offices have come to Delhi during the last five years. So far, the local government authorities have not been involved in any significant way in the development of the existing urban area, in a manner indicated by the master plan. Legally, except for those areas which are specifically declared as 'development areas' (the undeveloped fringe around the urbanized area), all other areas are to be developed or redeveloped by the local authorities themselves according to approved zonal plans.

The master plan, and especially its implementation during the last five years, seems totally inadequate to grapple firmly with problems like slum clearance and housing, water supply, and transportation. The backlog with respect to housing has increased as compared to the position when the plan was prepared, primarily because of the tremendous rate of population growth of Delhi and also due to the feeble housing programme in practice. The search for an adequate source of water supply has been equally futile, both within Delhi and also in the adjoining states. An efficient system of mass transportation is yet to come about in the shape of either a ring railway or an underground variant of it.

BOUNDARY PROBLEMS

The territorial problems of Delhi are essentially inter-state in nature. This has given rise to certain complications which indicate the type of problems one could expect when the process of urbanization enters into adjoining states in a federal system of government. In Delhi, the present urban area touches Haryana in the south and west and Uttar Pradesh in the east. The problem of regulating urban growth in those areas was realized in the master plan which included within the area delineated as metropolitan Delhi three urban areas of Haryana and one urban area of Uttar Pradesh. Similarly, in the national capital region and the zone of influence of Delhi, a much larger area consisting of the union territory and areas belonging to the States of Haryana, Rajasthan and Uttar Pradesh is included. The master plan contemplated joint action by the central and the two state governments in regional planning and its implementation.

In accordance with the spirit of the master plan, the central government created a 'high powered' board consisting of the representatives of the central ministries concerned, the Planning Commission, the chief ministers of Punjab (now Haryana) and Uttar Pradesh, the mayor and the chief commissioner (now lieutenant-governor) of Delhi under the chairmanship of the Prime Minister (now Union Home Minister). The board has been a signal failure. The experience of its working suggests that the state governments are jealous of their rights and not always mindful of their responsibilities. Not that this is unusual, but the practical demonstration of the negative or even passive attitude of the adjoining states poses the problem of the future growth of Delhi.

There are two solutions to this problem: (*a*) extending the territorial boundary, or (*b*) arming the central government with enough powers to force a decision on the adjoining states. The first solution would inevitably raise political dust, and the second problem cannot be solved except through changes in the Constitution, which means a political settlement.

There is, however, another aspect of the boundary problem. Recently, there has been a demand to create a Greater Haryana, fostered by the Vishal Haryana party of Haryana which wishes to amalgamate the State of Haryana with Delhi and certain other districts of Uttar Pradesh and Rajasthan. This is resisted by all the political parties in Delhi, including the Jana Sangh, who fear being submerged by rural interests. The claims are based on linguistic and cultural grounds. However, as long as the public opinion of Delhi and the attitude of the central government are against this move, there does not seem to be much future for it.

CONCLUSIONS

The picture sketched out so far about the city government, politics and planning of Delhi shows signs of disharmony and inadequacy. Perhaps this is primarily due to the rising expectations on the part of the citizens and the inability of the civic machinery coupled with a lack of political leadership to cope with the situation. Citizen interest in political participation is substantial, but this has to be geared to the needs of development. The municipal corporation has made worthwhile attempts at urban community development and by the end of 1964–65 the total population covered by the various community programmes amounted to 150,000. The general level of civic amenities and services is admittedly low, but the reasons for inadequacy are somewhat involved and diffused. The gordian knot can be cut only by enlightened political leadership and the identification of the citizens with the civic government.

Various reform measures for improving the city government in Delhi are under consideration, like the supersession of the municipal corporation, the mayor-in-council proposal, *ad hoc* bodies for the municipal undertakings and so on. These are only temporary palliatives. The way Delhi will be governed will depend primarily upon the forces of public opinion in the capital and the country at large.

Ibadan

LESLIE GREEN

Born 1918. Graduated B.Sc.(Econ.) London; M.Sc.(London) in Political Science; Ph.D. Natal in Local Government. Has lectured in public administration and local government in several universities. Has held appointments as adviser and research worker to Johannesburg City Council, 1954–57; as Simon Senior Research Fellow, Manchester University, 1957–58, to report on metropolitan problems of South-East Lancashire with particular reference to local government; as director of an International Urban Studies programme of the Institute of Public Administration, New York, for which he was stationed in Calcutta, 1961–65; and as a Ford Foundation regional and urban planning specialist, in the Ministry of Lands and Housing, Western Nigeria, 1966–68, and, since 1968, in the Nigerian Institute of Social and Economic Research, University of Ibadan.

His published books include: *History of Local Government in South Africa: an Introduction* (1957); *Provincial Metropolis: The Future of Local Government in South East Lancashire* (1959); *Development in Africa: A Study in Regional Analysis with special reference to Southern Africa* (1962) with T. J. D. Fair; *Special Agencies in Metropolitan Calcutta* (1967) with A. Datta.

He is the author of many reports and articles on local government problems.

Ibadan

VERY early in the 1820s, Ibadan was an uninhabited village, deserted by its Egba farmers who had fled westwards before the advance of a victorious Yoruba army. Today, it is the capital city of the Western State of Nigeria, the social and commercial hub of Yorubaland and one of the largest urban concentrations in West Africa. It lies seven degrees north of the Equator at a mean altitude of about seven hundred feet above sea level. Its mean daily temperature varies between 69° and 93°F, its mean annual rainfall is 48·4 inches, its mean relative humidity is 65 per cent, and its cloud cover is intense throughout most of the year.[1]

THE RISE OF AN AFRICAN CITY

Conceived and nurtured in war for seventy years, and still bubbling with suppressed conflicts that spasmodically erupt, Ibadan owes its rise to a strategic location and freedom from the constraints of age-old customs. The allied army did not disband after fighting the Egba. It settled in Ibadan because, as Awe points out,[2] the village stood on Mapo, the southernmost of seven hills strung out from north to south between the northern savannahs and southern forests. It thus offered excellent hill defences against Egba infantry attacking from Abeokuta in the west, and comparable forest protection from Fulani cavalry sweeping down from Ilorin in the north.

Being a military headquarters, the new town did not observe all the rites, usages and traditions restricting urban life elsewhere, and it quickly attracted the noncomformist and adventurer from all corners of Yorubaland. Sons from every tribe flocked to join the original warriors of Ife, Ijebu and Old Oyo stock—from the Ekiti, Ijesha, Ondo, Egbado and even the Egba themselves. Pagans, Muslims and, later, Christians were thrown together in a military melting-pot. The warriors settled in tribal camps, each under a war captain who divided the camp area into 'family lands'. A 'family land' was owned

---

[1] L. Green and V. Milone: *Physical Planning in Western Nigeria*, Ministry of Lands and Housing, Ibadan, October 1967, para. 18; Ministry of Information, Western Nigeria, *Ibadan*, Government Printer, Ibadan (no date).

[2] B. Awe: 'The Growth of Ibadan in the 19th Century', in *Ibadan in the Changing Nigerian Scene*, Seminar Papers, Institute of African Studies, Ibadan University, Ibadan, 1964 (unpublished); see also B. Awe: 'The Rise of Ibadan as a Yoruba Power in the 19th Century', D.Phil. thesis, Oxford, 1964 (unpublished). Except where indicated by other references, this historical introduction is based on Awe's seminar paper.

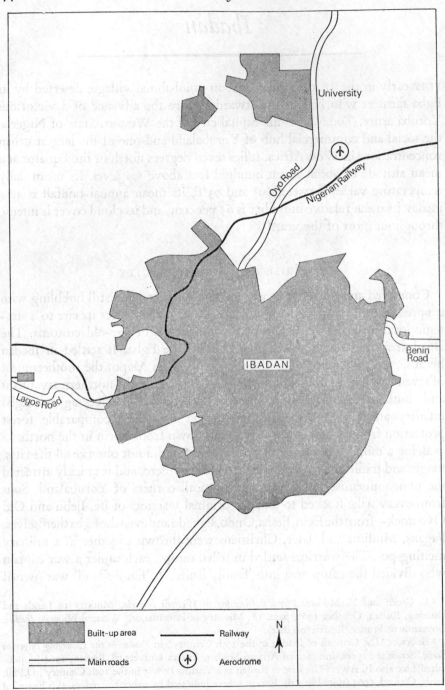

No municipal boundaries were settled or known at time of going to press

MAP 13   IBADAN

by an extended family or clan group of related families, who built their permanent dwellings there within a walled compound.[1] In course of time, a compound would shelter from perhaps forty to four hundred and more people.[2] As it became too congested, it would bud off other compounds so that, as the town grew by immigration and natural increase, the compounds spread haphazardly in all directions from the original nucleus, camp by camp.

In 1851, David Hinderer,[3] the first Christian missionary, estimated Ibadan's population at between 60,000 and 100,000 people. They inhabited an area of some sixteen square miles, which was enclosed by a defensive wall ten miles in circumference and dominated by the heights of Mapo, Are, Sapati, Oke-Aremo and lesser hills. The wall was pierced by four main gates, whence roads led south-west to Abeokuta, south to Ijebu, north to Oyo and north-east to Iwo and Ife. Through these gates flocked traders bringing arms, ammunition, salt and foreign goods, by way of Ijebu and Egba country from Lagos and Badagry on the coast; and cloth, ivory, rock salt and cattle from Oyo, Ilorin and farther north. From the same four gates spilled columns of slaves destined for shipment to the Americas, and crowds of townsmen-cultivators, who grew yams, beans and corn on their farms situated up to thirty miles outside the walls. Naturally, the principal markets sprang up at these gateways. Naturally, too, the old village site on Mapo, where stood the compounds of the original families and greatest warriors, became the town centre, the seat of government and the chief meeting-place of Oja'ba, or the great Iba market, since a market was a social as well as an economic pheno-menon. And, just as naturally, the war encampment's needs attracted hun-dreds of craftsmen—iron smelters, blacksmiths, saddlers, leather dressers, tanners, weavers, dyers, tailors, sawyers, carpenters, potters and makers of soap, nut-oil and palm-oil. Many of the market traders and most of the soap makers and dyers were women, for the non-craftsmen were engaged in either farming or fighting wars.

[1] S. A. Aribisala: 'Geology, Soil Types and Vegetation of Ibadan', in *Ibadan* (a brochure published under the auspices of the University College, Ibadan, for the Third International West African Conference held at Ibadan, December 1949), Zaria, 1949. See also P. C. Lloyd: *Yoruba Land Law*, London, 1962.

[2] D. Forde: 'The Yoruba-speaking Peoples of South-western Nigeria', *Ethnographic Survey of Africa, Western Africa*, Part IV, International African Institute, London, 1951, p. 11; B. Le Vine: 'Indigenous Ibadan' in *Ibadan in the Changing Nigerian Scene*.

[3] This paragraph summarizes quotations from D. Hinderer: *Journal*, Church Missionary Society, CA2/049, September 1851 (unpublished) appearing in B. Awe: 'The Growth of Ibadan in the 19th Century', and A. L. Mabogunje, 'Urbanization in Nigeria—A Constraint on Economic Development', *Economic Development and Cultural Change*, Vol. XIII, No. 4, Part I, July 1965, University of Chicago.

Because of their nonconformity, the people of Ibadan did not invite an hereditary priest-chief or *Oba* to rule over them. Physically, therefore, Ibadan differed from all other Yoruba towns, which were characterized by broad streets radiating from the *Oba's* central palace and adjacent market.[1] It differed politically, too, as its government was conducted by a *Bale*—elsewhere in Yorubaland no more than a village headman—and a council of chiefs comprising a civil line and a military line.[2] The *Bale* was head of the civil line and presided over the council; but his deputy was the *Balogun* or military leader, who generally succeeded the *Bale* on the latter's death. New chiefs were co-opted to the council after consulting an oracle, and usually on the basis of seniority, lineage, wealth, character and popularity. The townspeople owed allegiance to their chiefs by ties of family, clan and compound; and, because the majority of the people were of Old Oyo stock, the council in turn owed a token allegiance to the *Alafin* of Oyo, who was regarded by them as the spiritual head of the Yoruba and their paramount chief. But, especially after 1863, the *Alafin* was forced to follow Ibadan's lead, as by continuous warfare it rapidly extended its influence and placed resident representatives in the territories it conquered, to exact tribute and military levies. Reaction followed this expansion, however, since Ibadan's growing hegemony instilled fear and resentment to the west, south and east. By the end of the 1870s, it was fighting on five fronts at once, and inter-tribal hostilities were not finally halted until the British government intervened, instituted a round of treaty-making and eventually established a resident in the town in 1893.

For the next sixty-seven years, British influences helped to shape Ibadan's growth and government as the *de facto* capital of Yorubaland.[3] First, through Lord Lugard's system of indirect rule begun in 1913, which mistakenly placed the *Alafin* in ultimate charge of the town's administration and divested the chiefs of their former governmental functions. Secondly, through Sir Donald Cameron's system of local self-administration introduced from 1931 onwards, under which, in 1936, the translation of the *Bale* to the eminence of an *Olubadan* and the re-association of Ibadan's senior chiefs with the town's administration, marked the end of the *Alafin's* overlordship. Thirdly, through the development of a system of local self-government from 1952 onwards, at the instance of Chief Awolowo and the Action Group Party, which culminated in the passage of the Western Nigeria Local Government Law of 1957 and the granting of city status in 1961.

[1] A. L. Mabogunje: *Yoruba Towns: A Lecture*, Ibadan, 1962.
[2] For the traditional political organization of Ibadan described here and below, see D. Forde: *op. cit.*, pp. 39–41.
[3] G. D. Jenkins: 'Politics in Ibadan', in *Ibadan in the Changing Nigerian Scene*.

IBADAN TODAY

According to the 1963 census, Ibadan City then embraced 635,011 people, the great majority of whom were Yorubas. There were, however, substantial pockets of Hausas from Northern Nigeria, Ibos from the Eastern Region and Niger delta, and expatriates from Britain and America. With the outbreak of civil war in 1967, most of the Ibos fled by mammy wagon, bus and taxi; but the city yet[1] contains at least 630,000 people. They inhabit an area of about forty square miles at an average density of some 15,660 to the square mile, or three times the density of Hinderer's days. The Oke Aremo ridge still towers over Ibadan. From its forest-clad heights 933 feet above sea level, an amorphous mass of rust-brown, corrugated iron roofs tumbles 300 feet in congested disorder to engulf Mapo (now the seat of the city council) and lesser hills, to surge across the shallow valleys worn on either side of the ridge by two perennial streams, the Kudeti and Gege (now canalized), and to wash over the old city walls into the green bush beyond. Although the city is divided into at least thirty recognized quarters named after original camps and immigrant settlements, there is no geometric design in this maze of mud-walled houses, interspersed only by an occasional tree, a growing number of two-storeyed block-built dwellings, the minarets of a mosque or the steeple of a church. From the pillars of Mapo Hall to the green horizon, not a single row, crescent or circle of buildings can be seen.

On the eastern margins, this almost solid mass is contained by a green belt of playing fields, hospitals, colleges and schools. In the west, it gives way to government forests and agricultural plantations, the Liberty Sports Stadium, the beginnings of a new hospital, and government residential reservations. To the north stand an airfield, the wooded campus of Ibadan University, the wide expanse of Eleiyele reservoir, the Ibadan portion of Ife University, the Technical College, other government residential areas, the new Bodija housing estate, the grounds of the University College Hospital and the Secretariat and Legislative Assembly. To the south, the houses peter out in another belt of schools and the ubiquitous bush and forest. Most of the indigenous, old town crowds to the east of Oke Aremo, where, in some nine square miles of built-up confusion, live at least 400,000 people. Many of them reside in compounds, of which some two thousand still existed in 1954.[2] To the west and north of the ridge, beyond the former city wall, sprawls the new, surveyed and laid-out town of relatively recent immigrants from Ijebu, Benin, Enugu and the north, of government lands

---

[1] 1 October, 1967.

[2] N. C. Mitchell: 'Yoruba Towns', in *Essays in African Population* (K. M. Barbour and R. M. Prothero, eds.), London, 1961, pp. 279–301.

and institutions, and of expatriate homes, where densities sometimes fall to no more than a single house on an acre of land. Between the disorderly old and the orderly new soar a prestige skyscraper and a small cluster of high office blocks, marking Gbagi, the business hub of modern Ibadan.

Outside the old walled city and its peripheral built-up extensions, which together fill a rough circle some seven miles in diameter, the density of population drops dramatically. In 1963, a little over 514,000 people lived in the six surrounding district council areas covering between them more than 1,100 square miles. In this hinterland, Lalupon, with 30,800 inhabitants, was the single town of any size, and the vast majority of people lived in settlements of a few hundred persons only. Interestingly enough, Lalupon is listed by Awe[1] as one of the villages in which Ibadan's townsmen farmed in Hinderer's time, over a century ago; most of the main roads now radiating from the city through the surrounding countryside, are those mentioned by him; and the railway, built in 1901, follows the old roads to Abeokuta and Iwo. Indeed, virtually the same rural area today provides Ibadan with possibly a third of its traditional yams, cassava, corn and plantains.[2] Here, its townsmen-farmers still live for a few days at a time, or for one month or more—depending on the season, crops and personal circumstances—in hamlets and villages where even the more permanent householders maintain residences in Ibadan, to which they return at intervals on ceremonial and other social occasions. In this sense, the rural hinterland is an economic and social extension of the city; but there is no daily commuting of thousands of workers between Ibadan and the surrounding settlements, nor any metropolitan region in the sense understood in Europe or America. The farmers leave their wives in the city (to run the daily markets) and, when not tending their farms, many of them continue to earn cash incomes in Ibadan as carpenters, weavers, petty contractors, tailors and bricklayers.[3] Many, too, grow cocoa for export overseas, although swollen-shoot disease has decimated their plantations in recent years; and some now produce small quantities of lettuce, tomatoes, carrots and cucumbers from city lands for upper-income Nigerians and overseas expatriates.

Together with two or three thousand expatriates, this new Nigerian

---

[1] B. Awe: 'The Growth of Ibadan in the 19th Century', who also mentions the villages of Apomu, Ojo and Iroko, which likewise fall within a 20-mile radius of Ibadan.

[2] H. A. Oluwasanmi: 'The Agricultural Environment of Ibadan', in *Ibadan in the Changing Nigerian Scene*, but the present author's estimate of volume based on research by R. Gusten, provisionally reported in *Studies in the Staple Food Economy of Western Nigeria*, N.I.S.E.R. 1967.

[3] *Ibid.* for this and the following information on farming habits, crops and occupations.

élite (which dates from the mid-1930s and, on Lloyd's definition,[1] must now account for some 25,000 people of all ages) reflects an administrative, commercial and, lately, industrial development that may well transform much of Ibadan's economic and social life in a decade or two. According to Akinola,[2] in 1963–64, the city already housed forty-seven industrial units employing more than ten workers each, of which the most important were tobacco, plastics, canning, tyre re-treading, furniture and bottling factories and electricity and light engineering works. There were over two thousand smaller-scale units, and some 4,800 workers were employed in all kinds of transport services. But the number of traditional craftsmen possibly aggregates fifteen thousand[3] and, apart from a handful of large departmental stores and wholesale distributors run by expatriate firms in Gbagi, trading remains almost wholly in the hands of thousands of women who throng the city's markets—Oja'ba (with its cooked foods and large night market), Oje (for cloth), Gege (for meat and farm produce) and Dugbe (for imported goods, especially china and enamelware).[4] Moreover in all probability, about one-third of the townspeople are still directly connected with farming.[5]

Because of this largely traditional economic structure, the annual income earned by Ibadan's inhabitants possibly approximates to only £20 million a year; which is little more than £30 per head of the total population.[6] It is by no means a rich city, therefore, and its hinterland is even poorer (having an income of possibly £20 per head). Nor is its life sophisticated, like that of Lagos one hundred miles away. To some people it is little more than a vastly over-grown collection of villages. To others, it is the colourful epitome of an indigenous urbanism which is nearly one thousand years old, and distinguishes Yorubaland from the whole of the rest of Africa south of the Sahara.

[1] P. C. Lloyd: 'The Elite of Ibadan' in *Ibadan in the Changing Nigerian Scene*, who sets a standard equivalent to a car-owning government servant earning £600 a year in 1964.

[2] R. A. Akinola: 'The Industrial Structure of Ibadan', *Nigerian Geographical Journal*, Vol. 7, No. 2, December 1964. See also A. Callaway: 'Crafts and Industries' in *Ibadan in the Changing Nigerian Scene*.

[3] Personal communication from Mr. Michael Koll who is undertaking a census of crafts and small-scale industries in Ibadan at the Nigerian Institute of Social and Economic Research, University of Ibadan. See also A. Callaway: *op. cit.*

[4] N. C. Mitchell: *op. cit.*, and A. L. Mabogunje: 'Ibadan: Black Metropolis', *Nigerian Magazine*, Vol. 67, March 1961.

[5] H. A. Oluwasanmi: *op. cit.*

[6] According to the 1963 population census, the P.A.Y.E. breakdown in Table I and tax data published in *Western Nigeria Statistical Bulletin*, Vol. VIII, Nos 1 and 2, Statistics Division, Ministry of Economic Planning and Social Development, Ibadan, June and December 1966, the *per capita* income is £25. But allowance must be made for under-assessment, tax evasion and tax-exempt women.

GOVERNMENT IN IBADAN

Since January 1966, Nigeria has been administered by a military government, political parties have been banned, and Ibadan, with its city government in ruins, has been placed under an administrator appointed by the military governor of the Western Region (now the Western State). So soon after a bitterly fought civil war, no one can say when a civil administration will once again rule from Mapo Hall, nor what form it will take, nor what area will fall under its jurisdiction. One can be certain only that a veritable web of public authorities will continue to meet the city's needs for works and services, and that its local government will not revert wholly to the system existing prior to 1952.

Between 1936 and 1952, Ibadan's immediate local government authority was a district council headed by the *Olubadan* and an inner council of chiefs. The latter comprised the *Olubadan* as chairman, ten senior chiefs and twelve literate councillors. Six of the councillors were selected from untitled members of the community (the newly emergent élite), and six from the junior chiefs and compound heads (or *mogajis*). The inner council acted as the town's executive. It was assisted by a joint advisory board of thirty members native to Ibadan, who were elected partly by electoral colleges of representatives from the traditional quarters, and partly by representatives of the junior chiefs and *mogajis*. The inner council and joint advisory board held monthly meetings to discuss matters of public interest and, if necessary, to tender advice to the Ibadan Divisional Council. The latter was a higher authority which met quarterly and exercised jurisdiction over sixteen constituent district councils, including Ibadan's. The *Olubadan* also presided over the divisional council, which consisted of the inner council of chiefs and two representatives each from the other fifteen district councils.[1]

Thus, while the inner council of chiefs was responsible for the internal administration of Ibadan town, together with the *Olubadan* it was also directly involved in the government of a very much wider region, extending for over 4,500 square miles and including not only Ibadan's own immediate hinterland but the distant towns of Oshogbo, Ogbomosho, Ede and Iwo. And while the former influence of the traditional rulers is unlikely to be restored, the re-association of Ibadan's élite with the city's administration might possibly rescue it from its current depression, and the federal principle

[1] This description of local government in Ibadan before 1952 is based on S. A. Oloko: 'Ibadan Local Government', in *Ibadan* (a brochure . . .). E. D. O. John identifies the *mogaji* as the clan head (although the term *bale* is also used) and adds that, ideally, all clan members should live within a single compound: 'A Description of the Town', in *Ibadan* (a brochure . . .).

permitting the marriage of town and country for local government purposes could undoubtedly be revived.

The divorce between town and country took place in only 1961. Although the old divisional administration was abolished by a Local Government Law of 1952, Ibadan's new local government, as confirmed under a similar law of 1957, consisted of an all-purpose district council having jurisdiction over the town itself and the surrounding rural areas. This meant that a single local authority of fifty-two elected and nineteen traditional members administered a vast tract of nearly 3,000 square miles, which stretched far beyond the city's probable economic and social hinterland. It is thus hardly surprising that a basic reorganization took place nine years later. Indeed, in 1956, five years before the basic reorganization, the district council was superseded and a management committee appointed by the Western Region government.

From 1961 onwards, in token recognition of its function as a regional capital, Ibadan's status was raised to that of the only city in Western Nigeria. Outside the forty square miles falling within the city's limits, the remaining areas of the former district council were divided between seven new district councils, six of which had common boundaries with the city. In consequence, the local government of the city and its hinterland came to be shared between the Ibadan City Council (which could exercise no more than district council powers in spite of its status), and the Ibadan North, Ibadan East, Ibadan South-east, Ibadan South, Ibadan South-west and Ibadan West District Councils. This reorganization no longer contained a federal principle, in the shape of an overall divisional council co-ordinating the activities of the separate district councils. But a joint education board was appointed for the city and its hinterland, and important services were beginning to be operated by other public authorities having jurisdictions not limited to Ibadan alone.

THE CITY COUNCIL

Under the 1961 reorganization, the members of the Ibadan City Council consisted of the *Olubadan*, as president in virtue of his office, fifteen traditional chiefs appointed for an indefinite period, and forty-six councillors elected by single-member wards for three years at a time. A traditional member had to be the holder of a chieftaincy recognized under the Chiefs Law. An elected member had to be a Nigerian national over twenty years old, native to Ibadan and a resident of the city for at least two consecutive years preceding his election.[1] The *Olubadan* presided over the council's meetings, and standing

[1] The information for this section on the working of the former city council was kindly

committees were elected by and from the council 'to regulate and manage' its business. The appointment of a finance committee 'to regulate and control' the finances of the council was mandatory, all other committees were permissive, and matters were both referred and delegated to them.

In short, apart from the traditional members (who were superficially reminiscent of the aldermen of an English borough), the roles, structure and procedures of the council and its committees closely paralleled those of the English county council system. The Local Government Law in fact uses the terminology of the county council legislation in respect of the standing committees, although it also permits a council to appoint town, village or area committees in addition to such committees. The Ibadan City Council never used this latter power, however, and it thus appointed standing committees for only general purposes, finance, health, works, transport, markets, lands, staff and scholarships (the vestige of a former mandatory education committee). It also appointed a tenders board, which was in law no more than yet another standing committee, and the system pivoted on the general purposes and finance committees.

As in the English county council, these committees were intended to act as the buckles binding together the council, as a deliberative and directing organ of government, and the executive machinery of its several departments. The executive machinery was headed by a secretary[1] and a treasurer, whose appointment by the council was obligatory. The secretary was statutorily described as 'the chief executive and administrative officer of the council' who was 'responsible for co-ordinating the whole of the work of the council'. He was also statutorily responsible for convening all council and committee meetings, for preparing their minutes and reports, and for generally advising them and the president as required.

Today, with an appointed administrator in charge of Ibadan's city government, this system is in abeyance. There are no traditional or elected councillors; there are no committees. The secretary remains the chief executive and administrative officer, but he is now responsible only to the administrator,

supplied by the Secretary, Ibadan City Council. A person could also be barred from standing for election if currently serving or sentenced to a term of imprisonment exceeding three months, if of unsound mind, if holding a paid office or place of profit in the gift of the council (or one of its committees), if a federal or regional government minister or Parliamentary secretary to such a minister, if in default of paying income tax due during the two years preceding the election, if in default of paying any council rate due within three months prior to the election, or if he had within ten years preceding the election been an unsuccessful candidate for a chieftaincy in or associated with the area of the council and had not obtained the governor's consent to stand for election.

[1] Prior to 1961 the secretary was an expatriate British officer. The present secretary is a Nigerian who has had training in both the U.K. and U.S.A. and is primarily an administrator.

acting as his right-hand man. And the six district councils surrounding the city are similarly bereft of their former lay members, in each case being run by their secretary, who is answerable to an appointed divisional officer. The latter represents the military governor, and is placed in overall charge of the area falling under their combined jurisdictions.

OTHER PUBLIC AUTHORITIES

It would be a serious error, however, to believe that the government of the state's capital city is now wholly or mainly the responsibility of a single administrator. Reality has always been much more complex. As may be gathered from the description of governmental functions given below, a very wide range of works and services is permitted to a local government council by the Local Government, Education and other Laws. But many of the functions so authorized to the Ibadan City Council are also authorized to other public bodies by the same and other laws—to the federal and state governments, public corporations, joint boards, other corporate authorities and even voluntary agencies. These include the federal prisons department, federal and state hospitals, state and voluntary teacher-training colleges, a state malaria control unit, a state chest clinic, a federal police service, a state fire service, a state catering rest house, federal and state ministries of works, a state library, state and voluntary schools, the Ibadan Town Planning Authority, the Western Nigeria Housing Corporation and the Western Nigeria Water Supply Corporation.

Many other essential works and services provided in Ibadan are non-local government in character. Necessarily, they are functions of organs other than the city council. The most important of the national organs are the federal university and teaching hospital, the Electricity Corporation of Nigeria, the Nigerian Railways Corporation, the Nigerian Posts and Telecommunications Department, the Geological Survey, the Ibadan employment exchanges, the Nigerian Broadcasting Corporation, the Agricultural and Forest Research Departments, the Cocoa Research Institute, the National Archives, the Central Bank of Nigeria and the Nigeria Airways. The Western State organs extend to the Ibadan branch of Ife University, a technical college, the Ministry of Finance (for the collection of income tax), the Ministry of Works and Transport (for government buildings and reservations), the Ministry of Education (for trade schools), the Ministry of Lands and Housing (for the survey and registration of land), the Ministry of Health (for leprosy control) and the Judicial Department (for the High Court and magistrates' courts). Voluntary associations run blind schools and orphanages, and the Western

P

Nigeria Broadcasting Corporation and a state newspaper must also be included in any list of non-local government services operated in the city by public and semi-public agencies.

CITY POLITICS

Prior to the military takeover, the governmental stature of the city council had for long been further diminished by the fact that effective political power lay in the legislative assembly and secretariat, sited in the north-western corner of Ibadan beyond its obliterated city wall. If the majority party in control at Mapo Hall formed the minority opposition in the assembly and secretariat, the city council was in danger of supersession. If the same party ruled in both places, the power of decision in all important civic issues lay with its leaders, who held the principal ministerial posts in the regional government. As in many other capital cities, local political power was centralized at the regional and not city level.[1]

At the same time, the political leaders were mostly chiefs who necessarily took some cognizance of the views of the traditional hierarchy. To further complicate the political scene, the origins of the local people, in whom family, lineage and tribal loyalties continued to reign supreme, were most polyglot. Yet only men born in Ibadan could become councillors. The numerous immigrant groups could not easily secure representation on the city council through their own kith and kin, whether elected or appointed. To obtain a place in the sun, they needed to capture the regional (now state) government, and local and regional politics thus became inextricably mixed (especially because the Action Group Party attempted to base its strength on the local government councils). To embitter the political atmosphere still further, the sons of Ibadan were mainly of Old Oyo stock; the spearhead of the new immigrants came from Ijebu. Antipathy between them was etched deeply in the history of Yorubaland, let alone Ibadan. And not only did the struggle for control have these very old roots, but the tactics of temporary alliances, developed during the long warfare between Ibadan and its enemies during the previous century, were repeated in earnest from 1952 onwards.

To trace all the causes of the shifts in political alignments is thus impossible, since they reflected so many issues, local, regional and, ultimately, federal.[2]

[1] A. L. Mabogunje: 'The Urban Landscape of Ibadan' in *Ibadan in the Changing Nigerian Scene*.

[2] The following account of party politics is based on G. D. Jenkins: *op. cit.* See also G. D. Jenkins: 'Politics in Ibadan', Ph.D. thesis, Evanston University, 1965 (unpublished); G. D. Jenkins and K. Post: *The Price of Freedom*, to be published; P. C. Lloyd: 'Local Government in Yoruba Town', D.Phil. thesis, Oxford University, 1958 (unpublished).

But most alignments tended to form around two main poles. On the one hand, there was the Action Group led by Chief Awolowo. The latter was an Ijebu, who began his political career through a Yoruba cultural association, the *Egbe Omo Oduduwa*, but who was also general secretary of the Native Settlers' Union, which represented the Ijebu influx into Ibadan. Opposing the Action Group was the National Convention of Nigeria and the Cameroons (later renamed the National Convention of Nigerian Citizens). Although its national leader was an Ibo and it had strong connections with Lagos, its local leader was Chief Adelabu, a son of Ibadan and founder of a significantly named *Mabolaje* or chieftaincy party. Chief Adelabu's increasingly corrupt administration of the Ibadan District Council was abruptly concluded by supersession in 1956, under a regional government controlled by the Action Group. His accidental death in 1958 sparked off riots in which many Action Group supporters were killed. And the ensuing political in-fighting led to a general breakdown of government in Western Nigeria in 1962, to rampant ballot-stuffing in the 1965 elections, to widespread civil disorders and, finally, to the military takeover of January 1966. Since then, investigations into the activities of politicians and officials of the regional government, city council and other public bodies have revealed a degree of corruption and financial misappropriation unsurpassed in Ibadan's turbulent history.

During these years of conflict, the N.C.N.C. controlled the council from 1954 to 1956, when the Action Group formed the regional government. Warfare between Mapo Hall and the secretariat was inevitable, and it was temporarily stilled only by the appointment of a caretaker committee, which lasted from 1956 until 1960 and was favourable to the Action Group. Between 1960 and 1962, the latter controlled both seats of government; from 1962 to 1965, the United Progressive Party (a splinter group of the Action Group) followed in its footsteps; and in 1965, dissidents from both the Action Group and the N.C.N.C. formed the Nigerian National Democratic Party, to win control over both city and region until the final *débâcle*.[1]

While the party system thus rapidly disintegrated, the city's affairs were increasingly ignored to the point of virtual exclusion from the arithmetic of politics. They were certainly a dead issue as far as the counting of votes in the regional elections of 1965 was concerned. Indeed, according to Awe and Jenkins,[2] they had been a really live issue only in the 1930s (and during the Second World War). Only from 1936 onwards was the good of its citizens

[1] This paragraph is based on data compiled for the Ibadan Group's review of *Government, Administration and the Political Process* submitted to the Centennial Study and Training Programme on Metropolitan Problems, Toronto Bureau of Municipal Research, 1967.

[2] B. Awe: 'The Growth of Ibadan in the 19th Century', and G. D. Jenkins, *Politics in Ibadan*.

the approximate end of Ibadan's government. Then, the Ibadan Progressive Union, formed by the newly emerging élite, became a most influential body. Appointed as councillors who could merely advise the inner council of chiefs, its representatives nevertheless succeeded in initiating many improvements. By sedulously avoiding disputes with the traditional elements; by devoting their energies to the city's need for water, electric light, transport, storm-water drainage, housing, roads and health services, and by necessarily limiting the horizons of their political ambitions to Ibadan alone, they ushered in and nurtured a brief era of civic development that has never been equalled (even though the improvements tended to be located in their own immigrant areas). But since 1952 the potential horizons have widened to those of Western Nigeria, and since 1956 they have widened still farther to encompass the entire Federation. The special circumstances in which the Progressive Union operated cannot be repeated, unless the military government were now to lift the ban on political parties at the local level, while retaining it at the state and national levels.

Even so, the innumerable pressure groups existing in Ibadan, and the endemic factionalism characterizing its fragmented society, would remain formidable obstacles to a local political renaissance. In 1967, for example, riots resulted not only from inter-tribal suspicions, but from a taxi-drivers' strike in protest against a city council proposal to issue permits to ply for hire; and the strike provided an opportunity for other scores to be settled, especially against the town planning authority. Apart from organized groups —ranging from the Ibadan Chamber of Commerce to the Taxi Owners' Association, the Taxi Drivers' Union, the Farmers' Union, the Market Women and Women Traders' Association, the Butchers' Union, the Teachers' Association, the Sports Council and affiliated bodies, the *Mabolaje* association to preserve the chieftaincy system, the many guilds or craft unions controlling the goldsmiths, tinkers, carpenters, blacksmiths and fifteen thousand other craftsmen, the local improvement associations, and the local co-operative savings associations or *esusu*—there are ill-defined but no less significant sectional interests of expatriate commercial houses, civil servants, university academic staff and other professional persons. All can exert various kinds of pressures on government. And often working at cross-purposes with these interests and groups, there are the paramount familial, clan and wider kinship ties, differentiating, for instance, sons of Ife from sons of Ado-Ekiti, Abeokuta or Ondo; the extremely strong tribal unions or associations of Ibos, Mid-Westerners and Hausas (very few of whom seem to consider themselves as primarily citizens of Ibadan[1]); and the Muslim and Christian

[1] Cf. C. Okonjo: 'Western Ibos in Ibadan' in *Ibadan in the Changing Nigerian Scene*, who

religious institutions, which are especially active in the fields of education and health.

So far, political institutions have clearly failed to digest this multiplicity of diverse groups, and to resolve the conflicts arising from so many disparate and incompatible pressures, ethnic, economic and cultural in origin. The social fabric of the city seems too loosely woven to provide the essential backcloth needed to enact the drama—and comedy—of local party politics according to principles of the English county council system. Family and tribe especially demand too high a loyalty; wards tend to be determined traditionally and ethnically rather than economically or physically; nepotism is no crime in the eyes of those who still expect a successful son to look after his own kith and kin first.[1] And rule by majority opinion, as measured by the simple counting of heads, is a concept difficult to implant in a society where, for centuries, governmental decisions have been handed down by *Obas* as a result of discussions held within co-opted councils of chiefs. For, in these discussions, deference to seniority and the preservation of internal communal peace have been essential principles; and the popular election of rulers has been unknown.[2] It would thus be naïve to expect instant political success of a fledgeling city council called upon to govern Ibadan's heterogeneous peoples by means of simple majority voting, in which each vote is to be of equal value.

THE LEGAL POWERS OF LOCAL GOVERNMENT COUNCILS

Under the Local Government Law, a district council is *obliged* to prevent crime and breaches of the peace. It is *permitted* to provide and maintain the following:

(*a*) public works, including roads, bridges, motor parks and drainage systems;

(*b*) public health services, including hospitals, dispensaries, maternity homes, ambulances, refuse removal, sewerage systems, malaria eradication services, slaughterhouses, cemeteries and machinery for the abatement of nuisances;

states that very few Western Ibo immigrants consider themselves *in any way* citizens of Ibadan, and that even second-generation men born and bred in Ibadan mostly marry Western Ibos. (With the civil war, most Eastern Ibos have disappeared, and the Western Ibos are referred to as Mid-Westerners to distinguish them from the Eastern Ibos.)

[1] Cf. R. E. Wraith: *Local Government*, Penguin, Harmondsworth, 1953, p. 113: 'Nepotism . . . is widely and sincerely regarded as virtuous rather than reprehensible.'

[2] P. C. Lloyd: 'The Traditional Political System of the Yoruba', *Southwestern Journal of Anthropology*, Vol. 10, No. 4, 1954. See also P. C. Lloyd: 'Local Government in Yoruba Towns'.

(c) public utility and trading services, including transport, water supplies, markets, public lighting and any form of trade, commerce or industry;

(d) public housing, including housing estates, urban layouts and settlements, and schemes for planned rural development and settlement;

(e) public welfare services, including recreation grounds, parks, libraries, entertainments, child welfare services, social centres, institutions for old people, approved schools, remand homes and prisons; and

(f) miscellaneous services, including fire-fighting, night watchmen, public relations, rest houses, piers, weights and measures inspectors, soil erosion schemes, and schemes for the improvement of agriculture and livestock.

A district council may make by-laws in respect of all these matters, for the enforcement of which it may, under the Police Law, maintain a local government police force. Under the Education Law, 1955, as a local education authority it is obliged to establish and maintain such primary schools, secondary modern schools and teacher-training institutions as the state government directs, and it is permitted to run nursery schools and special schools for disabled children. The Local Government Law and the Income Tax Law, 1957, as amended, permit a council to levy general and special rates on either a capitation or property basis, and to collect directly-assessed income tax on all incomes up to £300 a year *in lieu* of a general rate on income and an education rate. Under the Town and Country Planning Law, a local government council may be appointed as a local planning authority and, under the Customary Courts Law, it may co-operate with the state in operating customary courts.

As will have become apparent from the agencies and activities already listed as being located or undertaken in Ibadan, in spite of its status the functions actually discharged by the city council itself are but a tithe of those authorized by law to even a district council. They extend for the most part to education (in so far as it has a financial responsibility for services run by the joint board), health and medical services, roads and bridges, customary courts, public transport (which it is currently losing), water supplies (which will soon be wholly transferred), refuse removal (which is a rather skeletal service) and sewerage (which over a large area consists of night-soil removal only). Any analysis of government functions in Ibadan must thus necessarily range well beyond the field so precariously occupied by the city council.

EDUCATION

Higher education is a function of the Federal University of Ibadan, the Federal University College Hospital, the State University of Ife, and the

Ibadan Technical College, owned and operated by the state. On its part, the city council finances twenty-six primary schools, three secondary modern schools, a secondary grammar school and a teacher-training college;[1] it provides secondary school scholarships for needy children and it runs a small library service. But the main public library in Ibadan is maintained by the state government, and the University of Ibadan has the largest collection of books. Three more teacher-training colleges are owned by religious denominations (Methodist and Anglican); one secondary grammar school is operated by the state (which also runs a trades school) and thirty-two are maintained by religious denominations (Methodist, Anglican, Baptist, Roman Catholic, Muslim and the African Church) and by private persons; nineteen secondary modern schools belong to these same religious groups and to private persons; and, in all probability, at least seventy-five primary schools are non-government owned.[2]

In consequence, although the city council is statutorily obliged to finance free primary education, and secondary modern schools, it is in practice most probably responsible for underwriting the education of no more than one-quarter of the city's school children, or 16 per cent of its school-age children.[3] Moreover, as indicated above, a joint education board has managed and controlled local government schools in Ibadan since 1961. This separate, corporate body exercises all the powers of a local education authority, other than the levying of a rate, borrowing of money and making of by-laws. It has jurisdiction over the city and the six surrounding district council areas, and consists of representatives drawn from all seven local authorities. In the six-council ring around Ibadan, however, voluntary agencies maintain the only four secondary grammar schools and thirteen of the fourteen secondary modern schools.

In spite of such vigorous, voluntary efforts, it is very possible that every third child in Ibadan never enters school. But even this proportion is a great advance. Only one of the existing secondary modern schools and seven of the secondary grammar schools were founded before 1955. Prior to the Second

[1] From information kindly supplied by the Secretary, Ibadan City Council.

[2] Statistics of schools in this and the following two paragraphs are derived from *Western Nigeria Annual Abstract of Education Statistics*, Vol. 6, 1966, Statistics Division, Ministry of Economic Planning and Social Development, Ibadan, 1967.

[3] In 1963, enrolments in primary schools in Western Nigeria totalled 730,000 and in secondary schools 104,000, as against a probable 1·8 million children in the 7–14 years age group. Enrolments in Ibadan City are no doubt higher than the regional average, but can hardly be greater than two-thirds of its school-age children. Calcott estimates that only 51 per cent of boys and 38 per cent of girls in the 6–12 years age group were enrolled in 1964 in Ibadan Division (D. Calcott: *Education in a Rural Area of Western Nigeria*. I.L.O. Mission Report, Ministry of Economic Planning and Social Development, Western Nigeria, 1967).

World War, there were no more than four secondary schools in Ibadan, which already had a population of 400,000 and probably 70,000 children between 7 and 14 years of age. Relatively speaking, therefore, enormous strides have been made in the last decade, if mainly by voluntary agencies.

PUBLIC HEALTH

Eleven years before Ibadan's first secondary school was founded in 1913, a public dispensary was completed.[1] Annual outbreaks of smallpox led to the appointment of a board of health in 1904, the building of a government hospital at Jericho in 1905 and the introduction of compulsory vaccination in the same year. Malaria, yellow fever, guinea-worm and dysentery continued to take a high annual toll of the population, however, and besides introducing health regulations, the local authority built its own hospital at Adeoyo in 1928. Today, Adeoyo (with 277 beds)[2] is run by the state government as a specialist hospital serving a much wider area than Ibadan, the state also maintains the Jericho Nursing Home (built in 1928 and having 33 beds) and it has begun work on a new specialist hospital. The federal government has built the University College Hospital, which has 507 beds and serves much of Nigeria, but mainly the Western State. The city council, having lost its hospital, now concentrates on the provision of dispensaries, clinics, medical services that are preventive and not curative, and environmental health services (including refuse collection, malaria control and street cleaning).

Nevertheless, as Ogunlesi emphasizes,[3] since 1964 the city's medical officer of health has been responsible for the preventive services of the whole of Ibadan Division, including not only Ibadan itself and the six adjacent district council areas, but the areas also of the Ibarapa West District Council and Ibarapa East Provincial Authority, which now form a new division. In 1963, these nine local authorities together covered no less than 2,221 square miles inhabited by nearly 1,269,000 people. The medical officer's responsibilities in this vast region extend to environmental health (including refuse services and the cleaning of streets and water courses), the control of communicable

[1] See S. A. Agbaje: 'Reflections on the Progress of Health in Ibadan', in *Ibadan* (a brochure . . .), for this and other historical information appearing in this section.

[2] Statistics of health institutions in this section are based on data compiled for the Ibadan Town Planning Authority (Mr. O. Adedapo, Chief Executive Officer), and *Western Nigeria Abstract of Local Government Statistics*, Vol. 1, No. 1, Statistics Division, Ministry of Economic Planning and Social Development, December 1966.

[3] T. O. Ogunlesi: 'Health in Ibadan', in *Ibadan in the Changing Nigerian Scene*.

diseases, the supervision of school clinics, the operation of fifteen maternity and child welfare centres, and the maintenance of personal health services provided in twenty-four dispensaries. Apparently, the reason for this unique and still unratified regional organization, which is financed by the city and district councils with state assistance, is personal to the incumbent medical officer, who is seconded by the council to the state, and it would cease to exist upon his resignation or retirement. Undoubtedly, it cannot expect to provide a satisfactory level of services. For example, the total staff employed in 1964–65 numbered no more than 335, or one to every 3,800 persons.

Although voluntary agencies in Ibadan maintain twenty maternity and general hospitals, together with the federal and state institutions only 983 general beds and 168 maternity beds are thus made available for the 1·3 million people living in the area of the city and the two divisions, discounting any beds needed for patients from the rest of the state and federation. In Ibadan itself, the shortage of beds is in fact acute and the military government has placed a high priority on the building of the new specialist hospital. To add to the difficulties of the public health services, there is a shortage of medical and nursing staff, there is no compulsory registration of births and deaths, medical practitioners themselves are only now being completely registered, and deaths from communicable diseases are grossly under-reported. Malaria and infectious hepatitis are known to be widespread, diarrhoeal diseases are rampant, there is a host of virus infections and typhoid is common; but the true incidence of these and other diseases can only be guessed at in the absence of compulsory returns.[1]

On the other hand, in spite of these obvious deficiencies, cholera is unknown, smallpox immunization programmes have effectively halted epidemics, neither typhoid nor hepatitis reaches explosive proportions, diarrhoea and dysentery could be much worse, guinea-worm infection is kept relatively low, and malaria is suppressed by acquired immunity, personal preventive measures and oil-spraying. Ibadan's canalized streams and open storm-water drains are polluted, although the council does its best to clean them. Its refuse collection by means of 146 cemented street-pens, some two thousand metal bins and a working fleet of seventeen covered lorries, can operate effectively in only the newer areas of the city. Water-borne sewage is confined very largely to the suburbs, because of the built-up confusion of the old city where, pending the results of a W.H.O. feasibility study, a night-soil system must continue to be run by the council. Side-streets and compounds are more often than not littered and malodorous, in spite of the

[1] *Ibid.*

P*

street-cleaning service. Water supplies are irregular, ill-distributed and inadequate. Nevertheless, there are few violent outbreaks of any major disease. The solution to this paradox, however, is very probably to be found in a high infant mortality rate, which compulsory registration and reporting might only too plainly confirm.

WATER

First contemplated in 1912, the Council's present waterworks were commissioned in 1943, and in 1949 capacity was increased from 1·5 million to 6 million gallons a day supplied from the Eleiyele reservoir. By 1963, without any further expansion in spite of a population growth from 450,000 to 627,000, the daily capacity thus averaged no more than ten gallons a head in a city only seven degrees from the equator. In 1966, however, with the assistance of United States aid, the state government began construction of another dam at Asejire capable of providing twenty-five million gallons a day.[1] When this dam is completed it will be possible to develop a daily supply of thirty-six million gallons of potable water for the city, and for villages in the area of the Ibadan East District Council. Since the latter's population reached 219,000 in 1963, over forty gallons per head per day should be attainable for the population potentially concerned, which in all the circumstances should be a satisfactory standard.

But it is notoriously difficult to lay pipes in the old town because of the intricate pattern of its compounds, the absence of streets, the consequent failure to enforce any kind of building lines, the lack of planned layouts and the broken terrain. The existing supplies are frequently interrupted for urgent repairs to outworn machinery and, probably because of the variations in pressure, seepage occurs permitting contamination of supplies after their filtration. In addition, especially because of the heavy capital expenditure incurred in providing adequate, regular supplies throughout Western Nigeria, the state government has now established the Western Nigeria Water Supply Corporation, to which all water undertakings are being transferred. The city council will thus lose control over its water supply system before the new dam and extensions have been completed, just as it has already lost control over its hospital and schools. Whether or not the efficiency of the system will be improved cannot be forecast at present. The latest information suggests that Ibadan's water supplies will be increased to 18 million gallons a day by not earlier than 1970, instead of by the end of 1968 as planned when work began on the Asejire dam.

[1] Press statement by Project Manager, Asejire Dam, *Daily Sketch*, Ibadan, June 20, 1967.

TRANSPORT

The city council is also being deprived of its public transport system begun in 1964, an Ibadan Joint Transport Board having been initiated in July, 1967.[1] The Board is to consist of four members appointed by the council, two by the State Ministry of Works and Transport, and one by the military governor. It is to operate according to instructions issued by the ministry, and independently of the council except in so far as it is prohibited from publishing by-laws, levying a rate and borrowing money.

Again, the effect of the transfer on the efficiency of the transport undertaking is difficult to forecast. The board has yet to meet and, while its personnel will be freed from service regulations and procedures that are inappropriate to a commercial venture, it will be unable to expand its facilities without going cap-in-hand to the city council for loans, and will be able to cover temporary losses by transfers from council revenues only with the agreement of the dispossessed former owners. The undertaking has never operated more than twenty single-decker buses, of which not more than ten are now in service. It has been confined very largely to routes in the newer suburbs and to the few main roads driven through the dense mass of the old town, particularly because of the hazards of attempting to operate buses in the latter's unpaved alleyways and winding, narrow streets.

The only motor transport capable of threading a way through the maze of compounds and corrugated iron roofs is a small taxi, and there are no less than four thousand privately-operated taxis crowding Ibadan's streets, carrying passengers from one side of the city to the other for only sixpence a head. A public transport system, consisting of single-decker buses and subject to minimum wage legislation, cannot possibly compete with this private motorized fleet. It is true that the bus fare is fourpence per head, but the few vehicles normally in service have no hope of vying with the taxis for convenience, speed and ubiquity except, for instance, if used for conveying children to and from school. Nor are they likely to compete on favourable terms with mammy wagons in Ibadan's rural hinterland, unless they are adapted to carry goods as well as passengers.

ROADS AND BRIDGES

The city council has constructed and maintains about seventy-five miles of metalled roads and streets,[2] of which in 1964–65 about five miles consisted of

---

[1] Information for this section was kindly supplied by the Secretary, Ibadan City Council.
[2] *Ibid.*

trunk B roads—a state responsibility—and fifty-three miles consisted of trunk C roads—a council responsibility.[1] The latter are not necessarily tarred, and many city streets are in fact surfaced with only laterite and are liable to deep erosion during the rainy season. In the six surrounding district council areas, 32 miles of trunk B roads and 538 miles of trunk C roads were reported as being locally maintained in 1964–65. The major arteries, however, are the federal trunk A roads radiating from Ibadan westwards to Abeokuta, northwards to Oyo, north-eastwards to Ife and southwards to Lagos, which, except in the latter case, follow old routes.

None of these roads can compare with those of, say, Lagos as regards capacity and surface, the accident rate on the trunk A roads is especially high, and the goods traffic is heavy. It has been estimated that, in 1963–64, nearly 363,000 tons of non-export non-foreign goods flowed between Northern Nigeria and Western Nigeria and Lagos combined.[2] The main tonnage consisted of foodstuffs, kolanuts, livestock, timber and building materials. At the same time, 249,000 tons of cocoa were moved from the Western markets for the most part through Ibadan; 500,000 tons of groundnuts and 75,000 tons of cottonseed were carried from Northern Nigeria to the coast; and some 500,000 tons of fuel oils were transported from Lagos for distribution in the Western Region. At least half of this traffic was carried by road, and all north–south trunk A roads pass through Ibadan. The movement of passengers cannot be estimated, but 3·3 million people lived in Ibadan province in 1963, and the city is a principal staging-post for all long-distance, through traffic. Sooner or later, therefore, a regional view will have to be taken of its road system and traffic, resulting in an inevitable loss of control by the city council over the planning, construction and, possibly, maintenance of its highway network.

POWER

Ibadan's first electric power station was built by the city and commissioned in 1939. Today, this is another undertaking lost to the Council, as the generation and distribution of electricity are now the prerogatives of the Electricity Corporation of Nigeria, which is a national body. By 1966, the whole of Western Nigeria was to have been supplied in bulk from the Corporation's three units at Ijora in Lagos, having a combined capacity of 107,000

[1] From a special tabulation kindly made by the Acting Chief Statistician, Ministry of Economic Planning and Social Development. See also *Western Nigeria Abstract of Local Government Statistics*, Vol. 1, No. 1.
[2] L. Green and V. Milone: *op. cit.*, para. 136.

kW.[1] But demands grew much more rapidly than anticipated, and the two Ibadan units with a combined capacity of 11,700 kW were re-commissioned. They will certainly remain in operation until the Niger dam undertaking at Kainji begins generating in 1968–69. From then onwards, however, the local power station should be closed down again, and power should be received and distributed from Kainji. In the meantime, because of under-capacity, Ibadan must continue to tolerate load-shedding and power failures that reach their peak in the hot and dry first quarter of the year. In the circumstances, it is probably fortunate that the city has only rudimentary public street lighting and not a single illuminated traffic signal.

The city has never operated a coal gas plant as there are no coal mines in Western Nigeria, but natural gas from the recently exploited eastern oil-fields is now becoming available. In the not too distant future, it may well be commercially possible to pipe gas to Ibadan from storage tanks in Lagos. For the present, however, gas for cooking will continue to be supplied in small domestic containers by private companies. The supplies are adequate and convenient.

TOWN PLANNING AND HOUSING

Although a Nigerian Town and Country Planning Ordinance was gazetted in 1946, and a town planning authority appointed in Ibadan in 1949, these measures produced very little, if any, tangible results. Financial backing was lacking, technical personnel were quite unavailable and the authority soon vanished.[2] Ten years later, as an unprecedented prelude to the federal and state elections of 1959, held prior to Nigeria assuming full independence, money was found to resuscitate many authorities, one of which was Ibadan's. Under the Western Nigeria Town and Country Planning Law, 1956, that very closely reproduces the older ordinance, these planning authorities are corporate bodies appointed by the state and empowered to frame *and execute* approved planning schemes for any area proclaimed by the state on an authority's recommendation. These schemes are not confined to urban areas nor are they limited to the planned control of land uses. They may in fact take the form of comprehensive development projects potentially embracing every economic, social and physical facet of the areas to which they apply. Moreover, once a scheme has been gazetted, the management and control of all local government services existing in the area of the scheme (including

[1] *Ibid.*, paras. 72–4.
[2] This section is based on data given in V. Milone and L. Green: *Administration of Physical Planning in Western Nigeria*, Ministry of Lands and Housing, Ibadan, October 1967.

similar services undertaken by the state and any other public body), auto-matically transfer to the planning authority, which can request the former operators to continue to function, if it is unable to assume their responsibilities itself.

The Ibadan Town Planning Authority (whose boundaries form a circle of six miles radius from the general post office in Gbagi) has hardly begun to use these wide-ranging, potential powers. A planning scheme prepared in 1959 has never got off the ground for lack of capital funds. Its chief executive officer has invariably been seconded from the Town Planning Division of the Ministry of Lands and Housing because of the dearth of trained personnel. It has always occupied inadequate, rented accommodation as if it were intended to be no more than a temporary experiment. It has never been able to initiate any kind of scheme or control in the old town, where planned redevelopment is most urgently needed. Its has been constantly bedevilled by the perennial problem of who owns land originally occupied by ex-tended families or clans, and still kept in trust for them by a headman or *mogaji*.

Between 1961 and 1966, the only funds given to the authority by the state comprised a grant of £6,300 in 1966 for general purposes, and an earlier subvention of £11,300 made in 1964 to enable it to start work on a master plan. For some time, however, the preparation of the plan (which is not a scheme under the Town and Country Planning Law) has been the intermit-tent responsibility of one and sometimes two officers in the town planning division, because the authority has employed no sufficiently competent officer not otherwise engaged. Needless to say, as a result, very wide gaps in know-ledge have still to be closed if the plan is to be based on a through analysis of the city's social, economic and physical structure. For instance, no full-scale housing survey or origin-and-destination traffic count has ever been made. A detailed land use survey of the old town would require an army of workers. A thorough census of crafts has only just been started on a sample basis by a private investigator,[1] who experienced great difficulty in deciding on the boundaries of the quarters into which the city is traditionally divided. Neither the town planning authority nor the town planning division has so far been able to employ a single industrial economist, urban sociologist or economic geographer to make an authentic analysis of the city's economic base, which is so unique an amalgam of traditional and modern commerce, craft and factory-operated industries, and subsistence and market-oriented agriculture. If the master plan is published without closing these and other

[1] Mr. Michael Koll, *vide supra*. But see also A. Callaway: *op. cit.*, for a former study of crafts in Ibadan.

gaps in essential data, it will be founded on seriously inadequate information. Without the appointment of special staff, it will necessarily be the
product of one or two hard-pressed town planners, whose understanding of
the city's social, economic and physical structure will be, by no fault of their
own, in part superficial and in part intuitive. A bad plan is worse than no
plan at all. There is grave danger that, in the present stringent and unsatisfactory circumstances, Ibadan's master plan will indeed be a partially
defective one, although one would expect a capital city to provide a model
for others to emulate.

Even if, in spite of these handicaps, a really acceptable plan is produced,
unfortunately there will be little likelihood of its effective application, unless
there is a drastic change in the attitude of the state and city council towards
town planning.[1] The former places so low a priority on physical planning
that no capital provision for it seems to be contemplated in the five-year
development plan which began in 1968, and the official economists are
certainly opposed to 'urban investment' because of its alleged unproductive-
ness.[2] The city council has never made any financial contribution to the town
planning authority as provided in the law; it threw out a slum improvement
scheme because the old town would naturally be affected, to the possible
advantage of immigrant sections;[3] and a second such scheme, scheduled to be
undertaken during the current six-year development plan period, has been
a dead letter since its conception.

These attitudes run deep. They are not merely a product of bias on the part
of economic planners. In 1967, the town planning authority's offices were
wrecked and the life of its chief executive officer was physically threatened
during the taxi-drivers' strike by elements opposed to the authority's
activities, although these activities have extended to little more than the
inspection and approval of building plans, and the enforcement of building
regulations in the more accessible parts of the city. In the same year, the
authority's officers were set upon by an armed mob when attempting to
enforce a building line by the demolition of an unauthorized mosque, for
which no plans had ever been submitted.

Lawlessness, rioting and the physical intimidation of officers are symptoms
of a social malaise that must itself be diagnosed for town planning purposes,
if the end of planning is to be the good of the planned. It is doubtful, however, if the master plan for Ibadan presently being framed will be primarily

[1] See V. Milone and L. Green: *op. cit.*, paras. 106–8.
[2] *Ibid.*, and *Guideposts for Second National Development Plan*, Federal Ministry of Economic
Development, Lagos, June 1966, paras. 30 and 31.
[3] A. L. Mabogunje: *Ibadan: Black Metropolis*.

concerned to identify and ameliorate conditions which promote social discord. These conditions do not necessarily arise in slum-like areas. Mabogunje points out, for instance, that the traditional residential pattern tends to make these areas the safest parts of the city.[1] He asks if town planning can preserve old cultural values and, if so, which if any of them should be preserved. As far as is known, the master plan will not ask these or similar questions, let alone attempt to solve them.

The Western Nigeria Housing Corporation has also failed to focus its efforts on this fundamental social problem. Although both the city council and the town planning authority are authorized to lay out housing estates and build dwellings, separate legislation was introduced in 1958 to establish a corporation with these special functions (later extended to the development of industrial estates) and with ability to operate in any part of the region (now state). As authorized by the government, it chose to begin its activities in Ibadan and Ikeja (near Lagos), and, in contrast to the authorities whose powers it thus usurped, the corporation has been well endowed with state funds, enabling it to engage adequate professional staff and to progress rapidly with large housing schemes. The Ibadan scheme has been located at Bodija, on four hundred acres of undeveloped land situated north of the city's former wall and lying between the university and the secretariat.[2] Conceived, it seems, as a low-income-group estate, Bodija in fact consists of mostly high-cost houses, of which the corporation has built some two hundred. These houses are suitable only for senior civil servants, senior university staff, prominent businessmen and expatriates. Thus, the scheme can hardly be said to have contributed towards the solution of a social problem connected with the less sophisticated of the city's peoples. Potential residents of Bodija are the most likely to welcome and respect the rule of law, and the least likely to riot, burn and pillage.

JUDICIAL AND POLICE SERVICES

Since the local government police force is not controlled by the city council which partly finances it, but by the Ibadan Divisional Constabulary Council, which has jurisdiction over the entire division (now formed of the city and the six adjacent district council areas); and since Ibadan is the regional headquarters of the larger federal police force, including the traffic police; the only major law-enforcement functions for which the city council

[1] A. L. Mabogunje: 'The Urban Landscape of Ibadan'. See also his 'The Growth of Residential Districts in Ibadan', *Geographical Review*, Vol. 52, No. 1, January 1962.
[2] See V. Milone and L. Green: *op. cit.*, paras. 88 and 89.

itself bears a substantial responsibility are those discharged by the customary courts and its prisons department. Under the Customary Courts Law, 1957–58, these courts have been established in Ibadan by the state to deal with land disputes, debts, divorce cases, other civil matters and minor criminal offences. Their members are appointed by the state local government service board, but their clerks, bailiffs, messengers and other officers and servants are appointed by the city council, which pays all members, officers and servants, and supplies the court buildings. In return for these disbursements, all fees, fines and proceeds of sales ordered by the courts accrue to the city council. By contrast, the magistrates' courts, dealing with major civil and criminal offences, the High Court and the Western Court of Appeal are established, staffed, paid and administered by the judicial department of the state government, as in England and Wales.

The courts have not been seriously affected by the social cleavages which have so insidiously undermined party politics, and the non-customary courts have certainly emerged today as singular examples of probity and honesty in a governmental *débâcle* notorious for its dishonesty and corruption. Presumably, their ability to withstand the corrosion of public life lies in the social status, training and sense of responsibility of their incumbents; but it may also derive from the fact that those incumbents are not elected to their offices.

OTHER SERVICES

The city council's own buildings, and the land on which they are sited, are managed by its estates section, which also supervises the city markets; and, as previously noted, the council operates a refuse service on a fee-paying basis. But the affairs of the markets have for many years been the concern of the Market Women and Women Traders' Association, and each market usually appoints its own headwoman to settle disputes and represent it.[1] The University of Ibadan operates its own refuse service. The small fire service of half a dozen modern fire-fighting vehicles is located at the secretariat and run by the state. Directly assessed income tax on annual incomes over £300, and all P.A.Y.E. income tax, is assessed and collected by the Regional Tax Board of the Ministry of Finance, which also issues all motor-vehicle licences and driving licences. The television and radio services are a state responsibility; the forest plantations are now mostly owned and managed by the federal and state governments; the airport, which is large enough for only domestic services, is operated by the Nigeria Airways Corporation; the

[1] For an account of 'Queen Mothers' in similar Ghanaian markets, see R. M. Lawson's letter 'Markets in Ghana', *West Africa*, No. 2556, May 28, 1966, p. 597.

railway connecting Ibadan to Lagos and the sea, to the northern states and, *via* the north, to the eastern parts of Nigeria, is a federal undertaking, as is the post and telecommunications service.

The adequacy of some of these services and undertakings can hardly be assessed from Ibadan's standpoint. But, for instance, a fire service of this size cannot be expected to serve the 1·1 million people living in Ibadan and the six surrounding district council areas, except in a token manner. Postal deliveries are not made to all areas of Ibadan, and it is particularly difficult to locate addresses in the built-up maze of the old town. In 1965, Ibadan had on the average only one telephone for every hundred inhabitants, *including* some two thousand telephones in government offices, which thus accounted for nearly one-third of the total.[1] And not even the railway's own management considers it to be an efficient undertaking.[2]

LOCAL GOVERNMENT FINANCE

To analyse the finances of the web of government agencies operating in Ibadan and its rural environs is a task far beyond the capacity of this short study. The accounts of national public corporations are not presented in a manner facilitating a breakdown of income and expenditure on revenue account for such an area. To allocate capital expenditure regionally or zonally is even more difficult. Similar problems arise in connection with federal government departments and institutions, except in the cases of the University and University College Hospital. Even state undertakings and departments present problems of allocation that can be solved only by much more research. Nevertheless, an attempt should certainly be made to frame comprehensive accounts for the capital city and its hinterland, especially for the purposes of economic and fiscal planning. That no one has any inkling of the magnitude of these accounts, in spite of an unbroken series of development plans beginning in 1945, exposes a serious weakness in the current practice of state planning which should be rectified as soon as possible. One solution is suggested in the conclusions below, under *The Future Government of Ibadan.*

Revenue and expenditure

For lack of data, in this study information on only local government

[1] L. Green and V. Milone: *op. cit.*, para. 81 and Table 25.
[2] Press reports of proceedings of a Tribunal of Inquiry into the Nigerian Railway Corporation, 1966–67.

income and expenditure can be presented and analysed. The results of a special tabulation of returns for the financial year ending on March 31, 1965, are summarized in Tables I and II.[1] That these tables cannot be reconciled is but a further indication of the paucity of reliable information. If, however, allowance is made for the fact that the P.A.Y.E. revenue was actually received in 1965–66, the *percentage* distributions of total revenue and expenditure do tally quite closely.

Concentrating on percentages, therefore, it will be seen that the Ibadan City Council accounted for about 74 per cent of the income and expenditure of the seven councils, and thus dominated both tables. As regards revenue, nearly 39 per cent was accounted for by the council's rates. These consisted of a water rate and an electricity rate. The former was charged at 12s. per head per year on all persons having no taps of their own and thus using street stand-pipes. Householders connected to the mains were charged according to floor area, and institutional consumers were metered. The electricity rate was charged at a flat 3s. per head per annum, and was intended to defray the cost of street lighting. A further 31 per cent of revenue was accounted for by personal income tax. This accrued to the council either by way of a sum paid annually in arrears by the regional state government and equivalent to the receipts of all tax deductions made by employers under the P.A.Y.E. scheme from wages and salaries of persons resident in Ibadan and earning not more than £300 a year, or by way of the proceeds of income tax directly assessed and collected by the council on all persons resident in Ibadan earning not more than £300 a year and not falling under the P.A.Y.E. scheme. Fines and fees, totalling 11 per cent of the council's revenue, accrued from the customary courts and from bicycle and dog licences. Grants aggregating 6 per cent of revenue were received from the regional government for public health purposes; nearly 7 per cent was accounted for by trading, that is, by receipts from the public transport undertaking; and a little over 6 per cent consisted of rents from council properties (shown under 'miscellaneous').

The revenue of the six district councils closely followed this pattern, except that they lacked a trading undertaking and relied very much more on directly assessed income tax receipts (since the P.A.Y.E. scheme applies mainly to government servants and the employees of large businesses, who for the most part reside in the city).

[1] Prepared from detailed returns kindly tabulated by the Acting Chief Statistician, Ministry of Economic Planning and Social Development, and from additional data supplied by the Assistant Secretary, Ministry of Local Government and Chieftancy Affairs, Western State. See also *Western Nigeria Abstract of Local Government Statistics*, Vol. 1, No. 1, *op. cit.*

TABLE I

Ibadan Councils: Local Government Revenue, 1964–65

Council	Rates £	%	D.A. tax £	%	P.A.Y.E.* £	%	Fines and Fees £	%	Grants £	%	Trading £	%	Miscellaneous £	%	Total £	%
Ibadan City Council	502,428	38·5	87,008	6·7	316,790	24·3	147,665	11·3	81,453	6·3	84,587	6·5	83,510	6·4	1,303,441	74·6
Ibadan East D.C.	51,634	45·8	46,163	40·9	4,613	4·1	6,161	5·5	3,959	3·5	—		260	0·2	112,810	6·5
Ibadan North D.C.	47,647	48·3	38,196	38·7	4,704	4·8	7,355	7·4	327	0·3	—		510	0·5	98,739	5·6
Ibadan South D.C.	17,160	46·9	16,105	44·0	1,579	4·3	1,318	3·6	383	1·0	—		57	0·2	36,602	2·1
Ibadan South-east D.C.	30,961	46·8	26,461	40·0	2,659	4·0	4,674	7·1	1,360	2·0	—		85	0·1	66,200	3·8
Ibadan South-west D.C.	24,208	41·5	20,235	34·7	5,524	9·4	5,184	8·9	3,073	5·3	—		141	0·2	58,365	3·3
Ibadan West D.C.	35,852	49·9	29,454	41·0	2,402	3·4	3,734	5·2	302	0·4	—		82	0·1	71,826	4·1
Total	709,890	40·6	263,622	15·1	338,271	19·4	176,091	10·1	90,877	5·2	84,587	4·8	84,645	4·8	1,747,983	100·0

* Paid in arrears in 1965–66.

D.C. = district council.

D.A. Tax = directly assessed income tax.

P.A.Y.E. = income tax withheld from monthly salary payments.

Sources: Council Returns, 1964–65, Ministry of Economic Planning and Social Development, Western State; Ministry of Local Government and Chieftaincy Affairs, Western State.

TABLE II

Ibadan Councils: Local Government Expenditure, 1964-65

Council		Council Allowances	Secretary's dept.	Precepts	Treasurer's dept.	General	Works (recurrent)	Works (capital)	Prisons	Judicial	Police	Education	Survey	Public health	Forests	Trading	Traditional Offices	Total
Ibadan City Council	£	1,218	28,664	85,182	39,653	86,112	290,427	13,823	19,750	35,743	20,207	11,914	9,319	91,278	5,535	66,427	12,879	818,131
	%	0·15	3·50	10·41	4·85	10·52	25·50	1·69	2·41	4·37	2·47	1·46	1·14	11·16	0·68	8·12	1·57	73·52
Ibadan East District Council	£	740	1,740	26,402	9,342	4,764	4,011	23,318	—	3,100	550	840	—	5,915	—	—	1,869	82,591
	%	0·89	2·11	31·97	11·31	5·77	4·86	28·23	—	3·75	0·67	1·02	—	7·16	—	—	2·26	7·42
Ibadan North District Council	£	1,100	1,828	8,459	8,205	541	14,621	6,702	—	3,647	712	1,047	—	9,262	1,534	—	1,602	59,269
	%	1·87	3·08	14·27	13·85	0·91	24·67	11·31	—	6·15	1·20	1·77	—	15·63	2·59	—	2·70	5·33
Ibadan South District Council	£	465	2,103	—	3,257	549	2,830	—	620	3,344	2,890	2,095	—	1,025	—	—	296	19,474
	%	2·39	10·80	—	16·73	2·82	14·53	—	3·18	17·17	14·84	10·76	—	5·26	—	—	1·52	1·75
Ibadan South-east District Council	£	828	1,542	11,819	5,344	1,427	8,758	490	—	3,206	—	990	—	3,486	—	—	235	38,125
	%	2·17	4·04	31·00	14·02	3·74	22·97	1·29	—	8·41	—	2·60	—	9·14	—	—	0·62	3·43
Ibadan South-west District Council	£	638	1,375	10,208	4,030	2,245	5,647	4,124	—	3,343	159	1,118	—	3,828	12,446	—	710	49,871
	%	1·28	2·76	20·47	8·08	4·50	11·32	8·27	—	6·70	0·32	2·24	—	7·68	24·96	—	1·42	4·48
Ibadan West District Council	£	642	2,206	11,117	5,567	—	16,620	—	—	3,597	340	704	—	3,610	336	—	521	45,260
	%	1·42	4·87	24·56	12·30	—	36·72	—	—	7·95	0·75	1·56	—	7·98	0·74	—	1·15	4·07
Total	£	5,640	39,458	153,187	75,398	95,638	342,914	48,457	20,370	55,980	24,858	18,708	9,319	118,494	19,851	66,427	18,112	1,112,721
	%	0·51	3·55	13·77	6·78	8·59	30·82	4·35	1·83	5·03	2·23	1·68	0·84	10·64	1·78	5·97	1·63	100·00

Source: Council Returns, 1964-65, Ministry Economic Planning and Social Development, Western State.

As regards the city council's expenditure, 37 per cent was accounted for by its public works, essentially those concerned with the maintenance of roads and water supplies. The only other substantial outlays were incurred by public health activities (11 per cent), which included both environmental and personal health services; by education (12 per cent), which reflected precepts made by the joint education board and scholarship payments; by the transport undertaking (8 per cent); by the prevention of crime (9 per cent), involving local government police, officers of the customary courts and prison expenses; and under miscellaneous heads (nearly 11 per cent). The six district councils also tended to spend most heavily on public works, education (comprising precepts and scholarships), health and the prevention of crime. But their cost of tax collection and administration seems to have been proportionately much higher than in Ibadan itself, presumably because P.A.Y.E. deductions were paid into the regional government's own tax office, and the administrative costs involved were thus borne by the latter.

An alternative source of revenue

Since nearly 70 per cent of the city council's revenue was derived from rates and taxes, they obviously constituted the controlling factors in its overall expenditure. And since personal income tax formed so large a proportion of total receipts, undoubtedly the council was, and is, in a favourable position relative to local authorities in most other parts of the world. Indeed, on the basis of published statistics, the local councils of Ibadan Division received 45 per cent of all personal income tax revenues raised in the division in 1964–65.[1] Nevertheless there are two pitfalls. On the one hand, the city council will soon be deprived of its water-rate powers, or act merely as a conduit for the precepts of the Water Supply Corporation. On the other hand, the state is in straitened circumstances and there is no constitutional obstacle to its reduction of the quantum of income tax receipts currently accruing to the local councils. Thus, the city council has already approached the Ministry of Local Government for authority to levy a general rate on immovable property.

To levy a property rate in Ibadan, however, would be no easy matter, especially because of the history and nature of land ownership. When the land was originally given to an extended family it was held in trust by the *mogaji*, no family member owned any portion of the land individually, and every member had the right to cultivate any portion which was not being

1 *Western Nigeria Statistical Bulletin*, Vol. VIII, Nos. 1 and 2, and *Western Nigeria Abstract of Local Government Statistics*, Vol. 1, No. 1. plus information on P.A.Y.E. allocations made by the Ministry of Local Government.

used by another member. The boundaries of the areas associated with individual members through such usage were naturally ill-defined, dependent on personal industry and unstable. Permanent cultivation and the construction of houses by individuals tended to stabilize this fluid situation, and eventually established prescriptive rights of ownership of the crops and buildings. In some instances, portions of family land even became recognized as being individually owned. But, as a rule, the family has remained the collective owner of the land, and it still retains the right to prevent any member from alienating the portion he occupies or owns, except by transfer or bequest to another member.[1] In principle, therefore, only the family can sell the land, and what constitutes the family today may well be obscure and disputable. The state government maintains a voluntary deeds registry, but it cannot guarantee title to any land registered, the boundaries of the areas surveyed and registered frequently overlap, as many as ten claimants will dispute the title to the same piece of land, and land is often transferred by persons who have no legal right to do so.[2]

In these circumstances, it is well-nigh impossible to levy a rate on the land which is payable by the owner. Moreover, even when land is in fact sold, the relevant documents are unlikely to reflect the actual price paid for it, since there is a long tradition of tax evasion.[3] The same problem arises with the sale of houses; but in the immigrant areas these are more likely to be leased or rented, and the traditional house in Ibadan is designed to accommodate a varying number of related nuclear families, each paying some form of rent to an individual owner.[4] Hence, contrary to the principles of local taxation in developing countries,[5] the only practicable solution seems to be a rate levied on buildings according to their assessed annual value. Unfortunately, the Local Government Law authorizes the levy of a rate on tenements, and defines a tenement as land *including* buildings. Unless and until the law is changed, therefore, in order to permit the separate rating of buildings, it is really not feasible to introduce any kind of general property tax. Certainly, to levy a rate on land is, for all practical purposes, out of the question; unless, for instance, the trusteeship vested in the *mogajis* were to be assumed by the state, which then allocated the land to individual members of each family as a

---

[1] S. A. Aribisala: *op. cit.*, and P. C. Lloyd: *Yoruba Land Law*.
[2] V. Milone and L. Green: *op. cit.*, paras. 57 and 62.
[3] See G. O. Orewa: *Taxation in Western Nigeria*, London, 1962, Chs. 2 and 9.
[4] See A. L. Mabogunje: 'The Growth of Residential Districts in Ibadan'.
[5] As enunciated, for instance, by U. K. Hicks: *Development from Below*, London, 1961, Ch. 16. For property rating previously practised in Mid-Western Nigeria (formerly Western Nigeria) see G. O. Orewa: *op. cit.*, Ch. 10, who also argues in favour of a general introduction of such rating.

land reform measure. But the trust extends to all past and future generations, as well as the present.

GOVERNMENT STAFF

As in the case of finance, no reliable estimate can be made of the total staff employed by the web of public and semi-public agencies operating in Ibadan and the surrounding district council areas. But, in 1964–65, there were about 3,100 teachers in the teacher-training colleges and secondary and primary schools of this composite area, of whom at least 2,350 worked in Ibadan itself.[1] The Western Nigerian statutory corporation employees numbered 2,057, the majority of whom lived in the same area, and mostly in the city. The staff of the regional government in Western Nigeria totalled 11,977, many of whom were directly or indirectly engaged on works and services connected with Ibadan and its rural hinterland.[2]

At a very conservative estimate, therefore, in 1964–65 at least 6,000 people were most probably employed in such locally oriented activities by public and semi-public agencies *other than* local government councils and federal authorities (including the federal police force and post and telephone services). By contrast, the local government staff of the Ibadan City Council and six adjacent district councils numbered no more than 1,641, excluding the local government police who totalled 686. Of this local government staff, 18 were employed in the administrative grade, 21 in the executive and higher technical grades, 988 in the clerical and junior technical grades, and 614 in other grades (consisting of messengers and manual workers). In Ibadan itself, the city council employed 800 persons in eight departments, namely, the secretary's department, the treasurer's department, the public health department, the city engineer's department (including the waterworks and survey), the judicial department, the prisons department, forestry and the passenger transport service.[3]

[1] See *Western Nigeria Annual Abstract of Education Statistics*, Vol. 6.

[2] See *Western Nigeria Statistical Bulletin*, Vol. VIII, Nos. 1 and 2, for statistics of employees of statutory corporations and civil servants.

[3] These statistics are derived from a special tabulation kindly made by the Acting Chief Statistician, Ministry of Economic Planning and Social Development, and *Western Nigeria Abstract of Local Government Statistics*, Vol. 1, No. 1. In 1964–65, the Ibadan City Council employed the following staff: secretary's dept., 131; treasurer's dept., 138; public health dept., 102; city engineer's dept. (including waterworks and survey) 134; judicial dept., 135; prisons dept., 49; forestry, 6; public transport service, 131. Of these, 17 were in the administrative grade, 14 in the executive and higher technical grades, 749 in the clerical and junior technical grades, and 20 in other grades. Of the six district councils, only Ibadan South had an officer in the administrative grade, all had one in the executive and higher technical grades (except for Ibadan East, which had two), and most employees fell into the category of 'other grades'.

The Local Government Service Board

For the last ten years, personnel in the administrative, executive and higher technical grades have been appointed to the local government councils by a Local Government Service Board, together with the members of customary courts and superintendents or supervisors of education in the service of joint boards of education. The board consists of a chairman and three permanent members appointed by the state government. It is empowered to make all appointments and promotions in the unified service, to transfer personnel between posts and councils, and to discipline them.

The problems of a unified service

The advantages to the local government councils are the removal of obstacles to the transfer of personnel to gain experience or to help new councils, the standardization of emoluments and conditions of service, the improvement of status and morale, and the possibilities of formal training provided by a larger service (e.g. potential higher-grade administrative officers receive from six to nine months' training at a local government school in Ibadan). By the same token, however, the grading of councils for salary purposes can lead to the loss of a good secretary or treasurer who must be transferred to reach the top of his scale; an administrator may have difficulty in appreciating to the full the special problems of local communities if he is moved too frequently; and, if movement is minimal, a family man may experience serious personal problems upon being uprooted from a community in which, for instance, his children have been born and bred. Transfer from community to community within Western Nigeria is not to be compared with transfer from department to department within the secretariat. Nevertheless, in principle, the advantages appear to lie with unification, although it does entail a substantial state invasion of local self-government preserves.

Unfortunately, hoped-for improvements in salary scales have still to be realized, so that a relatively young man who reached the top in, say, 1961, continues to receive the same monthly pay cheque and has no prospect of a further increase unless he leaves the service. In Ibadan itself, the city engineer and water superintendent are seconded from state government service, and the medical officer of health is appointed on special terms which have yet to be ratified. In short, the basic problem of assembling and keeping sufficient, skilled personnel to form an adequate and talented local government service has yet to be solved. Since it is the calibre of this service that will ultimately determine the calibre of local government, a high priority should clearly be given to the early solution of this complex and fundamental problem.

INTER-GOVERNMENTAL RELATIONS

The informal and volatile power relationships obtaining between the city council and the state government before the military takeover have already been described. Now, of course, party politics are banned and the formal relationships more nearly reflect reality; that is, the council is headed by an administrator appointed by the state, who is responsible to the military governor through the Ministry of Local Government and Chieftaincy Affairs. The result of this chain of responsibility, and of the facts that two state officers are seconded as departmental heads and the senior officers are not appointed, promoted, transferred or disciplined by the council, is apparently some ambivalence on the part of council officials, whose criticism of state policy in city matters tends to be inhibited. But, if so, this reticence is a small price to pay for saving government from complete collapse.

Prior to the advent of the military government, most formal controls were exercised by the Ministry of Local Government and Chieftaincy Affairs (most directly through inspectors appointed under the Local Government Law) and, before 1961, by the Ministry of Education. The law empowers the state to create a council by an instrument variable, as to constitution, powers and functions, within defined statutory limits; and to revoke the instrument at any time, after giving the council an opportunity to make representations. Where councils set up a joint board to operate a common service, the instrument creating it is subject to state approval; and the state can itself set up a joint board by its own instrument, with the concurrence of one or more councils. All by-laws are subject to state approval; the latter can initiate inquiries at any time into any council activity; it is empowered to dissolve a council (replacing it by either a committee of management or an administrator); the Ministry of Local Government can prohibit a council from incurring expenditure where it considers the latter has failed to levy a sufficient tax or to collect sufficient proceeds of a tax; and the state can carry out any work and enforce any by-law or function in default of a council, either by the council itself on the state's direction, or by any other body or person.

As already observed, the Ibadan City Council, which is statutorily obliged to appoint a secretary and treasurer, has long ceased to exercise control over its senior officers, as they fall under the jurisdiction of the state-appointed Local Government Service Board; nor does it appoint the members of its customary courts who, together with superintendents or supervisors of education, are also subject to the board's administration. Financial control over the council's operations is exercised by the state in respect of the approval of all borrowings and investments, and all advances and loans; the Ministry of Local Government circulates memoranda setting forth the mandatory procedures to be followed in the Council's financial business; all of its estimates of expenditure must be submitted to the Ministry for approval and, if necessary, modification; debts aggregating more than £250 in any financial year may be written off only with prior Ministerial approval; and its accounts are audited by a state appointee and rendered annually to the ministry.

Problems of control and co-ordination

All these provisions apply to the city council and district councils under the present military government, and certainly provide many opportunities for the close supervision of the principal local government functions and procedures. In comparison with the situation obtaining in, say, the United States or Great Britain, the controls in fact extend well beyond the legitimate frontiers of state intervention. But the situation in Ibadan is by no means identical. The capital territory of Washington has never enjoyed local self-government, and the extent of state controls in Western Nigeria has actually been declining in recent years, in so far as the councils have been increasingly deprived of former functions to which controls were attached. Furthermore, a proper appreciation of the controlling hand of the state in Ibadan today demands a review of its relations not only with the city and district councils, but with every other public and semi-public agency involved. In this short study, such a review is not possible. One can only comment that the very complexity of the capital's administrative web presents a governmental problem of the first order.

This problem of co-ordination and control is far from being officially recognized. Yet knowledgeable opinion holds that, in spite of the five-year development plans, each agency has tended to go its own way, in its own time, often in ignorance of what others might be planning or doing. Communication and co-operation between and within ministries, between statutory bodies and their parent ministries, and between statutory bodies themselves (including local government councils), have been intermittent and generally minimal. Perverseness has tended to cloud their relationships. A case in point, with direct repercussions on Ibadan, is the recurrent by-passing of the Town Planning Division of the Ministry of Lands and Housing in respect of its statutory responsibility for controlling land uses, exerciseable by itself and through the Ibadan Town Planning Authority.[1] Other ministries have frequently decided on the siting of development without prior reference to either the division or the authority; another division of the same ministry has even done so. For example, at one time neither agency was apparently consulted beforehand by the Lands Division in respect of the acquisition of land in Ibadan for petrol pumps and service stations, which were consequently sited at busy intersections and traffic roundabouts; nor at other times were they consulted beforehand by the Housing Corporation in connection with the location and planning of the Bodija housing estate, or by the Ministry of Health in connection with the proposed installation of a major sewerage system and the location of the new specialist hospital, or by the federal government in connection with the siting of new housing for police on the Oyo Road.

This perverseness in inter-agency relations seems to have been a growing disease of the regional government since at least its first breakdown in 1962. Certainly, as the Somolu Tribunal hearings confirm,[2] co-ordinated control of public agencies, undertakings and activities plunged to a nadir by 1965, undermined by graft, political chicanery and a naked struggle for power. The government tottered on the verge of collapse again in January 1966. Whatever formal controls over local government and other public agencies in Ibadan may have existed, their operation had fallen into the hands of unprincipled political manipulators. The task is now one of reconstruction, in which there are obviously great opportunities for reorganizing the city's administration in the light of its recent traumatic experiences.

THE FUTURE GOVERNMENT OF IBADAN

The accelerating trend to deprive the city council of its former functions; the consequent operation of a growing number of services by federal ministries, state ministries, federal and state public corporations, joint boards, other statutory bodies and voluntary organizations; and the subsequent mounting complexity of government in Ibadan, all spring ultimately from deep-seated social and political causes. For one thing, a repeated resort to unbridled violence, bribery and intimidation is wholly incompatible with the principles of representative and responsible government enshrined in the Western Nigeria Local Government Law. Secondly, that form of

[1] See V. Milone and L. Green: *op. cit.*, paras. 53, 59, 87 and 89.
[2] Set up in 1967 to investigate the assets of former members of the Western Region Government and senior civil servants since 1956.

government can function only in a society enjoying a wide consensus of opinion on fundamental ends, and means to their attainment. The warlike circumstances attending Ibadan's formative years, the fissures still existing between its ethnic components and the anarchy yet surfacing at times of tension, have all conspired to deny to representative and responsible government the stable foundations essential to its flowering in the city today. Ends remain socially disruptive; means to their attainment are incompatible with the rule of law; consensus of opinion is not apparent.

Thirdly, besides virtually ignoring Ibadan's function as a regional capital, the constitution created for the city council in 1961 has compounded the hazards of government. The twin bases have been a century-old institution of civil and military chiefs, and a Victorian-inspired English county council system. The former, founded ultimately on the extended family and clan, was appropriate to a polyglot association of tribal warriors, it is deeply rooted in the old, indigenous Yoruba culture, and it is naturally highly conservative in character. The latter is a product of entirely foreign circumstances, and traceable to the English Municipal Corporations Act of 1835. Formulated during an industrial revolution, this seminal legislation was the child of reforming Whig lawyers who fused the new radicalism of eighteenth-century Europe with older traditions of city government. The twin bases of the Ibadan City Council thus differ as chalk from cheese; and they are both inappropriate to the city's current development needs. For example, the one basis is dependent upon the perpetuation of an indigenous cultural nucleus—the extended family—which is difficult to reconcile with the organizational requirements of modern commerce and industry, where the family business is being outmoded and contractual relations must replace kinship ties. The other basis pertains to *laissez-faire* capitalism, which can hardly be made compatible with the concept of economic, physical and social planning by the state governments of developing countries.

Possible solutions

The rapid emasculation and demotion of a city council established in only 1961 bear witness to the anachronisms of its constitution, and to the inherent structural weaknesses of its social foundations. What kind of government should replace this wreckage of past hopes and fears? Perhaps the short-run answer lies in trends already nascent in the devolution of functions to single-purpose, appointed authorities, each having jurisdiction over Ibadan and the surrounding district council areas. In principle, a heterogeneous collection of agencies, both public and private, would but hold a mirror to the city's differentiated society. Their proliferation would present the unscrupulous politician with too many heads to corrupt, prevent any one ethnic group from seizing all the reins of government, and, by fostering inter-agency competition, tend to diminish that disinterested lethargy which only too often characterizes the operation of public services.

The dangers of deliberately encouraging a heterogeneous collection of agencies at the expense of a most-purpose city council are real and obvious, particularly as the present trend is towards *appointed* boards. The devolution of functions would have to be made with discretion and logic, and the public's active participation in the management of its own affairs could hardly be permanently denied, in spite of the traditional procedures ossified in the chieftaincy system. But, even using appointed boards, very wide scope indeed could be provided for voluntary work, especially in the fields of education, public health, maternity and child welfare, community development (including the maintenance and cleaning of streets, refuse collection and water distribution), other local capital works (including housing), craft co-operatives, marketing and industrial and agricultural development. Public participation in these fields by way of voluntary organizations is already immense, as briefly indicated in this study. There is every reason to suggest that government in Ibadan should build still further on the innumerable interest groups already honey-combing the city's society. Government should actively seek them out, recognize them for financial and technical assistance, and use them on a large scale to operate services for which they have been voluntarily created.

There are dangers, too, in encouraging a proliferation of agencies without introducing a very firm hand to guide and co-ordinate their activities and finances. A gross duplication of facilities and services can easily arise. Excursions into the Parkinsonian wastes of empire-building can be all too frequent; but a concentration of money and men is required to achieve a progressive improvement of physical living conditions in urban areas so congested as old Ibadan's.

Very possibly, part of the answer to these problems lies in distinguishing between (i) the continuing, day-to-day operation of services over the city and its immediate hinterland by single-purpose agencies, such as joint education, health, transport, works, highways and water boards, and (ii) the once-and-for-all comprehensive development of limited areas of the city and its hinterland by a special, multi-purpose authority. The former could permit voluntary bodies to play a leading role in their activities, and could consist very largely of appointed representatives of such bodies. The latter necessarily demands cadres of highly trained technical and professional officers, advanced managerial and engineering techniques, a tightly knit organization, vast powers and ample financial resources. Very possibly, also, part of the answer lies in the continuous planning of Ibadan's physical development, by means of which the controlling hand of a higher government authority may, especially by regulating the pattern and timing of the use of land, weave together and programme the activities of many local agencies according to priorities determined in conjunction with the state's economic and social planning. Yet another part of the answer possibly lies in just as firm fiscal planning, financial programming and budgetary control by a higher authority, according to the same development priorities. And, finally, Ibadan's capital status needs to be recognized by something more than an empty city title.

If so much of the answer to the city's problems of government lies in these possible directions, there is good reason to suggest that the multi-purpose development authority required could be fashioned out of the present Housing Corporation,[1] which could act as an expert, executive arm of the state under the control of a Ministry of Town and Country Planning (in place of the existing Ministry of Lands and Housing). There is also good reason to suggest that the city council could be divested of its remaining service functions by devolving them to joint boards, and be reconstituted as a state-appointed physical and fiscal planning authority. The boards and this authority could exercise jurisdiction on behalf of the state over Ibadan and its immediate environs, which could be designated as the state's capital territory and include the areas of the six district councils. Since the joint boards would then assume the district councils' functions, too, the latter would naturally be dissolved; the Water Supply Corporation could either be replaced by a joint board for this composite area, or be subjected to the physical and fiscal planning controls of the new city council in relation to such area; and the Ibadan Town Planning Authority would be merged with the city council to form part and parcel of its machinery. While the council's fiscal, financial and budgetary controls could not apply to federal agencies, they could certainly extend to the operations of all joint boards and state and voluntary bodies within the capital territory; and its physical planning controls should undoubtedly apply to all users of land, whether public or private, or local, state or federal.

These suggestions would not violate the Housing Corporation, Town and Country Planning and Local Government Laws, and could be implemented

---

[1] See V. Milone and L. Green: *op. cit.*, paras. 128–9; for a suggested reorganization of the Ministry, see paras. 113–19. At the same time, the state would have to revise its attitude to town and country planning.

for the most part without statutory innovation or amendment. The Housing Corporation Law already contains most extensive powers of development; the members of a local government council can already be appointed as the sole members of a local planning authority; and joint boards are already obliged to precept on their parent councils, as they are prohibited from levying a rate (and from borrowing money themselves). As a planning authority appointed under the Town and Country Planning Law, the city council could become a regional body exercising on behalf of the state the functions of research, analysis, programming and planning in connection with the social, economic and physical development of the capital territory. It could also provide the information, guidance and, where necessary, initiative needed by the other, primarily voluntary, agencies to manage their particular services in this area. As a fiscal, financial and budgetary authority operating on behalf of the state under the Local Government and other Laws, the council could levy all local rates and taxes, receive all authorized personal income tax revenue, charge all permitted fees, receive all customary court fines, approve and if necessary modify all annual budgets of locally-operating public agencies (other than federal agencies), receive all grants and raise all moneys for the capital territory. And it could generally inform and advise all such agencies on fiscal, financial and budgetary programmes, whether federal or not.

Doubtless, in the first instance and if only because of Ibadan's official status as the state capital, the new city council would be a state-appointed authority. In later years, however, it could increasingly represent the territorial community it would help to stabilize, shape and organize. Mapo Hall might then rise above not a confusion of roofs and people notorious for disorder and conflict, but a well-knit African city renowned for the responsibility and dignity of its civic life. Yet, it must be recognized that no real progress towards self-government could come to pass without the enduring support of the mass of the people. And one should not expect a lasting consensus of opinion on any major issue in this volatile city, unless, perhaps, the new élite were once more to grasp the nettle of civic leadership. But, generally speaking, this élite is Christian and immigrant; the mass of the people are Muslim and native to Ibadan. Through lineage, family and custom they still cling to the traditional hierarchy of chiefs, clothe the *Olubadan* with the authority of history, and reject the stranger who would seek to lead them. Quite possibly, only a social revolution could dissolve the impasse.

ACKNOWLEDGEMENTS

This study could not have been written without the active assistance of many people, and without drawing upon many sources of information. The sources are acknowledged in the footnotes. In addition, a special debt of gratitude is owed to the following persons: Mr. A. O. Ogunniyi, Acting Chief Statistician, Ministry of Economic Planning and Social Development, Western State; Mr. S. O. Tokun, Principal Town Planning Officer, Ministry of Lands and Housing, Western State; Mr. R. H. Whittam, C.F.R., C.B.E., Adviser on Internal Revenue, Ministry of Finance, Western State; Mr. M. A. Adesiyun, Assistant Secretary, Ministry of Local Government and Chieftaincy Affairs, Western State; Mr. Abebisi Aladejana, Assistant Librarian, Reference Library, Ibadan University (for a bibliography of works on Ibadan); Mr. Olutinwo Ajibola, Secretary, Ibadan City Council; and the author's colleague, Mr. Vincent Milone Ford Foundation Adviser, Town Planning Division, Ministry of Lands and Housing, Western State, who gave up much valuable time to discuss many of the issues involved. All expressions of opinion are, however, the author's and they are not to be attributed to either the Ministry of Lands and Housing or the Ford Foundation.

Bibliography on Great Cities in General

Amsterdam University, Sociographical Department. *Urban Core and Inner City*. Leiden, 1967.

Ash, Maurice. *Regions of Tomorrow: towards the open city*. Evelyn, Adams & Mackay, London, 1969.

Bollens, John Constantinus, and Schmandt, Henry J. *The Metropolis: its people, politics, and economic life*. Harper & Row, New York, 2nd edn. 1970.

Botero, Giovanni. *Reason of State and the Greatness of Cities*. English transl., Routledge, London, 1956.

Daland, Robert T. (ed.). *Comparative Urban Research: the administration and politics of cities* (Seminar held at the University of North Carolina, 1967). Beverly Hills, 1969,

Dickinson, Robert E. *City and Region: a geographical interpretation*. Humanities Press, New York, 1964.

Doxiadis, Konstantinos A. *Ekistics: an introduction to the science of human settlements*. O.U.P., London, 1968.

Geddes, Patrick. *Cities in Evolution*. London, rev. edn. Williams & Norgate, 1949.

Greer, Scott. *Emerging City*. Free Press of Glencoe, New York, 1962.

Greer, Scott. *Metropolitics: a study of political culture, etc*. New York, Wiley, 1963.

Halász, D. (compiler). *Metropolis: a select bibliography of administrative and other problems in metropolitan areas throughout the world*, 2nd edn. Nijhoff, The Hague, 1967.

Hall, Peter. *The World Cities*. London, Faber, 2nd edn. 1969.

Howard, Ebenezer. *Garden Cities of Tomorrow*. London, 1902.

Jacob, Philip Ernest, and Tuscano, James V. (eds.). *The Integration of Political Communities*. Lippincott, Philadelphia, 1964.

Jones, Victor. *Metropolitan Government*. University Press, Chicago, 1942.

Mandelker, Daniel R. *Green Belts and Urban Growth*. Univ. of Wisconsin Press, Madison, 1962.

Meyerson, Martin, *et al*. *Face of the Metropolis*. Random House, New York, 1963.

Ministry of Transport, U.K. *Traffic in Towns* (Buchanan Report). H.M.S.O., London, 1963.

Mumford, Lewis. *The City in History: its origins, its transformations, and its prospects*. Secker & Warburg, London, 1961.

Mumford, Lewis. *The Culture of Cities*. Harcourt, New York, 1938.

Osborn, Frederic J. *Green-belt Cities*, 2nd edn. Schocken, New York, 1969.

Osborn, Frederic, and Whittick, A. *New Towns: the answer to Megalopolis*. Hill, London, 1963.

Parkins, Maurice Frank. *City Planning in Soviet Russia: with an interpretative bibliography*. University Press, Chicago, 1953.

Robson, William A. *Local Government in Crisis*, 2nd English edn. Allen & Unwin, London, 1968.

Royal Commission on Local Government in England. *Report* Cmnd. 4040. London, 1969.

Scott, Stanley, and Bollens, John C. *Governing a Metropolitan Region*. Institute of Governmental Studies, Berkeley, California, 1968.

Self, Peter. *Cities in Flood*, Faber, 2nd edn. London, 1961.

Senior, Derek, *The Regional City*. Longmans, London, 1966.

United Nations, Department of Economic and Social Affairs, 1967. *Planning of Metropolitan Areas and New Towns* (papers given at two conferences). New York, 1967.

Walsh, Ann Marie Hauck. *The Urban Challenge to Government: an international comparison of thirteen cities.* Praeger, New York, 1969.

Select Bibliography

CLASSIFIED BY CITIES

AMSTERDAM

Brugmans, H. *Het Nieuwe Amsterdam*. Amsterdam, 1925.

Buriks, A. *Inleiding tot het Gemeenterecht* (Part I), and *De Nederlandse Gemeenten* (Part II). Alphen aan de Rijn, 1955.

D'Ailly, A. E. *Zeven eeuwen Amsterdam*. 1944. 6 vols.

Delfgaauw, G. T. S. *De Grondpolitiek van de Gemeente Amsterdam*. Amsterdam, 1934.

van der Does, J., de Jager, J. and Nolten, A. H. *Ons Amsterdam*. Amsterdam, 1950.

Hoogland, P. *Vijf en twintig Jaren sociaal-democratie in de Hoofdstad*. Amsterdam, 1928.

Leemans, A. F. *Eenheid in het Bestuur der Grote Stad* (Integration of Policy-making in a large City). Leiden, 1967.

de Miranda, S. R. *Amsterdam en zijn Bevolking in de negentiende Eeuw*. Amsterdam, undated.

van der Pot, C. W. *Handboek van het Nederlandse Staatsrecht*. Zwolle, 1968.

Sluyser, M. and Thomas, F. *Twaalf burgemeesters; vijfhonderd jaar Amsterdam*. Amsterdam, 1939.

van Tijn, Th. *Twintig jaren Amsterdam; de Hoofdstad van de jaren 50 der vorige eeuw tot 1876*. Amsterdam, 1965.

Vermooten, W. H. *Hervormd Amsterdam en zijn maatschappelijke achtergrond in de 19e en 20ste eeuw*, in *Handboek Pastorale sociologie*, The Hague, 1960.

de Vries, J. *Amsterdam-Rotterdam, rivalen in economisch-historisch perspectief*, Bussum, 1965.

Yearbooks of the City of Amsterdam.

Yearbooks of the Genootschap Amstellodamun.

Nota over de Economisch structuur van Amsterdam, published by the City of Amsterdam, Amsterdam, 1960.

Town planning and ground exploitation in Amsterdam (in English), published by the City of Amsterdam, Amsterdam, 1967. Second white paper on the Amsterdam City centre (draft), 1968.

De Interne stedelijke bestuursorganisatie van Amsterdam, Parts I and II, published by the City of Amsterdam, Amsterdam ,1959.

BELGRADE

Godišniak Grada Beograda (izdavač do 1967. godine Novinsko-izdavačko preduzeće 'Sedma sila', od 1968. godine Muzej grada Beograda, Beograd, godišnja publikacija).

Popović, J. dr Dušan, *Beograd kroz Vekove* (ed. 'Turistička štampa', Beograd, 1964).

New Beograd (ed. Direkcija za izgradnju Novog Beograda, štampa 'Export-press', Beograd, 1967—in English).

Belgrade—Review, October 1964 (ed. 'Turistička štampa', Beograd, 1964).

60. Godina Beogradskog Javnog Saobraćaja 1892–1952 (Beograd, 1953. str. 94).

Susedski Odnosi u Naseljima Novog Beograda (izdanje Saveznog zavoda za urbanizam i komunalna i stambena pitanja, Beograd, 1967).

Pešić, Branko, *Belgrade—Capital of Yugoslavia* ('Komuna', published by the Standing Conference of Towns of Yugoslavia, Belgrade, Year XII, Special Issue, June 1965, p. 38).

Stijović, Milosav, *Položaj Grada i Opština u Nacrtu Novog Statuta Beograda* ('Komuna', časopis Stalne konferencije gradova Jugoslavije, br. 1/1968, str. 10).

Papić, Josif, *Gradovi Podeljeni na Opštine Specifične Društveno-Političke Zajednice* ('Komuna', časopis Stalne konferencije gradova Jugoslavije, Beograd, br. 9/1968, str. 10).

Neograd of Today and Tomorrow (*Beograd of Today*; *Evolution of Beograd and Town-Planning Problems of Present Interest*; *Urbanization of the Area of Beograd and Town-Planning Measures for directing it*; *Traffic Problems of Beograd*; *Communal Equipment of Beograd*; *Role and Importance of Regularization plans in the Elaboration of the General Town Plan*; *Transformation of the Old Beograd*; *Detailed Town Plan of the Local Community in the Block 28*; *Town-Planning and Development Problems of Zemun*; *Beograd on the Left Bank of the Danube*; *Survey of the Development of Town-Planning Service in Beograd from 1944 to 1959*; *Tasks and Organization of the Town-Planning Institute of the City of Beograd*— 'Arhitektura Urbanizam', časopis Saveza arhitekata Jugoslavije i Urbanističkog saveza Jugoslavije, Beograd, br. 41–42, 1966).

Aktuelni Problemi Društveno-Političke Struckture Beograda (Materijal Komisije Skupštine grada Beograda za organizaciju i razvoj samoupravnog sistema u gradu, Beograd, 1966, 3 knjige i 10 priloga).

Šakić, Miladin, *O Nekim Iskustvima Sprovodjenja Stambene Reforme u Beogradu* ('Komuna', časopis Stalne konferencije gradova Jugoslavije, Beograd, br. 5/1968, str. 10).

Knežević, dr Novica, *Kreditiranje, Stambeno-Komunalne Izgradnje u Poslovnoj Politici Beogradske Udružene Banke* ('Stambena I komunalna privreda', časopis Centra za informacije i publicitet, Zagreb, br. 6/1968, str. 50)

BIRMINGHAM

Briggs, A. *Victorian Cities*, Odhams, 1963. Chapter on Birmingham.

Gill, C., and Briggs, A. *The History of Birmingham*. O.U.P., 1952.

Long, J. R., *et al.* 'The Wythall Inquiry', in *The Estate Gazette*, 1961.

Morris, D. S., and Newton, K. *Discussion Papers, Series F*. University of Birmingham, 1968–69.

Patterns of growths, H.M.S.O., 1965.

Report of the Committee on the Management of Local Government. (Maud Committee.) H.M.S.O., 1967.

Report of the Committee on the Staffing of Local Government. (Mallaby Committee.) H.M.S.O., 1967.

Royal Commission on Local Government: Research Studies, Vols. 7 and 10, *Aspects of Administration in a Large Local Authority*. H.M.S.O., 1968–69.

Smith, B. *Industrial Location Working Paper No. 19*. University of Birmingham, 1968.

West Midlands Study. H.M.S.O., 1965.

Worcestershire County Council. *Birmingham: Overspill Study*. 1967.

BUENOS AIRES

Bercaitz, M. A. *Procedimiento administrativo municipal*. Buenos Aires, 1946.

Bielsa, Rafael. *Principios de derecho administrativo*, 2nd edn. Buenos Aires, 1949.

Bielsa, Rafael. *Principios de régimen municipal*, 2nd edn. Buenos Aires, 1940.

Carril, B. del. *Buenos Aires frente al pais*. Buenos Aires, 1944.

Germani, Gino. *Encuestas en la población de Buenos Aires*. Buenos Aires Universidad, Instituto de Sociologia, Trabajos e Investigaciones. Colecion Datos, Buenos Aires, 1962.

Gómez Forgues, M. T. 'El régimen municipal en la capital federal' in *Revista de la Faculdad de Derecho y Ciencias Sociales*, No. 13, 1949.

Greca, A. *Derecho y ciencia de la administración municipal*, 2nd edn. Santa Fe, 1943.

Korn Villafañe, A. *Derecho municipal y provincial*. Buenos Aires, 1936–39.

Macdonald, A. F. 'The City of Buenos Aires', in his *Government of the Argentine Republic*. Crowell, New York, 1942.

Mouchet, Carlos. *Pasado y restauración del regimen municipal*. Editorial Perrot, Buenos Aires, 1952.

Municipalidad de la Ciudad de Buenos Aires, Organización del Plan Regulador. *Buenos Aires: Informe Preliminar Etapa 1959–60*. Buenos Aires, 1968.

Municipalidad de la Ciudad de Buenos Aires, Organización del Plan Regulador. *Buenos Aires: Synthetic Plan Description*. Buenos Aires, 1968.

Sarrailh, Edwardo J. 'Esquema de organización intermunicipal entre la Comuna de Buenos Aires y sus municipios limítrofes para crear una misma área de planeamiento,' *Revista municipal interamericana*, vol. 9 Nos. 3-4, 1959.

Scobie, James R. *Argentina: A City and a Nation*, O.U.P., New York, 1964.

Zabala, R., and Gandía, E. de. *Historia de la ciudad de Buenos Aires*. Buenos Aires, 1936–37, 2 vols.

Zavalia, C. *Tratado de derecho municipal*. Buenos Aires, 1941.

Zavalia, C. 'El gobierno de la ciudad de Buenos Aires' in *Revista de Derecho y Administración Municipal*, February 1940.

CAIRO

Russell, Dorothea. *Medieval Cairo*. London, Weidenfeld & Nicolson, 1962.

Stewart, Desmond. *Cairo*. London, Phoenix House, 1965, Cities of the World series.

Wiet, Gaston. *Cairo: city of art and commerce*, translated by Feiler Seymour. Norman Univ. of Oklahoma Press, 1964.

In Arabic

Ibrahim Galal. *Moeizeldine Allah El Fatemi wa Tashiid El Qaherah* (The construction of Cairo by Moeizeldine). Dar El Fekr Arabi, 1963.

Mohafazat El Qaherah. *Takrir A'n A'mal Majlis Mohafaza El Qaherah* (Year Book on the achievements of Cairo Governorate Council in 1962). Al Matba' El Amireya, 1962.

Mohamed Mu'tasam Sayed. *Al Qaherah wa El Hadarah wa Al Islam fi Afriqya* (Cairo, civilization and Islam in Africa). Al Qaherah, Al Majlis Al A'la lel Shu'un Al Islameya, 1965.

Mounir El Barbari. *Mashakel El Mourour Li Madinet Al Qaherah wa Torok Halaha* (Traffic problems in Cairo and their solutions). Game'yet Al Mohandesin Al Masreya, 1954.

Selim Hassan. *Masr El Kadimah* (Old Cairo). Goz' 14, Matba't, Al Qaherah, 1959.

Shehata Eissa Ibrahim. *Al Qaherah* (Cairo). Dar El Nahda, 1959.

Soad Maher. *Al Qaherah Al Kadima wa Ahyaiha* (Old Cairo and its districts). Dar Al Kalam, 1962.

Niazi Mustafa. *Al Qaherah-Derassat Takhtiteya fi Al Nakl* (Cairo—a study in planning transportation and traffic). Maktabet El Anglo, 1958.

CALCUTTA

Public Documents, Reports

Corporation of Calcutta. *Annual Reports of the Municipal Administration*. The Corporation Press, Calcutta, various years.

Year Book, 1961–62. The Corporation Press, Calcutta, 1961.

Year Book, 1964–65. The Corporation Press, Calcutta, 1964.

Calcutta Municipal Gazettes. The Corporation Press, Calcutta, various years.

The Calcutta Municipal Gazette, Silver Jubilee Number. The Corporation Press, Calcutta, 1950.

Commissioner's Budget Estimates, 1964. The Corporation Press, Calcutta, 1964.

Minutes of Proceeding, Calcutta, various years.

Calcutta Corporation Tubewell Case, Special Judge Bagchi, 1959.

Calcutta Improvement Trust. *Annual Report*, 1959–60. Calcutta Improvement Trust, Calcutta, 1960.

Calcutta Metropolitan Planning Organization. *First Report*, 1962. Calcutta Metropolitan Planning Organization, 1963.

Government of India. *Report of the Rural–Urban Relationship Committee*, 1966.

Gurner, C. W. *Report on the Finances of the Calcutta Corporation*. Calcutta, 1943.

The International Bank for Reconstruction and Development. *Mission Report*, 1960.

India, A. Mitra. *Census of India*, 1951, Vol. VI, Part III (Calcutta City). Manager of Publications, Delhi, 1954.

India, Ministry of Information and Broadcasting. *India, a Reference Annual*, 1964. Director, Publications Division, Delhi, 1964.

India, Ministry of Finance. *Report of the Taxation Enquiry Commission*, 1953–54, Vols. I–IV. Manager of Publications, Delhi, 1955.

India, Planning Commission. *The Second Five Year Plan; A Tentative Framework*. Manager of Publications, Delhi, 1955.

India, Planning Commission. *The Third Five Year Plan; Summary*. Director, Publications Division, Delhi, 1961.

West Bengal, Local Self-Government Department. *Report of the Calcutta Corporation Investigation Commission*, 1950, Vol. I, Part I (Interim Report, 1950). West Bengal Government Press, Alipore, 1950–51.

West Bengal, Local Self-Government and Panchayats Department. *Report of the Corporation of Calcutta Enquiry Committee*, Vol. I. Calcutta State Transport Corporation, 1962.

West Bengal, State Statistical Bureau. *Report on the Bustee Survey in Calcutta*, 1958–59. West Bengal Government Press, Alipore, 1963.

World Health Organization. *Assignment Report on Water Supply and Sewage Disposal, Greater Calcutta*. World Health Organization, Regional Office for South East Asia, New Delhi, 1960.

Books

Aiyar and Srinivasan. *Studies in Indian Democracy*, chapter on Urban Politics.

Banerjea, Surendranath. *A Nation in Making*. Oxford University Press, Calcutta, 1963.

Basu, Durga Das. *Shorter Constitution of India*. S. C. Sarkar & Sons, Calcutta, 1964.

Bhattacharya, M. *Rural Self-Government in Metropolitan Calcutta*, Calcutta Research Studies No. 5. Published for the Institute of Public Administration, New York. Asia Publishing House, Bombay, 1965.

Bhattacharya, M., Singh, M. M., and Tysen, Frank J. *Government in Metropolitan Calcutta: A Manual*, Calcutta Research Studies No. 1. Published for the Institute of Public Administration, New York. Asia Publishing House, Bombay, 1965.

Chakrabarty, Syamal. *Housing Conditions in Calcutta*. Bookland Private Ltd., Calcutta, 1958.

Citizens' Club. *Better Calcutta Exhibition, 1962*. Citizens' Club, Calcutta, 1962.

Datta, Abhijit. *Inter-Governmental Grants in Metropolitan Calcutta*, Calcutta Research Studies No. 10. Published for the Institute of Public Administration, New York. Asia Publishing House, Bombay, 1965.

Datta, Abhijit, and Ranney, David C. *Municipal Finances in the Calcutta Metropolitan District: A Preliminary Survey*, Calcutta Research Studies No. 3. Published for the Institute of Public Administration, New York. Asia Publishing House, Bombay, 1965.

Goldsmith, E. H., *Municipal Government in Calcutta: The Calcutta Corporation*. University of California, Berkeley, 1961 (unpublished master's thesis).

Goode, S. W. *Municipal Calcutta*. Calcutta Corporation, Calcutta, 1916.

Green, Leslie, and Datta, Abhijit, *Special Agencies in Metropolitan Calcutta: A Comparative Study*, Calcutta Research Studies No. 8. Published for the Institute of Public Administration, New York. Asia Publishing House, Bombay, 1966.

Gupta, S. K. 'Second Thoughts on Problems of Municipal Relationships', in *Improving City Government*. Indian Institute of Public Administration, New Delhi, 1958.

Hicks, Ursula. *Development from Below*. Oxford University Press, London, 1951.

Mitra, Asok. *Calcutta India's City*. New Age Publishers Private Ltd., Calcutta, 1963.

Sen, S. N. *The City of Calcutta*. Bookland Private Ltd., Calcutta, 1960.

Singh, M. M. *Municipal Government in the Calcutta Metropolitan District: A Preliminary Survey*, Calcutta Research Studies No. 2. Published for the Institute of Public Administration, New York. Asia Publishing House, Bombay, 1965.

Singh, M. M. *Municipal Government in the Calcutta Metropolitan District: A Preliminary Survey*, Calcutta Research Studies No. 2. Published for the Institute of Public Administration, New York. Asia Publishing House, Bombay, 1965.

Spate, O. H. K. *India and Pakistan*. Methuen & Co., London, 1957.

Articles

Green, L. P. 'Observations on Munipical Government', *Proceedings* of Annual Conference, Institute of Municipal Treasurers and Accounts, South Africa, 1952.

Lamb, Helen. 'The Indian Business Communities and the Evolution of an Industrial Class', *Pacific Affairs*, 1955.

Seal, S. C., and Mathew, K. K. 'A Study of the Concentration of Social Factors to the Continued Prevalence of Cholera in the City of Calcutta', *Indian Journal of Public Health*, inaugural issue, October 1956.

CHICAGO

Banfield, Edward C. *Political Influence*. The Free Press, New York, 1961.

Burnham, D. H. *Plan of Chicago*. Commercial Club of Chicago, Chicago, 1949.

Chicago Department of City Planning. *The Chicago Plan Commission; a historical sketch, 1909–1960*. Chicago, 1961.

Chicago Department of Development and Planning. *The Comprehensive Plan of Chicago*. Chicago, 1966.

Chicago Home Rule Commission. *Modernizing a City Government*. University of Chicago Press, Chicago, 1954.

Chicago Plan Commission. *Rebuilding Old Chicago*. Chicago, 1941.

Committee on Urban Progress. *A Pattern for Greater Chicago*. Chicago, 1965.

Democratic Party of Cook County. *Your Neighborhood Today and Tommorrow*. Chicago, 1967.

Dreiske, John. *Your Government and Mine: Metropolitan Chicago*. Oceana Publications, New York, 1959.

Goode, J. P. *The Geographic Background of Chicago*. University of Chicago Press, Chicago, 1928.

Goshel, H. F. *Machine Politics: Chicago Model*. University of Chicago Press, Chicago, 1937.

Gottfried, Alex. *Boss Cermak of Chigao: A Study of Political Leadership*. University of Washington Press, Seattle, 1962.

Hodge, Patricia and Kitagawa, Evelyn. *Population Projections for the City of Chicago and the Chicago Standard Metropolitan Statistical Area 1970 and 1980*. Population Research and Training Center and Chicago Community Inventory, University of Chicago, Chicago, 1964.

Karlen, Harvey M. *The Governments of Chicago*. Courier Publishing Company, Chicago, 1958.

Kitagawa, Evelyn M., and Tauber, Karl E., eds. *Local Community Fact Book Chicago Metropolitan Area 1960*. Chicago Community Inventory, University of Chicago, 1963.

League of Women Voters of Chicago. *The Key to Our Local Government*. Citizen Information Service of Metropolitan Chicago, Chicago, 1966.

Liebling, A. J. *Chicago: the Second City*, New York, Alfred A. Knopf, 1952.

Mayer, Harold M., *Chicago: City of Decisions*, edited by Chauncey D. Harris. The Geographic Society, Chicago, 1955.

Mayor's Committee for Economic and Cultural Development. *Mid-Chicago Economic Development Study*. Chicago, 1966.

Mayor's Office of Inquiry and Information. *Know Your City Government*. Chicago, 1960.

Merriam, C. E. *Chicago: a More Intimate View of Urban Politics*. New York, Macmillan, 1929.

Merriam, C. E. et al. *The Government of the Metropolitan Region of Chicago*. University of Chicago Press, Chicago, 1933.

Meyerson, Martin, and Banfield, Edward. *Politics, Planning and The Public Interest*. The Free Press, Glencoe, 1955.

Municipal Reference Library. *The Government of The City of Chicago*, prepared by Richard J. Wolfert, revised by Joyce Malden. Chicago, 1966.

Northeastern Illinois Metropolitan Area Local Governmental Services Commission. *Governmental Problems in the Chicago Area: a Report*, edited by Leverett S. Lyon. University of Chicago Press, Chicago, 1957.

Northeastern Illinois Metropolitan Area Local Governmental Services Commission. *Metropolitan Area Services*, edited by Gilbert Y. Steiner and Lois M. Pelekoudas. Institute of Government and Public Affairs, University of Illinois, Urbana, 1959.

Pierce, B. L. *A History of Chicago*. Knopf, New York, 1937–40.

Rakove, Milton. *The Changing Patterns of Suburban Politics in Cook County, Illinois*. Loyola University Press, Chicago, 1965.

Rakove, Milton. 'State Action in Illinois: Some Political Considerations' in *The State and Its Cities*. Institute of Government and Public Affairs, University of Illinois, Urbana, 1967.

Small, Joseph F. *Governmental Alternatives Facing the Chicago Metropolitan Area*. Loyola University Press, Chicago, 1966.

Spear, Allan H. *Black Chicago: the Making of a Negro Ghetto, 1890–1920*. University of Chicago Press, Chicago, 1967.

Steiner, Gilbert Y. *Metropolitan Government and the Real World: The Case of Chicago*. Loyola University Press, Chicago, 1966.

Walker, R. A. 'Chicago: Planning in Evolution' in *The Planning Function in Urban Government*. University of Chicago Press, Chicago, 1950.

Wendt, Lloyd, and Kogan, Herman. *Lords of the Levee: the Story of Bathhouse John and Hinky Dink*. The Bobbs Merrill Company, Indianapolis and New York, 1943.

Wendt, Lloyd and Kogan, Herman. *Big Bill of Chicago*. The Bobbs Merrill Company, Indianapolis, 1953.

Wilson, James Q. *Negro Politics The Search for Leadership*. The Free Press, Glencoe, 1960.

Wilson, James Q. *The Amateur Democrat*. University of Chicago Press, 1962. Chicago.

Articles

Bowen, W. 'Chicago: They Didn't have to Burn it Down After all', *Fortune*, January 1965, pp. 142–6.

Bruno, H. 'Chicago Ain't Ready for Reform'. *Reporter*, 28 March 1963, pp. 41–3.

Dugan, J. 'Mayor Daley's Chicago', *Holiday*, December 1963, pp. 84–93.

Gilbreth, E. S. 'Making Book on Mr Daley', *Nation*, 27 March 1967, pp. 395–6.

Higdon, H. 'Minority Objects but Daley is Chicago', *New York Times Magazine*, 11 September 1966, pp. 84–5+.

Lens, S. 'Daley of Chicago', *The Progressive*, March 1966, pp. 15–21.

Rakove, 'Daley's Balance of Power', *Chicago Sun Times*, 9 April 1967, II, 4.

Wheeler, K. 'Last Big Boss on U.S. Scene', *Life*, 8 February 1960, pp. 138–40.

COPENHAGEN

Bruun, C. *Kjøbenhavn: en illustreret skildring af dets historie, mindesmaerker og institutioner*. Philipsen, Kjøbenhavn, 1887–1901, 3 vols.

Dahl, F. *Københavns bystyre gennem 300 år.*, Vol. I, 1648–1858. Munksgaard, København, 1943.

Det danske Selskab. *Capital of a Democracy*. 1964.

Holm, Axel. *Københavns kommunes forfatning*, 3rd edn. København, 1964.

Holm, Axel, and Johansen, K. *Kobenhavn 1840–1940: det københavnske bysamfund og kommunens økonomi*. Nyt Nordisk Forlag, København, 1941.

Jørgensen, H. (ed.). *København fra boplads til storby*. Hirschsprung, København, 1948, 2 vols.

Københavns kommunalbestyrelse. *Københavns kommune 1940–55*.

Nielsen, O. *Kiøbenhavns historie og beskrivelse*. Gad, Kjøbenhavn, 1877–92, 6 vols.

Ramsing, H. U. *Københavns historie og topografi i middelalderen*. Munksgaard, København, 1940, 3 vols.

Rasmusing, Steen Eiler. *Københavnsegnens Planlægning, status 1950*.

Trap, J. P. *Storkøbenhavn I–III*, Gad, København, 1960.

Annuals

Historiske Meddelelser om København, 1907–.

Københavns Borgerrepraesentanters Forhandlinger 1840–.

Københavns Kommunalkalender, Annual. 1931–.
Samling af Bestemmelser vedrørende Købehnavns Kommune, Annual.
Statistik Årbog for København, Frederiksberg og Gentofte Kommune, Annual 1919–.

DELHI

Books
Chandra, Jag Parvesh. *New Set-up for Delhi, Fears and Hopes Examined*. The Author, Delhi, 1955.
Bopegamage, A. *Delhi: A Study in Urban Sociology*. University of Bombay, Bombay, 1957.
Samaj, Bharat Sevak. *Slums of Old Delhi*. Atma Ram, Delhi, 1958.
Rao, V. K. R. V., and Desai, P. B. *Greater Delhi: A Study in Urbanisation—1940–1957*. Asia Publishing House, Bombay, 1965.

Official Reports and Documents
Census of India, 1951, *Delhi State, District Census Handbook*, Vol. 27, Delhi State Government, Delhi, 1953.
Census of India, 1961, *Delhi: District Census Hand Book*. Delhi Administration, Delhi, 1964.
Census of India, 1961, Vol. XIX, *Delhi (Part I-A); General Report of the Census*. Delhi Administration, Delhi, 1964.
Delhi Development Authority. *Draft Master Plans for Delhi*, Vol. I, Text and Drawings, Vol. II, Appendices and Drawings. Authority, Delhi, 1960.
Delhi Development Authority. *Master Plan for Delhi*. Delhi, 1962.
Delhi Municipal Committee. *Survey of Activities, 1954–58*. Delhi, 1958.
Government of India. *Delhi Municipal Organisation Enquiry Committee Report*. Delhi, 1948.
Government of India. *States' Reorganization Commission Report*. Delhi, 1955.
Municipal Corporation of Delhi. *A brief review of the financial position of the general wing of the Corporation* (by K. L. Rathee). Delhi, 1967.
Municipal Corporation of Delhi. *Annual Administration Report for the years 1960–61. 1964–65*.

Acts
The Constitution of India (as modified up to 15 April 1967).
Delhi Municipal Corporation Act, 1957.
Delhi Development Act, 1957.
The Government of Union Territories Act, 1963.
Delhi Administration Act, 1966.

IBADAN

Akinola, R. A. 'The Industrial Structure of Ibadan', in *Nigeria Geographical Journal*, Vol. 7, No. 2, December 1964.
Awe, B. 'The Growth of Ibadan in the 19th Century' in *Ibadan in the Changing Nigerian Scene* (unpublished seminar papers, Institute of African Studies, Ibadan University, 1964).
Awe, B. *The Rise of Ibadan as a Yoruba Power in the 19th Century* (unpublished D.Phil. thesis, University of Oxford, 1964).
Campbell, M. J., Brierly, T. G., and Blitz, L. F. *The Structure of Local Government in West Africa*. I.U.L.A., The Hague, 1965.

Cowan, L. G. *Local Government in West Africa*. A.M.S. Press, New York, 1958.

Green, L., and Milone, V. *Physical Planning in Western Nigeria* (unpublished). Ministry of Lands and Housing, Ibadan, 1967.

Jenkins, G. D. *Politics in Ibadan* (unpublished Ph.D. thesis, Evanston University, 1965).

Lloyd, P. C. *Local Government in Yoruba Towns* (unpublished D.Phil. thesis, Oxford University, 1958).

Lloyd, P. C. *Yoruba Land Law*. O.U.P., London, 1962.

Lloyd, P. C. *et al. City of Ibadan*. C.U.P., London, 1967.

Mabogunje, A. L. 'Ibadan: Black Metropolis', in *Nigeria Magazine*, Vol. 67, March 1961.

Okin, Theophilus A. *Urbanised Nigerian*. Exposition Press, New York, 1968.

University College, Ibadan. *Ibadan: a brochure*. For 3rd International West African Conference, Zaria, 1949.

Wraith, R. E. *Local Government in West Africa*. Allen & Unwin, London, 1964.